THE

HISTORICAL EVIDENCES

OF THE

TRUTH OF THE SCRIPTURE RECORDS.

Τῷ μὲν γὰρ ἀληθεῖ πάντα συνᾴδει τὰ ὑπάρχοντα· τῷ δὲ ψευδεῖ ταχὺ διαφωνεῖ τἀληθές.—ARISTOTLE.

(FOR WITH THE TRUE ALL THINGS THAT EXIST ARE IN HARMONY; BUT WITH THE FALSE THE TRUE AT ONCE DISAGREES.)

Ὁ χρόνος εὑρετής. (TIME IS THE DISCOVERER.)

THE

HISTORICAL EVIDENCES

OF THE

TRUTH OF THE SCRIPTURE RECORDS

STATED ANEW,

WITH SPECIAL REFERENCE TO THE DOUBTS AND DISCOVERIES OF MODERN TIMES.

IN

EIGHT LECTURES DELIVERED IN THE OXFORD UNIVERSITY PULPIT, IN THE YEAR 1859,

ON

The Bampton Foundation.

BY

GEORGE RAWLINSON, M.A.,

LATE FELLOW AND TUTOR OF EXETER COLLEGE; EDITOR OF "THE HISTORY OF HERODOTUS," ETC.

FROM THE LONDON EDITION, WITH THE NOTES TRANSLATED,

BY REV. A. N. ARNOLD.

BOSTON:

GOULD AND LINCOLN,

59 WASHINGTON STREET.

NEW YORK: SHELDON AND COMPANY.

CINCINNATI: GEO. S. BLANCHARD.

1860.

ELECTROTYPED AT THE
BOSTON STEREOTYPE FOUNDRY.

EXTRACT

FROM

THE LAST WILL AND TESTAMENT

OF THE

REV. JOHN BAMPTON,

CANON OF SALISBURY.

. . . . "I give and bequeath my Lands and Estates to the Chancellor Masters, and Scholars of the University of Oxford for ever, to have and to hold all and singular the said Lands or Estates upon trust, and to the intents and purposes hereinafter mentioned; that is to say, I will and appoint that the Vice-Chancellor of the University of Oxford for the time being shall take and receive all the rents, issues, and profits thereof, and (after all taxes, reparations, and necessary deductions made) that he pay all the remainder to the endowment of eight Divinity Lecture Sermons, to be established for ever in the said University, and to be performed in the manner following:

"I direct and appoint, that, upon the first Tuesday in Easter Term, a Lecturer be yearly chosen by the Heads of Colleges only, and by no others, in the room adjoining to the Printing-House, between the hours of ten in the morning and two in the afternoon, to preach eight Divinity Lecture Sermons, the year following, at St. Mary's in Oxford, between the commencement of the last month in Lent Term, and the end of the third week in Act Term.

"Also I direct and appoint, that the eight Divinity Lecture Sermons shall be preached upon either of the following Subjects — to confirm and establish the Christian Faith, and to confute all heretics and schismatics — upon the divine authority of the holy Scriptures — upon the authority of the writings of the primitive Fathers, as to the faith and practice of the primitive Church — upon the Divinity of our Lord and Saviour Jesus Christ — upon the Divinity of the Holy Ghost — upon the Articles of the Christian Faith, as comprehended in the Apostles' and Nicene Creeds.

"Also I direct, that thirty copies of the eight Divinity Lecture Sermons shall be always printed, within two months after they are preached, and one copy shall be given to the Chancellor of the University, and one copy to the Head of every College, and one copy to the Mayor of the city of Oxford, and one copy to be put into the Bodleian Library; and the expense of printing them shall be paid out of the revenue of the Land or Estates given for establishing the Divinity Lecture Sermons; and the Preacher shall not be paid, nor be entitled to the revenue, before they are printed.

"Also I direct and appoint, that no person shall be qualified to preach the Divinity Lecture Sermons, unless he hath taken the degree of Master of Arts at least, in one of the two Universities of Oxford or Cambridge; and that the same person shall never preach the Divinity Lecture Sermons twice."

PUBLISHERS' ADVERTISEMENT

TO

THE AMERICAN EDITION.

THE present work, though it belongs to the same series, and has the same general design, with Prof. Mansel's Lectures on the Limits of Religious Thought, deals with very different materials, and employs very different modes of reasoning. Instead of abstruse inquiries into the subtle conditions and laws of thought, the business of our author is with the concrete facts of history, and the explicit records of the past. The two works thus represent the opposite poles of scientific inquiry. They are like two buttresses, built up of different materials, but of equal strength, on opposite sides of the citadel of our Christian faith.

Mr. Rawlinson has been peculiarly happy in the facilities which he has enjoyed for combining with his own extensive and accurate knowledge of the literary monuments of antiquity the latest results of the remarkable discoveries of his distinguished brother and other successful explorers in those rich mines of history, more precious than of gold, which have so recently been opened in the valleys of the Euphrates and the Nile. Some general knowledge of these results, as confirmatory of the historical accuracy of the Sacred Scriptures, has already been widely diffused; but there was needed a thorough and scholarly work upon this particular subject, which, by combining a complete survey and a logical method with copious specific proofs and illustrations, should stamp with a more unquestionable certainty, and estimate with a more critical exactness, these reputed confirmations of Scripture history. This is the task which Mr. Rawlinson has undertaken in these "Bampton Lectures;" and we are confident that the verdict of his own countrymen, as to the signal ability and success with which he has accomplished it, will be fully indorsed by his American readers.

But it would be unjust to the author to intimate that the value of his book is measured only by the skilful and exhaustive use which he has made of recent discoveries in the East: the plan of his work covers a broader field, including all the testimonies of ancient literature to the facts of Christianity, and the veracity of the Inspired Volume. But as most of these testimonies of Pagan, Jewish, and Christian writers have become familiarly known to those who have studied the Christian evidences, the main interest of these Lectures, for a large class of readers, will probably be found in the fresher contribution which they bring to this subject, from the recently deciphered hieroglyphics of Egypt, and the still more recent excavations on the sites of the ancient cities of Assyria.

As this work promises, from its less abstract character, to interest a larger proportion of the reading public than the excellent volume by Prof. Mansel, there was a still stronger reason than in the case of that work for making the valuable Notes intelligible to all, by translating such portions of them as were given in foreign languages in the English edition. These Notes were mostly in the Greek language; and the translations have been made by the Rev. A. N. Arnold, who was for many years a resident in Greece. The translator has not had access to all the Greek and Latin writers from whom the author has quoted in his proofs; and hence it is not impossible that some trifling inaccuracies have resulted from the want of that light which the connection would have shed upon these fragmentary sentences.

It is a happy omen, that, while so much of the literature of our times is marked by a tone of infidelity, and especially by a disparagement of the evidences of the authenticity and inspiration of the Scriptures, there is in other quarters an increasing readiness to make the choicest gifts of modern science and learning tributary to the word of God. The eclipse of faith is not total. And it is an additional cause for gratitude to the God of Providence and of Revelation, that, even at this remote distance of time from the date of the Sacred Oracles, new evidences of their credibility and accuracy are continually coming to light. How much may yet remain, buried under barren mounds, or entombed in pyramids and catacombs, or hidden in the yet unexplored pages of some ancient literature, it were vain to conjecture; but of this we may be sure, that if any new forms of evidence should hereafter be needed, to meet any new forms of unbelief, and authenticate afresh the word of truth, they will be found deposited somewhere, waiting for the fulness of time; and God will bring them forth in their season, from the dark hieroglyphics, or the desert sands, or the dusty manuscripts, to confound the adversaries of his word, and to "magnify it above all his name."

PREFACE.

THESE Lectures are an attempt to meet that latest phase of modern unbelief, which, professing a reverence for the name and person of Christ, and a real regard for the Scriptures as embodiments of what is purest and holiest in religious feeling, lowers Christ to a mere name, and empties the Scriptures of all their force and practical efficacy, by denying the historical character of the Biblical narrative. German Neology (as it is called) has of late years taken chiefly this line of attack, and has pursued it with so much vigor and apparent success, that, according to the complaints of German orthodox writers, "no objective ground or stand-point" is left, on which the believing Theological science can build with any feeling of security.[1] Nor is the evil in question confined to Germany. The works regarded as most effective in destroying the historical faith of Christians abroad, have received an English dress, and are, it is to be feared, read by numbers of persons very ill prepared by historical studies to withstand their specious reasonings, alike in our own country and in America. The tone, moreover, of German historical writings generally is

1 See Keil's Preface to his *Comment on Joshua*, quoted in Note XXIV. to Lecture I.

tinged with the prevailing unbelief; and the faith of the historical student is liable to be undermined, almost without his having his suspicions aroused, by covert assumptions of the mythical character of the sacred narrative, in works professing to deal chiefly, or entirely, with profane subjects. The author had long felt this to be a serious and a growing evil. Meanwhile his own studies, which have lain for the last eight or nine years almost exclusively in the field of Ancient History, had convinced him more and more of the thorough truthfulness and faithful accuracy of the historical Scriptures. Circumstances had given him an intimate knowledge of the whole course of recent cuneiform, and (to some extent) of hieroglyphical discovery; and he had been continually struck with the removal of difficulties, the accession of light, and the multiplication of minute points of agreement between the sacred and the profane, which resulted from the advances made in deciphering the Assyrian, Babylonian, Persian, and Egyptian records. He therefore ventured, at the earliest moment which engagements of long standing would allow, to submit to the Heads of Colleges, electors to the office of Bampton Lecturer under the will of the Founder, the scheme of the following Discourses. His scheme having at once met with their approval, it only remained for him to use his best efforts in the elaboration of the subject which he had chosen.

Two modes of meeting the attacks of the Mythical School presented themselves. He might make it his main object to examine the arguments of their principal writers *seriatim*, and to demonstrate from authentic records their weakness, perverseness, and falsity. Or touching only slightly on this purely controversial ground, he might endeavor to exhibit clearly and forcibly the argument from the positive agreement between Scripture and profane history, which they ignored altogether. The latter mode of treatment appeared to him at once the more convincing to young minds, and the more suitable for a set of Lectures. For these reasons he adopted it. At the same time he has occasionally, both in the Text and in the Notes, addressed himself to the more important of the reasonings by which the school of Strauss and De Wette seek to overthrow the historical authority of the Sacred documents.

The Notes have run to a somewhat unusual length. The author thought it important to exhibit (where possible) the authorities for his statements in full; and to collect into a single volume the chief testimonies to the historical truth and accuracy of the Scripture records. If in referring to the cuneiform writings he has on many occasions stated their substance, rather than cited their exact words, it is because so few of them have as yet been translated by competent scholars, and because in most cases his own knowledge is limited to an acquaintance with the substance, derived from frequent conversations with his gifted brother. It is to be hoped that no long time will elapse before some one of the four *savans*, who have proved their capacity to render the ancient

2

Assyrian,[1] will present the world with a complete translation of all the historical inscriptions hitherto recovered.

The author cannot conclude without expressing his acknowledgments to Dr. Bandinel, Chief Librarian of the Bodleian, for kind exertions in procuring at his instance various foreign works; and to Dr. Pusey, Professor Stanley, and Mr. Mansel for some valuable information on several points connected with the Lectures. He is bound also to record his obligations to various living or recent writers, whose works have made his task easier, as Professors Keil, Hävernick, and Olshausen in Germany, and in England Dr. Lardner, Dr. Burton, and Dean Alford. Finally, he is glad once more to avow his deep obligations to the learning and genius of his brother, and to the kind and liberal communication on his part of full information upon every point where there seemed to be any contact between the sacred history and the cuneiform records. The novelty of the Lectures will, he feels, consist chiefly, if not solely, in the exhibition of these points of contact and agreement; and the circumstance of his having this novelty to offer was his chief inducement to attempt a work on the subject. It is his earnest prayer that, by the blessing of God, his labors may tend to check the spread of unbelief, and to produce among Scripture students a more lively appreciation of the reality of those facts which are put before us in the Bible.

OXFORD, *November* 2, 1859.

1 See the *Inscription of Tiglath-Pileser I., king of Assyria, B. C.* 1150, as translated by Sir Henry Rawlinson, Fox Talbot, Esq., Dr. Hincks, and Dr. Oppert; published by the Royal Asiatic Society, London, Parker, 1857.

CONTENTS.

LECTURE I.

LECTURE II.

LECTURE III.

LECTURE IV.

LECTURE V.

LECTURE VI.

LECTURE VII.

LECTURE VIII.

THE

HISTORICAL EVIDENCES

OF THE

TRUTH OF THE SCRIPTURE RECORDS.

LECTURE I.

LET ALL THE NATIONS BE GATHERED TOGETHER, AND LET THE PEOPLE BE ASSEMBLED: WHO AMONG THEM CAN DECLARE THIS, AND SHOW US FORMER THINGS? LET THEM BRING FORTH THEIR WITNESSES, THAT THEY MAY BE JUSTIFIED: OR LET THEM HEAR, AND SAY, IT IS TRUTH. —ISAIAH XLIII. 9.

Christianity—including therein the dispensation of the Old Testament, which was its first stage—is in nothing more distinguished from the other religions of the world than in its objective or historical character. The religions of Greece and Rome, of Egypt, India, Persia, and the East generally, were speculative systems, which did not even seriously postulate an historical basis. If they seemed to do so to some extent, if for instance the mythological ideas of the Greeks be represented under the form of a mythological *period*, which moreover blends gradually and almost imperceptibly with the historical, still in the minds of the Greeks themselves the periods were separate and distinct, not merely in time, but in character; and the objective reality of the scenes and events described as belonging to each was not conceived of as parallel, or even similar, in the two cases.[1] The modern distinction between the legend and the myth, properly so called,[2] was felt, if not formally recognized, by the Greek mind; and the basis of fact, which is of the essence of the former, was regarded as absent from the latter, which thus ceased altogether to be history. Mahometanism again, and the other religious systems which have started with an individual, and which so far bear a nearer resemblance to the religions of Moses and of Christ, than those that have grown up and been developed gradually out of the feeling and imagination of a people, are very slightly, if at all, connected with any body of important facts, the due attestation of which and their accordance with other known facts might be made the subject of critical examination. We may concede the truth of the whole story of Mahomet, as it was related by his early followers, and this concession in no sort carries with it even the probable truth of the religion.[3] But it is otherwise with the religion of the Bible. There, whether we look to the Old or the New Testament, to the Jewish dispensation or to the Christian, we find a scheme of doctrine which is bound up with facts; which depends absolutely upon them; which is null and void without them; and which may be regarded as for all practical purposes established if they are shown to deserve acceptance.

It is this peculiar feature of Christianity — a feature often noticed by its apologists[4] — which brings it into such a close relation to historical studies and investigations. As a religion of fact, and not merely of opinion, — as one whose chief scene is this world, and whose main doctrines are events exhibited openly before the eyes of men — as one moreover which, instead of affecting a dogmatic form, adopts from first to last, with very rare exceptions, the historical shape, it comes necessarily within the sphere of the historical inquirer, and challenges him to investigate it according to what he regards as the principles of his science. Moreover, as Christianity is in point of fact connected intimately with certain records, and as those records extend over a period of several thousands of years, and "profess to contain a kind of abridgment of the history of the world," (5) its points of contact with profane history are (practically speaking) infinite; and it becomes impossible for the historical inquirer to avoid the question, in what light he is to view the documents which, if authentic, must exercise so important an influence over his studies and conclusions.

Christianity then cannot complain if, from time to time, as historical science advances, the question is raised afresh concerning the real character of those events which form its basis, and the real value of those documents on which it relies. As an historical religion, it invites this species of inquiry, and is glad that it should be made and repeated. It only complains in one of two cases — when either principles unsound and wrong in themselves, having been assumed as proper *criteria* of historic truth, are applied to it for the purpose of disparagement; or when, right principles being assumed, the application of them, of which it is the object, is unfair and illegitimate.

It is the latter of these two errors which seems to me to be the chief danger of the present day. Time was — and that not very long ago — when all the relations of ancient authors concerning the old world were received with a ready belief; and an unreasoning and uncritical faith accepted with equal satisfaction the narrative of the campaigns of Cæsar and of the doings of Romulus, the account of Alexander's marches and of the conquests of Semiramis.

We can most of us remember when in this country the whole story of Regal Rome, and even the legend of the Trojan settlement in Latium, were seriously placed before boys as history, and discoursed of as unhesitatingly, and in as dogmatic a tone, as the tale of the Catiline conspiracy, or the conquest of Britain. "All ancient authors were" at this time, as has been justly observed, "put upon the same footing, and regarded as equally credible;" while "all parts of an author's work were supposed to rest on the same basis." (6) A blind and indiscriminate faith of a low kind — acquiescence rather than actual belief — embraced equally and impartially the whole range of ancient story, setting aside perhaps those prodigies which easily detached themselves from the narrative, and were understood to be embellishments on a par with mere graces of composition.

But all this is now changed. The last century has seen the birth and growth of a new science — the science of Historical Criticism. Beginning in France with the labors of Pouilly and Beaufort, (7) it advanced with rapid strides in Germany under the guidance of Niebuhr, (8) Otfried Müller, (9) and Böckh, (10) and finally, has been introduced and naturalized among ourselves by means of the writings of our best living historians. (11)

Its results in its own proper and primary field are of the most extensive and remarkable character. The whole world of profane history has been revolutionized. By a searching and critical investigation of the mass of materials on which that history rested, and by the application to it of Canons embodying the judgments of a sound discretion upon the value of different sorts of evidence, the views of the ancient world formerly entertained have been in ten thousand points either modified or reversed — a new antiquity has been raised up out of the old — while much that was unreal in the picture of past times which men had formed to themselves has disappeared, consigned to that "Limbo large and broad" into which "all things transitory and vain" are finally received, a fresh revelation has in many cases taken the place of the old view, which has dissolved before the wand of the critic; and a firm and strong fabric has arisen out of the shattered *débris* of the fallen systems. Thus the results obtained have been both positive and negative; but, it must be confessed, with a preponderance of the latter over the former. The scepticism in which the science originated has clung to it from first to last, and in recent times we have seen not only a greater leaning to the destructive than to the constructive side, but a tendency to push doubt and incredulity beyond due limits, to call in question without cause, and to distrust what is sufficiently established. This tendency has not, however, been allowed to pass unrebuked;[12] and viewing the science as developed, not in the writings of this or that individual, but in the general conclusions in which it has issued, we may regard it as having done, and as still prepared to do, good service in the cause of truth.

It was not to be expected — nor was it, I think, to be wished — that the records of past times contained in the Old and New Testament should escape the searching ordeal to which all other historical documents had been subjected, or remain long, on account of their sacred character, unscrutinized by the inquirer. Reverence may possibly gain, but Faith, I believe, — real and true Faith — greatly loses by the establishment of a wall of partition between the sacred and the profane, and the subtraction of the former from the domain of scientific inquiry. As truth of one kind cannot possibly be contradictory to truth of another, Christianity has nothing to fear from scientific investigations; and any attempt to isolate its facts and preserve them from the scrutiny which profane history receives must, if successful, diminish the fulness of our assent to them — the depth and reality of our belief in their actual occurrence. It is by the connection of sacred with profane history that the facts of the former are most vividly apprehended, and most distinctly felt to be real; to sever between the two is to make the sacred narrative grow dim and shadowy, and to encourage the notion that its details are not facts in the common and every-day sense of the word.

When therefore, upon the general acceptance of the principles laid down with respect to profane history by Otfried Müller and Niebuhr, theological critics in Germany proceeded, as they said, to apply the new canons of historical criticism to the Gospels and to the historical books of the Old Testament, there was no cause for surprise, nor any ground for extreme apprehension. There is of course always danger when science alone, disjoined from religious feeling, undertakes, with its purblind sight and limited means of knowing, to examine, weigh, and decide matters of the highest import. But there did not appear to be in this instance any reason for special alarm. The great Master-spirit, he to whom the new science owed, if not its existence, yet at any rate its advancement and the estimation in which it was generally held — had distinctly accepted the mass of the Scripture history as authentic, and was a sincere and earnest believer.[(13)] It was hoped that the inquiry would be made in his spirit, and by means of a cautious application of his principles. But the fact has unfortunately been otherwise. The application of the science of historical criticism to the narrative of Scripture has been made in Germany by two schools — one certainly far less extravagant than the other — but both wanting in sound critical judgment, as well as in a due reverence for the Written Word. It will be necessary, in order to make the scope of these Lectures clearly intelligible, to give an account at some length of the conclusions and reasonings of both classes of critics.

The portion of the Scripture history which was first subjected to the application of the new principles was the historical part of the Old Testament. It was soon declared that a striking parallelism existed between this history and the early records of most heathen nations. (14) The miracles in the narrative were compared with the prodigies and divine appearances related by Herodotus and Livy. (15) The chronology was said to bear marks, like that of Rome and Babylon, of artificial arrangement; the recurrence of similar numbers, and especially of round numbers, particularly indicating its unhistorical character. (16) The names of kings, it was observed, were frequently so apposite, that the monarchs supposed to have borne them must be regarded as fictitious personages, (17) like Theseus and Numa. Portions of the sacred narrative were early declared to present every appearance of being simply myths; (18) and by degrees it was sought to attach to the whole history, from first to last, a legendary and unreal character. All objections taken by rationalists or infidels to particular relations in the sacred books being allowed as valid, it was considered a sufficient account of such relations to say, that the main source of the entire narrative was oral tradition — that it first took a written shape many hundreds of years after the supposed date of the circumstances narrated, the authors being poets rather than historians, and bent rather on glorifying their native country than on giving a true relation of facts — and that in places they had not even confined themselves to the exaggeration and embellishment of actual occurrences, but had allowed imagination to step in and fill up blanks in their annals.[(19)] By some, attempts were made to disentangle the small element of fact which lay involved in so much romance and poetry from the mass in which it was embedded;[(20)] but the more logical minds rejected this as a vain and useless labor, maintaining that no separation which was other than arbitrary could be effected; and that the events themselves, together with the dress in which they appeared, "constituted a whole belonging to the province of poetry and mythus."[(21)] It was argued that by this treatment the sacredness and divinity, and even the substantial truth of the Scriptures, was left unassailed;[(22)] the literal meaning only being discarded, and an allegorical one substituted in its place. Lastly, the name of Origen was produced from the primitive and best ages of Christianity to sanction this system of interpretation, and save it from the fatal stigma of entire and absolute novelty.[(23)]

When the historical character of the Old Testament, assailed on all sides by clever and eloquent pens, and weakly defended by here and there a single hesitating apologist, seemed to those who had conducted the warfare irretrievably demolished and destroyed,[(24)] the New Testament became, after a pause, the object of attack to the same school of writers. It was felt, no doubt, to be a bold thing to characterize as a collection of myths the writings of an age of general enlightenment[(25)] — nay, even of incredulity and scepticism; and perhaps a lingering regard for what so many souls held precious,[(26)] stayed the hands of those who nevertheless saw plainly, that the New Testament was open to the same method of attack as the Old, and that an inexorable logic required that both should be received or neither. A pause therefore ensued, but a pause of no long duration. First, particular portions of the New Testament narrative, as the account of our Lord's infancy,(27) and of the Temptation,(28) were declared to possess equal tokens of a mythic origin with those which had been previously regarded as fatal to the historical character of Old Testament stories, and were consequently singled out for rejection. Then, little by little, the same system of explanation was adopted with respect to more and more of the narrative;(29) till at last, in the hands of Strauss, the whole came to be resolved into pure myth and legend, and the historical Christ being annihilated, the world was told to console itself with a "God-man, eternally incarnate, not an individual, but an idea;"(30) which, on examination, turns out to be no God at all, but mere man — man perfected by nineteenth-century enlightenment — dominant over nature by the railroad and the telegraph, and over himself by the negation of the merely natural and sensual life, and the substitution for it of the intellectual, or (in the nomenclature of the school) the spiritual.

"In an individual," says Strauss, "the properties which the Church ascribes to Christ contradict themselves; in the *idea of the race* they perfectly agree. *Humanity is* the union of the two natures — God become man, the infinite manifesting itself in the finite, and the finite spirit remembering its infinitude; it is the child of the visible Mother and the invisible Father, Nature and Spirit; it is the worker of miracles, in so far as in the course of human history the spirit more and more completely subjugates nature, both within and around man, until it lies before him as the inert matter on which he exercises his active power; it is the sinless existence, for the course of its development is a blameless one; pollution cleaves to the individual only, and does not touch the race or its history. It is Humanity that dies, rises, and ascends to Heaven; for from the negation of its phenomenal life there ever proceeds a higher spiritual life; from the suppression of its mortality as a personal, national, and terrestrial spirit, arises its union with the infinite spirit of the heavens. *By faith in this Christ*, especially in his death and resurrection, man is justified before God; that is, by the kindling within him of the idea of Humanity, the individual man partakes of the divinely human life *of the species*."[(31)]

Such are the lengths to which speculation, professedly grounding itself on the established principles of historical criticism, has proceeded in our day; and such the conclusions recommended to our acceptance by a philosophy which calls itself preëminently spiritual. How such a philosophy differs from Atheism, except in the use of a religious terminology, which it empties of all religious meaning, I confess myself unable to perceive. The final issue of the whole seems to be simply that position which Aristotle scouted as the merest folly, that "man is the highest and most divine thing in the universe,"[(32)] and that God consequently is but a name for humanity when perfected.

More dangerous to faith, because less violent in its methods, and less sweeping in the conclusions to which it comes, is the moderate rationalism of another school, a school which can with some show of reason claim to shelter itself under the great name and authority of Niebuhr. Notwithstanding the personal faith of Niebuhr, which cannot be doubted, and the strong expressions of which he made use against the advocates of the mythical theory,[(33)] he was himself upon occasions betrayed into remarks which involved to a great extent their principles, and opened a door to the thorough-going scepticism from which he individually shrank with horror. For instance, in one place Niebuhr says, with respect to the Book of Esther, "I am convinced that this book is not to be regarded as historical, and I have not the least hesitation in here stating it publicly. Many entertain the same opinion. Even the early fathers have tormented themselves with it; and St. Jerome, as he himself clearly indicates, was in the greatest perplexity through his desire to regard it as an historical document. At present no one looks upon the Book of Judith as historical, and neither Origen nor St. Jerome did so; *the same is the case with Esther;* it is *nothing more than a poem* on the occurrences." (34) The great historical critic here (so far as appears, on mere subjective grounds, because the details of the narrative did not appear to him probable) surrendered to the mythical interpreters a book of Scripture — admitted that to be "a poem *and nothing more*," which, on the face of it, bore the appearance of a plain matter-of-fact history — put a work which the Church has always regarded as canonical and authoritative on a par with one which was early pronounced apocryphal, — not, certainly, moved to do so by any defect in the external evidence, (35) though a vague reference is made to "early fathers;" but on account of internal difficulties, either in the story itself, or in the manner of its narration. I cannot see that it is possible to distinguish the principle of this surrender from that asserted by the mythical school; or that the principle once admitted, any ground can be shown for limiting its application to a single book of Scripture, or indeed to any definite number of such books. Let it be once allowed that we may declare any part of Scripture which seems to us improbable, or which does not approve itself to our notions of what revelation should be, "a poem and nothing more," and what security is there against the extremest conclusions of the mythologists? One book will naturally be surrendered after another,(36) and the final result will not be distinguishable from that at which the school of De Wette and Strauss professedly aims — the destruction of all trust in the historical veracity of the Scripture narrative.

The partial scepticism of Niebuhr has always had followers in Germany — men who are believers, but who admit the principles of unbelief — who rationalize, but who think to say to the tide of rationalism, "Thus far shalt thou go, and no farther." I shall not detain my hearers with a long array of instances in this place. Suffice it to adduce the teaching of a single living writer, whose influence is very considerable both in Germany and in our own country. On the ground that Egypt has a continuous history, commencing more than six thousand years before the Christian era, we are required to reject the literal interpretation of the sixth, seventh, and eighth chapters of Genesis, and to believe that the Flood was no more than a great catastrophe in Western Asia, which swept away the inhabitants of that region, but left Egypt and the greater part of the world untouched. Ham, we are told, is not a person, but the symbolical representative of Egypt; and he is the elder brother, because Egyptian Hamitism is older than Asiatic Semitism. The expression that Canaan is the son of Ham "must be interpreted geographically;" it means, that the Canaanitic tribes which inhabited historical Canaan came from Egypt, where they had previously had their abode. Nimrod is said to have been begotten by Cush; but he was no more a Cushite by blood than Canaan was an Egyptian; he is called a Cushite, because the people represented by him came from the part of Africa called Cush or Ethiopia (which they had held as conquerors) back into Asia, and there established an empire.(37) Again, "the family tree of Abraham is an historical representation of the great and lengthened migrations of the primitive Asiatic race of man, from the mountains of Armenia and Chaldæa, through Mesopotamia, to the north-east frontier of Egypt, as far as Amalek and Edom. It represents the connection between nations and their tribes, *not personal connection between father and son*, and records consequently epochs, *not real human pedigrees*."(38) The early Scriptures are devoid altogether of an historical chronology. When the sojourn of the children of Israel in Egypt is said to have been four hundred and thirty years, of which one half, or two hundred and fifteen years, was from Abraham's going down into Egypt to Jacob's, the other from Jacob's going down to the Exodus, the number must be regarded as "conventional and unhistorical;"(39) as "connected with the legendary genealogies of particular families;"(40) as formed, in fact, artificially by a doubling of the first period; which itself only "represents the traditionary accounts of the primitive times of Canaan, as embodied in a genealogy of the three patriarchs,"(41) and "cannot possibly be worthy of more confidence than the traditions with regard to the second period," which are valueless.(42) Of course the earlier lists of names and calculations of years are looked upon with still less favor. "The Jewish tradition, in proportion as its antiquity is thrown back, bears on its face less of a chronological character," so that "no light is to be gleaned from it" for general purposes.(43) Even in the comparatively recent times of David and Solomon, there is no coherent or reliable chronology; the round number forty being still met with, which is taken to be an indubitable sign of arbitrary and artificial arrangement.(44)

Such are some of the results which have, in fact, followed from the examination by historical critics, possessed of more or less critical acumen, of those sacred records, which are allowed on all hands to be entitled to deep respect, and which we in this place believe to be, not indeed free from such small errors as the carelessness or ignorance of transcribers may have produced, but substantially "the Word of God." I propose at the present time, in opposition to the views which I have sketched, to examine the Sacred Narrative *on the positive side.* Leaving untouched the question of the inspiration of Scripture, and its consequent title to outweigh all conflicting testimony whatever, I propose briefly to review the historical evidence for the orthodox belief. My object will be to meet the reasoning of the historical sceptics on their own ground. I do not, indeed, undertake to consider and answer their minute and multitudinous cavils, which would be an endless task, and which is moreover unnecessary, as to a great extent the cavillers meet and answer one another;(45) but I hope to show, without assuming the inspiration of the Bible, that for the great facts of revealed religion, the miraculous history of the Jews, and the birth, life, death, resurrection, and ascension of Christ, as well as for his miracles and those of his apostles, the historical evidence which we possess is of an authentic and satisfactory character. I shall review this evidence in the light and by the laws of the modern historical criticism, so far as they seem to be established. Those laws appear to me to be sound; and their natural and real bearing is to increase instead of diminishing the weight of the Christian evidences. It is not from a legitimate and proper application of them that faith has suffered, but partly from their neglect or misapplication, partly from the intrusion among them of a single unproved and irrational opinion.

I am not aware that the laws in question have ever been distinctly laid down in a compendious, or even in an abstract form. They are assumed throughout the writings of our best historians, but they are involved in their criticisms rather than directly posited as their principles. I believe, however, that I shall not misrepresent them if I say, that, viewed on their positive side, they consist chiefly of the four following Canons:—

1. When the record which we possess of an event is the writing of a contemporary, supposing that he is a credible witness, and had means of observing the fact to which he testifies, the fact is to be accepted, as possessing the first or highest degree of historical credibility. Such evidence is on a par with that of witnesses in a court of justice, with the drawback, on the one hand, that the man who gives it is not sworn to speak the truth, and with the advantage, on the other, that he is less likely than the legal witness to have a personal interest in the matter concerning which he testifies. (46)

2. When the event recorded is one which the writer may be reasonably supposed to have obtained directly from those who witnessed it, we should accept it as probably true, unless it be in itself very improbable. Such evidence possesses the second degree of historical credibility. (47)

3. When the event recorded is removed considerably from the age of the recorder of it, and there is no reason to believe that he obtained it from a contemporary writing, but the probable source of his information was oral tra-

dition; still, if the event be one of great importance, and of public notoriety, if it affected the national life, or prosperity, — especially if it be of a nature to have been at once commemorated by the establishment of any rite or practice, — then it has a claim to belief as probably true, at least in its general outline. (48) This, however, is the third, and a comparatively low, degree of historical credibility.

4. When the traditions of one race, which, if unsupported, would have had but small claim to attention, and none to belief, are corroborated by the traditions of another, especially if a distant or hostile race, the event which has this double testimony obtains thereby a high amount of probability, and, if not very unlikely in itself, thoroughly deserves acceptance. (49) The degree of historical credibility in this case is not exactly commensurable with that in the others, since a new and distinct ground of likelihood comes into play. It may be as strong as the highest, and it may be almost as weak as the lowest, though this is not often the case in fact. In a general way we may say that the weight of this kind of evidence exceeds that which has been called the third degree of historical probability, and nearly approaches to the second.

To these Canons may be added certain corollaries, or dependent truths, — with respect to the relative value of the materials from which history is ordinarily composed, — important to be borne in mind in all inquiries like that on which we are entering. Historical materials may be divided into direct and indirect, — direct, or such as proceed from the agents in the occurrences; indirect, or such as are the embodiment of inquiries and researches made by persons *not* themselves engaged in the transactions. The former are allowed, on all hands, to be of primary importance. There is indeed a drawback upon their value, arising out of the tendency of human vanity to exalt self at the expense of truth; but where the moral character of the writer is a security against wilful misrepresentation, or where the publicity of the events themselves would make misrepresentation folly, the very highest degree of credit is to be given to direct records. These may be either public inscribed monuments, such as have frequently been set up by governments and kings; state papers, such as we hear of in the books of Ezra and Esther;[(50)] letters, or books. Again, books of this class will be either commentaries, (or particular histories of events in which the authors have taken part;) autobiographies, or accounts which persons have given of their own lives up to a certain point; or memoirs; i. e., accounts which persons have given of those with whom they have had some acquaintance. These are the best and most authentic sources of history; and we must either be content with them, or regard the past as absolutely shrouded from our knowledge by a veil which is impenetrable. Indirect records — the compilations of diligent inquirers concerning times or scenes in which they have themselves had no part — are to be placed on a much lower footing; they must be judged by their internal character, by their accord with what is otherwise known of the times or scenes in question, and by the apparent veracity and competency of their composers. They often have a high value; but this value cannot be assumed previously to investigation, depending as it does almost entirely on the critical judgment of their authors, on the materials to which they had access, and on the use that they actually made of them.

The force of cumulative evidence has often been noticed. No account of the grounds of historic belief would be complete, even in outline, which failed to notice its applicability to this field of investigation, and its great weight and importance in all cases where it has any place. "Probable proofs," says Bishop Butler, "by being added, not only increase the evidence, but *multiply* it." (51) When two independent writers witness to the same event, the probability of that event is increased, not in an arithmetical but in a geometrical ratio, not by mere addition, but by multiplication. (52) "By the mouth of two or three witnesses," the word to which such witness is borne is "*established*." [1] And the agreement is the more valuable if it be — so to speak — incidental and casual; if the two writers are contemporary, and their writings not known to one another; if one only alludes to what the other narrates; if one appears to have been an actor, and the other merely a looker-on; if one gives events, and the other the feelings which naturally arise out of them: in these cases the conviction which springs up in every candid and unprejudiced mind is absolute; the element of doubt which hangs about all matters of mere *belief* being reduced to such infinitesimal proportions as to be inappreciable, and so, practically speaking, to disappear altogether.

To the four Canons which have been already enumerated as the *criteria* of historic truth, modern Rationalism would add a fifth, an *a priori* opinion of its own — the admission of which would put a stop at once to any such inquiry as that upon which we are now entering. "No just perception of the true nature of history is possible," we are told, "without a perception of the inviolability of the chain of finite causes, and of the *impossibility of miracles*." (53) And the mythical interpreters insist, that one of the essential marks of a mythical narrative, whereby it

[1] Deut. xix. 15.

may be clearly distinguished from one which is historical, is, its "presenting an account of events which are either absolutely or relatively beyond the reach of (ordinary) experience, such as occurrences connected with the spiritual world, or its dealing in the supernatural." (54) Now, if miracles cannot take place, an inquiry into the historical evidences of Revealed Religion is vain; for Revelation is itself miraculous, and therefore, by the hypothesis, impossible. But what are the grounds upon which so stupendous an assertion is made, as that God cannot, if He so please, suspend the working of those laws by which He commonly acts upon matter, and act on special occasions differently? Shall we say that He cannot, because of His own immutability — because He is a being "with whom is no variableness, neither shadow of turning?"[1] But, if we apply the notion of a Law to God at all, it is plain that miraculous interpositions on fitting occasions may be as much a regular, fixed, and established rule of His government, as the working ordinarily by what are called natural laws. Or shall we say that all experience and analogy is against miracles? But this is either to judge, from our own narrow and limited experience, of the whole course of nature, and so to generalize upon most weak and insufficient grounds; or else, if in the phrase "all experience" we include the experience of others, it is to draw a conclusion directly in the teeth of our data; for many persons well worthy of belief have declared that they have witnessed and wrought miracles. Moreover, were it true that all known experience was against miracles, this would not even prove that they had not happened — much less that they are impossible. If they are impossible, it must be either from something in the nature of things, or from something in the

[1] James i. 17.

nature of God. That the immutability of God does not stand in the way of miracles has been already shown; and I know of no other attribute of the Divine Nature which can be even supposed to create a difficulty. To most minds it will, if I do not greatly mistake, rather appear, that the Divine Omnipotence includes in it the power of working miracles. And if God created the world, He certainly once worked a miracle of the most surpassing greatness. Is there then any thing in the nature of things to make miracles impossible? Not unless things have an independent existence, and work by their own power. If they are in themselves nought, if God called them out of nothing, and but for His sustaining power they would momentarily fall back into nothing; if it is not they that work, but He who works in them and through them; if growth, and change, and motion, and assimilation, and decay, are His dealings with matter, as sanctification, and enlightenment, and inward comfort, and the gift of the clear vision of Him, are His dealings with ourselves; if the Great and First Cause never deserts even for a moment the second Causes, but He who "upholdeth all things by the word of His power,"[1] and is "above all and *through* all,"[2] is also (as Hooker says) "the Worker of all in all" (55)—then certainly things in themselves cannot oppose any impediment to miracles, or do aught but obsequiously follow the Divine fiat, be it what it may. The whole difficulty with regard to miracles has its roots in a materialistic Atheism, which believes things to have a force in and of themselves; which regards them as self-sustaining, if not even as self-caused; which deems them to possess mysterious powers of their own uncontrollable by the Divine Will; which sees in the connection of physical cause and effect, not a

[1] Heb. i. 3. [2] Eph. iv. 6.

sequence, not a law, but a necessity; which, either positing a Divine First Cause to bring things into existence, then (like Anaxagoras) makes no further use of Him;[56] or does not care to posit any such First Cause at all, but is content to refer all things to a "course of nature," which it considers eternal and unalterable, and on which it lavishes all the epithets that believers regard as appropriate to God, and God only. It is the peculiarity of Atheism at the present day that it uses a religious nomenclature — it is no longer dry, and hard, and cold, all matter of fact and common-sense, as was the case in the last century, — on the contrary, it has become warm in expression, poetic, eloquent, glowing, sensuous, imaginative — the "Course of Nature," which it has set up in the place of God, is in a certain sense deified, — no language is too exalted to be applied to it, no admiration too great to be excited by it — it is "glorious," and "marvellous," and "superhuman," and "heavenly," and "spiritual," and "divine" — only it is "IT," not "HE," — a fact or set of facts, and not a Person; — and so it can really call forth no love, no gratitude, no reverence, no personal feeling of any kind — it can claim no willing obedience — it can inspire no wholesome awe — it is a dead idol after all, and its worship is but the old nature worship, — man returning in his dotage to the follies which beguiled his childhood — losing the Creator in the creature, the Workman in the work of his hands.

It cannot therefore be held on any grounds but such as involve a real, though covert Atheism, that miracles are impossible, or that a narrative of which supernatural occurrences form an essential part is therefore devoid of an historic character. Miracles are to be viewed as in fact a part of the Divine Economy, — a part as essential as any other, though coming into play less frequently. It has already been observed, that the creation of the world was a miracle, or rather a whole array of miracles; and any true historical account of it must "deal in the supernatural." A first man was as great a miracle — may we not say a greater miracle? — than a raised man. Greater, inasmuch as to create and unite a body and soul is to do more than merely to unite them when they have been created. And the occurrence of miracles at the beginning of the world established a precedent for their subsequent occurrence from time to time with greater or less frequency, as God should see to be fitting. Again, all history abounds in statements that miracles have in fact from time to time occurred; and though we should surrender to the sceptic the whole mass of Heathen and Ecclesiastical miracles, which I for one do not hold to be necessary,[57] yet still fictitious miracles imply the existence of true ones, just as hypocrisy implies that there is virtue. To reject a narrative, therefore, simply because it contains miraculous circumstances, is to indulge an irrational prejudice — a prejudice which has no foundation, either in *a priori* truths or in the philosophy of experience, and which can only be consistently held by one who disbelieves in God.

The rejection of this negative Canon, which a pseudo-critical School has boldly but vainly put forward for the furtherance of its own views with respect to the Christian scheme, but which no historian of repute has adopted since the days of Gibbon, will enable us to proceed without further delay to that which is the special business of these Lectures — the examination, by the light of those Canons whose truth has been admitted, of the historic evidences of Revealed Religion. The actual examination must, however, be reserved for future Lectures. Time will not permit of my attempting to do more in the brief remainder of the present Discourse than simply to point out the chief kinds or branches into which the evidence divides itself, and to indicate, somewhat more clearly than has as yet been done, the method which will be pursued in the examination of it.

The sacred records themselves are the main proof of the events related in them. Waiving the question of their inspiration, I propose to view them simply as a mass of documents, subject to the laws, and to be judged by the principles, of historical criticism; I shall briefly discuss their genuineness, where it has been called in question, and vindicate their authenticity. Where two or more documents belong to the same time, I shall endeavor to exhibit some of their most remarkable points of agreement: I shall not, however, dwell at much length on this portion of the inquiry. It is of preëminent importance, but its preëminence has secured it a large amount of attention on the part of Christian writers; and I cannot hope to add much to the labors of those who have preceded me in this field. There is, however, a second and distinct kind of evidence, which has not (I think) received of late as much consideration as it deserves — I mean the *external* evidence to the truth of the Bible records, whether contained in monuments, in the works of profane writers, in customs and observances now existing or known to have existed, or finally in the works of believers nearly contemporary with any of the events narrated. The evidence under some of these heads has recently received important accessions, and fresh light has been thrown in certain cases on the character and comparative value of the writers. It seems to be time to bid the nations of the earth once more "bring forth their witnesses," and "declare" and "show us" what it is which they record of the "former things" —

that they may at once justify and "be justified"—in part directly confirming the Scripture narrative, in part silent but not adverse, content to "hear, and say, 'It is truth.'" "Ye are my witnesses, saith the Lord"—even "the blind people, that have eyes; and the deaf, that have ears"—"Ye are my witnesses—*and* my servant whom I have chosen."[1] The testimony of the sacred and the profane is not conflicting, but consentient—and the comparison of the two will show, not discord, but harmony.

[1] Isaiah xliii. 8, 10.

LECTURE II.

INQUIRE, I PRAY THEE, OF THE FORMER AGE, AND PREPARE THYSELF TO THE SEARCH OF THEIR FATHERS; (FOR WE ARE BUT OF YESTERDAY, AND KNOW NOTHING, BECAUSE OUR DAYS UPON EARTH ARE A SHADOW;) SHALL NOT THEY TEACH THEE, AND TELL THEE, AND UTTER WORDS OUT OF THEIR HEART?—JOB VIII. VERSES 8 TO 10.

In every historical inquiry it is possible to pursue our researches in two ways: we may either trace the stream of time upwards, and pursue history to its earliest source; or we may reverse the process, and beginning at the fountain-head follow down the course of events in chronological order to our own day. The former is the more philosophical, because the more real and genuine method of procedure: it is the course which in the original investigation of the subject must, in point of fact, have been pursued: the present is our standing point, and we necessarily view the past from it; and only know so much of the past as we connect, more or less distinctly, with it. But the opposite process has certain advantages which cause it commonly to be preferred. It is the order of the actual occurrence, and therefore has an objective truth which the other lacks. It is the simpler and clearer of the two, being synthetic and not analytic; commencing with little, it proceeds by continual accretion, thus adapting itself to our capacities, which cannot take in much at once; and further, it has the advantage of conducting us out of comparative darkness into a light which brightens and broadens as we keep advancing, "shining more and more unto the perfect day."[1] Its difficulties and inconveniences are at the first outset, when we plunge as it were into a world unknown, and seek in the dim twilight of the remote past for some sure and solid ground upon which to plant our foot. On the whole there is perhaps sufficient reason for conforming to the ordinary practice, and adopting the actual order of the occurrences as that of the examination upon which we are entering.

It will be necessary, however, in order to bring within reasonable compass the vast field that offers itself to us for investigation, to divide the history which is to be reviewed into periods, which may be successively considered in their entirety. The division which the sacred writings seem to suggest is into five such periods. The first of these extends from the Creation to the death of Moses, being the period of which the history is delivered to us in the Pentateuch. The second extends from the death of Moses to the accession of Rehoboam, and is treated in Joshua, Judges, Ruth, the two Books of Samuel, and some portions of the Books of Kings and Chronicles. The third is the period from the accession of Rehoboam to the Captivity of Judah, which is treated of in the remainder of Kings and Chronicles, together with portions of Isaiah, Jeremiah, Ezekiel, Hosea, Joel, Amos, Jonah, Micah, Nahum, and Zephaniah. The fourth extends from the Captivity to the reform of Nehemiah; and its history is contained in Daniel, Ezra, Esther, and Nehemiah, and illustrated by Haggai and Zechariah. The fifth is the period of the life of Christ and the preaching and establishment of Christianity, of which the history is given in the New Testament. The first four periods will form the subject of the present and

[1] Proverbs iv. 18.

three following Lectures. The fifth period, from its superior importance, will require to be treated at greater length. Its examination is intended to occupy the remainder of the present Course.

The sacred records of the first period have come down to us in the shape of five Books, the first of which is introductory, while the remaining four present us with the history of an individual, Moses, and of the Jewish people under his guidance. Critically speaking, it is of the last importance to know by whom the books which contain this history were written. Now the ancient, positive, and uniform tradition of the Jews assigned the authorship of the five books, (or Pentateuch,) with the exception of the last chapter of Deuteronomy, to Moses;[(1)] and this tradition is *prima facie* evidence of the fact, such as at least throws the burden of proof upon those who call it in question. It is an admitted rule of all sound criticism, that books are to be regarded as proceeding from the writers whose names they bear, unless very strong reasons indeed can be adduced to the contrary.[(2)] In the present instance, the reasons which have been urged are weak and puerile in the extreme; they rest in part on misconceptions of the meaning of passages,[(3)] in part, upon interpolations into the original text, which are sometimes very plain and palpable.[(4)] Mainly, however, they have their source in arbitrary and unproved hypotheses, as that a contemporary writer would not have introduced an account of miracles;[(5)] that the culture indicated by the book is beyond that of the age of Moses;[(6)] that if Moses had written the book, he would not have spoken of himself in the third person;[(7)] that he would have given a fuller and more complete account of his own history;[(8)] and that he would not have applied to himself terms of praise and expressions of honor.(9) It is enough to observe of these objections, that they are such as might equally be urged against the genuineness of St. Paul's epistles, which is allowed even by Strauss(10) — against that of the works of Homer, Chaucer, and indeed of all writers in advance of their age — against Cæsar's Commentaries, and Xenophon's Expedition of Cyrus — against the Acts of the Apostles,(11) and against the Gospel of St. John. St. Paul relates contemporary miracles; Homer and Chaucer exhibit a culture and a tone which, but for them, we should have supposed unattainable in their age; Cæsar and Xenophon write throughout in the third person; St. Luke omits all account of his own doings at Philippi; St. John applies to himself the most honorable of all titles — "the disciple whom Jesus loved."[1] *A priori* conceptions of how an author of a certain time and country would write, of what he would say or not say, or how he would express himself, are among the weakest of all presumptions, and must be regarded as outweighed by a very small amount of positive testimony to authorship. Moreover, for an argument of this sort to have any force at all, it is necessary that we should possess, from other sources besides the author who is being judged, a tolerably complete knowledge of the age to which he is assigned, and a fair acquaintance with the literature of his period.(12) In the case of Moses our knowledge of the age is exceedingly limited, while of the literature we have scarcely any knowledge at all,(13) beyond that which is furnished by the sacred records next in succession — the Books of Joshua and Judges, and (perhaps) the Book of Job — and these are so far from supporting the notion that such a work as the Pentateuch could not be produced in the age of Moses, that they furnish a very strong argument

[1] John xiii. 23; xix. 26, &c.

to the contrary. The diction of the Pentateuch is older than that of Joshua and Judges, (14) while its ideas are presupposed in those writings, (15) which may be said to be based upon it, and to require it as their antecedent. If, then, they could be written at the time to which they are commonly and (as will be hereafter shown) rightly assigned, (16) the Pentateuch not only may, but must, be as early as Moses.

Vague doubts have sometimes been thrown out as to the existence of writings at this period. (17) The evidence of the Mosaic records themselves, if the true date of their composition were allowed, would be conclusive upon the point; for they speak of writing as a common practice. Waiving this evidence, we may remark that hieroglyphical inscriptions upon stone were known in Egypt at least as early as the fourth dynasty, or B. C. 2450, (18) that inscribed bricks were common in Babylonia about two centuries later, (19) and that writing upon papyruses, both in the hieroglyphic and hieratic characters, was familiar to the Egyptians under the eighteenth and nineteenth dynasties, (20) which is exactly the time to which the Mosaic records would, if genuine, belong. It seems certain that Moses, if educated by a daughter of one of the Ramesside kings, and therefore "learned" (as we are told he was) "in all the wisdom of Egypt,"[1] would be well acquainted with the Egyptian method of writing with ink upon the papyrus; while it is also probable that Abraham, who emigrated not earlier than the nineteeth century before our era from the great Chaldæan capital, Ur, would have brought with him and transmitted to his descendants the alphabetic system with which the Chaldæans of his day were acquainted. (21) There is thus every reason to suppose that writing was

[1] Acts vii. 22.

familiar to the Jews when they quitted Egypt; and the mention of it as a common practice in the books of Moses is in perfect accordance with what we know of the condition of the world at the time from other sources.

To the unanimous witness of the Jews with respect to the authorship of the Pentateuch may be added the testimony of a number of heathen writers. Hecatæus of Abdera,[(22)] Manetho,[(23)] Lysimachus of Alexandria,[(24)] Eupolemus,[(25)] Tacitus,[(26)] Juvenal,[(27)] Longinus,[(28)] all ascribe to Moses the institution of that code of laws by which the Jews were distinguished from other nations; and the majority distinctly[(29)] note that he committed his laws to writing. These authors cover a space extending from the time of Alexander, when the Greeks first became curious on the subject of Jewish history, to that of the emperor Aurelian, when the literature of the Jews had been thoroughly sifted by the acute and learned Alexandrians. They constitute, not the full voice of heathenism on the subject, but only an indication of what that voice was. It cannot be doubted that if we had the complete works of those many other writers to whom Josephus, Clement, and Eusebius refer as mentioning Moses,[(30)] we should find the amount of heathen evidence on this point greatly increased. Moreover, we must bear in mind that the witness is unanimous, or all but unanimous.[(31)] Nor is it, as an objector might be apt to urge, the mere echo of Jewish tradition faintly repeating itself from far off lands; in part at least it rests upon a distinct and even hostile authority — that of the Egyptians. Manetho certainly, and Lysimachus probably, represent Egyptian, and not Jewish, views; and thus the Jewish tradition is confirmed by that of the only nation which was sufficiently near and sufficiently advanced in the Mosaic age to make its testimony on the point of real importance.

To the external testimony which has been now adduced must be added the internal testimony of the work itself, which repeatedly speaks of Moses as writing the law, and recording the various events and occurrences in a book, and as reading from this book to the people.(32) The modern rationalist regards it as a "most unnatural supposition," that the Pentateuch was written during the passage of the Israelites through the wilderness;(33) but this is what every unprejudiced reader gathers from the Pentateuch itself, which tells us that God commanded Moses to "write" the discomfiture of Amalek "in a book;"[1] that Moses "wrote all the words of the law,"[2] and "took the book of the covenant, and read it in the audience of the people,"[3] and "wrote the goings out of the people of Israel according to their journeys, by the commandment of the Lord;"[4] and, finally, "made an end of writing the words of the law in a book, until they were finished;"[5] and bade the Levites, who bare the ark of the covenant, "take that book of the law, and put it in the side of the ark of the covenant of the Lord, that it might be there for a witness against the people."[6] A book, therefore — a "book of the covenant" — a book out of which he could read the whole law(34) — was certainly written by Moses; and this book was deposited in the ark of the covenant, and given into the special custody of the Levites, who bare it, with the stern injunction still ringing in their ears, "Ye shall not add unto the word, neither diminish aught from it;"[7] and they were charged "at the end of every seven years, in the year of release, in the feast of tabernacles, to read it before all Israel in their hearing;"[8] and, further, a command was

[1] Exod. xvii. 14. [2] Ibid. xxiv. 4. [3] Ibid. ver. 7.
[4] Numb. xxxiii. 2. [5] Deut. xxxi. 24. [6] Ibid. ver. 26.
[7] Deut. iv. 2. [8] Ibid. xxxi. 10, 11.

given, that, when the Israelites should have kings, each king should "write him a copy of the law in a book, out of that which was before the priests the Levites, that he might read therein all the days of his life."[1] Unless, therefore, we admit the Pentateuch to be genuine, we must suppose that the book which (according to the belief of the Jews) Moses wrote, which was placed in the ark of God, over which the Levites were to watch with such jealous care, which was to be read to the people once in each seven years, and which was guarded by awful sanctions from either addition to it or diminution from it — we must suppose, I say, that this book perished; and that another book was substituted in its place — by an unknown author — for unknown objects — professing to be the work of Moses, (for that is allowed,)[(35)] and believed to be his work thenceforth, without so much as a doubt being breathed on the subject either by the nation, its teachers, or even its enemies, for many hundreds of years.[(36)] It has often been remarked, that the theories of those who assail Christianity, make larger demands upon the faith of such as embrace them than the Christian scheme itself, marvellous as it is in many points. Certainly, few suppositions can be more improbable than that to which (as we have seen) those who deny the Pentateuch to be genuine must have recourse, when pressed to account for the phenomena. It is not surprising that, having to assign a time for the introduction of the forged volume, they have varied as to the date which they suggest by above a thousand years, while they also differ from one another in every detail with which they venture to clothe the transaction.[(37)]

I have dwelt the longer upon the genuineness of the Pentateuch, because it is admitted, even by the extremest

[1] Deut. xvii. 18, 19.

sceptics, that the genuineness of the work carries with it the authenticity of the narrative, at least in all its main particulars. "It would most unquestionably," says Strauss, "be an argument of *decisive* weight in favor of the credibility of the Biblical history, could it indeed be shown that it was written by eye-witnesses." "Moses, being the leader of the Israelites on their departure from Egypt, would undoubtedly give a faithful history of the occurrences, unless" (which is not pretended) "he designed to deceive." And further, "Moses, if his intimate connection with Deity described in these books" (i. e. the last four) "be historically true, was likewise eminently qualified, by virtue of such connection, to produce a credible history of the earlier periods."[(37)] If Moses indeed wrote the account which we possess of the Exodus and of the wanderings in the wilderness; and if, having written it, he delivered it to those who knew the events as well as he, the conditions, which secure the highest degree of historical credibility, so far at least as regards the events of the last four books, are obtained. We have for them the direct witness of a contemporary writer — not an actor only, but the leader in the transactions which he relates — honest evidently, for he records his own sins and defects, and the transgressions and sufferings of his people; and honest necessarily, for he writes of events which were public and known to all — we have a work, which, by the laws of historical criticism, is thus for historical purposes just as reliable as Cæsar's Commentaries or Xenophon's Retreat of the Ten Thousand — we have that rare literary treasure, the autobiography of a great man, engaged in great events, the head of his nation at a most critical period in their annals; who commits to writing as they occur the various events and transactions in which he is engaged, wherever they have a national or public character.(38) We must therefore consider, even setting aside the whole idea of inspiration, that we possess in the last four books of the Pentateuch as reliable an account of the Exodus of the Jews, and their subsequent wanderings, as we do, in the works of Cæsar and Xenophon, of the conquest of Britain, or of the events which preceded and followed the battle of Cunaxa.

The narrative of Genesis stands undoubtedly on a different footing. Our confidence in it must ever rest mainly on our conviction of the inspiration of the writer. Still, setting that aside, and continuing to judge the documents as if they were ordinary historical materials, it is to be noted, in the first place, that, as Moses was on the mother's side grandson to Levi, he would naturally possess that fair knowledge of the time of the first going down into Egypt, and of the history of Joseph, which the most sceptical of the historical critics allow that men have of their own family and nation to the days of their grandfathers.(39) He would thus be as good an historical authority for the details of Joseph's story, and for the latter part of the life of Jacob, as Herodotus for the reign of Cambyses, or Fabius Pictor for the third Samnite War. Again, with respect to the earlier history, it is to be borne in mind through how very few hands, according to the numbers in the Hebrew text, this passed to Moses.(40) Adam, according to the Hebrew original, was for two hundred and forty-three years contemporary with Methuselah, who conversed for one hundred years with Shem. Shem was for fifty years contemporary with Jacob, who probably saw Jochebed, Moses' mother. Thus Moses might, by mere oral tradition, have obtained the history of Abraham, and even of the Deluge, at third hand; and that of the Temptation and the Fall, at fifth hand. The patriarchal longevity had the effect of reducing centuries to little more than lustres, so far as the safe transmission of historical events was concerned; for this does not depend either upon years or upon generations, but upon the number of links in the chain through which the transmittal takes place. If it be granted, as it seems to be, (41) that the great and stirring events in a nation's life will, under ordinary circumstances, be remembered (apart from all written memorials) for the space of one hundred and fifty years, being handed down through five generations, it must be allowed (even on mere human grounds) that the account which Moses gives of the Temptation and the Fall is to be depended on, if it passed through no more than four hands between him and Adam. And the argument is of course stronger for the more recent events, since they would have passed through fewer hands than the earlier. (42)

And this, be it remembered, is on the supposition that the sole human source from which Moses composed the Book of Genesis was oral tradition. But it is highly probable that he also made use of documents. So much fanciful speculation has been advanced, so many vain and baseless theories have been built up, in connection with what is called the "document-hypothesis" concerning Genesis, (43) that I touch the point with some hesitation, and beg at once to be understood as not venturing to dogmatize in a matter of such difficulty. But both *a priori* probability, and the internal evidence, seem to me to favor the opinion of Vitringa (44) and Calmet, (45) that Moses consulted monuments or records of former ages, which had descended from the families of the patriarchs, and by collecting, arranging, adorning, and, where they were deficient, completing them, composed his history. What we know of the antiquity of writing, both in Egypt and Babylonia, (46) renders it not improbable that the art was known and practised soon after the Flood, if it was not even (as some have supposed) a legacy from the antediluvian world.(47) Abraham can scarcely have failed to bring with him into Palestine a knowledge which had certainly been possessed by the citizens of Ur for several hundred years before he set out on his wanderings. And if it be said that the art, though known, might not have been applied to historical records in the family of Abraham at this early date, — yet, at any rate, when the Israelites descended into Egypt, and found writing in such common use, and historical records so abundant as they can be proved to have been in that country at that period, it is scarcely conceivable that they should not have reduced to a written form the traditions of their race, the memory of which their residence in a foreign land would be apt to endanger. And these probabilities are quite in accordance with what appears in the Book of Genesis itself. The great fulness with which the history of Joseph is given, and the *minutiæ* into which it enters, mark it as based upon a contemporary, or nearly contemporary, biography; and the same may be said with almost equal force of the histories of Jacob, Isaac, and even Abraham. Further, there are several indications of separate documents in the earlier part of Genesis, as the superscriptions or headings of particular portions, the change of appellation by which the Almighty is distinguished, and the like; which, if they do not certainly mark different documents, at least naturally suggest them. If we then upon these grounds accept Vitringa's theory, we elevate considerably what I may call the human authority of Genesis. Instead of being the embodiment of oral traditions which have passed through two, three, four, or perhaps more hands, previously to their receiving a written form, the Book of

Genesis becomes a work based in the main upon contemporary, or nearly contemporary, documents — documents of which the venerable antiquity casts all other ancient writings into the shade, several of them dating probably from times not far removed from the Flood, while some may possibly descend to us from the antediluvian race. The sanction which the Book of Genesis thus obtains is *additional*, it must be remembered, to what it derives from Moses; who is still the responsible author of the work; who selected the documents, and gave them all the confirmation which they could derive from his authority, whether it be regarded as divine or human, as that of one "learned" in man's "wisdom,"[1] or that of an inspired teacher — "a prophet, raised up by God."[2]

Thus far we have been engaged in considering the weight which properly attaches to the Pentateuch itself, viewed as an historical work produced by a certain individual, under certain circumstances, and at a certain period. It remains to examine the external evidence to the character of the Mosaic narrative which is furnished by the other ancient records in our possession, so far at least as those records have a fair claim to be regarded as of any real historic value.

Records possessing even moderate pretensions to the character of historic are, for this early period, as we should expect beforehand, extremely scanty. I cannot reckon in the number either the primitive traditions of the Greeks, the curious compilations of the Armenians,(48) the historical poems of the Hindoos,(49) or the extravagant fables of the Chinese.(50) A dim knowledge of certain great events in primeval history — as of the Deluge — may indeed be traced in all these quarters;(51) but the historical element

[1] Acts vii. 22. [2] Deut. xviii. 15.

to be detected is in every case so small, it is so overlaid by fable, and intermixed with what is palpably imaginative, that no manner of reliance can be placed upon statements merely because they occur in these pretended histories; nor have they the slightest title to be used as tests whereby to try the authenticity of any other narrative. The only reliable materials that we possess, besides the Pentateuch, for the history of the period which it embraces, consist of some fragments of Berosus and Manetho, an epitome of the early Egyptian history of the latter, a certain number of Egyptian and Babylonian inscriptions, and two or three valuable papyri.

If it be asked on what grounds so strong a preference is assigned to these materials, the answer is easy. The records selected are those of Egypt and Babylon. Now these two countries were, according to the most trustworthy accounts, both sacred and profane,[(52)] the first seats of civilization: in them writing seems to have been practised earlier than elsewhere; they paid from the first great attention to history, and possessed, when the Greeks became acquainted with them, historical records of an antiquity confessedly greater than that which could be claimed for any documents elsewhere. Further, in each of these countries, at the moment when, in consequence of Grecian conquest and the infusion of new ideas, there was the greatest danger of the records perishing or being vitiated, there arose a man — a native — thoroughly acquainted with their antiquities, and competently skilled in the Greek language, who transferred to that tongue, and thus made the common property of mankind, what had previously been a hidden treasure — the possession of their own priests and philosophers only. The value of the histories written by Manetho the Sebennyte, and Berosus the Chaldæan, had long been suspected by the learned;[53] but it remained for the present age to obtain distinct evidence of their fidelity — evidence which places them, among the historians of early times, in a class by themselves, greatly above even the most acute and painstaking of the Greek and Roman compilers. Herodotus, Ctesias, Alexander Polyhistor, Diodorus Siculus, Trogus Pompeius, could at best receive at second hand such representations of Babylonian and Egyptian history as the natives chose to impart to them, and moreover received these representations (for the most part) diluted and distorted by passing through the medium of comparatively ignorant interpreters. Manetho and Berosus had free access to the national records, and so could draw their histories directly from the fountain-head. This advantage might, of course, have been forfeited by a deficiency on their part of either honesty or diligence; but the recent discoveries in the two countries have had the effect of removing all doubt upon either of these two heads from the character of both writers. The monuments which have been recovered furnish the strongest proof alike of the honest intention and of the diligence and carefulness of the two historians; who have thus, as profane writers of primeval history, a preëminence over all others.[54] This is perhaps the chief value of the documents obtained, which do not in themselves furnish a history, or even its framework, a chronology;[55] but require an historical scheme to be given from without, into which they may fit, and wherein each may find its true and proper position.

If we now proceed to compare the Mosaic account of the first period of the world's history with that outline which may be obtained from Egyptian and Babylonian sources, we are struck at first sight with what seems an enormous difference in the chronology. The sum of the years in Manetho's scheme, as it has come down to us in Eusebius, is little short of thirty thousand;(56) while that in the scheme of Berosus, as reported by the same author,(57) exceeds four hundred and sixty thousand! But upon a little consideration, the greater part of this difficulty vanishes. If we examine the two chronologies, we shall find that both evidently divide at a certain point, above which all is certainly mythic, while below all is, or at least may be, historical. Out of the thirty thousand years contained (apparently) in Manetho's scheme, nearly twenty-five thousand belong to the time when Gods, Demigods, and Spirits had rule on earth; and the history of Egypt confessedly does not begin till this period is concluded, and Menes, the first Egyptian king, mounts the throne.(58) Similarly, in the chronology of Berosus, there is a sudden transition from kings whose reigns are counted by *sossi* and *neri*, or periods respectively of sixty and six hundred years, to monarchs the average length of whose reigns very little exceeds that found to prevail in ordinary monarchies. Omitting in each case what is plainly a mythic computation, we have in the Babylonian scheme a chronology which mounts up no higher than two thousand four hundred and fifty-eight years before Christ, or eight hundred years after the Deluge, (according to the numbers of the Septuagint;) while in the Egyptian we have at any rate only an excess of about two thousand years to explain and account for, instead of an excess of twenty-seven thousand.

And this latter discrepancy becomes insignificant, if it does not actually disappear, upon a closer scrutiny. The five thousand years of Manetho's dynastic lists were reduced by himself (as we learn from Syncellus) to three thousand five hundred and fifty-five years,(59) doubtless because he was aware that his lists contained in some cases contemporary dynasties; in others, contemporary kings in the same dynasty, owing to the mention in them of various royal personages associated on the throne by the principal monarch. Thus near fifteen hundred years are struck off from Manetho's total at a blow; and the chronological difference between his scheme and that of Scripture is reduced to a few hundred years — a discrepancy of no great moment, and one which might easily arise, either from slight errors of the copyists, or from an insufficient allowance being made in Manetho's scheme, in respect of either or both of the causes from which Egyptian chronology is always liable to be exaggerated. Without taxing Manetho with conscious dishonesty, we may suspect that he was not unwilling to exalt the antiquity of his country, if he could do so without falsifying his authorities; and from the confusion of the middle or Hyksos period of Egyptian history, and the obscurity of the earlier times, when there were as yet no monuments, he would have had abundant opportunity for chronological exaggeration by merely regarding as consecutive dynasties all those, which were not certainly known to have been contemporary. The real duration of the Egyptian monarchy depends entirely upon the proper arrangement of the dynasties into synchronous and consecutive — a point upon which the best Egyptologers are still far from agreed. Some of the greatest names in this branch of antiquarian learning are in favor of a chronology almost as moderate as the historic Babylonian; the accession of Menes, according to them, falling about 2660 B. C., or more than six hundred years after the Septuagint date for the Deluge.[(60)]

The removal of this difficulty opens the way to a consideration of the positive points of agreement between the

Scriptural narrative and that of the profane authorities. And here, for the earliest times, it is especially Babylon which furnishes an account capable of being compared with that of Moses. According to Berosus, the world when first created was in darkness, and consisted of a fluid mass inhabited by monsters of the strangest forms. Over the whole dominated a female power called Thalatth, or Sea. Then Belus, wishing to carry on the creative work, cleft Thalatth in twain; and of the half of her he made the earth, and of the other half the heaven. Hereupon the monsters, who could not endure the air and the light, perished. Belus upon this, seeing that the earth was desolate, yet teeming with productive power, cut off his own head, and mingling the blood which flowed forth with the dust of the ground, formed men, who were thus intelligent, as being partakers of the divine wisdom. He then made other animals fit to live on the earth: he made also the stars, and the sun and moon, and the five planets. The first man was Alôrus, a Chaldæan, who reigned over mankind for thirty-six thousand years, and begat a son, Alaparus, who reigned ten thousand eight hundred years. Then followed in succession eight others, whose reigns were of equal or greater length, ending with Xisuthrus, under whom the great Deluge took place.(61) The leading facts of this cosmogony and antediluvian history are manifestly, and indeed confessedly,(62) in close agreement with the Hebrew records. We have in it the earth at first "without form and void," and "darkness upon the face of the deep."[1] We have the Creator dividing the watery mass and making the two firmaments, that of the heaven and that of the earth, first of all; we have Light spoken of before the sun and moon; we have their creation, and that of the stars,

[1] Genesis i. 2.

somewhat late in the series of events given; we have a divine element infused into man at his birth, and again we have his creation "from the dust of the ground."[1] Further, between the first man and the Deluge are in the scheme of Berosus ten generations, which is the exact number between Adam and Noah; and though the duration of human life is in his account enormously exaggerated, we may see even in this exaggeration a glimpse of the truth, that the lives of the Patriarchs were extended far beyond the term which has been the limit in later ages. This truth seems to have been known to many of the ancients,(63) and traces of it have even been found among the modern Burmans and Chinese.(64)

The account which Berosus gives of the Deluge is still more strikingly in accordance with the narrative of Scripture. "Xisuthrus," he says, "was warned by Saturn in a dream that all mankind would be destroyed shortly by a deluge of rain. He was bidden to bury in the city of Sippara (or Sepharvaim) such written documents as existed; and then to build a huge vessel or ark, in length five furlongs, and two furlongs in width, wherein was to be placed good store of provisions, together with winged fowl and four-footed beasts of the earth; and in which he was himself to embark with his wife and children, and his close friends. Xisuthrus did accordingly, and the flood came at the time appointed. The ark drifted towards Armenia; and Xisuthrus, on the third day after the rain abated, sent out from the ark a bird, which, after flying for a while over the illimitable sea of waters, and finding neither food nor a spot on which it could settle, returned to him. Some days later, Xisuthrus sent out other birds, which likewise returned, but with feet covered with mud. Sent out a third

[1] Genesis ii. 7.

time, the birds returned no more; and Xisuthrus knew that the earth had reappeared. So he removed some of the covering of the ark, and looked, and behold the vessel had grounded upon a high mountain, and remained fixed. Then he went forth from the ark, with his wife, his daughter, and his pilot, and built an altar, and offered sacrifice; after which he suddenly disappeared from sight, together with those who had accompanied him. They who had remained in the ark, surprised that he did not return, sought him; when they heard his voice in the sky, exhorting them to continue religious, and bidding them go back to Babylonia from the land of Armenia, where they were, and recover the buried documents, and make them once more known among men. So they obeyed, and went back to the land of Babylon, and built many cities and temples, and raised up Babylon from its ruins."(65)

Such is the account of Berosus; and a description substantially the same is given by Abydenus,(66) an ancient writer of whom less is known, but whose fragments are generally of great value and importance. It is plain that we have here a tradition not drawn from the Hebrew record, much less the foundation of that record;(67) yet coinciding with it in the most remarkable way. The Babylonian version is tricked out with a few extravagances, as the monstrous size of the vessel, and the translation of Xisuthrus; but otherwise it is the Hebrew history *down to its minutiæ.* The previous warning, the divine direction as to the ark and its dimensions, the introduction into it of birds and beasts, the threefold sending out of the bird, the place of the ark's resting, the egress by removal of the covering, the altar straightway built, and the sacrifice offered, constitute an array of exact coincidences which cannot possibly be the result of chance, and of which I see no plausible account that can be given except that it is the harmony of truth. Nor are these minute coincidences counterbalanced by the important differences which some have seen in the two accounts. It is not true to say (as Niebuhr is reported to have said) that "the Babylonian tradition differs from the Mosaic account by stating that not only Xisuthrus and his family, but *all pious men*, were saved; and also by making the Flood not universal, but only partial, and *confined to Babylonia*." (66) Berosus does indeed give Xisuthrus, as companions in the ark, not only his wife and children, but a certain number of "close friends;" and thus far he differs from Scripture; but these friends are not represented as numerous, much less as "all pious men." And so far is he from making the Flood partial, or confining it to Babylonia, that his narrative distinctly implies the contrary. The warning given to Xisuthrus is that "mankind" (τοὺς ἀνθρώπους) is about to be destroyed. The ark drifts to Armenia, and when it is there, the birds are sent out, and find "an illimitable sea of waters," and no rest for the sole of their feet. When at length they no longer return, Xisuthrus knows "that land has reappeared," and leaving the ark, finds himself "on a mountain in Armenia." It is plain that the waters are represented as prevailing above the tops of the loftiest mountains in Armenia, — a height which must have been seen to involve the submersion of all the countries with which the Babylonians were acquainted.

The account which the Chaldæan writer gave of the events following the Deluge is reported with some disagreement by the different authors through whom it has come down to us. Josephus believed that Berosus was in accord with Scripture in regard to the generations between the Flood and Abraham, which (according to the Jewish historian) he correctly estimated at ten.(67) But other writers introduce in this place, as coming from Berosus, a series of eighty-six kings, the first and second of whom reign for above two thousand years, while the remainder reign upon an average three hundred and forty-five years each. We have here perhaps a trace of that gradual shortening of human life which the genealogy of Abraham exhibits to us so clearly in Scripture; but the numbers appear to be artificial,(68) and they are unaccompanied by any history. There is reason, however, to believe that Berosus noticed one of the most important events of this period, in terms which very strikingly recall the Scripture narrative. Writers, whose Babylonian history seems drawn directly from him, or from the sources which he used, give the following account of the tower of Babel, and the confusion of tongues — "At this time the ancient race of men were so puffed up with their strength and tallness of stature, that they began to despise and contemn the gods; and labored to erect that very lofty tower, which is now called Babylon, intending thereby to scale heaven. But when the building approached the sky, behold, the gods called in the aid of the winds, and by their help overturned the tower, and cast it to the ground. The name of the ruins is still called Babel; because until this time all men had used the same speech, but now there was sent upon them a confusion of many and diverse tongues."(69)

At the point which we have now reached, the sacred narrative ceases to be general, and becomes special or particular. It leaves the history of the world, and concentrates itself on an individual and his descendants. At the moment of transition, however, it throws out, in a chapter of wonderful grasp and still more wonderful accuracy, a sketch of the nations of the earth, their ethnic affinities, and to some extent their geographical position and boundaries. The *Toldoth Beni Noah* has extorted the admiration of modern ethnologists, who continually find in it anticipations of their greatest discoveries. For instance, in the very second verse the great discovery of Schlegel,(70) which the word Indo-European embodies — the affinity of the principal nations of Europe with the Arian or Indo-Persic stock — is sufficiently indicated by the conjunction of the Madai or Medes (whose native name was *Mada*) with Gomer or the Cymry, and Javan or the Ionians. Again, one of the most recent and unexpected results of modern linguistic inquiry is the proof which it has furnished of an ethnic connection between the Ethiopians or Cushites, who adjoined on Egypt, and the primitive inhabitants of Babylonia; a connection which (as we saw in the last Lecture) was positively denied by an eminent ethnologist only a few years ago, but which has now been sufficiently established from the cuneiform monuments.(71) In the tenth of Genesis we find this truth thus briefly but clearly stated — "And Cush begat Nimrod," the "beginning of whose kingdom was Babel."[1] So we have had it recently made evident from the same monuments, that "out of that land went forth Asshur, and builded Nineveh"[2] — or that the Semitic Assyrians proceeded from Babylonia and founded Nineveh long after the Cushite foundation of Babylon.(72) Again, the Hamitic descent of the early inhabitants of Canaan, which had often been called in question, has recently come to be looked upon as almost certain, apart from the evidence of Scripture;(73) and the double mention of Sheba, both among the sons of Ham, and also among those of Shem,[3] has been illustrated by the discovery that there are

[1] Gen. x. 8 and 10.
[2] Ibid. verse 11.
[3] Ibid. verses 7 and 28.

two races of Arabs — one (the Joktanian) Semitic, the other (the Himyaric) Cushite or Ethiopic.(74) On the whole, the scheme of ethnic affiliation given in the tenth chapter of Genesis is pronounced "safer" to follow than any other; and the *Toldoth Beni Noah* commends itself to the ethnic inquirer as "the most authentic record that we possess for the affiliation of nations," and as a document "of the very highest antiquity."(75)

The confirmation which profane history lends the Book of Genesis from the point where the narrative passes from the general to the special character, is (as might be expected) only occasional, and for the most part incidental. Abraham was scarcely a personage of sufficient importance to attract much of the attention of either the Babylonian or the Egyptian chroniclers. We possess, indeed, several very interesting notices of this Patriarch and his successors from heathen pens;(76) but they are of far inferior moment to the authorities hitherto cited, since they do not indicate a separate and distinct line of information, but are, in all probability, derived from the Hebrew records. I refer particularly to the passages which Eusebius produces in his Gospel Preparation from Eupolemus, Artapanus, Molo, Philo, and Cleodemus or Malchas, with regard to Abraham, and from Demetrius, Theodotus, Artapanus, and Philo, with respect to Isaac and Jacob. These testimonies are probably well known to many of my hearers, since they have been adduced very generally by our writers.(77) They bear unmistakably the stamp of a Jewish origin; and show the view which the more enlightened heathen took of the historical character of the Hebrew records, when they first became acquainted with them; but they cannot boast, like notices in Berosus and Manetho, a distinct origin, and thus a separate and independent authority. I shall therefore content myself with this brief mention of them here, which is all that time will allow; and proceed to adduce a few direct testimonies to the later narrative, furnished either by the native writers, or by the results of modern researches.

There are three points only in this portion of the narrative which, being of the nature of public and important events, might be expected to obtain notice in the Babylonian or Egyptian records — the expedition of Chedor-laomer with his confederate kings, the great famine in the days of Joseph, and the Exodus of the Jews. Did we possess the complete monumental annals of the two countries, or the works themselves of Berosus and Manetho, it might fairly be demanded of us that we should adduce evidence from them of all the three. With the scanty and fragmentary remains which are what we actually possess, it would not be surprising if we found ourselves without a trace of any. In fact, however, we are able to produce from our scanty stock a decisive confirmation of two events out of the three.

The monumental records of Babylonia bear marks of an interruption in the line of native kings, about the date which from Scripture we should assign to Chedor-laomer, and "point to Elymais (or Elam) as the country from which the interruption came." (78) We have mention of a king, whose name is on good grounds identified with Chedor-laomer, (79) as paramount in Babylonia at this time — a king apparently of Elamitic origin — and this monarch bears in the inscriptions the unusual and significant title of *Apda Martu*, or "Ravager of the West." Our fragments of Berosus give us no names at this period; but his dynasties exhibit a transition at about the date required, (80) which is in accordance with the break indicated by the monuments. We thus obtain a double witness to the remarkable fact of an interruption of pure Babylonian supremacy at this time; and from the monuments we are able to pronounce that the supremacy was transferred to Elam, and that under a king, the Semitic form of whose name would be Chedor-laomer, a great expedition was organized, which proceeded to the distant and then almost unknown west, and returned after "ravaging" but not conquering those regions.

The Exodus of the Jews was an event which could scarcely be omitted by Manetho. It was one however of such a nature — so entirely repugnant to all the feelings of an Egyptian — that we could not expect a fair representation of it in their annals. And accordingly, our fragments of Manetho present us with a distinct but very distorted notice of the occurrence. The Hebrews are represented as leprous and impious Egyptians, who under the conduct of a priest of Heliopolis, named Moses, rebelled on account of oppression, occupied a town called Avaris, or Abaris, and having called in the aid of the people of Jerusalem, made themselves masters of Egypt, which they held for thirteen years; but who were at last defeated by the Egyptian king, and driven from Egypt into Syria.[(81)] We have here the oppression, the name Moses, the national name, Hebrew, under the disguise of *Abaris*, and the true direction of the retreat; but we have all the special circumstances of the occasion concealed under a general confession of disaster; and we have a claim to final triumph which consoled the wounded vanity of the nation, but which we know to have been unfounded. On the whole we have perhaps as much as we could reasonably expect the annals of the Egyptians to tell us of transactions so little to their credit; and we have a narrative fairly confirming the principal facts, as well as very curious in many of its particulars.[(82)]

I have thus briefly considered some of the principal of those direct testimonies which can be adduced from ancient profane sources, in confirmation of the historic truth of the Pentateuch. There are various other arguments — some purely, some partly historic — into which want of space forbids my entering in the present Course. For instance, there is what may be called the historico-scientific argument, derivable from the agreement of the sacred narrative with the conclusions reached by those sciences which have a partially historical character. Geology — whatever may be thought of its true bearing upon other points — at least witnesses to the recent creation of man, of whom there is no trace in any but the latest strata. (83) Physiology decides in favor of the unity of the species, and the probable derivation of the whole human race from a single pair. (84) Comparative Philology, after divers fluctuations, settles into the belief that languages will ultimately prove to have been all derived from a common basis. (85) Ethnology pronounces that, independently of the Scriptural record, we should be led to fix on the plains of Shinar as a common centre, or focus, from which the various lines of migration and the several types of races originally radiated. (86) Again, there is an argument perhaps more convincing than any other, but of immense compass, deducible from the indirect and incidental points of agreement between the Mosaic records and the best profane authorities. The limits within which I am confined compel me to decline this portion of the inquiry. Otherwise it might be shown that the linguistic, geographic, and ethologic notices contained in the books of Moses are of the most veracious character, (87) stamping the whole narration with an unmistakable air of authenticity. And this, it may be remarked, is an argument to which modern research is perpetually adding fresh weight. For instance, if we look to the geography, we shall find that till within these few years, "Erech, and Accad, and Calneh, in the land of Shinar"[1]—Calah and Resen, in the country peopled by Asshur[2]—Ellasar, and "Ur of the Chaldees,"[3] were mere names; and beyond the mention of them in Genesis, scarcely a trace was discoverable of their existence. (88) Recently, however, the mounds of Mesopotamia have been searched, and bricks and stones buried for near three thousand years have found a tongue, and tell us exactly where each of these cities stood, (89) and sufficiently indicate their importance. Again, the power of Og, and his "threescore cities all fenced with high walls, gates, and bars, besides unwalled towns a great many,"[4] in such a country as that to the east of the Sea of Galilee, whose old name of Trachonitis indicates its barrenness, seemed to many improbable — but modern research has found in this very country a vast number of walled cities still standing, which show the habits of the ancient people, and prove that the population must at one time have been considerable. (90) So the careful examination that has been made of the valley of the Jordan, which has resulted in a proof that it is a unique phenomenon, utterly unlike any thing elsewhere on the whole face of the earth, (91) tends greatly to confirm the Mosaic account, that it became what it now is by a great convulsion; and by pious persons will, I think, be felt as confirming the miraculous character of that convulsion. Above all, perhaps, the absence of any counter-evidence — the fact that each accession to our knowledge of the ancient times, whether historic or geographic, or ethnic, helps to remove difficulties, and to produce a perpetual

[1] Gen. x. 10.
[2] Ibid. verses 11 and 12.
[3] Ibid. xi. 31; xiv. 1.
[4] Deut. iii. 5.

supply of fresh illustrations of the Mosaic narrative; while fresh difficulties are not at the same time brought to light — is to be remarked, as to candid minds an argument for the historic truth of the narrative, the force of which can scarcely be over-estimated. All tends to show that we possess in the Pentateuch, not only the most authentic account of ancient times that has come down to us, but a history absolutely and in every respect true. All tends to assure us that in this marvellous volume we have no old wives' tales, no "cunningly devised fable;"[1] but a "treasure of wisdom and knowledge"[2] — as important to the historical inquirer as to the theologian. There may be obscurities — there may be occasionally, in names and numbers, accidental corruptions of the text — there may be a few interpolations — glosses which have crept in from the margin; but upon the whole it must be pronounced that we have in the Pentateuch a genuine and authentic work, and one which — even were it not inspired — would be, for the times and countries whereof it treats, the leading and paramount authority. It is (let us be assured) "MOSES," who is still "read in the synagogues every sabbath day;"[3] and they who "resist" him, by impugning his veracity, like Jannes and Jambres of old, "resist the *truth*."[4]

[1] 2 Pet. i. 16.
[2] Col. ii. 3.
[3] Acts xv. 21.
[4] 2 Tim. iii. 8.

LECTURE III.

WHEN HE HAD DESTROYED SEVEN NATIONS IN THE LAND OF CHANAAN, HE DIVIDED THEIR LAND TO THEM BY LOT. AND AFTER THAT HE GAVE THEM JUDGES ABOUT THE SPACE OF FOUR HUNDRED AND FIFTY YEARS, UNTIL SAMUEL THE PROPHET. AND AFTERWARD THEY DESIRED A KING. — ACTS XIII. 19–21.

THE period of Jewish history, which has to be considered in the present Lecture, contains within it the extremes of obscurity and splendor, of the depression and the exaltation of the race. The fugitives from Egypt, who by divine aid effected a lodgment in the land of Canaan, under their great leader, Joshua, were engaged for some hundreds of years in a perpetual struggle for existence with the petty tribes among whom they had intruded themselves, and seemed finally on the point of succumbing and ceasing altogether to be a people, when they were suddenly lifted up by the hand of God, and carried rapidly to the highest pitch of greatness whereto they ever attained. From the time when the Hebrews "hid themselves in holes,"[1] for fear of the Philistines, and were without spears, or swords, or armorers, because the Philistines had said, "Lest the Hebrews make themselves swords or spears,"[2] to the full completion of the kingdom of David by his victories over the Philistines, the Moabites, the Syrians, the Ammonites, and the Amalekites, together with the submission of the Idumæans,[3] was a space little, if at all, exceeding half a

[1] 1 Sam. xiv. 11. [2] Ibid. xiii. 19–22. [3] 2 Sam. viii.

century. Thus were brought within the lifetime of a man the highest glory and the deepest shame, oppression and dominion, terror and triumph, the peril of extinction and the establishment of a mighty empire. The very men who "hid themselves in caves and in thickets, in rocks, and in high places, and in pits,"[1] or who fled across the Jordan to the land of Gad and Gilead,[2] when the Philistines "pitched in Michmash," may have seen garrisons put in Damascus and "throughout all Edom,"[3] and the dominion of David extended to the Euphrates.[4]

The history of this remarkable period is delivered to us in four or five Books, the authors of which are unknown, or at best uncertain. It is thought by some that Joshua wrote the book which bears his name, except the closing verses of the last chapter; (1) and by others, (2) that Samuel composed twenty-four chapters of the first of those two books which in our Canon bear the title of Books of Samuel; but there is no such uniform tradition (3) in either case as exists respecting the authorship of the Pentateuch, nor is there the same weight of internal testimony. On the whole, the internal testimony seems to be against the ascription of the Book of Joshua to the Jewish leader; (4) and both it, Judges, and Ruth, as well as Kings and Chronicles, are best referred to the class of βιβλια ἀδέσποτα, or books the authors of which are unknown to us. The importance of a history, however, though it may be enhanced by our knowledge of the author, does not necessarily depend on such knowledge. The Turin Papyrus, the Parian Marble, the Saxon Chronicle, are documents of the very highest historic value, though we know nothing of the persons who composed them; because there is reason to

[1] 1 Sam. xiii. 6.
[2] Ibid. verse 7.
[3] 2 Sam. viii. 14.
[4] Ibid. verse 3.

believe that they were composed from good sources. And so it is with these portions of the Sacred Volume. There is abundant evidence, both internal and external, of their authenticity and historic value, notwithstanding that their actual composers are unknown or uncertain. They have really the force of State Papers, being authoritative public documents, preserved among the national archives of the Jews so long as they were a nation; and ever since cherished by the scattered fragments of the race as among the most precious of their early records. As we do not commonly ask who was the author of a State Paper, but accept it without any such formality, so we are bound to act towards these writings. They are written near the time, sometimes by eye-witnesses, sometimes by those who have before them the reports of eye-witnesses; and their reception among the sacred records of the Jews stamps them with an authentic character.

As similar attempts have been made to invalidate the authority of these books with those to which I alluded in the last Lecture, as directed against the Pentateuch, it will be necessary to state briefly the special grounds, which exist in the case of each, for accepting it as containing a true history. Having thus vindicated the historical character of the Books from the evidence which they themselves offer, I shall then proceed to adduce such confirmation of their truth as can be obtained from other, and especially from profane, sources.

The Book of Joshua is clearly the production of an eye-witness. The writer includes himself among those who passed over Jordan dryshod.[1] He speaks of Rahab the harlot as still "dwelling in Israel" when he writes;[2] and of Hebron as still in the possession of Caleb the son of

[1] Josh. v. 1. [2] Ibid. vi. 25.

Jephunneh.[1] He belongs clearly to the "elders that outlived Joshua, which had known all the works of the Lord that he had done for Israel;"[2] and is therefore as credible a witness for the events of the settlement in Palestine, as Moses for those of the Exodus and the passage through the wilderness. Further, he undoubtedly possesses documents of authority, from one of which (the Book of Jasher) he quotes;[3] and it is a reasonable supposition that his work is to a great extent composed from such documents, to which there are several references,[4] besides the actual quotation. (5)

The Book of Judges, according to the tradition of the Jews, was written by Samuel. (6) There is nothing in the work itself that very distinctly marks the date of its composition. From its contents we can only say that it must have been composed *about* Samuel's time; that is, after the death of Samson, and before the capture of Jerusalem by David. (7) As the events related in it certainly cover a space of some hundreds of years, the writer, whoever he be, cannot be regarded as a contemporary witness for more than a small portion of them. He stands rather in the position of Moses with respect to the greater part of Genesis, being the recorder of his country's traditions during a space generally estimated as about equal to that which intervened between the call of Abraham and the birth of Moses. (8) Had these traditions been handed down entirely by oral communication, still, being chiefly marked and striking events in the national life, they would have possessed a fair title to acceptance. As the case actually stands, however, there is every reason to believe that national records, which (as we have seen) existed in the

[1] Josh. xiv. 14.
[2] Ibid. xxiv. 31.
[3] Ibid. x. 13.
[4] Ibid. xviii. 9; xxiv. 26.

days of Moses and Joshua, were continued by their successors, and that these formed the materials from which the Book of Judges was composed by its author. Of such records we have a specimen in the Song of Deborah and Barak, an historical poem embodying the chief facts of Deborah's judgeship. It is reasonable to suppose that there may have been many such compositions, belonging to the actual time of the events, of which the historian could make use; and it is also most probable that chronicles were kept even at this early date, like those to which the writers of the later historical books refer so constantly.[1]

The two Books of Samuel are thought by some to form, together with the two Books of Kings, a single work, and are referred to the time of the Babylonish captivity;[(9)] but this view is contrary both to the internal and to the external evidence. The tradition of the Jews is, that the work was commenced by Samuel, continued by Gad, David's seer, and concluded by Nathan the prophet;[(10)] and this is — to say the least — a very probable supposition. We know from a statement in the First Book of Chronicles, that "the acts of David the king, *first and last*, were written in the book of Samuel the seer, and in the book of Nathan the prophet, and in the book of Gad the seer;"[2] and these writings, it is plain, were still extant in the Chronicler's time. If then the Books of Samuel had been a compilation made during the Captivity, or earlier, it would have been founded on these books, which could not but have been of primary authority; in which case the compiler could scarcely have failed to quote them, either by name, as the Chronicler does in the place which has been

[1] 1 Kings xi. 41; xiv. 19 and 29; xv. 7; xvi. 5, 14, 20, 27, &c.; 1 Chron. xxvii. 24; 2 Chron. xii. 15; xiii. 22; xx. 34, &c.

[2] 1 Chron. xxix. 29.

cited, or under the title of "the Chronicles of David," as he seems to do in another.[1] But there is no quotation, direct or indirect, no trace of compilation, no indication of a writer drawing from other authors, in the two Books of Samuel, from beginning to end. In this respect they contrast most strongly with both Chronicles and Kings, where the authors at every turn make reference to the sources from which they derive their information. These books therefore are most reasonably to be regarded as a primary and original work—the work used and quoted by the Chronicler for the reign of David—and a specimen of those other works from which the authors of Kings and Chronicles confessedly compiled their histories. We have thus, in all probability, for the times of Samuel, Saul, and David, the direct witness of Samuel himself, and of the two prophets who were in most repute during the reign of David.

The writer of the first Book of Kings derives his account of Solomon from a document which he calls "the Book of the Acts of Solomon;"[2] while the author of the second Book of Chronicles cites three works as furnishing him with materials for this part of his history—"the book of Nathan the prophet, the prophecy of Abijah the Shilonite, and the visions of Iddo the seer against Jeroboam the son of Nebat."[3] These last were certainly the works of contemporaries;[(11)] and the same may be presumed of the other; since the later compiler is not likely to have possessed better materials than the earlier. We may therefore conclude that we have in Kings and Chronicles the history of Solomon's reign—not perhaps exactly in the words of contemporary writers—but substantially as they delivered it. And the writers were persons who held the same high

[1] 1 Chron. xxvii. 24. [2] 1 Kings xi. 41. [3] 2 Chron. ix. 29.

position under Solomon, which the composers of the Books of Samuel had held under Saul and David.

It is also worthy of remark, that we have the histories of David and Solomon from two separate and distinct authorities. The writer of Chronicles does not draw even his account of David wholly from Samuel, but adds various particulars, which show that he had further sources of information.(12) And his account of Solomon appears not to have been drawn from Kings at all, but to have been taken quite independently from the original documents.

Further, it is to be noted that we have in the Book of Psalms, at once a running comment, illustrative of David's personal history, the close agreement of which with the historical books is striking, and also a work affording abundant evidence that the history of the nation, as it is delivered to us in the Pentateuch, in Joshua, and in Judges, was at least believed by the Jews to be their true and real history in the time of David. The seventy-eighth Psalm, which certainly belongs to David's time, is sufficient proof of this: it contains a sketch of Jewish history, from the wonders wrought by Moses in Egypt to the establishment of the ark in mount Zion by David, and refers to not fewer than fifty or sixty of the occurrences which are described at length in the historical writings.(13) It is certain, at the least, that the Jews of David's age had no other account to give of their past fortunes than that miraculous story which has come down to us in the Books of Exodus, Numbers, Deuteronomy, Joshua, Judges, and Samuel.

We have now further to consider what amount of confirmation profane history lends to the truth of the sacred narrative during the period extending from the death of Moses to the accession of Rehoboam. This period, it has been observed above, comprises within it the two most opposite conditions of the Jewish race: during its earlier portion the Israelites were a small and insignificant people, with difficulty maintaining themselves in the hill-country of Palestine against the attacks of various tribes, none of whom have made any great figure in history: while towards its close a Jewish Empire was formed — an Empire perhaps as great as any which up to that time had been known in the Eastern world, and which, if not so extensive as some that shortly afterwards grew up in Western Asia, at any rate marks very distinctly the period when the power and prosperity of the Jews reached its *acmé*.

It was not to be expected that profane writers would notice equally both of these periods. During the obscure time of the Judges, the Jews could be little known beyond their borders; and even had Assyria and Egypt been at this time flourishing and aggressive states, had the armies of either or both been then in the habit of traversing Palestine in the course of their expeditions, the Israelites might easily have escaped mention, since they occupied only a small part of the country, and that part the least accessible of the whole. (14) It appears, however, that in fact both Assyria and Egypt were weak during this period. The expeditions of the former were still confined within the Euphrates, or, if they crossed it on rare occasions, at any rate went no farther than Cappadocia and Upper Syria, or the country about Aleppo and Antioch. (15) And Egypt from the time of Ramesses the third, which was not long after the Exodus, to that of Shishak, the contemporary of Solomon, seems to have sent no expeditions at all beyond its own frontier. (16) Thus the annals of the two countries are necessarily silent concerning the Jews during the period in question; and no agreement between them and the Jewish records is possible, except that tacit one which is found in fact to exist. The Jewish records are silent concerning Egypt, from the Exodus to the reign of Solomon; which is exactly the time during which the Egyptian records are silent concerning the Jews. And Assyria does not appear in Scripture as an influential power in Lower Syria and Palestine till a time considerably later than the separation of the kingdoms; while similarly the Assyrian monuments are without any mention of expeditions into these parts during the earlier period of the empire. Further, it may be remarked that from the mention of Chushan-Rishathaim, king of Aram-Naharaim, (or the country about Harran,) as a powerful prince soon after the death of Joshua, it would follow that Assyria had not at that time extended her dominion even to the Euphrates; a conclusion which the cuneiform records of perhaps two centuries later entirely confirm,[(17)] since they show that even then the Assyrians had not conquered the whole country east of the river.

Besides the points of agreement here noticed, which, though negative, are (I think) of no slight weight, we possess one testimony belonging to this period of a direct and positive character, which is among the most curious of the illustrations, that profane sources furnish, of the veracity of Scripture. Moses of Chorêne, the Armenian historian,[(18)] Procopius, the secretary of Belisarius,[(19)] and Suidas the Lexicographer,[(20)] relate, that there existed in their day at Tingis, (or Tangiers,) in Africa, an ancient inscription to the effect that the inhabitants were the descendants of those fugitives who were driven from the land of Canaan by Joshua the son of Nun, the plunderer. It has been said that this story "can scarcely be any thing but a Rabbinical legend, which Procopius may have heard from African Jews."[21] But the independent testimony of the three writers, who do not seem to have copied from one another, is an argument of great weight; and the expressions used, by Procopius especially, have a precision and a circumstantiality, which seem rather to imply the basis of personal observation. "There stand," he says, "two pillars of white marble near the great fountain in the city of Tigisis, bearing an inscription in Phœnician characters, and in the Phœnician language, which runs as follows." I cannot see that there would be any sufficient reason for doubting the truth of this very clear and exact statement, even if it stood alone, and were unconfirmed by any other writer. Two writers, however, confirm it—one of an earlier and the other of a later date; and the three testimonies are proved, by their slight variations, to be independent of one another. There is then sufficient reason to believe that a Phœnician inscription to the effect stated existed at Tangiers in the time of the Lower Empire; and the true question for historical criticism to consider and determine is, what is the weight and value of such an inscription.[22] That it was not a Jewish or a Christian monument is certain from the epithet of "plunderer" or "robber" applied in it to Joshua. That it was more ancient than Christianity seems probable from the language and character in which it was written.[23] It would appear to have been a genuine Phœnician monument, of an antiquity which cannot now be decided, but which was probably remote; and it must be regarded as embodying an ancient tradition, current in this part of Africa in times anterior to Christianity, which very remarkably confirms the Hebrew narrative.

There is another event of a public nature, belonging to this portion of the history, of which some have thought to find a confirmation in the pages of a profane writer. "The Egyptians," says Herodotus,(24) "declare that since Egypt was a kingdom, the sun has on four several occasions moved from his wonted course, twice rising where he now sets, and twice setting where he now rises." It has been supposed (25) that we have here a notice of that remarkable time when "the sun stood still in the midst of heaven, and hasted not to go down about a whole day;"[1] as well as of that other somewhat similar occasion, when "the sun returned ten degrees" on the dial of Ahaz.[2] But the statement made to Herodotus by the Egyptian priests would very ill describe the phenomena of these two occasions, however we understand the narratives in Joshua and Kings; and the fact which they intended to convey to him was probably one connected rather with their peculiar system of astronomical cycles, than with any sudden and violent changes in the celestial order. If the narrative in Joshua is to be understood astronomically, of an actual cessation or retardation of the earth's motion, (26) we must admit that profane history fails to present us with any mention of an occurrence, which it might have been expected to notice with distinctness. But at the same time we must remember how scanty are the remains which we possess of this early time, and how strictly they are limited to the recording of political events and dynastic changes. The astronomical records of the Babylonians have perished; and the lists of Manetho contain but few references to natural phenomena, which are never introduced except when they have a political bearing. No valid objection therefore can be brought against the literal truth of the narrative in Joshua from the present want of any profane confirmation of it. Where the records of the

[1] Josh. x. 13. [2] Isa. xxxviii. 8.

past are so few and so slight, the argument from mere silence has neither force nor place.

The flourishing period of Jewish history, which commences with the reign of David, brought the chosen people of God once more into contact with those principal nations of the earth, whose history has to some extent come down to us. One of the first exploits of David was that great defeat which he inflicted on the Syrians of Damascus, in the vicinity of the Euphrates, when they came to the assistance of Hadedezer king of Zobah — a defeat which cost them more than twenty thousand men, and which was followed by the temporary subjection of Damascus to the Israelites; since "David put garrisons in Syria of Damascus, and the Syrians became servants to David, and brought gifts."[1] This war is mentioned not only by Eupolemus,(27) who appears to have been well acquainted with the Jewish Scriptures, but also by Nicolas of Damascus, the friend of Augustus Cæsar, who clearly draws his history from the records of his native place. "After this," says Nicolas, "there was a certain Hadad, a native Syrian, who had great power: he ruled over Damascus, and all Syria, except Phœnicia. He likewise undertook a war with David, the king of Judæa, and contended against him in a number of battles; in the last of them all — which was by the river Euphrates, and in which he suffered defeat — showing himself a prince of the greatest courage and prowess."(28) This is a testimony of the same nature with those already adduced from Berosus and Manetho; it is a separate and independent notice of an event in Jewish history, which has come down to us from the other party in the transaction, with particulars not contained in the Jewish account, yet compatible with all that is so

[1] 2 Sam. viii. 6. Comp. 1 Chr. xviii. 6.

contained, and strictly corroborative of the main circumstances of the Hebrew narrative.

The other wars of the son of Jesse were with enemies of inferior power and importance, as the Philistines, the Moabites, the Ammonites, the Idumæans, and the Amalekites. Eupolemus mentions most of these successes; (29) but otherwise we have no recognition of them by profane writers, which cannot be considered surprising, since there are no ancient histories extant wherein these nations are mentioned otherwise than incidentally. We have, however, one further point of contact between sacred and profane history at this period which is of considerable interest and importance, and which requires separate consideration. I speak of the connection, seen now for the first time, between Judæa and Phœnicia, which, separated by natural obstacles, (30) and hitherto, perhaps, to some extent by intervening tribes, only began to hold relations with each other when the conquests of David brought Judæa into a new position among the powers of these regions. It was necessary for the commerce of Phœnicia that she should enjoy the friendship of whatever power commanded the great lines of inland traffic, which ran through Cœle-Syria and Damascus, by Hamath and Tadmor, to the Euphrates. (31) Accordingly we find that upon the "establishment" and "exaltation" of David's kingdom,[1] overtures were at once made to him by the chief Phœnician power of the day; and his good will was secured by benefits of the most acceptable kind — the loan of skilled artificers and the gift of cedar-beams "in abundance"[2] — after which a firm friendship was established between the two powers,[3] which continued beyond the reign of David into that of Solomon his son.[4] Now here it is most

[1] 2 Sam. v. 11, 12.
[2] 1 Chr. xxii. 4.
[3] 1 Kings v. 1.
[4] Ibid. verse 12.

interesting to see whether the Hebrew writer has correctly represented the condition of Phœnicia at the time; whether the name which he has assigned to his Phœnician prince is one that Phœnicians bore or the contrary; and finally, whether there is any trace of the reign of this particular prince at this time.

With regard to the first point, it is to be observed, that the condition of Phœnicia varied at different periods. While we seem to trace throughout the whole history a constant recognition of some one city as predominant among the various towns, if not as sovereign over them, we do not always find the same city occupying this position. In the most ancient times it is Sidon which claims and exercises this precedency and preëminence;(32) in the later times the dignity has passed to Tyre, which is thenceforward recognized as the leading power. Homer implies,(33) Strabo(34) and Justin(35) distinctly assert, the ancient superiority of Sidon, which was said to have been the primitive settlement, whence the remainder were derived. On the other hand, Dius(36) and Menander,(37) who drew their Phœnician histories from the native records, clearly show that at a time anterior to David, Tyre had become the leading state, which she continued to be until the time of Alexander.(38) The notices of Phœnicia in Scripture are completely in accordance with what we have thus gathered from profane sources. While Sidon alone appears to have been known to Moses,[1] and Tyre occurs in Joshua as a mere stronghold in marked contrast with imperial Sidon, ("great Zidon," as she is called more than once)[2] — whose dominion seems to extend along the coast to Carmel,(39) and certainly reaches inland as far as Laish[3] — in Samuel and Kings the case is

[1] Gen. x. 15; xlix. 13. [2] Josh. xi. 8; xix. 28.

[3] Judges xvii. 7 and 28.

changed; Sidon has no longer a distinctive epithet;[1] and it is the "king of Tyre" who on behalf of his countrymen makes advances to David, and who is evidently the chief Phœnician potentate of the period.

Further, when we look to the name borne by this prince — the first Phœnician mentioned by name in Scripture — we are at once struck with its authentic character. That Hiram was really a Phœnician name, and one which kings were in the habit of bearing, is certain from the Assyrian Inscriptions(40) and from Herodotus,(41) as well as from the Phœnician historians, Dius and Menander. And these last-named writers not only confirm the name as one which a king of Tyre might have borne, but show moreover that it was actually borne by the Tyrian king contemporary with Solomon and David, of whom they relate circumstances which completely identify him with the monarch who is stated in Scripture to have been on such friendly terms with those princes. They do not indeed appear to have made any mention of David; but they spoke distinctly of the close connection between Hiram and Solomon; adding facts, which, though not contained in Scripture, are remarkably in accordance with the sacred narrative. For instance, both Menander and Dius related that "hard questions" were sent by Solomon to Hiram to be resolved by him;(42) while Dius added, that Hiram proposed similar puzzles to Solomon in return, which that monarch with all his wisdom was unable to answer.(43) We may see in this narrative, not only a resemblance to the famous visit of the "Queen of the South,"[2] who, "when she heard of the fame of Solomon, came to prove him with hard questions;"[3] but also an illustration of the statement that "all the earth sought to Solomon to hear his wisdom, which God had put in his

[1] 2 Sam. xxiv. 6. [2] Matt. xii. 42. [3] 1 Kings x. 1.

heart."[1] Again, Menander stated that Hiram gave his daughter in marriage to Solomon.(44) This fact is not recorded in Scripture; but still it is illustrative of the statement that "King Solomon loved many strange women, together with the daughter of Pharaoh, women of the Moabites, Ammonites, Edomites, *Zidonians*, and Hittites. . . . And he had seven hundred wives, *princesses*."[2] One of these we may well conceive to have been the daughter of the Tyrian king.

The relations of Solomon with Egypt have received at present but little illustration from native Egyptian sources. Our epitome of Manetho gives us nothing but a bare list of names at the period to which Solomon must belong; and the Egyptian monuments for the time are particularly scanty and insignificant.(45) Moreover the omission of the Jewish writers to place on record the distinctive name of the Pharaoh whose daughter Solomon married, forbids his satisfactory identification with any special Egyptian monarch. Eupolemus indeed professed to supply this omission of the older historians,(46) and enlivened his history with copies of the letters which (according to him) passed between Solomon and Vaphres or Apries, king of Egypt; but this name is clearly taken from a later portion of Egyptian history, and none at all similar to it is found either on the monuments or in the dynastic lists for the period. The Egyptian marriage of Solomon, therefore, and his friendly connection with a Pharaoh of the twenty-first dynasty, have at present no confirmation from profane sources, beyond that which it derives from Eupolemus; but the change in the relations between the two courts towards the close of Solomon's reign, which is indicated by the protection extended to his enemy Jeroboam by a new king, Shishak,

[1] 1 Kings x. 24. [2] Ibid. xi. 1–3.

receives some illustration and confirmation both from the monuments and from the native historian. Shishak makes his appearance at a suitable point, so far as chronology is concerned,(47) in the lists of Manetho, where he is called Sesonchis or Sesonchôsis;(48) and his name occurs likewise in the sculptures of the period under its Egyptian form of Sheshonk.(49) The confirmation which the monuments lend to the capture of Jerusalem by this king will be considered in the next Lecture. At present, we have only to note, besides the occurrence of the name at the place where we should naturally look for it in the lists, the fact that it occurs *at the commencement of a new dynasty*—a dynasty furnished by a new city, and quite of a different character from that preceding it—which would therefore be in no way connected with Solomon, and would not be unlikely to reverse the policy of the house which it had supplanted.

The wealth and magnificence of Solomon were celebrated by Eupolemus and (50) Theophilus,(51) the former of whom gave an elaborate account of the temple and its ornaments. As, however, these writers were merely well-informed Greeks who reported to their countrymen the ideas entertained of their history by the Jews of the third and fourth centuries B. C., I forbear to dwell upon their testimonies. I shall therefore close here the direct confirmations from profane sources of this portion of the Scripture narrative, and proceed to consider briefly some of the indirect points of agreement, with which this part of the history, like every other, abounds.

First, then, it may be observed, that the empire ascribed to David and Solomon is an empire of *exactly that kind* which alone Western Asia was capable of producing, and did produce, about the period in question. The modern system of centralized organization by which the various provinces of a vast empire are cemented into a compact mass, was unknown to the ancient world, and has never been practised by Asiatics. The satrapial system of government, or that in which the provinces retain their individuality, but are administered on a common plan by officers appointed by the crown — which has prevailed generally through the East since the time of its first introduction — was the invention of Darius Hystaspis. Before his time the greatest monarchies had a slighter and weaker organization. They were in all cases composed of a number of separate *kingdoms*, each under its own native king; and the sole link uniting them together and constituting them an empire, was the subjection of these petty monarchs to a single suzerain.(52) The Babylonian, Assyrian, Median, and Lydian, were all empires of this type — monarchies, wherein a sovereign prince at the head of a powerful kingdom was acknowledged as suzerain by a nnmber of inferior princes, each in his own right sole ruler of his own country. And the subjection of the inferior princes consisted chiefly, if not solely, in two points; they were bound to render homage to their suzerain, and to pay him annually a certain stated tribute. Thus, when we hear that "Solomon reigned over *all the kingdoms* from the river (Euphrates) unto the land of the Philistines and unto the border of Egypt"[1] — or again, that "he had dominion over all the region on this side the river, from Tiphsah (or Thapsacus on the Euphrates) to Azzah, (or Gaza, the most southern of the Philistine towns,) over *all the kings* on this side the river"[2] — and that "they *brought presents*"[3] — "a rate *year by year*"[4] — and "*served* Solomon all the days of

[1] 1 Kings iv. 21.
[2] Ibid. verse 24.
[3] Ibid. verse 21.
[4] Ibid. x. 25.

his life,"[1] we recognize at once a condition of things with which we are perfectly familiar from profane sources; and we feel that at any rate this account is in entire harmony with the political notions and practices of the day.

Similarly, with respect to the buildings of Solomon, it may be remarked, that they appear, from the description given of them in Kings and Chronicles, to have belonged exactly to that style of architecture which we find in fact to have prevailed over Western Asia in the earliest times, and of which we have still remains on the ancient sites of Nineveh, Susa, and Persepolis. The strong resemblance in general structure and arrangement of the palace of Esar-haddon to that which Solomon constructed for his own use, has been noticed by our great Mesopotamian excavator;(53) and few can fail to see in the "house of the forest of Lebanon,"[2] with its five-and-forty cedar pillars forming the "forest" from which the palace derived its name, a resemblance to the remarkable structures at Susa and Persepolis, in each of which the pillars on which the entire edifice rested form a sort of forest, amounting in number to seventy-two. It is true that in the Persian buildings the columns are of stone; but this is owing to the advance of art. The great chambers in the Assyrian palaces had no stone columns, but are regarded by those who have paid most attention to the subject, as having had their roofs supported by pillars of cedar.(54) Nor does the resemblance of which I am speaking consist only in the multiplicity of columns. The height of the Persepolitan columns, which is forty-four feet,(55) almost exactly equals the "thirty cubits" of Solomon's house; and there is even an agreement in the general character of the capitals, which has attracted notice from some who have written upon the history of art.(56)

[1] 1 Kings iv. 21. [2] Ibid. vii. 2.

Again, the copious use of gold in ornamentation,[1] which seems to moderns so improbable,(57) was a practice known to the Phœnicians, the Assyrians, and the Babylonians.(58) The brazen pillars, Jachin and Boaz, set up in the court of the temple,[2] recall the pillar of gold which Hiram, according to Menander,(59) dedicated in the temple of Baal, and the two pillars which appear in the coins of Cyprus before the temple of the Phœnician Venus.(60) The "throne of ivory"[3] has its parallel in the numerous ivory carvings lately brought from Mesopotamia, which in many cases have plainly formed the covering of furniture.(61) The lions, which stood beside the throne,[4] bring to our mind at once the lions' feet with which Assyrian thrones were ornamented,(62) and the gigantic sculptured figures which commonly formed the portals of the great halls. In these and many other points the state and character of art, which the Hebrew writers describe as existing in Solomon's time, receives confirmation from profane sources, and especially from those remains of a time not long subsequent, which have been recently brought to light by the researches made in Mesopotamia.

Once more — the agreement between the character of the Phœnicians as drawn in Kings and Chronicles, and that which we know from other sources to have attached to them, is worthy of remark. The wealth, the enterprise, the maritime skill, and the eminence in the arts, which were the leading characteristics of the Phœnicians in Homer's time, are abundantly noted by the writers of Kings and Chronicles; who contrast the comparative ignorance and rudeness of their own nation with the science and "cunning" of their neighbors. "Thou

[1] 1 Kings vi. 20, 21, 28, 30, 32, &c. [2] Ibid. vii. 15–22.
[3] Ibid. x. 19. [4] Ibid. verses 19 and 20.

knowest," writes king Solomon to Hiram, "that there is not among us any that can skill to hew timber like the Sidonians."[1] "Send me a man," again he writes, "cunning to work in gold, and in silver, and in brass, and in iron, and in purple, and crimson, and blue, and that can skill to grave with the cunning men which are with me in Judah and in Jerusalem, whom David my father did provide."[2] And the man sent, "a man of Tyre, a worker in brass, filled with wisdom, and understanding, and cunning to work all works in brass, came to king Solomon, and *wrought all his work.*"[3] So too when Solomon "made a navy of ships in Ezion-geber, on the shore of the Red Sea," Hiram "sent in the navy his servants, *shipmen that had knowledge of the sea*, with the servants of Solomon."[4] It has been well remarked,(62) that "we discover the greatness of Tyre in this age, not so much from its own annals as from those of the Israelites, its neighbors." The scanty fragments of the Phœnician history which alone remain to us are filled out and illustrated by the more copious records of the Jews; which, with a simplicity and truthfulness that we rarely meet with in profane writers, set forth in the strongest terms their obligations to their friendly neighbors.

These are a few of the indirect points of agreement between profane history and this portion of the sacred narrative. It would be easy to adduce others;(63) but since, within the space which an occasion like the present allows, it is impossible to do more than broadly to indicate the sort of evidence which is producible in favor of the authenticity of Scripture, perhaps the foregoing specimens may suffice. It only remains therefore to sum up briefly the results to which we seem to have attained.

[1] 1 Kings v. 6.
[2] 2 Chron. ii. 7.
[3] 1 Kings vii. 14.
[4] Ibid. ix. 26, 27.

We have been engaged with a dark period — a period when the nations of the world had little converse with one another, when civilization was but beginning, when the knowledge of letters was confined within narrow bounds, when no country but Egypt had a literature, and when Egypt herself was in a state of unusual depression, and had little communication with nations beyond her borders. We could not expect to obtain for such a period any great amount of profane illustration. Yet the Jewish history of even this obscure time has been found to present points of direct agreement with the Egyptian records, scanty as they are for it, with the Phœnician annals, with the traditions of the Syrians of Damascus, and with those of the early inhabitants of Northern Africa. It has also appeared that the Hebrew account of the time is in complete harmony with all that we otherwise know of Western Asia at the period in question, of its political condition, its civilization, its arts and sciences, its manners and customs, its inhabitants. Illustrations of these points have been furnished by the Assyrian inscriptions, the Assyrian and Persian palaces, the Phœnician coins and histories, and the earliest Greek poetry. Nor is it possible to produce from authentic history any contradiction of this or any other portion of the Hebrew records. When such a contradiction has seemed to be found, it has invariably happened that in the progress of historical inquiry, the author from whom it proceeds has lost credit, and finally come to be regarded as an utterly untrustworthy authority.[64] Internally consistent, externally resting upon contemporary or nearly contemporary documents, and both directly and indirectly confirmed by the records of neighboring nations, the Hebrew account of this time is entitled to be received as a true and authentic history on almost every ground upon which such a claim can be rested. It was then justly and with sufficient reason that the Proto-martyr in his last speech,[1] and the great Apostle of the Gentiles, in his first public preaching as an Apostle,[2] assumed as certain the simple, literal, and historic truth of this portion of the sacred narrative. Through *God's good providence, there is no break in that historic* chain which binds the present with the past, the new covenant with the old, Christ with Moses, the true Israel with Abraham. A "dark age"—a time of trouble and confusion, undoubtedly supervened upon the establishment of the Israelites in Canaan; but amid the gloom the torch of truth still passed from hand to hand—prophets arose at intervals—and the main events in the national life were carefully put on record. Afterwards—from the time of Samuel—a more regular system was introduced; events were chronicled as they occurred; and even the sceptic allows that "with the Books of Samuel, the history assumes an appearance far more authentic than that of the contemporary history of any other ancient nation."(65) This admission may well be taken to render any further argument unnecessary, and with it we may properly conclude this portion of our inquiry.

[1] Acts vii. 45–47. [2] Ibid. xiii. 19–22.

LECTURE IV.

AND AHIJAH SAID TO JEROBOAM, TAKE THEE TEN PIECES: FOR THUS SAITH THE LORD, THE GOD OF ISRAEL, BEHOLD, I WILL REND THE KINGDOM OUT OF THE HAND OF SOLOMON, AND WILL GIVE TEN TRIBES TO THEE: BUT HE SHALL HAVE ONE TRIBE FOR MY SERVANT DAVID'S SAKE.—1 KINGS XI. 31, 32.

THE subject of the present Lecture will be the history of the chosen people from the separation of the two kingdoms by the successful revolt of Jeroboam, to the completion of the Captivity of Judah, upon the destruction of Jerusalem, in the nineteenth year of Nebuchadnezzar, king of Babylon. The space of time embraced is thus a period of about four centuries. Without pretending to a chronological exactitude, for which our data are insufficient, we may lay it down as tolerably certain, that the establishment of the two kingdoms of Israel and Judah on the ruins of Solomon's empire is an event belonging to the earlier half of the tenth century before our era; while the destruction of Jerusalem may be assigned with much confidence to the year B. C. 586.

These centuries constitute a period second in importance to none of equal length. They comprise the great development, the decadence and the fall of Assyria—the sudden growth of Media and Babylon—the Egyptian revival under the Psammetichi—the most glorious time of the Phœnician cities—the rise of Sparta and Athens to preëminence in Greece—the foundation of Carthage and of

Rome — and the spread of civilization by means of the Greek and Phœnician colonies, from the Palus Mæotis to the Pillars of Hercules. Moreover, they contain within them the transition time of most profane history — the space within which it passes from the dreamy cloud-land of myth and fable into the sober region of reality and fact, exchanging poetic fancy for prosaic truth, and assuming that character of authenticity and trustworthiness, which is required to fit it thoroughly for the purpose whereto it is applied in these Lectures. Hence, illustrations of the sacred narrative, hitherto somewhat rare and infrequent, will now crowd upon us, and make the principal difficulty at the present stage that of selection. Egypt, Assyria, Babylon, Phœnicia, Greece, will vie with each other in offering to us proofs that the Hebrew records, for this time, contain a true and authentic account of the fortunes of the race; and instead of finding merely a few points here and there to illustrate from profane sources, we shall now be able to produce confirmatory proof of almost every important event in the history.

Before entering, however, on this branch of the inquiry, some consideration must be given to the character of the documents in which this portion of the history has come down to us, and to the confirmation which those documents obtain from other Books in the Sacred Canon.

It was observed in the last Lecture, that the Books of Kings and Chronicles are compilations from State Papers preserved in the public archives of the Jewish nation,(1) the authors of those papers being probably, in most cases, the Prophets in best repute at the time of their composition. This is particularly apparent from the Second Book of Chronicles, where the author, besides citing in several places[1] "the Book of the Chronicles of the Kings of Israel and Judah," particularizes no fewer than thirteen works of prophets, some of which he expressly states to have formed a portion of the general "Book of the Chronicles,"[2] while most of the others may be probably concluded to have done the same. The Books of Samuel, of Nathan, and of Gad, the Prophecy of Ahijah the Shilonite, and the Visions of Iddo the seer, which are among the works quoted by the Chronicler, have been already noticed.(2) To these must now be added, "the Book of Shemaiah the Prophet,"[3] "the Book of Iddo the seer, concerning genealogies,"[4] "the Story or Commentary of the Prophet Iddo,"[5] "the Book of Jehu the son of Hanani,"[6] "the Acts of Uzziah by Isaiah,"[7] "the Vision of Isaiah,"[8] and the book of "the Sayings of the Seers"[9] — all works which served as materials to the Chronicler, and to which he refers his readers. We found reason to believe, in the last Lecture, that our Book (or Books) of Samuel is the very work which the Chronicler quotes under the three names of the Book of Samuel, the Book of Nathan, and the Book of Gad. Similarly the Book of the Acts of Solomon[10] would seem to have been composed of a Book of Nathan, a Book of Ahijah the Shilonite, and a portion of a Book of Iddo the seer.[11] And the Book, or rather the two Books,(3) of the Chronicles of the Kings of Israel and Judah, would appear to have been carried on in the same way; first, by Iddo, in his "Story," or "Com-

[1] 2 Chron. xvi. 11; xxv. 26; xxvii. 7; xxviii. 26; xxxii. 32; xxxiii. 18; and xxxv. 27.

[2] Ibid. xx. 34; and xxxiii. 32.

[3] Ibid. xii. 15.

[4] Ibid.

[5] Ibid. xiii. 22.

[6] Ibid. xx. 34.

[7] Ibid. xxvi. 22.

[8] Ibid. xxxii. 32.

[9] Ibid. xxxiii. 19.

[10] 1 Kings xi. 41.

[11] 2 Chron. ix. 29.

mentary;" then by Jehu, the son of Hanani, in the Book which we are told was made to form a part of the Book of the Kings of Israel; (4) and afterwards by other prophets and seers, among whom were certainly Isaiah and Jeremiah. That Isaiah wrote the history of the reign of Uzziah is expressly stated;[1] and it is also said that his account of the acts of Hezekiah formed a portion of the Book of the Kings of Judah; (5) besides which, the close verbal agreement between certain historical chapters in Isaiah and in Kings, (6) would suffice to prove that this part of the state history was composed by him. A similar agreement between portions of Kings and of Jeremiah, leads to a similar conclusion with respect to that prophet. (7) Thus Samuel, Gad, Nathan, Ahijah, Shemaiah, Iddo, Jehu, Isaiah, Jeremiah, and other prophets contemporary with the events, are to be regarded as the real authorities for the Jewish history as it is delivered to us in Kings and Chronicles. "The prophets, who in their prophecies and addresses held forth to the people, not only the law as a rule and direction, but also the history of the past as the mirror and example of their life, must have reckoned the composition of the theocratic history among the duties of the call given to them by the Lord, and composed accordingly the history of their time by noting down public annals, in which, without respect of persons, the life and conduct of the kings were judged and exhibited according to the standard of the revealed law." (8) With this judgment of a living German writer, there is sufficient reason to concur; and we may therefore conclude that the history in Kings and Chronicles rests upon the testimony of contemporary and competent witnesses.

The only objection of any importance that Rationalism

[1] 2 Chron. xxvi. 22.

makes to the conclusion which we have here reached, is drawn from the circumstances of the time when the books were composed; which is thought to militate strongly against their having been drawn directly from the sources which have been indicated. The authority of the writers of these Books, we are told,(9) "cannot have been the official annals" of the kingdoms; for these must have perished at their destruction, and therefore could not have been consulted by authors who lived later than the Captivity. It may be granted that the mass of the State Archives are likely to have perished with Samaria and Jerusalem, if we understand by that term the bulky documents which contained the details of official transactions: but there is no more difficulty in supposing that the digested annals which the prophets had composed escaped, than there is in understanding how the Prophecy of Isaiah and the rest of the Sacred Volume were preserved. At any rate, if there be a difficulty, it is unimportant in the face of the plain and palpable fact, that the authors of the two Books speak of the annals as existing, and continually refer their readers to them for additional information. However we may account for it, the "Books of the Chronicles of the Kings of Israel and Judah," the different portions of which had been written by the prophets above mentioned, were still extant when the authors of Kings and Chronicles wrote their histories, having escaped the dangers of war, and survived the obscure time of the Captivity. It is not merely that the writers in question profess to quote from them; but they constantly appeal to them as books the contents of which are well known to their own readers.

The confirmation which the Books of Kings and Chronicles lend to each other, deserves some notice while we are engaged with this portion of the inquiry. Had the later composition uniformly followed, and, as it were, echoed the earlier, there would have been but little advantage in the double record. We should then only have known that the author of the Book of Chronicles regarded the Book of Kings as authentic. But the Chronicler — I use the term in no offensive sense — does not seem really in any case merely to follow the writer of Kings.(10) On the contrary, he goes straight to the fountain-head, and draws his materials partly from the sources used by the earlier writer, partly (as it seems) from contemporary sources which that writer had neglected. He is thus, throughout, a distinct and independent authority for the history of his nation, standing to the writer of Kings as Africanus stands to Eusebius, in respect of the history of Egypt.(11) As the double channel by which Manetho's Egyptian history is conveyed to us, renders our hold upon that history far more firm and secure than would have been the case had we derived our knowledge of it through one channel only, so the two parallel accounts, which we possess in Kings and Chronicles, of the history of Solomon and his successors, give us a hold upon the original annals of this period which we could not have had otherwise. The Chronicler, while he declines to be beholden to the author of Kings for any portion of his narrative, and does not concern himself about apparent discrepancies between his own work and that of the earlier writer, confirms the whole general course of that writer's history, repeating it, illustrating it, and adding to it, but never really differing from it, except in such minute points as are readily explainable by slight corruptions of the text in the one case or the other.(12)

Further, the narrative contained in Kings and Chronicles receives a large amount of illustration, and so of confirmation, from the writings of the contemporary Prophets, who exhibit the feelings natural under the circumstances described by the historians, and incidentally allude to the facts recorded by them. This point has been largely illustrated by recent writers on the prophetical Scriptures, who find the interpretation of almost every chapter "bound up with references to contemporary events, political and social," and discover in this constant connection at once a "source of occasional difficulty," and a frequent means of throwing great additional light on the true meaning of the prophetical writers.(13) The illustration thus afforded to prophecy by history is reflected back to history from prophecy; and there is scarcely an event in the Jewish annals after the reign of Uzziah — which is the time of the earliest of the extant prophetical writings(14) — that is not illuminated by some touch from one prophet or another. To take the case of a single writer — Isaiah mentions the succession of Jewish kings from Uzziah to Hezekiah,[1] the alliance of Rezin, king of Syria, and Pekah, the son of Remaliah, king of Israel, against Ahaz,[2] the desolation of their country which shortly followed,[3] the plunder of Damascus, and the spoiling of Samaria at this time,[4] the name of the then high priest,[5] the Assyrian conquests of Hamath, Aradus, and Samaria,[6] the close connection about this time of Egypt and Ethiopia,[7] the inclination of the Jewish monarchs to lean on Egypt for support against Assyria,[8] the conquest by Sennacherib of the "fenced cities" of Judah,[9] the embassy of Rabshakeh,[10] the sieges of Libnah and

[1] Isaiah i. 1. [2] Ibid. vii. 1, 2. [3] Ibid. verse 16.
[4] Ibid. viii. 4. Compare 2 Kings xvi. 9.
[5] Ibid. verse 2. Compare 2 Kings xvi. 10–16.
[6] Ibid. x. 9–11. [7] Ibid. xx. 3–5.
[8] Ibid. xxx. 2, 3, &c.; xxxi. 1–3. [9] Ibid. xxxvi. 1.
[10] Ibid. verses 2–22.

Lachish,[1] the preparations of Tirhakah against Sennacherib,[2] the prayer of Hezekiah,[3] the prophecy of Isaiah in reply,[4] the destruction of Sennacherib's host,[5] the return of Sennacherib himself to Nineveh,[6] his murder and the escape of his murderers,[7] Hezekiah's illness and recovery,[8] and the embassy sent to him by Merodach-Baladan, king of Babylon;[9]—he glances also at the invasion of Tiglath-Pileser, and the destruction then brought upon a portion of the kingdom of Israel,[10] at the oppression of Egypt under the Ethiopian yoke,[11] at the subjection of Judæa to Assyria during the reign of Ahaz,[12] and at many other events of less consequence. About half the events here mentioned are contained in the three historical chapters of Isaiah,[13] which are almost identical with three chapters of the second Book of Kings:[14] but the remainder occur merely incidentally among the prophecies; and these afford the same sort of confirmation to the plain narrative of Kings and Chronicles, as the Epistles of St. Paul have been shown to furnish to the Acts.(15) Jeremiah, Amos, Hosea, Micah, and Zephaniah, contain numerous allusions of a similar character, illustrative of the history at this time and subsequently. Jeremiah, in particular, is as copious in notices bearing upon Jewish history for the time extending from Josiah to the Captivity, as Isaiah is for the reigns of Ahaz and Hezekiah.

Having thus briefly noticed the character of the documents in which this portion of the history has come down to us, and drawn attention to the weight of the scriptural

[1] Isaiah xxxvii. 8. [2] Ibid. verse 9. [3] Ibid. verses 15–20.
[4] Ibid. verses 22–35. [5] Ibid. verse 36. [6] Ibid. verse 37.
[7] Ibid. verse 38. [8] Ibid. xxxviii. [9] Ibid. xxxix. 1, 2.
[10] Ibid. ix. 1. [11] Ibid. xix. 4, &c. [12] Ibid. xiv. 24–28.
[13] Chaps, xxxvi. xxxvii. and xxxviii. [14] Chaps. xviii. xix. and xx.

evidence in favor of its authenticity, I proceed to the consideration of that point which is the *special* subject of these Lectures—the confirmation which this part of the narrative receives from profane sources.

The separate existence of the two kingdoms of Israel and Judah is abundantly confirmed by the Assyrian inscriptions. Kings of each country occur in the accounts which the great Assyrian monarchs have left us of their conquests—the names being always capable of easy identification with those recorded in Scripture, and occurring in the chronological order which is there given. (16) The Jewish monarch bears the title of "King of Judah," while his Israelitish brother is designated after his capital city; which, though in the earlier times not called Samaria, is yet unmistakably indicated under the term *Beth-Khumri*, (17) "the house or city of Omri," that monarch having been the original founder of Samaria, according to Scripture.[1]

The first great event in the kingdom of Judah after the separation from Israel, was the invasion of Judæa by Shishak, king of Egypt, in the fifth year of Rehoboam. Shishak came up against Jerusalem with "twelve hundred chariots and threescore thousand horsemen," besides a host of footmen who were "without number."[2] He "took the fenced cities which pertained to Judah," and was proceeding to invest the capital, when Rehoboam made his submission, delivered up the treasures of the temple, and of his own palace, and became one of the "servants" or tributaries of the Egyptian king.[3] This success is found to have been commemorated by Shishak on the outside of the great temple at Karnac; and here in a long list of captured towns and districts, which Shishak boasts of

[1] 1 Kings xvi. 24. [2] 2 Chron. xii. 3. [3] Ibid. verse 8.

having added to his dominions, occurs the "*Melchi Yuda*," or kingdom of Judah, (18) the conquest of which by this king is thus distinctly noticed in the Egyptian records.

About thirty years later Judæa was again invaded from this quarter. "Zerah the Ethiopian," at the head of an army of "a thousand thousand"[1]—or a million of men—who were chiefly Ethiopians and Libyans,[2] made war upon Asa, and entering his kingdom at its south-western angle, was there met by the Jewish monarch and signally defeated by him.[3] In this case we cannot expect such a confirmation as in the last instance; for nations do not usually put on record their great disasters. It appears, however, that at the time indicated, the king of Egypt was an Osorkon (19)—a name identical in its root consonants with *Zerach;* and it appears also that Egypt continued to decline from this period till the time of Psammetichus, a natural result of such a disaster as that which befell the invading host. The only difficulty which meets us is the representation of Zerah as *an Ethiopian*—a fact not at present confirmed by the monuments. Perhaps, though an Egyptian, he was regarded as an Ethiopian, because he ruled over Ethiopia, and because his army was mainly composed of men belonging to that country. Or perhaps, though we have no positive evidence of this, he may have been really of Ethiopian extraction. Osorkon the Second, who is the natural contemporary of Asa, was not descended from the earlier kings of the dynasty. He was the *son-in-law* of his predecessor, and reigned in right of his wife. It is therefore not at all impossible that he may have been an Ethiopian by birth, and have ruled over both countries.

In the succeeding generation, the records of the other

[1] 2 Chron. xiv. 9. [2] Ibid. xvi. 8. [3] Ibid. xiv. 12, 13.

kingdom present us with some points of contact between the Jewish and the Phœnician annals, in which again we have all the agreement that is possible. Ahab, king of Israel, is represented as having sought to strengthen himself in the position which his father had usurped, by a marriage with a foreign princess, and as having made choice for the purpose of "Jezebel, daughter of Eth-baal, king of the Zidonians."[1] Here again not only have we a genuine Phœnician name, but we have the name of a king, who is proved by the Tyrian history of Menander to have been seated upon the throne exactly at this time. Eithobalus, the priest of Ashteroth (or Venus,) who by the murder of his predecessor, Pheles, became king of Tyre, mounted the throne just fifty years after the death of Hiram, the contemporary of Solomon.[(20)] Ahab mounted the throne of Israel fifteen or twenty years later, and was thus the younger contemporary of Eithobalus, or Eth-baal, who continued to reign at Tyre during a considerable portion of Ahab's reign in Israel. The only objection that can be taken to this identity — which is generally allowed[(21)] — turns upon the circumstance that Eth-baal is called in Scripture, not king of Tyre, but "king of the Zidonians." Sidon, it is probable, although a dependency of Tyre at this time, had her own line of kings; and if Eth-baal was one of these, the coincidence between his name and that of the reigning Tyrian monarch would be merely accidental, and the confirmation here sought to be established would fall to the ground. But the fact seems to be that the Jewish writers use the term "Zidonians" in two senses, one specific, and the other generic, — sometimes intending by it the inhabitants of Sidon alone, sometimes the Phœnicians generally.[(22)] And it is *probably* in this latter sense that

[1] 1 Kings xvi. 31.

the title "king of the Zidonians" is applied to the father of Jezebel.

Menander also related that during the reign of Eth-baal, which (as we have seen) coincided in a great measure with that of Ahab in Israel, there was a remarkable drought, which continued in Phœnicia for the full space of a year. (23) This drought is fairly connected with the still longer one in the land of Israel, which Elijah announced to Ahab,[1] and which led to the destruction of the priests of Baal upon Mount Carmel.[2]

The most remarkable feature in the external history of Israel during the reign of Ahab, is the war which raged towards its close between the Israelites and the Syrians of Damascus. The power and greatness of the Damascene king, who bears the name of Ben-hadad, are very strikingly depicted. He comes against Samaria at the head of no fewer than thirty-two subject or confederate "kings,"[3] with "horses" and with "chariots,"[4] and a "great multitude."[5] Though defeated with great slaughter on his first attempt, he is able to bring into the field another army of equal strength in the ensuing year.[6] The exact number of his troops is not mentioned, but it may be conjectured from the losses in his second campaign, which are said to have amounted to one hundred and twenty-seven thousand men.[7] Even this enormous slaughter does not paralyze him: he continues the war for three years longer; and in the third year fights the battle in which Ahab is slain.[8] Now, of this particular struggle we have no positive confirmation, owing to the almost total loss of the ancient Syrian records. (24) But we have, in the cuneiform annals

[1] 1 Kings xvii. 1. [2] Ibid. chap. xviii. [3] Ibid. xx. 1.
[4] Ibid. [5] Ibid. verse 13. [6] Ibid. xx. 25.
[7] Ibid. verses 28 and 29. [8] Ibid. xxii. 1–36.

of an Assyrian king, a very curious and valuable confirmation of the power of Damascus at this time — of its being under the rule of a monarch named Ben-hadad, who was at the head of a great confederacy of princes, and who was able to bring into the field year after year vast armies, with which he repeatedly engaged the whole force of Assyria. We have accounts of three campaigns between the Assyrians on the one side, and the Syrians, Hittites, Hamathites, and Phœnicians, united under the command of Ben-hadad, upon the other,(25) in which the contest is maintained with spirit, the armies being of a large size, and their composition and character such as we find described in Scripture.(26)

The same record further verifies the historical accuracy of the Books of Kings by a mention of Hazael as king of Damascus immediately after Ben-hadad,(27) and also by the synchronism which it establishes between this prince and Jehu, who is the first Israelite king mentioned by name on any Inscription hitherto discovered. Jehu appears by the monument in question to have submitted himself to the great Assyrian conqueror;(28) and it may be suspected that from this date both the Jewish and the Israelitish kings held their crowns as fiefs dependent on the will of the Assyrian monarch, with whom it formally lay to "confirm" each new prince "in his kingdom."[1]

A break now occurs in the series of profane notices, which have extended, without the omission of a generation, from the time of David to that of Jehu. During the century which follows on the death of that monarch we are able to adduce from profane sources no more than one or two doubtful illustrations of the Sacred Narrative. Here, however, it is to be remarked, that the absence of

[1] 2 Kings xiv. 5; xv. 19.

profane confirmation is coincident with, and must fairly be regarded as resulting from, a want of sufficient materials. There is a great dearth of copious Assyrian inscriptions from the time of the monarch who made Jehu tributary to that of the Tiglath-Pileser of Scripture.(29) For this time too the Tyrian records are an absolute blank,(30) while the Egyptian are but little better; and moreover there seems to have been no political contact between these countries and Palestine during the period in question. We cannot therefore be surprised at the deficiency here noted; nor would it be right to view it as having the slightest tendency to weaken the force of our previous reasoning.

The Hebrew annals touch no foreign country, of which we have any records at all, from the time of Jehu to that of Menahem. In the reign of this latter prince occurs the first direct mention of Assyria as a power actively interfering in Palestine, and claiming and exercising political influence. We are told that in the reign of Menahem, "Pul, the king of Assyria, came up against the land; and Menahem gave Pul a thousand talents of silver, that his hand might be with him, to confirm the kingdom in his hand."[1] There is some difficulty in identifying the Assyrian monarch here mentioned, who not only took this large tribute, but (as appears from Chronicles)[2] led a portion of the nation into captivity. In the Hebrew Scriptures he appears as Pul, or rather Phul; and this is also the form of the name which the Armenian Eusebius declares to have been used by Polyhistor,(31) who followed Berosus; but in the Septuagint he is called Phalôch, or Phalôs,(32) a form of which the Hebrew word seems to be an abbreviation. The Assyrian records of the time present us with no name very close to this; but there

[1] 2 Kings xv. 19. [2] 1 Chron. v. 26.

is one which has been read variously, as *Phal-lukha*, *Vul-lukha*, and *Iva-lush*, wherein it is not improbable that we may have the actual appellation of the Biblical Phul, or Phaloch. The annals of this monarch are scanty; but in the most important record which we possess of his reign, there is a notice of his having taken tribute from *Beth-Khumri*, or Samaria, as well as from Tyre, Sidon, Damascus, Idumæa, and Philistia. (33) Neither the name of the Israelitish king, nor the amount of his tribute, is mentioned in the Assyrian record; but the amount of the latter, which may to many appear excessive, receives illustration, and a certain degree of confirmation, from a fact which happens to be recorded on the monument — namely, that the Assyrian monarch took at this time from the king of Damascus a tribute considerably greater than that which, according to the author of Kings, he now exacted from Menahem. From Menahem he received one thousand talents of silver; but from the Damascene king the tribute taken was twenty-three hundred of such talents, together with three thousand talents of copper, forty of gold, and five thousand of some other metal. (34)

The expedition of Pul against Menahem is followed by a series of attacks on the independence of the two kingdoms, which cause the sacred history to be very closely connected, for the space of about a century, with the annals of Assyria. The successors of Pul are presented to us by the Biblical writers, apparently in a continuous and uninterrupted line — Tiglath-Pileser, Shalmaneser, Sargon, Sennacherib, and Esar-haddon, all of them carrying their arms into Palestine, and playing an important part in the history of the favored race. It happens most fortunately (may we not say, providentially?) that records of all these monarchs — the greatest which Assyria produced — have been recovered; and these in some cases are sufficiently full to exhibit a close agreement with the sacred narrative, while throughout they harmonize with the tenor of that narrative, only in one or two cases so differing from the Hebrew text as to cause any difficulty. I shall proceed to exhibit this agreement with the brevity which my limits necessitate, before noticing the confirmation which this portion of the history derives also from the Egyptian and Babylonian records.

The chief events related of Tiglath-Pileser in Scripture are his two invasions of Israel — once when he "took Ijon, and Abel-beth-maachah, and Janoah, and Kedesh, and Hazor, and Gilead, and Galilee, and all the land of Naphtali, and carried them captive to Assyria;"[1] and again, when he came at the invitation of Ahaz, and not only chastised Pekah, but "took Damascus, and slew Rezin."[2] Of the first of these two campaigns we have no profane confirmation; but some account of the second is given in an Assyrian fragment, where Tiglath-Pileser speaks of his defeating Rezin, and capturing Damascus, and also of his taking tribute from the king of Samaria. The monarch indeed from whom he takes the tribute is called Menahem, instead of Pekah; and this constitutes a discrepancy — the first that we have found — between the Assyrian and the Hebrew records: but the probability is that Pekah is intended, and that the official who composed, or the workman who engraved, the Assyrian document made a mistake in the name.(35)

Tiglath-Pileser is also stated in Scripture to have been visited at Damascus by the Jewish king Ahaz; and the result of this visit was that Ahaz set up a new altar in the temple at Jerusalem, according to the pattern of an altar

[1] 2 Kings xv. 29. [2] Ibid. xvi. 7–9.

which he had seen at Damascus.[1] It has been generally supposed that this altar was Syrian; (36) and its establishment has been connected with the passage in Chronicles, where Ahaz is said to have "sacrificed to the gods of Damascus, which smote him;"[2] but few things can be more improbable than the adoption of the gods of a foreign nation at the moment when they had been proved powerless. The strange altar of Ahaz was in all probability not Syrian, but Assyrian; and its erection was in accordance with an Assyrian custom, of which the Inscriptions afford abundant evidence — the custom of requiring from the subject nations some formal acknowledgment of the gods and worship of the sovereign country. (37)

The successor of Tiglath-Pileser seems to have been Shalmaneser — a king, whose military exploits in these regions were celebrated by Menander in his history of Tyre. (38) He appears, from the narrative in Kings, to have come up twice against Hoshea, the last king of Israel,[3] — on the first occasion merely enforcing the tribute which was regarded as due, but on the second proceeding to extremities, in order to punish Hoshea for contracting an alliance with Egypt, laying siege to Samaria, and continuing to prosecute the siege for the space of three years. The records of Shalmaneser have been so mutilated by his successors, that they furnish only a very slight confirmation of this history. The name of Hoshea, however, king of Samaria, is found in an inscription, which has been with reason assigned to Shalmaneser; (39) and though the capture of Samaria is claimed by his successor, Sargon, as an exploit of his own in his first year, (40) yet this very claim confirms the Scriptural account of Shalmaneser's commencing the

[1] 2 Kings xvi. 10–16. [2] 2 Chron. xxviii. 23.
[3] 2 Kings xvii. 3 and 5.

siege, which began three years before the capture;[1] and it is easily brought into harmony with the Scriptural account of the actual capture, either by supposing that Sargon claimed the success as falling into his own reign, (which had then begun at Nineveh,) though Shalmaneser was the real captor; or by regarding (as we are entitled to do) the king of Assyria, who is said to have taken Samaria in the Book of Kings, as a distinct person from the king who commenced the siege.(41)

Of Shalmaneser's successor, Sargon, Scripture contains but one clear historic notice. In the twentieth chapter of Isaiah, we are told that "in the year that Tartan came unto Ashdod, (when Sargon, the king of Assyria, sent him,) and fought against Ashdod, and took it,"[2] certain directions were given by the Lord to the prophet. It was formerly supposed that Sargon was another name for one of the Assyrian monarchs mentioned in the Book of Kings;(42) but since the discovery that the king of Assyria, who built the great palace at Khorsabad, actually bore this appellation, which continued to attach to its ruins until the Arab conquest,(43) it has been generally admitted that we have in Isaiah a reference to an Assyrian ruler distinct from all those mentioned in Kings, and identical with the Khorsabad monarch, who was the father of Sennacherib. Now of this monarch we find it related in his annals that he made war in Southern Syria, *and took Ashdod.*(44) Thus the sole fact which Scripture distinctly assigns to the reign of Sargon is confirmed by the native records; which likewise illustrate the two or three other facts probably intended to be assigned to him by the sacred writers. Isaiah apparently means Sargon in the fourth verse of his twentieth chapter, when he prophesies that "the king of Assyria shall

[1] 2 Kings xvii. 3, 5, and xviii. 9, 10.

[2] Isaiah xx. 1.

lead away the Egyptians prisoners, and the Ethiopians captives, young and old, naked and barefoot, even with their buttocks uncovered, to the shame of Egypt." If this be allowed, we obtain a second illustration of Sargon's reign from the monuments; which represent him as warring with Egypt, and forcing the Pharaoh of the time to become his tributary, and which also show that Egypt was at this time in just that close connection with Ethiopia (45) which the prophet's expressions indicate.[1] Again, if we may presume that Sargon is intended by the king of Assyria who took Samaria,[2] and carried the Israelites away captive;[3] then there is derivable from the monuments a very curious illustration of the statement of Scripture, that the monarch, who did this, placed his captives, or at least a portion of them, "in the cities of the Medes."[4] For Sargon seems to have been the first Assyrian monarch who conquered Media; and he expressly relates that, in order to complete its subjection, he founded there a number of cities, which he planted with colonists from other portions of his dominions. (46)

The Assyrian monarch who appears in Scripture as most probably the successor of Sargon is Sennacherib, whom the monuments show to have been his son. Two expeditions of this prince against Hezekiah are related; and each of them receives a very striking confirmation from a profane source. The sacred writers tell us that on the first occasion, Hezekiah having thrown off the allegiance[5] which the kings of Judah appear to have paid to Assyria at least from the time of Ahaz' message to Tiglath-Pileser,[6] "Sennacherib, king of Assyria, came up against all the fenced cities of Judah, and took them: and Hezekiah, king of Judah sent

[1] Isaiah xx. 3 and 4. [2] 2 Kings xvii. 6. [3] Ibid. xviii. 11.
[4] Ibid. [5] Ibid. xvii. 7. [6] Ibid. xvi. 7.

to the king of Assyria to Lachish, saying, 'I have offended; return from me: that which thou puttest upon me, I will bear:' and the king of Assyria appointed unto Hezekiah, king of Judah, three hundred talents of silver and thirty talents of gold."[1] The annals of Sennacherib contain a full account of this campaign. "And because Hezekiah, king of Judah," says Sennacherib, "would not submit to my yoke, I came up against him, and by force of arms and by the might of my power I took *forty-six of his strong fenced cities;* and of the smaller towns which were scattered about, I took and plundered a countless number. And from these places I captured and carried off as spoil two hundred thousand one hundred and fifty people, old and young, male and female, together with horses and mares, asses and camels, oxen and sheep, a countless multitude. And Hezekiah himself I shut up in Jerusalem, his capital city, like a bird in a cage, building towers round the city to hem him in, and raising banks of earth against the gates, so as to prevent escape. . . . Then upon this Hezekiah there fell the fear of the power of my arms, and he sent out to me the chiefs and the elders of Jerusalem *with thirty talents of gold*, and eight hundred talents of silver, and divers treasures, a rich and immense booty. . . . All these things were brought to me at Nineveh, the seat of my government, Hezekiah having sent them by way of tribute, and as a token of his submission to my power." (47) It is needless to particularize the points of agreement between these narratives. The only discrepancy is in the amount of the silver which Sennacherib received; and here we may easily conceive, either that the Assyrian king has exaggerated, or that he has counted in a portion of the spoil, while the

[1] 2 Kings xviii. 13, 14. Compare Isaiah xxxvi. 1, and 2 Chron. xxxii. 1–8.

sacred writer has merely mentioned the sum agreed to be paid as tribute.(48)

The second expedition of Sennacherib into Syria seems to have followed very shortly upon the first. In neither case was Judæa the sole, or even the main object of attack. The real purpose of both expeditions was to weaken Egypt; and it was by his Egyptian leanings that Hezekiah had provoked the anger of his suzerain.[1] No collision appears to have taken place on this second occasion between the Assyrians and the Jews. Hezekiah was threatened; but before the threats could be put in execution, that miraculous destruction of the Assyrian host was effected which forms so striking a feature of this portion of the sacred narrative. "The angel of the Lord went out, and smote in the camp of the Assyrians" (which was at Libnah on the borders of Egypt) "a hundred fourscore and five thousand; and when they arose early in the morning, they were all dead corpses."[2] It has been generally seen and confessed, that the marvellous account which Herodotus gives of the discomfiture of Sennacherib by Sethôs(49) is the Egyptian version of this event, which was (naturally enough) ascribed by that people to the interposition of its own divinities.

The murder of Sennacherib by two of his sons,[3] though not mentioned in the Assyrian Inscriptions, (which have never been found to record the death of a king,) appears to have been noticed by Berosus; from whom were derived in all probability the brief allusions to the event which are met with in the fragments of Alexander Polyhistor and Abydenus.(49) The escape of the murderers into Armenia[4] is in harmony with what is known of the condition of that

[1] 2 Kings xviii. 21 and 24.
[2] Ibid. xix. 35.
[3] Ibid. verse 37.
[4] Ibid.

country at the time; for it appears as an independent state generally hostile to the Assyrian monarchs, in the cuneiform records of this period;(50) and it is further perhaps worthy of remark, that the Armenian traditions spoke distinctly of the reception of the two refugees, and of the tracts respectively assigned to them.(51)

Esarhaddon is distinctly stated in Scripture to have been the son and successor of Sennacherib.[1] As usual, the monuments are in complete accordance.(52) Esarhaddon every where calls himself the son of Sennacherib; and there is no appearance in the native records of any king having intervened between the two.(53) The events belonging to the reign of Esarhaddon, which are introduced by the sacred writers into their narrative, are but few. As his father was contemporary with Hezekiah, we naturally regard him as falling into the time of Manasseh; and it has therefore been generally felt that he should be the king of Assyria, whose captains "took Manasseh among the thorns, and bound him with fetters, and *carried him to Babylon*."[2] The monuments confirm the synchronism which Scripture implies, by distinctly mentioning "Manasseh, king of Judah," among the tributaries of Esarhaddon;(54) and though no direct confirmation has as yet been found of the captivity and restoration of the Jewish monarch, yet the narrative contains an incidental allusion which is in very remarkable harmony with the native records. One is greatly surprised at first hearing that the generals of an *Assyrian* king, on capturing a rebel, carried him to *Babylon* instead of Nineveh — one is almost inclined to suspect a mistake. 'What has a king of Assyria to do with Babylon?' one naturally asks. The reply is, that Esarhaddon,

[1] 2 Kings xix. 37. Compare Isaiah xxxvii. 38.

[2] 2 Chron. xxxiii. 11.

and *he only of all the Assyrian kings*, actually was king of Babylon — that he built a palace, and occasionally held his court there (55) — and that consequently a captive was as likely to be brought to him at that city as at the metropolis of Assyria Proper. Had the narrative fallen under the reign of any other Assyrian monarch, this explanation could not have been given; and the difficulty would have been considerable. Occurring where it does, it furnishes no difficulty at all, but is one of those small points of incidental agreement which are more satisfactory to a candid mind than even a very large amount of harmony in the main narrative.

With Esarhaddon the notices of Assyria in the sacred history come to an end. Assyria herself shortly afterwards disappears; (56) and her place is taken by Babylon, which now for the first time becomes a great conquering power. This transfer of empire is abundantly confirmed by profane authorities; (57) but, as the historical character of the Biblical narrative in this respect has always been allowed, it is unnecessary in this place to dwell upon it. I proceed to consider the agreement between the sacred narrative and the native Egyptian and Babylonian records during the later times of the Hebrew monarchy.

Egyptian and Jewish history touch at four points during this period. Hoshea, the contemporary of Shalmaneser, makes a treaty with So, king of Egypt,[1] shortly before the capture of Samaria, or about the year B. C. 725. Sennacherib, not very long afterwards, on attacking the dependencies of Egypt, learns that Tirhakah, king of the Ethiopians, is gathering together an army to oppose him.[2] Nearly a century later, Pharaoh-Necho invades Judæa, defeats and kills the Jewish king Josiah, presses forward to the

[1] 2 Kings xvii. 4. [2] Ibid. xix. 9.

Euphrates, takes Carchemish and Jerusalem, leads Jehoahaz the son of Josiah into captivity, and establishes his dominion over the whole of Syria; but is shortly afterwards defeated by Nebuchadnezzar, king of Babylon, and dispossessed of all his conquests.[1] Finally, about twenty years after this, Pharaoh-Hophra is spoken of as encouraging the Jews to resist Nebuchadnezzar, and threatened with the wrath of that monarch, into whose hands it is said he will be delivered.[2]

Here, then, within about one hundred and forty years, we have the names of four kings of Egypt, one of whom is also the sovereign of Cush or Ethiopia. Let us see whether the Egyptian annals recognize the monarchs thus brought under our notice.

Neither Manetho nor the monuments present us with any name which at all closely resembles the word "So." If, however, we look to the Hebrew literation of that name, we shall find that the word is written with three letters, which may be (and probably are) all consonants. They may be read as S, V, H; and the name of the monarch thus designated may most properly be regarded as *Seveh.*(58) Now a king of the name of Sevech, or Sevechus, appears in the proper place in Manetho's lists; and the monuments show that two monarchs, (who seem to have been a father and a son,) *Shebek* I. and *Shebek* II., ruled Egypt about this period.(59) The former of the two is familiar to us under the name (which Herodotus assigns to him) of Sabaco;(60) and it is probably this prince of whom the Hebrew writer speaks. The fact that he came into contact with Assyria is confirmed by the discovery of his seal at Koyunjik; it had probably been affixed to a treaty

[1] 2 Kings xxiii. 29–35; xxiv. 7. Compare 2 Chron. xxxv. 20.

[2] Jerem. xliv. 30; xlvi. 13–26.

which, in consequence of his machinations, he had been forced to make with the triumphant Assyrian monarch.(61)

Tirhakah, who appears as king of the Ethiopians, yet at the same time as protector of Egypt, in the second Book of Kings, is manifestly the Tarcus or Taracus of Manetho,(62) the Tearchon of Strabo,(63) and the *Tehrak* of the monuments.(64) He succeeded the second *Shebek*, and is proved by his remains to have been king of both countries, but to have held his court in Ethiopia.

In the Pharaoh-Necho of Kings and Jeremiah,[1] it is impossible not to recognize the famous Egyptian monarch whom Manetho calls Nechao,(65) Herodotus Neco,(66) and the monuments *Neku*,(67) the son and successor of the first Psammetichus. The invasion of Syria by this prince, and his defeat of the Syrians in a great battle, are attested by Herodotus; who only commits a slight and very venial error, when he makes Magdolum instead of Megiddo the scene of the encounter.(68) It has been usual to regard Herodotus as also confirming the capture of Jerusalem by Necho;(69) but too much uncertainty attaches to the presumed identity of Cadytis with the Jewish capital, to make it wise that much stress should be laid on this imagined agreement.(70) We may with more confidence appeal for a confirmation of this fact, and of the captivity of Jehŏahaz, to the fragments of Manetho, who is reported both by Africanus and by Eusebius to have mentioned these Egyptian successes.(71)

Not less certain and unmistakable is the identity of the Scriptural Pharaoh-Hophra with Manetho's Uaphris, Herodotus's Apries, and the monumental *Haifra-het* or *Haifra*.(72) Egyptian chronology makes this prince contemporary with Nebuchadnezzar;(73) and if we may trust the

[1] Jerem. xlvi. 2-12.

abstracts which Eusebius and Africanus profess to give of Manetho, that writer mentioned the flight of the Jews into Egypt upon the destruction of their city, and their reception by Uaphris or Hophra.(74) The miserable end of Hophra, predicted by Jeremiah, is related from Egyptian traditions by Herodotus; and though it may be doubted whether his account of the occurrence is in its minuter circumstances altogether correct,(75) yet at any rate the facts of the deposition and execution of the Egyptian king must be accepted on his testimony; and these are the facts which especially illustrate the statements of Scripture.

Babylonian and Jewish history come into contact only at two points in the period under consideration. We are told that in the reign of Hezekiah, Merodach-Baladan, king of Babylon, sent letters and a present to that prince, partly because he had heard that he was sick,[1] partly because he wished to inquire concerning the wonder that had been done in the land,[2] when the shadow went back ten degrees on the dial of Ahaz. The name of Merodach-Baladan does not at first sight appear to be contained in the authentic list of Babylonian kings preserved to us in Ptolemy. But it is probable that the king in question does really occur in that list under the appellation of Mardoc-empad, or Mardoc-empal;(76) and there is abundant evidence from the inscriptions, not only of the existence of such a monarch, but of his having been contemporary with the Jewish king in whose reign his embassy is placed.(77) The fact of the embassy — which seems improbable if we only know the *general* condition of Babylon at the period to have been one of subjection to Assyria — becomes highly probable when we learn — both from Berosus(78) and the monuments(79) — that there was a fierce and bitter hostility between Mero-

[1] 2 Kings xx. 12. [2] 2 Chron. xxxii. 31.

dach-Baladan and the Assyrian monarchs, from whose oppressive yoke he more than once freed his country. The ostensible motive of the embassy — to inquire about an astronomical marvel — is also highly probable in the case of a country where astronomy held so high a rank, where the temples were observatories, and the religion was to a great extent astral.(80)

About a century later, Babylon is found in the Scripture history to have succeeded to the position and influence of Assyria over Palestine, and we have a brief relation, in Jeremiah, Ezekiel, and Kings, of several campaigns conducted by Nebuchadnezzar in these regions. Profane accounts are in accordance. The reconquest of Syria and Palestine from Necho by Nebuchadnezzar, which is mentioned by Jeremiah,[1] and glanced at in Kings,[2] was related at length by Berosus;(81) his prolonged siege of Tyre, which is spoken of by Ezekiel,[3] was attested by the Tyrian historians, who said that it lasted thirteen years;(82) while his destruction of the temple at Jerusalem, and his deportation of vast bodies of Jewish captives, were noticed by the native historian, who said that the captives were settled in convenient places in Babylonia.(83) As the rest of the acts of Nebuchadnezzar fall into our next period, the present review here comes to an end, and we may now close this portion of the inquiry with a brief summary of the evidence adduced in the course of it.

The period with which we have been dealing is one of comparative light. We possess, it is true, no continuous history of it besides that which the Sacred Volume furnishes; but we have abstracts of the writings of Berosus and Manetho, which contained the annals of Egypt and of Babylon during the space; we have considerable fragments

[1] Jerem. xlvi. 1–12. [2] 2 Kings xxiv. 7. [3] Ezek. xxix. 18.

of the Tyrian histories of the time; and in the latter portion of it we begin to enjoy the advantage of those investigations which the inquisitive Greeks pushed into the antiquities of all the nations wherewith they became acquainted. Above all we possess the contemporary records — often in a very copious form — of all the great Assyrian monarchs whose reigns fell within the period in question, while we derive likewise a certain amount of information from the monuments of Egypt. All these sources have been examined, and all have combined to confirm and illustrate the Scriptural narrative at almost every point where it was possible — or at any rate where it was probable — that they would have a bearing upon it. The result is a general confirmation of the entire body of leading facts — minute confirmation occasionally — and a complete absence of any thing that can be reasonably viewed as serious discrepancy. A few difficulties — chiefly chronological [84] — meet us; but they are fewer in proportion than are found in the profane history of almost any remote period; and the faith must be weak indeed to which they prove a stumbling-block. Generally, throughout this whole period, there is that "admirable agreement," which Niebuhr observes upon towards its close, [85] between the profane records and the accounts of Scripture. We have not for the most part by any labored efforts to harmonize the two — their accord is patent and striking; and is sufficiently exhibited by a mere juxtaposition of passages. The monarchs themselves, the order of their names, their relationship where it is indicated, their actions so far as they come under notice, are the same in both the Jewish and the native histories; which present likewise, here as elsewhere, numerous points of agreement, connected with the geography, religion, and customs of the various nations. [86] As discovery proceeds, these points of agreement are multiplied; obscurities clear up; difficulties are solved; doubts vanish. It is only where profane records are wanting or scanty, that the Sacred Narrative is unconfirmed and rests solely upon its own basis. Perhaps a time may come when through the recovery of the complete annals of Egypt, Assyria, and Babylon, we may obtain for the whole of the Sacred History that sort of illustration, which is now confined to certain portions of it. God, who disposes all things "after the counsel of his own will,"[1] and who has given to the present age such treasures of long buried knowledge, may have yet greater things in store for us, to be brought to light at His own good time. When the voice of men grows faint and feeble, then the very "stones" are made to "cry out."[2] "Blessed be the name of God forever and ever; for wisdom and might are his.... He revealeth the deep and secret things: He knoweth what is in the darkness, and the light dwelleth with Him."[3]

[1] Eph. i. 11. [2] Luke xix. 40. [3] Dan. ii. 20, 22.

LECTURE V.

BY THE RIVERS OF BABYLON, THERE WE SAT DOWN, YEA, WE WEPT, WHEN WE REMEMBERED ZION. WE HANGED OUR HARPS UPON THE WILLOWS IN THE MIDST THEREOF. FOR THEY THAT CARRIED US AWAY CAPTIVE REQUIRED OF US A SONG: AND THEY THAT WASTED US REQUIRED OF US MIRTH, SAYING, "SING US ONE OF THE SONGS OF ZION." HOW SHALL WE SING THE LORD'S SONG IN A STRANGE LAND? — PSALM CXXXVII. 1–4.

WE are brought now by the course of our inquiry to the fourth and closing period of the Old Testament History — a period which subdivides itself into two portions offering a marked contrast to each other, the time of the Captivity, or servitude in Babylon, and the time of the Return, or gradual reëstablishment of the Jews in their own country. From the direct historical writings of the chosen people the former time is omitted. The harp of the Historic Muse refuses to sound during this sad season; and it would form a blank in the Hebrew annals, did we not possess in the writings of one of the Prophets a personal narrative, which to some extent fills up the gap left between Kings and Ezra. Conformably with a custom which we find also in Isaiah and Jeremiah, Daniel combines history with prophecy, uniting in a single book the visions wherewith he was favored and an account of various remarkable events which he witnessed. He does not, however, confine himself strictly to the precedent which those writers had set him; but, as if aware that on him had devolved the double office of Prophet and Historian, and that future ages would learn the circumstances of this period from his pen only, he gives to the historical element in his work a marked and very unusual prominence. Hence we are still able to continue through the period in question the comparison (in which we have been so long engaged) between the History of the Jews as delivered by their own writers, and the records of those nations with which they came in contact.

If the book of Daniel be a genuine work, the narrative which it contains must possess the highest degree of historical credibility. The writer claims to be a most competent witness. He represents himself as having lived at Babylon during the whole duration of the Captivity, and as having filled situations of the highest trust and importance under the Babylonian and Medo-Persic monarchs. Those who have sought to discredit the Book, uniformly maintain that it is spurious, having been composed by an uninspired writer, who falsely assumed the name of an ancient prophet,[(1)] — or, according to some, of a mythic personage,[(2)] — but who lived really under Antiochus Epiphanes. The supposed proof of this last assertion is the minuteness and accuracy of the predictions, which tally so exactly with the known course of history, that it is said they must have been written after the events had happened. This objection, which was first made in the third century of our era by the heathen writer Porphyry,[(3)] has been revived in modern times, and is become the favorite argument of the Rationalists,[(4)] with whom Prophecy means nothing but that natural foresight whereby the consequences of present facts and circumstances are anticipated by the prudent and sagacious. I shall not stop at this time to examine an argument which can only persuade those who disbelieve in the prophetic gift altogether.(5) Suffice it to observe, that the book of Daniel, like the books of Ezra and Jeremiah, is written partly in Hebrew and partly in Chaldee, which peculiarity may fairly be said to fix its date to the time of the Captivity:(6) and that it was translated into Greek in the reign of Ptolemy Philadelphus, more than seventy years before the accession of Epiphanes.(7) There is therefore every reason to believe that it belongs to the age in which it professes to have been composed; while no sufficient ground has been shown for doubting that its writer was the Daniel whose history it records(8)—the prince,(9)—whose extraordinary piety and wisdom were commended by his contemporary, Ezekiel.[1](10)

The authenticity of the narrative has been denied on the ground that it is irreconcilable with what we know of profane history. According to De Wette, the book of Daniel is full of "historical inaccuracies, such as are contained in no other prophetical book of the Old Testament."(11) These pretended inaccuracies will best be considered in connection with that general comparison of the sacred narrative with the profane records of the period in question, on which (in pursuance of the plan uniformly adopted throughout these Lectures) we have now to enter.

The fundamental fact of the time—the Captivity itself—is allowed on all hands to admit of no reasonable doubt. Not only do we find, from the monuments of the Assyrian kings(12) and the subsequent history of Persia,(13) that such transfers of whole populations were common in the East in ancient times; but we have the direct evidence of Josephus to the fact, that Berosus mentioned the carrying

[1] Ezek. xiv. 14 and 20 xxviii. 3.

off of the Jews by Nebuchadnezzar and their settlement in parts of Babylonia. (14) Profane evidence, however, on this point is unnecessary; since it cannot be thought that any people would have invented a tale with regard to themselves which redounded so little to their credit, and from which it was impossible that they could gain any advantage.

The character of Nebuchadnezzar, the length of his reign, and the fact of his having uttered prophecies, are points in which there is a remarkable agreement between the sacred record and profane authorities. The splendor and magnificence which this prince displayed, his military successes, his devotion to his gods, and the pride which he took in adorning Babylon with great buildings, are noted by Berosus and Abydenus; (15) the latter of whom has a most curious passage, for the preservation of which we are indebted to Eusebius, on the subject of his having been gifted with prophetic powers. "The Chaldæans relate," says Abydenus, "that, after this, Nebuchadnezzar went up to his palace, and being seized with a divine *afflatus*, prophesied to the Babylonians the destruction of their city by the Medes and Persians, after which he suddenly disappeared from among them." (16) The details are incorrect; but it is at least remarkable that the particular prince, who alone, of all the heathen monarchs with whom the Jews were brought into contact, is said in Scripture to have had the future made known to him by God,[1] is also the only one of those persons who is declared to have had the prophetic gift by a profane writer.

The length of Nebuchadnezzar's reign is stated without any variety by Berosus, Polyhistor, and Ptolemy, (17) at forty-three years. The Babylonian monuments go near to

[1] Dan. ii. 28–9.

prove the same; for the forty-second year of Nebuchadnezzar has been found on a clay tablet. (18) Here Scripture is in *exact* accordance; for as the first year of Evil-Merodach, the son and successor of Nebuchadnezzar, is the thirty-seventh of the captivity of Jehoiachin,[1] who was taken to Babylon in Nebuchadnezzar's eighth year,[2] it is evident that just forty-three years are required for the reign of the great Chaldæan monarch. (19) This agreement, moreover, is incidental; for Evil-Merodach is not said in Scripture to have been the successor of Nebuchadnezzar: we only know this fact from profane sources.

It has been maintained that the book of Daniel misrepresents the condition of Babylonia under Nebuchadnezzar; (20) the points to which objection is especially taken being the account given of the Babylonian wise men, the admission of Daniel among them, and the apparent reference to something like a satrapial organization of the empire. (21) With respect to the first point, it would really be far more reasonable to adduce the descriptions in question as proof of the intimate knowledge which the writer possessed of the condition of learning among the Babylonians, than to bring them forward as indications of his ignorance. The wise men are designated primarily by a word which exactly suits the condition of literature in the time and country — a word derived from the root *cheret*, which means "a graving tool," exactly the instrument wherewith a Babylonian ordinarily wrote. (22) They are also termed Chasdim or Chaldæans, whereby a knowledge is shown beyond that of the earlier prophets — a knowledge of the fact that the term "Chaldæan" was not properly applied to the whole nation, but only to a learned caste or

[1] 2 Kings xxv. 27; Jer. lii. 31.

[2] 2 Kings xxiv. 12. Compare Jer. xxv. 1.

class, the possessors of the old wisdom, which was written in the Chaldæan tongue. (23)

The objection raised to the admission of Daniel among the "wise men," is based on the mistaken notion that they were especially a priestly caste, presiding over the national religion; whereas the truth seems to be that they were a learned class, including the priests, but not identical with them, and corresponding rather to the graduates of a university than to the clergy of an establishment. (24) Into such a class foreigners, and those of a different religion, might readily be admitted.

With respect to what has been called the "satrapial organization" of the empire under Nebuchadnezzar,[1] (and again under Darius the Mede,[2]) it is to be observed in the first place, that nothing like a general organization of the kind is asserted. We are told of certain "rulers of provinces," who were summoned to worship the golden image set up in the plain of Dura;[3] and we find that Judæa itself, after the revolt of Zedekiah, was placed under a "governor."[4] But the latter case was exceptional, being consequent upon the frequent rebellions of the Jewish people: and in the former we are probably to understand the chiefs of districts in the immediate vicinity of Babylonia, who alone would be summoned on such an occasion — not the rulers of all the conquered nations throughout the empire. Further, we must remark, that the system of Babylonian administration is but very little known to us; and that it *may to some extent have been satrapial.* Berosus, at any rate, speaks expressly of "the *Satrap* appointed by Nabopolassar to govern Phœnicia, Cœle-Syria, and Egypt;" (25) and it is not impossible that Darius

[1] Dan. iii. 2, &c. [2] Ibid. vi. 1, &c. [3] Ibid. iii 1, 2.
[4] 2 Kings xxv. 22. Compare Jer. xl. and xli.

Hystaspis, who is usually regarded as the inventor of the system, may have merely enlarged a practice begun by the Babylonians. (26)

There is thus no ground for the assertion that the general condition of Babylonia under Nebuchadnezzar is incorrectly represented in the book of Daniel. Daniel's representation agrees sufficiently with the little that we know of Babylon at this time from any authentic source, (27) and has an internal harmony and consistency which is very striking. We may therefore resume our comparison of the particulars of the civil history, as it is delivered by the sacred writers, and as it has come down to us from the Babylonians themselves.

Berosus appears to have kept silence on the subject of Nebuchadnezzar's mysterious malady. I cannot think, with Hengstenberg, (28) that either he or Abydenus intended any allusion to this remarkable fact in the accounts which they furnished of his decease. It was not to be expected that the native writer would tarnish the glory of his country's greatest monarch by any mention of an affliction which was of so strange and debasing a character. Nor is it at all certain that he would be aware of it. As Nebuchadnezzar outlived his affliction, and was again "established in his kingdom,"[1] all monuments belonging to the time of his malady would have been subject to his own revision; and if any record of it was allowed to descend to posterity, care would have been taken that the truth was not made too plain, by couching the record in sufficiently ambiguous phraseology. Berosus may have read, without fully understanding it, a document which has descended to modern times in a tolerably complete condition, and which seems to contain an allusion to the fact that the great king

[1] Dan. iv. 36.

was for a time incapacitated for the discharge of the royal functions. In the inscription known as the "Standard Inscription" of Nebuchadnezzar, the monarch himself relates, that during some considerable time — four years apparently — all his great works were at a stand — "he did not build high places — he did not lay up treasures — he did not sing the praises of his Lord, Merodach — he did not offer him sacrifice — he did not keep up the works of irrigation."(29) The cause of this suspension, at once of religious worship and of works of utility, is stated in the document in phrases of such obscurity as to be unintelligible; until therefore a better explanation is offered, it cannot but be regarded as at least highly probable, that the passage in question contains the royal version of that remarkable story with which Daniel concludes his notice of the great Chaldæan sovereign.

For the space of time intervening between the recovery of Nebuchadnezzar from his affliction and the conquest of Babylon by the Medo-Persians, which was a period of about a quarter of a century, the Biblical narrative supplies us with but a single fact — the release from prison of Jehoiachin by Evil-Merodach in the year that he ascended the throne of his father. It has been already remarked that the native historian agreed exactly in the name of this prince and the year of his accession; he added, (what Scripture does not expressly state,) that Evil-Merodach was Nebuchadnezzar's son.(30) With regard to the character of this monarch, there seems at first sight to be a contrast between the account of Berosus and the slight indications which the Scripture narrative furnishes. Berosus taxes Evil-Merodach with intemperance and lawlessness;(31) Scripture relates that he had compassion on Jehoiachin, released him from prison, and "spake kindly unto him"[1] — allowed him the rank of king once more, and made him a constant guest at his table, thus treating him with honor and tenderness during the short remainder of his life. Perhaps to the Babylonians such a reversal of the policy pursued by their great monarch appeared to be mere reckless "lawlessness;" and Evil-Merodach may have been deposed, in part at least, because of his departure from the received practice of the Babylonians with respect to rebel princes.

The successor of this unfortunate king was his brother-in-law, Neriglissar; who, although not mentioned in Scripture as a monarch, has been recognized among the "princes of the king of Babylon"[2] by whom Nebuchadnezzar was accompanied in his last siege of Jerusalem. A name there given, Nergal-shar-ezar, corresponds letter for letter with that of a king whose remains are found on the site of Babylon,(32) and who is reasonably identified with the Neriglissar of Berosus and the Nerigassolassar of Ptolemy's Canon. Moreover, the title of "Rab-Mag," which this personage bears in Jeremiah, is found attached to the name of the Babylonian monarch in his brick legends(33) — a coincidence of that minute and exact kind which is one of the surest indications of authentic history.

Of the son of Neriglissar, who was a mere child, and reigned but a few months, Scripture certainly contains no trace. Whether his successor, the last native king of the Canon, whose name is there given as Nabonadius, and who appears elsewhere as Nabannidochus, Nabonnedus, or Labynetus(34) — whether this monarch has a place in the Scriptural narrative or no, has long been a matter of dispute among the learned. That there is no name in the least resembling Nabonadius in the Bible, is granted. But

[1] 2 Kings xxv. 28. [2] Jerem. xxxix. 3 and 13.

it has been by many supposed that that prince must be identical with Daniel's Belshazzar [35] — the last native ruler mentioned in Scripture. The great diversity, however, of the two names, coupled with the fact that in every other case of a Semitic monarch — whether Assyrian or Babylonian — the Hebrew representative is a near expression of the vernacular term, has always made this theory unsatisfactory; and Rationalists, finding no better explanation than this of the acknowledged difficulty, [36] have been emboldened to declare that Daniel's account of Belshazzar is a pure invention of his own, that it *contradicts* Berosus, and is an unmistakable indication of the unhistorical character which attaches to the entire narrative. [37] It was difficult to meet the arguments of these objectors in former times. Not only could they point to the want of confirmation by any profane writer of the name Belshazzar, but they could urge further "contradictions." Berosus, they could say, made the last Babylonian monarch absent from the city at the time of its capture by the Persians. He spoke of him as taken prisoner afterwards at Borsippa, and as then not slain, but treated with much kindness by Cyrus. Thus the two narratives of the fall of Babylon appeared to be wholly irreconcilable, and some were driven to suppose two falls of Babylon, to escape the seeming contrariety. [38] But out of all this confusion and uncertainty a very small and simple discovery, made a few years since, has educed order and harmony in a very remarkable way. It is found that Nabonadius, the last king of the Canon, associated with him on the throne during the later years of his reign his son, *Bil-shar-uzur*, and allowed him the royal title. [39] There can be little doubt that it was this prince who conducted the defence of Babylon, and was slain in the massacre which followed upon the capture; while his father, who was at the time in Borsippa, surrendered, and experienced the clemency which was generally shown to fallen kings by the Persians.

If it be still objected that Belshazzar is, in Scripture, not the son of Nabonadius, but of Nebuchadnezzar,[1] and of the Nebuchadnezzar who carried off the sacred vessels from Babylon,[2] it is enough to reply, first, that the word "son" is used in Scripture not only in its proper sense, but also as equivalent to "grandson," or indeed any descendant; (40) and secondly, that *Bil-shar-uzur* (or Belshazzar) may easily have been Nebuchadnezzar's grandson, since his father may upon his accession have married a daughter of Nebuchadnezzar, and Belshazzar may have been the issue of this marriage. (41) A usurper in those days commonly sought to strengthen himself in the government by an alliance with some princess of the house, or branch, which he dispossessed.

There still remains one historical difficulty in the book of Daniel, which modern research has not yet solved, but of which Time, the great discoverer, will perhaps one day bring the solution. We can only at present indulge in conjectures concerning "Darius the Mede," who "took the kingdom" after Belshazzar was slain.[3] He has been identified with Astyages, (42) with Cyaxares, a supposed son of Astyages, (43) with Neriglissar, (44) and with Nabonadius; (45) but each of these suppositions has its difficulties, and perhaps it is the most probable view that he was a viceroy set up by Cyrus, of whom there is at present no trace in profane history. (46)

The fact of the sudden and unexpected capture of Babylon by a Medo-Persic army during the celebration of a festival, and of the consequent absorption of the Babylo-

[1] Dan. v. 11, 18, &c. [2] Ibid. verse 2. [3] Ibid. v. 31.

nian into the Medo-Persic Empire, is one of those manifest points of agreement between Scripture and profane authors (47) which speak for themselves, and on which all comment would be superfluous. The administration of the realm after the conquest by "the law of the Medes and Persians which altereth not,"[1] is at once illustrative of that unity of the two great Arian races which all ancient history attests, (48) and in harmony with that superiority of law to the king's caprice, which seems to have distinguished the Persian from most Oriental despotisms. (49) With respect to the "satrapial organization of the Empire," which is again detected in Daniel's account of the reign of Darius the Mede, (50) and which is supposed to have been transferred to this time from the reign of Darius Hystaspis by an anachronism, it may be observed, that the "one hundred and twenty princes" which "it pleased Darius to set over the kingdom,"[2] are not the satraps, perhaps not even provincial governors at all, but rather a body of councillors resident in or near the capital, and accustomed to meet together,[3] to advise the monarch. It is a mistake to suppose that Darius the Mede, like the Ahasuerus of Esther, with whom he has been compared, (51) rules over the East generally. He "was made king *over the realm of the Chaldæans*"[4] — that is, he received from Cyrus, the true conqueror of Babylon, the kingdom of Babylonia Proper, which he held as a fief under the Medo-Persic Empire. The one hundred and twenty princes are either his council, or at the most provincial governors in the comparatively small kingdom of Babylon; and the coincidence (if such it is to be considered) between their number and that of the one hundred and twenty-seven provinces of Ahasuerus,

[1] Dan. vi. 8.
[2] Ibid. verse 1.
[3] Ibid. verses 4–6.
[4] Ibid. ix. 1.

extending from Ethiopia to India,[1] is purely accidental. There is no question here of the administration of an Empire, but only of the internal regulations of a single province.

We have now reached the time when the Captivity of Judah approached its close. "In the first year of Darius, the son of Ahasuerus, of the seed of the Medes,"[2] Daniel, who naturally counted the Captivity from the time when he was himself carried off from Jerusalem,[3] perceiving that the period fixed by Jeremiah for the restoration of the Jews to their own land approached, "set his face to seek by prayer and supplications, with fastings, and sackcloth, and ashes,"[4] that God would "turn away his fury and anger from Jerusalem,"[5] and "cause his face to shine upon his sanctuary,"[6] and "do, and defer not."[7] It is evident therefore that, according to the calculations of Daniel, a space little short of seventy years had elapsed from the capture of Jerusalem in the reign of Jehoiakim to the first year of Darius the Mede. The close agreement of this chronology with the Babylonian is very remarkable. It can be clearly shown from a comparison of Berosus with Ptolemy's Canon, that, according to the reckoning of the Babylonians, the time between Nebuchadnezzar's first conquest of Judæa in the reign of Jehoiakim, and the year following the fall of Babylon, when Daniel made his prayer, was sixty-eight years,(52) or two years only short of the seventy which had been fixed by Jeremiah as the duration of the Captivity.

Attempts have been made to prove a still more exact agreement;(53) but they are unnecessary. Approximate

[1] Esther i. 1.
[2] Dan. ix. 1.
[3] Ibid. i. 1.
[4] Ibid. ix. 3.
[5] Ibid. verse 16.
[6] Ibid. verse 17.
[7] Dan. ix. 19.

coincidence is the utmost that we have any right to expect between the early chronologies of different nations, whose methods of reckoning are in most cases somewhat different; and in the present instance the term of seventy years, being primarily a prophetic and not an historic number, is perhaps not intended to be exact and definite.(54)

The restoration of the Jews to their own land, and their fortunes till the reform of Nehemiah, are related to us in the three historical books of Ezra, Nehemiah, and Esther; and receive illustration from the prophecies of Zechariah, Haggai, and Malachi. The generally authentic character of the books of Ezra and Nehemiah has never been questioned. They disarm the Rationalist by the absence from them of any miraculous, or even any very marvellous features; and the humble and subdued tone in which they are written, the weakness and subjection which they confess, mark in the strongest possible way the honesty and good faith of their composers. Under these circumstances the question of their genuineness becomes one of minor importance. If the relations are allowed to be true, it is of little consequence who was their author. I see, however, no reason to doubt that *in the main* the two books are the works of the individuals whose names they bear in the Septuagint and in our own Version. That some portions of the book of Ezra were written by Ezra, and that Nehemiah wrote the greater part of the book of Nehemiah, is allowed even by De Wette; who has not (I think) shown sufficient ground for questioning the integrity of either composition,(55) unless in respect of a single passage. The genealogy of the high priests in the twelfth chapter of Nehemiah[1] is a later addition to the book, which cannot have been inserted into it before the time of Alexander.(56)

[1] Verses 10 to 22.

It stands to the rest of Nehemiah as the genealogy of the Dukes of Edom[1] stands to Genesis, or that of the descendants of Jechoniah[2] to the rest of Chronicles.(57) But apart from this passage there is nothing in Nehemiah which may not have been written by the cupbearer of Artaxerxes Longimanus; while in Ezra there is absolutely nothing at all which may not easily have proceeded from the pen of the "ready scribe" who was in favor with the same monarch. It is objected that the book sometimes speaks of Ezra in the third, sometimes in the first person; and concluded from this fact that he did not write the parts in which the third person is used.(58) But the examples of Daniel(59) and Thucydides(60) are sufficient to show that an author may change from the one person to the other even more than once in the course of a work; and the case of Daniel is especially in point, as indicating the practice of the period. The same irregularity (it may be remarked) occurs in the Persian inscriptions.(61) It belongs to the simplicity of rude times, and has its parallel in the similar practice found even now in the letters of uneducated persons.

If then the books of Ezra and Nehemiah are rightly regarded as the works of those personages, they will possess the same high degree of historical credibility as the later portions of the Pentateuch. Ezra and Nehemiah were chief men in their nation — the one being the ecclesiastical, the other the civil head; and they wrote the national history of their own time, for which they are the most competent witnesses that could possibly have come forward. Ezra, moreover, resembles Moses in another respect; he not only gives an account of his own dealings with the Jewish people, but prefaces that account by a sketch of

[1] Gen. xxxvi. 31–43. [2] 1 Chron. iii. 17–24.

their history during a period with which he was personally unacquainted. As this period does not extend farther back than about eighty years from the time when he took the direction of affairs at Jerusalem,(62) and as the facts recorded are of high national importance, they would deserve to be accepted on his testimony, even supposing that he obtained them from mere oral tradition, according to the Canons of historical credibility which have been laid down in the first Lecture.(63) Ezra's sketch, however, (as many commentators have seen,) bears traces of having been drawn up from contemporary documents;(64) and we may safely conclude, that the practice of "noting down public annals," which we have seen reason to regard as a part of the prophetic office under the Kings,(65) was revived on the return from the Captivity, when Haggai and Zechariah may probably have discharged the duty which at an earlier period had been undertaken by Jeremiah and Isaiah.

While the historical authority of the books of Ezra and Nehemiah is recognized almost universally, that of Esther is impugned by a great variety of writers. Niebuhr's rejection of this book has been already noticed.(66) De Wette regards it as "consisting of a string of historical difficulties and improbabilities, and as containing a number of errors in regard to Persian customs."(67) Œder, Michaelis, Corrodi, Bertholdt, and others, throw more or less doubt upon its authenticity.(68) The Jews, however, have always looked upon it, not only as a true and authentic history, but as a book deserving of special honor;(69) and it seems impossible to account for its introduction into their Canon on any other ground than that of its historic truth. The feast of Purim, which the Jews still celebrate, and at which the book of Esther is always read, must be regarded as sufficiently evidencing the truth of the main facts of the narrative; (70) and the Jews would certainly never have attached to the religious celebration of that festival the reading of a document from which the religious element is absent, or almost absent, (71) had they not believed it to contain a correct account of the details of the transaction. Their belief constitutes an argument of very great weight; to destroy its force there is needed something more than the exhibition of a certain number of "difficulties and improbabilities," such as continually present themselves to the historic student in connection even with his very best materials. (72)

The date and author of the book of Esther are points of very great uncertainty. The Jews in general ascribe it to Mordecai; but some say that it was written by the High Priest, Joiakim; while others assign the composition to the Great Synagogue. (73) It appears from an expression at the close of the ninth chapter—"And the decree of Esther confirmed these matters of Purim, and *it was written in the book*"[1]—that the whole affair was put on record at once; but "the book" here spoken of is probably that "book of the Chronicles of the kings of Media and Persia,"[2] which had been mentioned more than once in the earlier part of the narrative.[3] To this work the actual writer of our book of Esther—whoever he may have been—evidently had access; and it is a reasonable supposition that in the main he follows his Persian authority. Hence probably that omission of the name of God, and of the distinctive tenets of the Israelites, which has been made an objection by some to the canonicity of this book. (74)

We have now to examine the narrative contained in Ezra, Nehemiah, and Esther, by the light which profane

[1] Esther ix. 32. [2] Ibid. x. 2. [3] Ibid. ii. 23; and vi. 1.

history throws on it, more particularly in respect of those points which have been illustrated by recent discoveries.

There are probably few things more surprising to the intelligent student of Scripture than the religious tone of the proclamations which are assigned in Ezra to Cyrus, Darius, and Artaxerxes. "*The Lord God of heaven*," says Cyrus, "hath given me all the kingdoms of the earth, and he hath charged me to build him a house at Jerusalem, which is in Judah. Who is there among you of all his people? His God be with him, and let him go up to Jerusalem, which is in Judah, and build the house of the Lord God of Israel (*he is the God*) which is in Jerusalem."[1] "I make a decree," says Darius, "that these men be not hindered... that which they have need of... for the burnt-offerings of *the God of heaven*... let it be given them day by day without fail; that they may offer sacrifices of sweet savors unto the God of heaven, and *pray for the life of the king* and of his sons."[2] "Artaxerxes, king of kings," writes that monarch, "unto Ezra the priest, the scribe of the law of *the God of heaven*, perfect peace, and at such a time... Whatsoever is commanded by the God of heaven, let it be diligently done for the house of the God of heaven; for *why should there be wrath against the realm of the king* and his sons?"[3] Two things are especially remarkable in these passages — first, the strongly marked religious character, very unusual in heathen documents; and secondly, the distinctness with which they assert the unity of God, and thence identify the God of the Persians with the God of the Jews. Both these points receive abundant illustration from the Persian cuneiform inscriptions, in which the recognition of a single supreme God, Ormazd, and the

[1] Ezra i. 2, 3. Compare 2 Chron. xxxvi. 23.

[2] Ibid. vi. 8–10.

[3] Ibid. vii. 12, 23.

clear and constant ascription to him of the direction of all mundane affairs, are leading features. In all the Persian monuments of any length, the monarch makes the acknowledgment that "Ormazd has bestowed on him his empire."(75) Every success that is gained is "by the grace of Ormazd." The name of Ormazd occurs in almost every other paragraph of the Behistun inscription. No public monuments with such a pervading religious spirit have ever been discovered among the records of any heathen nation as those of the Persian kings; and through all of them, down to the time of Artaxerxes Ochus, the name of Ormazd stands alone and unapproachable, as that of the Supreme Lord of earth and heaven. The title "Lord of Heaven," which runs as a sort of catchword through these Chaldee translations of the Persian records, is not indeed in the cuneiform monuments distinctly attached to him as an epithet; but the common formula wherewith inscriptions open sets him forth as "the great God Ormazd, who gave both earth and heaven to mankind."(76)

It is generally admitted that the succession of the Persian kings from Cyrus to Darius Hystaspis is correctly given in Ezra.(77) The names of the two intermediate monarchs are indeed replaced by others — and it is difficult to explain how these kings came to be known to the Jews as Ahasuerus and Artaxerxes, instead of Cambyses and Smerdis(78) — but the exact agreement in the number of the reigns, and the harmony in the chronology(79) have caused it to be almost universally allowed that Cambyses and Smerdis are intended. Assuming this, we may note that the only Persian king who is said to have interrupted the building of the temple is that Magian monarch, the Pseudo-Smerdis, who was opposed to the pure Persian religion, and who would therefore have been likely to reverse the religious policy of his predecessors. The Samaritans "weakened the hands of the people of Judah and troubled them in building"[1] during the reigns of Cyrus and Cambyses; but it was not till the letter of the Pseudo-Smerdis was received, that "the work of the house of God ceased."[2] The same prince, that is, who is stated in the inscriptions to have changed the religion of Persia,(80) appears in Ezra as the opponent of a religious work, which Cyrus had encouraged, and Cambyses had allowed to be carried on.

The reversal by Darius of the religious policy of the Magian monarch, and his recurrence to the line of conduct which had been pursued by Cyrus, as related in Ezra, harmonize completely with the account which Darius himself gives of his proceedings soon after his accession. "I restored to the people," he says, "the religious worship, of which the Magian had deprived them. As it was before, so I arranged it."(81) Of course, this passage refers primarily to the Persian Court religion, and its reëstablishment in the place of Magism as the religion of the state; but such a return to comparatively pure principles would involve a renewal of the old sympathy with the Jews and with the worship of Jehovah. Accordingly, while the letter of the Magus[3] is devoid of the slightest reference to religion, that of Darius exhibits — as has been already shown — the same pious and reverential spirit, the same respect for the God of the Jews, and the same identification of Him with the Supreme Being recognized by the Persians, which are so prominent in the decree of Cyrus. Darius is careful to follow in the footsteps of the great founder of the monarchy, and under him "the house of

[1] 1 Ezra iv. 4. [2] Ibid. verse 24. [3] Ibid. iv. 17 to 22.

God at Jerusalem," which Cyrus was "charged" to build,[1] is finally "builded and finished."[2]

A break occurs in the Biblical narrative between the sixth and seventh chapters of Ezra, the length of which is not estimated by the sacred historian, but which we know from profane sources to have extended to above half a century.(82) Into this interval falls the whole of the reign of Xerxes. The Jews in Palestine appear to have led during this time a quiet and peaceable life under Persian governors, and to have disarmed the hostility of their neighbors by unworthy compliances, such as intermarriages;[3] which would have tended, if unchecked, to destroy their distinct nationality. No history of the time is given, because no event occurred during it of any importance to the Jewish community in Palestine. It is thought, however, by many — and on the whole it is not improbable — that the history related in the Book of Esther belongs to the interval in question, and thus fills up the gap in the narrative of Ezra. The name Ahasuerus is undoubtedly the proper Hebrew equivalent for the Persian word which the Greeks represented by Xerxes.(83) And if it was Kish, the ancestor of Mordecai in the fourth degree, who was carried away from Jerusalem by Nebuchadnezzar, together with Jeconiah,[4] the time of Xerxes would be exactly that in which Mordecai ought to have flourished.(84) Assuming on these grounds the king intended by Ahasuerus to be the Xerxes of Greek history, we are at once struck with the strong resemblance which his character bears to that assigned by the classical writers to the celebrated son of Darius. Proud, self-willed, amorous, careless of contravening Persian customs; reckless of human life, yet not actually bloodthirsty; impetu-

[1] Ezra i. 2.
[2] Ibid. vi. 14.
[3] Ibid. ix. 2, &c.
[4] Esther ii. 5, 6.

ous, facile, changeable — the Ahasuerus of Esther corresponds in all respects to the Greek portraiture of Xerxes, which is not (be it observed) the mere picture of an Oriental despot, but has various peculiarities which distinguish it even from the other Persian kings, and which — I think it may be said — individualize it. Nor is there — as might so easily have been the case, were the book of Esther a romance — any contradiction between its facts and those which the Greeks have recorded of Xerxes. The third year of his reign, when Ahasuerus makes his great feast at Shushan (or Susa) to his nobles,[1] was a year which Xerxes certainly passed at Susa, (85) and one wherein it is likely that he kept open house for "the princes of the provinces," who would from time to time visit the court, in order to report on the state of their preparations for the Greek war. The seventh year, wherein Esther is made queen,[2] is that which follows the return of Xerxes from Greece, where again we know from the best Greek authority (86) that he resumed his residence at Susa. It is true that "after this time history speaks of other favorites and another wife of Xerxes, namely Amestris," (87) who can scarcely have been Esther, (88) since the Greeks declare that she was the daughter of a Persian noble; — but it is quite possible that Amestris may have been in disgrace for a time, and that Esther may have been temporarily advanced to the dignity of Sultana. We know far too little of the domestic history of Xerxes from profane sources to pronounce the position which Esther occupies in his harem impossible or improbable. True again that profane history tells us nothing of Haman or Mordecai — but we have absolutely no profane information on the subject of who were the great officers of the Persian court, or who had influence with Xerxes after the death of Mardonius.

[1] Esther i. 2, 3. [2] Ibid. ii. 16.

The intimate acquaintance which the Book of Esther shows in many passages with Persian manners and customs, has been acknowledged even by De Wette,(89) who regards it as composed in Persia on that account. I think it may be said that we have nowhere else so graphic or so just a portraiture of the Persian court, such as it was in the earlier part of the period of decline, which followed upon the death of Darius. The story of the Book is no doubt in its leading features — the contemplated massacre of the Jews, and the actual slaughter of their adversaries — wonderful and antecedently improbable; but these are exactly the points of which the commemorative festival of Purim is the strongest possible corroboration. And it may lessen the seeming improbability to bear in mind that open massacres of obnoxious persons were not unknown to the Persians of Xerxes' time. There had once been a general massacre of all the Magi who could be found; (90) and the annual observance of this day, which was known as "the Magophonia," would serve to keep up the recollection of the circumstance.

Of Artaxerxes Longimanus, the son and successor of Xerxes, who appears both from his name and from his time to be the monarch under whom Ezra and Nehemiah flourished, (91) we have little information from profane sources. His character, as drawn by Ctesias, is mild but weak, (92) and sufficiently harmonizes with the portrait in the first chapter of Nehemiah. He reigned forty years — a longer time than any Persian king but one; and it is perhaps worthy of remark that Nehemiah mentions his thirty-second year;[1] for this, which is allowable in his case, would have involved a contradiction of profane history, had it occurred in connection with any other Persian king mentioned in Scripture, excepting only Darius Hystaspis.

[1] Nehem. v. 14; xiii. 6.

The Old Testament history here terminates. For the space of nearly five hundred years — from the time of Nehemiah and Malachi to that of St. Paul — the Jews possessed no inspired writer; and their history, when recorded at all, was related in works which were not regarded by themselves as authoritative or canonical. I am not concerned to defend the historical accuracy of the Books of Maccabees; much less that of Judith and the second Esdras, which seem to be mere romances.(93) My task, so far as the Old Testament is concerned, is accomplished. It has, I believe, been shown, in the first place, that the sacred narrative itself is the production of eye-witnesses, or of those who followed the accounts of eye-witnesses, and therefore that it is entitled to the acceptance of all those who regard contemporary testimony as the main ground of all authentic history. And it has, secondly, been made apparent, that all the evidence which we possess from profane sources of a really important and trustworthy character tends to confirm the truth of the history delivered to us in the sacred volume. The monumental records of past ages — Assyrian, Babylonian, Egyptian, Persian, Phœnician — the writings of historians who have based their histories on contemporary annals, as Manetho, Berosus, Dius, Menander, Nicolas of Damascus — the descriptions given by eye-witnesses of the Oriental manners and customs — the proofs obtained by modern research of the condition of art in the time and country — all combine to confirm, illustrate, and establish the veracity of the writers, who have delivered to us, in the Pentateuch, in Joshua, Judges, Samuel, Kings and Chronicles, Ezra, Esther, and Nehemiah, the history of the chosen people. That history stands firm against all the assaults made upon it; and the more light that is thrown by research and discovery upon the times and countries with which it deals, the more apparent becomes its authentic and matter-of-fact character. Instead of ranging parallel with the mythical traditions of Greece and Rome, (with which some delight to compare it,) it stands, *at the least*, on a par with the ancient histories of Egypt, Babylon, Phœnicia, and Assyria; which, like it, were recorded from a remote antiquity by national historiographers. Sound criticism finds in the sacred writings of the Jews documents belonging to the times of which they profess to treat, and on a calm investigation classes them, not with romantic poems or mythological fables, but with the sober narratives of those other ancient writers, who have sought to hand down to posterity a true account of the facts which their eyes have witnessed. As in the New Testament, so in the Old, that which the writers "declare" to the world is in the main "that which they have heard, which they have seen with their eyes, which they have looked upon, and which their hands have handled."[1] It is not their object to amuse men, much less to impose on them by any "cunningly devised fables;"[2] but simply to record facts and "bear their witness to the truth."[3]

[1] 1 John i. 1. [2] 2 Pet. i. 16. [3] John xviii. 37.

LECTURE VI.

THAT WHICH WAS FROM THE BEGINNING, WHICH WE HAVE HEARD, WHICH WE HAVE SEEN WITH OUR EYES, WHICH WE HAVE LOOKED UPON, AND OUR HANDS HAVE HANDLED, OF THE WORD OF LIFE; (FOR THE LIFE WAS MANIFESTED, AND WE HAVE SEEN IT, AND BEAR WITNESS, AND SHOW UNTO YOU THAT ETERNAL LIFE, WHICH WAS WITH THE FATHER, AND WAS MANIFESTED UNTO US;) THAT WHICH WE HAVE SEEN AND HEARD DECLARE WE UNTO YOU.—1 JOHN I. 1–3.

The period of time embraced by the events of which we have any mention in the New Testament but little exceeds the lifetime of a man, falling short of a full century. The regular and continuous history is comprised within a yet narrower space, since it commences in the year of Rome 748 or 749, and terminates about sixty-three years later, in the fifth of Nero, Anno Domini 58.(1) If uniformity of plan were a thing of paramount importance, it would be my duty to subdivide this space of time into three portions, which might be treated separately in the three remaining Lectures of the present Course. Such a subdivision could be made without any great difficulty. The century naturally breaks into three periods—the time of our Lord's life, or that treated of in the Gospels; the time of the rapid and triumphant spread of Christianity, or that of which we have the history in the Acts; and the time of oppression and persecution without, of defection and heresy within, or that to which we have incidental allusions in the later Epistles and the Apocalypse. Or, if we confined our view to the space of time which is covered by the historical Books, and omitted the last of these three periods from our consideration, we might obtain a convenient division of the second period from the actual arrangement of the Acts, where the author, after occupying himself during twelve chapters with the general condition of the Christian community, becomes from the thirteenth the biographer of a single Apostle, whose career he thenceforth follows without interruption. But on the whole I think it will be more convenient, at some sacrifice of uniformity, to regard the entire space occupied by the New Testament narrative as a single period, and to substitute, at the present point, for the arrangement of time hitherto followed, an arrangement based upon a division of the *evidence*, which here naturally separates into three heads or branches. The first of these is the internal evidence, or that of the documents themselves, which I propose to make the subject of the present Lecture; the second is the testimony of adversaries, or that borne by Heathen and Jewish writers to the veracity of the narrative; the third is the testimony of believers, or that producible from the uninspired Christian remains of the times contemporary with or immediately following the age of the Apostles. The two last named branches will be treated respectively in the seventh and eighth Lectures.

The New Testament is commonly regarded too much as a single book, and its testimony is scarcely viewed as more than that of a single writer. No doubt, contemplated on its divine side, the work has a real unity, He who is with His church "always"[1] having designed the whole in His Eternal Counsels, and having caused it to take the shape that it bears; but regarded as the work of man, which it also is, the New Testament (it should be remembered) is a

[1] Matt. xxviii. 20.

collection of twenty-seven separate and independent documents, composed by eight or nine different persons, at separate times, and under varied circumstances. Of these twenty-seven documents, twenty-one consist of letters written by those who were engaged in the propagation of the new Religion to their converts, four are biographies of Christ, one is a short Church History, containing a general account of the Christian community for twelve or thirteen years after our Lord's ascension, together with a particular account of St. Paul's doings for about fourteen years afterwards; and one is prophetical, containing (as is generally supposed) a sketch of the future state and condition of the Christian Church from the close of the first century, when it was written, to the end of the world. It is with the historical Books that we are in the present review primarily concerned. I wish to show that for the Scriptural narrative of the birth, life, death, resurrection, and ascension of Christ, as well as for the circumstances of the first preaching of the Gospel, the historical evidence that we possess is of an authentic and satisfactory character.

As with that document which is the basis of Judaism,(2) so with those which are the basis of Christianity, it is of very great interest and importance to know by whom they were written. If the history was recorded by eye-witnesses, or even by persons contemporaneous with the events narrated, then it is allowed on all hands that the record containing it must have a very strong claim indeed to our acceptance. "But the alleged ocular testimony," we are told, "or proximity in point of time to the events recorded, is mere assumption — an assumption originating from the titles which the Biblical books bear in our Canon."(3) "Little reliance, however, can be placed on these titles, or on the headings of ancient manuscripts generally."(4) "The early Jewish and Christian writers—even the most reputable—published their works with the substitution of venerated names, without an idea that they were guilty of falsehood or deception by so doing."(5) In "sacred records" and "biblical books" this species of forgery obtained "more especially;"(6) and the title of works of this kind is scarcely any evidence at all of the real authorship. Further, the actual titles of our Gospels are not to be regarded as intended to assert the composition of the Gospel by the person named; all that they mean to assert is, the composition of the connected history "after the oral discourses, or notes," of the person named in the title. This is the true original meaning of the word translated by "according to;" which is improperly understood as implying actual authorship.(7)

Such are the assertions with which we are met, when we urge that for the events of our Lord's life we have the testimony of eye-witnesses, whose means of knowing the truth were of the highest order, and whose honesty is unimpeachable. These assertions (which I have given as nearly as possible in the words of Strauss) consist of a series of positions either plainly false, or at best without either proof or likelihood; yet upon these the modern Rationalism is content to base its claim to supersede Christianity. This end it openly avows, and it admits that, to make its claim good, the positions above given should be established. Let us then consider briefly the several assertions upon which we are invited to exchange the Religion of Christ for that of Strauss and Schleiermacher.

It is said, that "the alleged ocular testimony is an assumption originating from the titles which the Biblical books bear in our Canon." I do not know if any stress is intended to be laid on the last clause of this objection; but as it might mislead the unlearned, I may observe in passing, that the titles which the Books bear in the modern authorized versions of the Scriptures are literal translations from some of the most ancient Greek manuscripts, and descend to us at least from the times of the first Councils; while titles still more emphatic and explicit are found in several of the versions which were made at an early period.(8) Our belief in the authorship of the writings, no doubt, rests partly on the titles, as does our belief in the authorship of every ancient treatise; but it is untrue to say that these headings first originated the belief; for before the titles were attached, the belief must have existed. In truth, there is not the slightest pretence for insinuating that there was ever any doubt as to the authorship of any one of the historical books of the New Testament; which are as uniformly ascribed to the writers whose names they bear as the Return of the Ten Thousand to Xenophon, or the Lives of the Cæsars to Suetonius. There is indeed *far better* evidence of authorship in the case of the four Gospels and of the Acts of the Apostles, than exists with respect to the works of almost any classical writer. It is a very rare occurrence for classical works to be distinctly quoted, or for their authors to be mentioned by name, within a century of the time of their publication.(9) The Gospels, as we shall find in the sequel, are frequently quoted within this period, and the writers of three at least out of the four are mentioned within the time as authors of works corresponding perfectly to those which have come down to us as their compositions. Our conviction then of the genuineness of the Gospels does not rest exclusively, or even mainly, on the titles, but on the unanimous consent of ancient writers and of the whole Christian church in the first ages.

In the next place we are told that "little reliance can be placed on the headings of ancient manuscripts generally." Undoubtedly, such headings, when unconfirmed by further testimony, are devoid of any great weight, and may be set aside, if the internal evidence of the writings themselves disproves the superscription. Still they constitute important *primâ facie* evidence of authorship; and it is to be presumed that they are correct, until solid reasons be shown to the contrary. The headings of ancient manuscripts are, in point of fact, generally accepted as correct by critics; and the proportion, among the works of antiquity, of those reckoned spurious to those regarded as genuine, is small indeed.

But it is said that in the case of "sacred records" and "biblical books" the headings are "especially" untrustworthy. This, we are told, "is evident, and has long since been proved."(10) Where the proof is to be found, we are not informed, nor whence the peculiar untrustworthiness of what is "sacred" and "biblical" proceeds. We are referred, however, to the cases of the Pentateuch, the book of Daniel, and a certain number of the Psalms, as well known instances; and we shall probably not be wrong in assuming that these are selected as the most palpable cases of incorrect ascription of books which the Sacred Volume furnishes. We have already found reason to believe that in regard to the Pentateuch and the book of Daniel no mistake has been committed;(11) they are the works of the authors whose names they bear. But in the case of the Psalms, it must be allowed that the headings seem frequently to be incorrect. Headings, it must be remembered, are in no case any part of the inspired Word; they indicate merely the opinion of those who had the custody of the Word at the time when they were prefixed. Now in most cases the headings would be attached soon after the composition of the work, when its authorship was certainly known; but the Psalms do not appear to have been collected into a book until the time of Ezra,(12) and the headings of many may have been then first affixed, those who attached them following a vague tradition or venturing upon conjecture. Thus error has here crept in; but on this ground to assume that "sacred records" have a peculiar untrustworthiness in this respect, is to betray an irreligious spirit, and to generalize upon very insufficient data.

But, it is said, "the *most reputable* authors amongst the Jews *and early Christians* published their works with the substitution of venerated names, without an idea that they were guilty of falsehood or deception by so doing." What is the proof of this astounding assertion? What *early* Christian authors, reputable or no, can be shown to have thus acted? If the allusion is to the epistles of Hermas and Barnabas, it must be observed that the genuineness of these is still matter of dispute among the learned; if to such works as the Clementines, the interpolated Ignatius, and the like, that they are not "early" in the sense implied, for they belong probably to the third century.(13) The practice noted was common among heretical sects from the first, but it was made a reproach to them by the orthodox;(14) who did not themselves adopt it till the teaching of the Alexandrian School had confused the boundaries of right and wrong, and made "pious frauds" appear defensible. There is no reason to suppose that any orthodox Christian of the first century — when it is granted that our Gospels were written — would have considered himself entitled to bring out under a "venerated name" a work of his own composition.

Lastly, it is urged, "the titles of our Gospels are not intended to assert the composition of the works by the persons named, but only their being based upon a groundwork furnished by such persons, either orally, or in the shape of written notes."(15) "This seems to be the original meaning attached to the word κατά," we are told. No example, however, is adduced of this use, which is certainly not that of the Septuagint, where the book of Nehemiah is referred to under the name of "The Commentaries according to Nehemiah;"[1] and it cannot be shown to have obtained at any period of the Greek language.

It cannot therefore be asserted with any truth that the titles of the Gospels do not represent them as the compositions of the persons named therein. Nothing is more certain than that the object of affixing titles to the Gospels at all was to mark the opinion entertained of their authorship. This opinion appears to have been universal. We find no evidence of any doubt having ever existed on the subject in the early ages.(16) Irenæus, Tertullian, Clement of Alexandria, and Origen, writers in the latter half of the second or the beginning of the third century, not only declare the authorship unreservedly, but indicate or express the universal agreement of the Church from the first upon the subject.(17) Justin, in the middle of the second century, speaks of the "Gospels" which the Christians read in their Churches, as having been composed "by the Apostles of Christ and their companions;" and he further shows by his quotations, which are abundant, that he means the Gospels now in our possession.(18) Papias, a quarter of a century earlier, mentions the Gospels of St. Matthew and St. Mark as authoritative, and declares the latter writer to have derived his materials from St. Peter. Thus we are brought

[1] 2 Mac. ii. 13.

to the very age of the Apostles themselves; for Papias was a disciple of St. John the Evangelist.(19)

Further, in the case of three out of the five Historical Books of the New Testament, there is an internal testimony to their composition by contemporaries, which is of the last importance. "And *he that saw it*," says St. John, "bare record, and his record is true, and he knoweth that he saith true, that ye may believe."[1] And again, still more explicitly, after speaking of himself and of the circumstances which caused it to be thought that he would not die—"*This* is the disciple which testifieth of these things *and wrote these things:* and we know that his testimony is true."[2] Either therefore St. John must be allowed to have been the writer of the fourth Gospel, or the writer must be taxed with that "conscious intention of fiction," which Strauss with impious boldness has ventured to allege against him.(20)

That the Acts of the Apostles and the third Gospel have "a testimony of a particular kind," which seems to give them a special claim to be accepted as the works of a contemporary, is admitted even by this Prince of Sceptics. The writer of the Acts, he allows, "by the use of the first person identifies himself with the companion of St. Paul," and the prefaces of the two books make it plain that they "proceeded from the same author."(21) This evidence is felt to be so strong, that even Strauss does not venture to deny that a companion of St. Paul *may have* written the two works. He finds it "difficult" to believe that this was actually the case, and "suspects" that the passages of the Acts where the first person is used "belong to a distinct memorial by another hand, which the author of the Acts has incorporated into his history." But still he allows the

[1] John xix. 35. [2] Ibid. xxi. 24.

alternative — that "it is possible the companion of Paul may have composed the two works" — only it must have been "at a time when he was no longer protected by apostolic influence from the tide of tradition," and so was induced to receive into his narrative, and join with what he had heard from the apostle, certain marvellous (and therefore incredible) stories which had no solid or substantial basis.(22) To the objection that the Acts appear, from the fact of their terminating where they do, to have been composed at the close of St. Paul's first imprisonment at Rome, A. D. 58, (or A. D. 63, according to some(23) writers,) and that the Gospel, as being "the former treatise,"[1] was written earlier, Strauss replies, "that the breaking off of the Acts at that particular point might have been the result of many other causes; and that, at all events, such testimony *standing alone* is wholly insufficient to decide the historical worth of the Gospel."(24) He thus assumes that the testimony "stands alone," forgetting or ignoring the general voice of antiquity on the subject of the date and value of the Gospel,(25) while he also omits to notice the other important evidence of an early date which the Gospel itself furnishes — the declaration, namely, in the preface that what St. Luke wrote was delivered to him by those "which from the beginning were eye-witnesses and ministers of the Word."[2]

If the third Gospel be allowed to have been composed by one who lived in the apostolic age and companied with the apostles, then an argument for the early date of the first and second will arise from their accordance with the third — their resemblance to it in style and general character, and their diversity from the productions of any other period. The first three Gospels belong so entirely to the

[1] Acts i. 1. [2] Luke i. 2.

same school of thought, and the same type and stage of language, that on critical grounds they must be regarded as the works of contemporaries; while in their contents they are at once so closely accordant with one another, and so full of little differences, that the most reasonable view to take of their composition is that it was almost simultaneous.[(26)] Thus the determination of any one out of the three to the apostolic age involves a similar conclusion with respect to the other two; and if the Gospel ascribed to St. Luke be allowed to be probably his, there can be no reason to question the tradition which assigns the others to St. Matthew and St. Mark.

On the whole, therefore, we have abundant reason to believe that the four Gospels are the works of persons who lived at the time when Christianity was first preached and established. Two of the writers — St. Luke and St. John — fix their own date, which must be accepted on their authority, unless we will pronounce them impostors. The two others appear alike by their matter and their manner to be as early as St. Luke, and are certainly earlier than St. John, whose Gospel is supplemental to the other three, and implies their preëxistence. Nor is there any reasonable ground for doubting the authorship which Christian antiquity with one voice declares to us, and in which the titles of the earliest manuscripts and of the most ancient versions agree. The four Gospels are assigned to those four persons, whom the Church has always honored as Evangelists, on grounds very much superior to those on which the bulk of classical works are ascribed to particular authors. The single testimony of Irenæus is really of more weight than the whole array of witnesses commonly marshalled in proof of the genuineness of an ancient classic; and, even if it stood alone, might fairly be regarded as placing the question of the authorship beyond all reasonable doubt or suspicion.

If then the Gospels are genuine, what a wonderful historical treasure do we possess in them! Four biographies of the great Founder of our religion by contemporary pens, two of them the productions of close friends — the other two written by those who, if they had no personal acquaintance with the Saviour, at least were the constant companions of such as had had intimate knowledge of Him. How rarely do we obtain even two distinct original biographies of a distinguished person! In the peculiar and unexampled circumstances of the time it is not surprising that many undertook to "set forth in order a declaration of the things"[1] which constituted the essence of the new religion, namely, the life and teaching of Christ; but it is remarkable, and I think it may fairly be said to be providential, that four accounts should have been written possessing claims to attention so nearly equal, that the Church felt bound to adopt all into her Canon, whence it has happened that they have all come down to us. We should have expected, alike on the analogy of the Old Testament,[(27)] and on grounds of *a priori* probability, a single record. If an authentic account had been published early — that is, before the separation of the Apostles, and the formation of distinct Christian communities — it is probable that no second account would have been written, or at any rate no second account confirmatory to any great extent of the preceding one. A supplementary Gospel, like that of St. John, might of course have been added in any case; but had the Gospel of St. Matthew, for instance, been really composed, as some have imagined,[(28)] within a few years of our Lord's ascension, it would have been carried

[1] Luke i. 1.

together with Christianity into all parts of the world; and it is very unlikely that in that case the Gospels of St. Mark and St. Luke, which cover chiefly the same ground, would have been written. The need of written Gospels was not felt at first, while the Apostles and companions of Christ were in full vigor, and were continually moving from place to place, relating with all the fulness and variety of oral discourse the marvels which they had seen wrought, and the gracious words which they had heard uttered by their Master. But as they grew old, and as the sphere of their labors enlarged, and personal superintendence of the whole Church by the Apostolic body became difficult, the desire to possess a written Gospel arose; and simultaneously, in different parts of the Church, for different portions of the Christian body, the three Gospels of St. Matthew, St. Mark, and St. Luke, were published. This at least seems to be the theory which alone suits the phenomena of the case;[(29)] and as it agrees nearly with the testimony of Irenæus,[(30)] who is the earliest authority with regard to the time at which the Gospels were composed, it is well deserving of acceptance.

If this view of the independent and nearly simultaneous composition of the first three Gospels be admitted, then we must be allowed to possess in their substantial agreement respecting the life, character, teaching, miracles, prophetic announcements, sufferings, death, resurrection, and ascension of our Lord,[(31)] evidence of the most important kind, and such as is scarcely ever attainable with respect to the actions of an individual. Attempts have been made from time to time, and recently on a large scale, to invalidate this testimony by establishing the existence of minute points of disagreement between the accounts of the three Evangelists.[(32)] But the differences adduced consist almost entirely of omissions by one Evangelist of what is mentioned by another, such omissions being regarded by Strauss as equivalent to direct negatives.(33) The weak character of the argument *a silentio* is now admitted by all tolerable critics, who have ceased to lean upon it with any feeling of security except under very peculiar circumstances. In ordinary cases, and more particularly in cases where brevity has been studied, mere silence proves absolutely nothing; and to make it equivalent to counter-assertion is to confuse two things wholly different, and to exhibit a want of critical discernment, such as must in the eyes of all reasonable persons completely discredit the writer who is so unfair or so ill-judging. Yet this, I confidently affirm, is the ordinary manner of Strauss, who throughout his volumes conceives himself at liberty to discard facts recorded by one Evangelist only on the mere ground of silence on the part of the others. Whatever an Evangelist does not record, he is argued not to have known; and his want of knowledge is taken as a proof that the event could not have happened. It seems to be forgotten, that, in the first place, eye-witnesses of one and the same event notice a different portion of the attendant circumstances; and that, secondly, those who record an event which they have witnessed omit ordinarily, for brevity's sake, by far the greater portion of the attendant circumstances which they noticed at the time and still remember. Strauss's cavils could only have been precluded by the mere repetition on the part of each Evangelist of the exact circumstances mentioned by every other — a repetition which would have been considered to mark collusion or or unacknowledged borrowing, and which would have thus destroyed their value as distinct and independent witnesses.

It has been well observed,[34] that, even if all the difficulties and discrepancies, which this writer has thought to discover in the Gospels, were real and not merely apparent — if we were obliged to leave them as difficulties, and could offer no explanation of them[35] — still the general credibility of the Gospel History would remain untouched, and no more would be proved than the absence of that complete inspiration which the Church has always believed to attach to the Evangelical writings. The writers would be lowered from their preëminent rank as perfect and infallible historians, whose every word may be depended on; but they would remain historical authorities of the first order — witnesses as fully to be trusted for the circumstances of our Lord's life, as Xenophon for the sayings and doings of Socrates, or Cavendish for those of Cardinal Wolsey. The facts of the miracles, preaching, sufferings, death, resurrection, and ascension, would therefore stand firm, together with those of the choice of the Apostles, the commission given them, and the communication to them of miraculous powers; and these are the facts which establish Christianity, and form its historical basis — a basis which can be overthrown by nothing short of a proof that the New Testament is a forgery from beginning to end, or that the first preachers of Christianity were a set of impostors.

For the truth of the Gospel facts does not rest solely upon the Gospels — they are stated with almost equal distinctness in the Acts, and are implied in the Epistles. It is not denied that a companion of St. Paul may have written the account of the early spread of the Gospel which is contained in the Acts of the Apostles. But the Acts assume as indisputable the whole series of facts which form the basis on which Christianity sustains itself. They set forth "Jesus of Nazareth, a man approved of God by miracles and wonders and signs, which God did by Him in the midst of you, *as you yourselves also know*"[1]—a man "who went about doing good, and healing all that were oppressed of the devil"[2]—who "beginning from Galilee, after the baptism which John preached, published the word throughout all Judæa;[3] whom yet "they that dwelt at Jerusalem, and their rulers, because they knew him not, nor yet the voices of the Prophets which are read every Sabbath day, condemned, finding no cause of death in him, yet desiring of Pilate that he should be slain"[4]—who was "taken and crucified by wicked hands"[5]—"hanged upon a tree and slain"[6]—then "taken down from the tree and laid in a sepulchre,"[7] but "raised up the third day, and showed openly,"[8] "by many infallible proofs during the space of forty days,"[9] "not to all the people, but unto witnesses chosen before of God, who did eat and drink with him after he rose from the dead"[10]—and who, finally, "while his disciples beheld, was taken up into heaven, a cloud receiving him out of their sight."[11] The Acts further show that to the chosen "witnesses"—the Apostles to whom "the promise of the Father"[12] had been given, and to those whom they associated with them in the direction of the infant Church miraculous gifts were communicated, so that they prophesied,[13] cured lameness by a word or a touch,[14] spake languages of which they had no natural knowledge,[15] restored the bedridden to health,[16] handled serpents,[17] cast out devils,[18] inflicted blindness,[19] raised the

[1] Acts ii. 22.
[2] Ibid. x. 38.
[3] Ibid. verse 37.
[4] Ibid. xiii. 27–8.
[5] Ibid. ii. 23.
[6] Ibid. x. 39.
[7] Ibid. xiii. 29.
[8] Ibid. x. 40.
[9] Ibid. i. 3.
[10] Ibid. x. 41.
[11] Ibid. i. 9, 10.
[12] Ibid. verse 4.
[13] Ibid. v. 9; vi. 27, &c.
[14] Ibid. xiv. 10, and iii. 7.
[15] Ibid. ii. 4–13.
[16] Ibid. ix. 34.
[17] Ibid. xxviii. 5.
[18] Ibid. xvi. 18, &c.
[19] Ibid. xiii. 11.

dead to life,[1] and finally even in some cases cured men by the touch of their shadows[2] or by handkerchiefs and aprons from their persons.[3]

The substantial truth of the history contained in the Acts — so far at least as it concerns St. Paul — has been excellently vindicated, by a writer of our own nation and communion, from the undesigned conformity between the narrative and the Epistles ascribed to the great Apostle. Without assuming the genuineness of those Epistles, Paley has most unanswerably shown, that the peculiar nature of the agreement between them and the history of the Acts affords good reason to believe that "the persons and transactions described are real, the letters authentic, and the narration in the main true."(36) The *Horæ Paulinæ* establish these positions in the most satisfactory manner. I do not think that it is possible for any one to read them attentively without coming to the conclusion that the Epistles of St. Paul and the Acts of the Apostles bring us into contact with real persons, real scenes, real transactions — that the letters were actually written by St. Paul himself at the time and under the circumstances related in the history — and that the history was composed by one who had that complete knowledge of the circumstances which could only be gained by personal observation, or by intimate acquaintance with the Apostle who is the chief subject of the narrative. The effect of a perusal of this masterly work will scarcely be neutralized by the bare and unsupported assertion of Strauss, that "the details concerning Paul in the Book of the Acts are so completely at variance with Paul's genuine epistles, that it is extremely difficult to reconcile them with the notion that they were written by a compan-

[1] Acts ix. 37–41; xx. 9–12.

[2] Ibid. v. 15.

[3] Ibid xix. 12.

ion of the Apostle."(37) The *Horæ Paulinæ* should have been answered in detail, before such an assertion was adventured on. Boldly and barely made, without a tittle of proof, it can only be regarded as an indication of the utter recklessness of the new School, and of its striking deficiency in the qualities which are requisite for a sound and healthy criticism.

It is further to be remarked, that Paley's work, excellent and conclusive as it must be allowed to be, is far from being exhaustive. He has noticed, and illustrated in a very admirable way, the most remarkable of the undesigned coincidences between the Acts and the Pauline Epistles; but it would not be difficult to increase his list by the addition of an equal number of similar points of agreement, which he has omitted.(38)

Again, it is to be remarked, that the argument of Paley is applicable also to other parts of the New Testament. Undesigned coincidences of the class which Paley notes are frequent in the Gospels, and have often been pointed out in passing by commentators, though I am not aware that they have ever been collected or made the subject of a separate volume. When St. Matthew,[1] however, and St. Luke,[2] in giving the list of the Apostles, place them in pairs without assigning a reason, while St. Mark, whose list is not in pairs,[3] happens to mention that they were sent out "two and two;"[4] we have the same sort of recondite and (humanly speaking) accidental harmony on which Paley has insisted with such force as an evidence of authenticity and truth in connection with the history of the Acts. It would be easy to multiply instances; but my limits will not allow me to do more than briefly to allude to this head of evi-

[1] Matt. x. 2–4.
[2] Luke vi. 14–16.
[3] Mark iii. 16–19.
[4] Ibid. vi. 7.

dence, to which full justice could not be done unless by an elaborate work on the subject.[(39)]

Finally, let it be considered whether the Epistles alone, apart from the Gospels and the Acts, do not sufficiently establish the historic truth of that narrative of the life of Christ and foundation of the Christian Church, which it has been recently attempted to resolve into mere myth and fable. The genuineness of St. Paul's Epistles, with one or two exceptions, is admitted even by Strauss;[(40)] and there are no valid reasons for entertaining any doubt concerning the authorship of the other Epistles, except perhaps in the case of that to the Hebrews, and of the two shorter Epistles commonly assigned to St. John.[(41)] Excluding these, we have eighteen letters written by five of the principal Apostles of Christ, one by St. John, two by St. Peter, thirteen by St. Paul, one by St. James, and one by St. Jude, his brother—partly consisting of public addresses to bodies of Christians, partly of instructions to individuals—all composed for practical purposes with special reference to the peculiar exigencies of the time, but all exhibiting casually and incidentally the state of opinion and belief among Christians during the half century immediately following our Lord's ascension. It is indisputable that the writers, and those to whom they wrote, believed in the recent occurrence of a set of facts similar to, or identical with, those recorded in the Gospels and the Acts—more particularly those which are most controverted, such as the transfiguration, the resurrection, and the ascension. "Great is the mystery of godliness," says St. Paul. "God was manifest in the flesh, justified in the Spirit, seen of angels, preached unto the Gentiles, believed on in the world, received up into glory."[1] "Christ," says St. Peter, "suf-

[1] 1 Tim. iii. 16.

fered once for sins, the just for the unjust, that he might bring us to God, being put to death in the flesh, but quickened in the spirit."[1] "He received from God the Father honor and glory, when there came such a voice to him from the excellent glory, 'This is my beloved Son in whom I am well pleased;' and this voice which came from heaven we heard, when we were with him in the holy mount."[2] "God raised up Christ from the dead, and gave him glory"[3]—"He is gone into heaven, and is on the right hand of God, angels and authorities and powers being made subject to him."[4] "Remember," again St. Paul says, "that Jesus Christ of the seed of David was raised from the dead"[5]—"If Christ be not risen, then is our preaching vain, and your faith also is vain"[6]—"I delivered unto you first of all that which I also received, how that Christ died for our sins according to the Scriptures; and that he was buried, and that he rose again the third day according to the Scriptures; and that he was seen of Cephas, then of the twelve—after that he was seen of above five hundred brethren at once . . . after that, he was seen of James, then of all the apostles."[7] These are half a dozen texts out of hundreds, which might be adduced to show that the writers of the Epistles, some writing before, some after the Evangelists, are entirely agreed with them as to the facts on which Christianity is based, and as strongly assert their reality. We are told, that "the Gospel myths grew up in the space of about thirty years, between the death of Jesus and the destruction of Jerusalem."(42) But in the Epistles and the Acts there is evidence that throughout the whole of this time the belief of the Church was the same—the

[1] 1 Pet. iii. 18. [2] 2 Pet. i. 17, 18. [3] 1 Pet. i. 21.
[4] Ibid. iii. 22. [5] 2 Tim. ii. 8. [6] 1 Cor. xv. 14.
[7] Ibid. verses 3–7.

Apostles themselves, the companions of Christ, maintained from the first the reality of those marvellous events which the Evangelists have recorded — they proclaimed themselves the "witnesses of the resurrection"[1] — appealed to the "miracles and signs"[2] which Jesus had wrought — and based their preaching altogether upon the facts of the Gospel narrative. There is no historical ground for asserting that that narrative was formed by degrees; nor is there any known instance of a mythic history having grown up in such an age, under such circumstances, or with such rapidity as is postulated in this case by our adversaries. The age was an historical age, being that of Dionysius, Diodorus, Livy, Velleius Paterculus, Plutarch, Valerius Maximus, and Tacitus — the country was one where written records were kept, and historical literature had long flourished; it produced at the very time when the New Testament documents were being written, an historian of good repute, Josephus, whose narrative of the events of his own time is universally accepted as authentic and trustworthy. To suppose that a mythology could be formed in such an age and country, is to confuse the characteristics of the most opposite periods — to ascribe to a time of luxury, over-civilization, and decay, a phase of thought which only belongs to the rude vigor and early infancy of nations.

There is in very deed no other alternative, if we reject the historic truth of the New Testament, than that embraced by the old assailants of Christianity — the ascription of the entire religion to imposture. The mythical explanation seems to have been invented in order to avoid this harsh conclusion, which the moral tone of the religion and the sufferings of its first propagators in defence of it

[1] Acts i. 22; iv. 33, &c. [2] Ibid. ii. 22.

alike contradict. The explanation fails, however, even in this respect; for its great advocate finds it insufficient to explain the phenomena, and finally delivers it as his opinion, that in many places the authors of the Gospels consciously and designedly introduced fictions into their narratives.(43) If then we feel sure that in the books of the New Testament we have not the works of impostors, testifying to have seen that which they had not seen, and knew that they had not seen; if we are conscious in reading them of a tone of sincerity and truth beyond that of even the most veracious and simple-minded of profane writers; if we recognize throughout an atmosphere of fact and reality, a harmony of statement, a frequency of undesigned coincidence, an agreement like that of honest witnesses not studious of seeming to agree; we must pronounce utterly untenable this last device of the sceptic, which presents even more difficulties than the old unbelief. We must accept the documents as at once genuine and authentic. The writers declare to us that which they have heard and seen.[1] They were believed by thousands of their contemporaries, on the spot where they stated the most remarkable of the events to have taken place, and within a few weeks of the time. They could not be mistaken as to those events. And if it be granted that these happened — if the resurrection and ascension are allowed to be facts, then the rest of the narrative may well be received, for it is less marvellous. Vain are the "profane babblings," which ever "increase unto more ungodliness," of those whose "word doth eat like a canker . . . who concerning the truth have erred" — denying the resurrection of Christ, and "saying that the resurrection" of man "is past already," thus "overthrowing the faith of some."[2]

[1] 1 John i. 3. [2] 2 Tim. ii. 16–18.

"The foundation of God standeth sure."[1] "Jesus Christ of the seed of David was raised from the dead"[2]—Jesus Christ, the God-Man, is "ascended into the heavens."[3] These are the cardinal points of the Christian's faith. On these credentials, which nothing can shake, he accepts as certain the divine mission of his Saviour.

[1] 2 Tim. ii. 19. [2] Ibid. verse 8. [3] Acts ii. 34.

LECTURE VII.

IN THE MOUTH OF TWO OR THREE WITNESSES SHALL EVERY WORD BE ESTABLISHED. — 2 CORINTHIANS XIII. 1.

THE historical inquirer, on passing from the history of the Old Testament to that contained in the New, cannot fail to be struck with the remarkable contrast which exists between the two narratives in respect of their aim and character. In the Old Testament the writers seek to set before us primarily and mainly the history of their nation, and only secondarily and in strict subordination to this object introduce accounts of individuals.(1) Their works fall under the head of History Proper — History, no doubt, of a peculiar cast, — not secular, that is, but sacred or theocratic, — yet still History in the strictest sense of the term, — accounts of kings and rulers, and of the vicissitudes through which the Jewish nation passed, its sufferings, triumphs, checks, reverses, its struggles, ruin, and recovery. In the Historical Books of the New Testament, on the contrary, these points cease altogether to engage the writers' attention, which becomes fixed on an individual, whose words and actions, and the effect of whose teaching, it is their great object to put on record. The authors of the Gospels are biographers of Christ, not historians of their nation; they intend no account of the political condition of Palestine in their time, but only a narrative of the chief facts concerning our Lord — especially those of his public life and ministry.(2) Even the Evangelist, who in a second treatise carries on the narrative from the Ascension during the space of some thirty years to the first imprisonment of St. Paul at Rome, leaves untouched the national history, and confines himself (as the title of his work implies) to the "acts" of those who made the doctrine of Christ known to the world. Hence the agreement to be traced between the sacred narrative and profane history in this part of the Biblical records, consists only to a very small extent of an accord with respect to the main facts related, which it scarcely came within the sphere of the civil historian to commemorate; it is to be found chiefly, if not solely, in harmonious representations with respect to facts which in the Scriptural narrative are incidental and secondary, as the names, offices, and characters of the political personages to whom there happens to be allusion; the general condition of the Jews and heathen at the time; the prevalent manners and customs; and the like. The value of such confirmation is not, however, less, but rather greater, than that of the more direct confirmation which would result from an accordance with respect to main facts — in the first place, because it is a task of the extremest difficulty for any one but an honest contemporary writer to maintain accuracy in the wide field of incidental allusion;(3) and secondly, because exactness in such matters is utterly at variance with the mythical spirit, of which, according to the latest phase of unbelief, the narrative of the New Testament is the product. The detail and appearance of exactness, which characterizes the Evangelical writings, is of itself a strong argument against the mythical theory; if it can be shown that the detail is correct and the exactness that of persons intimately acquainted with the whole history of the time and bent on faithfully recording it, that theory may be considered as completely subverted and disproved. It will be the chief object of the present Lecture to make it apparent that this is the case with respect to the Evangelical writings — that the incidental references to the civil history of the time of which they treat, and to the condition of the nations with which they deal, are borne out, for the most part, by Pagan or Jewish authors, and are either proved thus to be correct, or are at any rate such as there is no valid reason, on account of any disagreement with profane authorities, seriously to question.

Before entering, however, on this examination of the incidental allusions or secondary facts in the New Testament narrative, it is important to notice two things with regard to the main facts; in the first place, that some of them (as the miracles, the resurrection, and the ascension) are of such a nature that no testimony to them from profane sources was to be expected, since those who believed them naturally and almost necessarily became Christians; and secondly, that with regard to such as are not of this character, there does exist profane testimony of the first order. The existence at this time of one called by his followers Christ, the place of his teaching, his execution by Pontius Pilate, Procurator of Judea under Tiberius, the rapid spread of his doctrine through the Roman world, the vast number of converts made in a short time, the persecutions which they underwent, the innocency of their lives, their worship of Christ as God — are witnessed to by Heathen writers of eminence, and would be certain and indisputable facts, had the New Testament never been written. Tacitus, Suetonius, Juvenal, Pliny, Trajan, Adrian, (4) writing in the century immediately following upon the death of Christ, declare these things to us, and establish, so firmly that no sceptic can even profess to doubt it, the historical character of (at least) that primary groundwork whereon the Christian story, as related by the Evangelists, rests as on an immovable basis. These classic notices compel even those who set no value on the historical Christ, to admit his existence;[(5)] they give a definite standing-point to the religion, which might otherwise have been declared to have no historical foundation at all, but to be purely and absolutely mythic; they furnish, taken by themselves, no unimportant argument for the truth of the religion, which they prove to have been propagated with such zeal, by persons of pure and holy lives, in spite of punishments and persecutions of the most fearful kind; and they form, in combination with the argument from the historic accuracy of the incidental allusions, an evidence in favor of the substantial truth of the New Testament narrative which is amply sufficient to satisfy any fair mind. As they have been set forth fully and with admirable argumentative skill by so popular a writer as Paley, I am content to make this passing allusion to them, and to refer such of my hearers as desire a fuller treatment of the point to the excellent chapter on the subject in the first part of Paley's Evidences.[(6)]

If an objection be raised against the assignment of very much weight to these testimonies of adversaries on account of their scant number and brevity; and if it be urged, that supposing the New Testament narrative to be true, we should have expected far more frequent and fuller notices of the religion and its Founder than the remains of antiquity in fact furnish,—if it be said (for instance) that Josephus ought to have related the miracles of Christ, and Seneca, the brother of Gallio, his doctrines; that the observant Pausanias, the voluminous Plutarch, the copious Dio, the exact Arrian, should have made frequent mention of Christianity in their writings, instead of almost wholly ignoring it;(7) let it be considered, in the first place, whether the very silence of these writers is not a proof of the importance which in their hearts they assigned to Christianity, and the difficulty which they felt in dealing with it — whether in fact it is not a *forced and studied* reticence — a reticence so far from being indicative of ignorance that it implies only too much knowledge, having its origin in a feeling that it was best to ignore what it was unpleasant to confess and impossible to meet satisfactorily. Pausanias must certainly have been aware that the shrines of his beloved gods were in many places deserted, and that their temples were falling into decay, owing to the conversion of the mass of the people to the new religion; we may be sure he inwardly mourned over this sad spirit of disaffection — this madness (as he must have thought it) of a degenerate age; but no word is suffered to escape him on the painful subject; he is too jealous of his gods' honor to allow that there are any who dare to insult them. Like the faithful retainer of a falling house he covers up the shame of his masters, and bears his head so much the more proudly because of their depressed condition. Again, it is impossible that Epictetus could have been ignorant of the wonderful patience and constancy of the Christian martyrs, of their marked contempt of death and general indifference to worldly things — he must, one would think, as a Stoic, have been moved with a secret admiration of those great models of fortitude, and if he had allowed himself to speak freely, could not but have made frequent reference to them. The one contemptuous notice, which is all that Arrian reports,(8) sufficiently indicates his knowledge; the entire silence, except in this passage,(9) upon what it so nearly concerned a Stoical philosopher to bring forward, can only be viewed as the studied avoidance of a topic which would have been unpalatable to his hearers, and to himself perhaps not wholly agreeable. The philosopher who regarded himself as raised by study and reflection to an exalted height above the level of ordinary humanity would not be altogether pleased to find that his elevation was attained by hundreds of common men, artisans and laborers, through the power of a religion which he looked on as mere fanaticism. Thus from different motives,—from pride, from policy, from fear of offending the Chief of the state, from real attachment to the old Heathenism and tenderness for it—the heathen writers who witnessed the birth and growth of Christianity, united in a reticence, which causes their notices of the religion to be a very insufficient measure of the place which it really held in their thoughts and apprehensions. A large allowance is to be made for this studied silence in estimating the value of the actual testimonies to the truth of the New Testament narrative adducible from heathen writers of the first and second centuries.(10)

And the silence of Josephus is, more plainly still, wilful and affected. It is quite impossible that the Jewish historian should have been ignorant of the events which had drawn the eyes of so many to Judæa but a few years before his own birth, and which a large and increasing sect believed to possess a supernatural character. Jesus of Nazareth was, humanly speaking, at least as considerable a personage as John the Baptist, and the circumstances of his life and death must have attracted at least as much attention. There was no good reason why Josephus, if he had been an honest historian, should have mentioned the latter and omitted the former. He had grown to manhood during the time that Christianity was being spread over the world;(11) he had probably witnessed the tumults excited against St. Paul by his enemies at Jerusalem;[1] he knew of the irregular proceedings against "James the Lord's brother;"[2](12) he must have been well acquainted with the various persecutions which the Christians had undergone at the hands of both Jews and heathen;(13) at any rate he could not fail to be at least as well informed as Tacitus on the subject of transactions, of which his own country had been the scene, and which had fallen partly within his own lifetime. When, therefore, we find that he is absolutely silent concerning the Christian religion, and, if he mentions Christ at all, mentions him only incidentally in a single passage, as, "Jesus, who was called Christ,"(14) without appending further comment or explanation; when we find this, we cannot but conclude that for some reason or other the Jewish historian practises an intentional reserve, and *will* not enter upon a subject which excites his fears,(15) or offends his prejudices. No conclusions inimical to the historic accuracy of the New Testament can reasonably be drawn from the silence of a writer who determinately avoids the subject.

Further, in estimating the value of that direct evidence of adversaries to the main facts of Christianity which remains to us, we must not overlook the probability that much evidence of this kind has perished. The books of the early opponents of Christianity, which might have been of the greatest use to us for the confirmation of the Gospel History,(16) were with an unwise zeal destroyed by the first Christian Emperors.(17) Other testimony of the greatest importance has perished by the ravages of time. It seems

[1] Acts xxi. 27, et seqq.; xxii. 22, 23; xxiii. 10.
[2] Gal. i. 19.

certain that Pilate remitted to Tiberius an account of the execution of our Lord, and the grounds of it; and that this document, to which Justin Martyr more than once alludes,(18) was deposited in the archives of the empire. The "Acts of Pilate," as they were called, seem to have contained an account, not only of the circumstances of the crucifixion, and the grounds upon which the Roman governor regarded himself as justified in passing sentence of death upon the accused, but also of the Miracles of Christ — his cures performed upon the lame, the dumb, and the blind, his cleansing of lepers, and his raising of the dead.(19) If this valuable direct testimony had been preserved to us, it would scarcely have been necessary to enter on the consideration of those indirect proofs of the historical truth of the New Testament narrative arising from the incidental allusions to the civil history of the times which must now occupy our attention.

The incidental allusions to the civil history of the times which the writings of the Evangelists furnish, will, I think, be most conveniently reviewed by being grouped under three heads. I shall consider, first of all, such as bear upon the general condition of the countries which were the scene of the history; secondly, such as have reference to the civil rulers and administrators who are represented as exercising authority in the countries at the time of the narrative; and, thirdly, such as touch on separate and isolated facts which might be expected to obtain mention in profane writers. These three heads will embrace all the most important of the allusions in question, and the arrangement of the scattered notices under them will, I hope, prove conducive to perspicuity.

I. The political condition of Palestine at the time to which the New Testament narrative properly belongs, was one curiously complicated and anomalous; it underwent frequent changes, but retained through all of them certain peculiarities, which made the position of the country unique among the dependencies of Rome. Not having been conquered in the ordinary way, but having passed under the Roman dominion with the consent and by the assistance of a large party among the inhabitants, it was allowed to maintain for a while a species of semi-independence, not unlike that of various native states in India which are really British dependencies. A mixture, and to some extent an alternation, of Roman with native power resulted from this arrangement, and a consequent complication in the political *status*, which must have made it very difficult to be thoroughly understood by any one who was not a native and a contemporary. The chief representative of the Roman power in the East — the President of Syria, the local governor, whether a Herod or a Roman Procurator, and the High Priest, had each and all certain rights and a certain authority in the country. A double system of taxation, a double administration of justice, and even in some degree a double military command, were the natural consequence; while Jewish and Roman customs, Jewish and Roman words, were simultaneously in use, and a condition of things existed full of harsh contrasts, strange mixtures, and abrupt transitions. Within the space of fifty years Palestine was a single united kingdom under a native ruler, a set of principalities under native ethnarchs and tetrarchs, a country in part containing such principalities, in part reduced to the condition of a Roman province, a kingdom reunited once more under a native sovereign, and a country reduced wholly under Rome and governed by procurators dependent on the president of Syria, but still subject in certain respects to the Jewish monarch of a neighboring territory. These facts we know from Josephus[(20)] and other writers, who, though less accurate, on the whole confirm his statements;[(21)] they render the civil history of Judæa during the period one very difficult to master and remember; the frequent changes, supervening upon the original complication, are a fertile source of confusion, and seem to have bewildered even the sagacious and painstaking Tacitus.[(22)] The New Testament narrative, however, falls into no error in treating of the period; it marks, incidentally and without effort or pretension, the various changes in the civil government — the sole kingdom of Herod the Great,[1] — the partition of his dominions among his sons,[2] — the reduction of Judæa to the condition of a Roman province, while Galilee, Ituræa, and Trachonitis continued under native princes,[3] — the restoration of the old kingdom of Palestine in the person of Agrippa the First,[4] and the final reduction of the whole under Roman rule, and reëstablishment of Procurators[5] as the civil heads, while a species of ecclesiastical superintendence was exercised by Agrippa the Second.[6][(23)] Again, the New Testament narrative exhibits in the most remarkable way the mixture in the government — the occasional power of the president of Syria, as shown in Cyrenius's "taxing;"[7] the ordinary division of authority between the High-Priest and the Procurator;[8] the existence of two separate taxations — the civil and the ecclesiastical, the "census"[9] and the "didrachm;"[10]

[1] Matt. ii. 1; Luke i. 5.

[2] Ibid. ii. 22, and xiv. 1; Luke iii. 1.

[3] Luke iii. 1, et passim.

[4] Acts xii. 1, et seqq.

[5] Ibid. xxiii. 24; xxiv. 27, &c.

[6] Ibid. xxv. 14, et seqq.

[7] Luke ii. 2. Compare Acts v. 37.

[8] Matt. xxvii. 1, 2; Acts xxii. 30; xxiii. 1–10.

[9] Ibid. xxii. 17.

[10] Ibid. xvii. 24.

of two tribunals,[1] two modes of capital punishment,(24) two military forces,[2] two methods of marking time;[3] at every turn it shows, even in such little matters as verbal expressions, the coexistence of Jewish with Roman ideas and practices in the country — a coexistence, which (it must be remembered) came to an end within forty years of our Lord's crucifixion. The conjunction in the same writings of such Latinisms as κεντυρίων,[4] λεγεών,[5] πραιτώριον,[6] κουστωδία,[7] κῆνσος,[8] κοδράντης,[9] δηνάριον,[10] ἀσσάριον,[11] σπεκουλάτωρ,[12] φραγελλώσας,[13] and the like,(25) with such Hebraisms as κορβᾶν,[14] ῥαββουνί,[15] δύο δύο,[16] πρασιαὶ πρασιαί,[17] τὸ βδέλυγμα

[1] John xviii. 28, 32, &c. [2] Matt. xxvii. 64, 65. [3] Luke iii. 1.

[4] Lat. *centurio* = Eng. "centurion." (Mark xv. 39, 44, 45.)

[5] Lat. *legio* = Eng. "legion." (Matt. xxvi. 53; Mark v. 9; Luke viii. 30.)

[6] Lat. *prætorium*, translated "common hall" in Matt. xxvii. 27; "judgment hall," or "hall of judgment," in John xviii. 28, 33; xix. 9; Acts xxiii. 35; "palace," in Phil. i. 13; "prætorium," in Mark xv. 16.

[7] Lat. *custodia* = Eng. "watch." (Matt. xxvii. 65, 66; xxviii. 11.)

[8] Lat. *census* = Eng. "tribute." (Matt. xvii. 25; xxii. 17, 19; Mark xii. 14.)

[9] Lat. *quadrans* = Eng. "farthing." (Matt. v. 26; Mark xii. 42.)

[10] Lat. *denarius* = Eng. "penny." (Matt. xviii. 28; xx. 2, 9, 10, 13; xxii. 19; Mark vi. 37; xii. 15; xiv. 5; Luke vii. 41; x. 35; xx. 24; John vi. 7; xii. 5; Rev. vi. 6.)

[11] Lat. *assarius* = Eng. "farthing." (Matt. x. 29; Luke xii. 6.)

[12] Lat. *speculator* = Eng. "executioner." (Mark vi. 27.)

[13] A participle of the verb φραγελλοῦν, formed from the Latin verb *flagellare* = to scourge, or from the noun *flagellum* = a scourge. It is translated, "when he had scourged." (Matt. xxvii. 26; Mark xv. 15.)

[14] Heb. קָרְבָּן = "corban." (Mark vii. 11.)

[15] Rabboni, John xx. 16, translated "Lord" in Mark x. 51.

[16] Literally, "two, two;" translated "by two and two" in Mark vi. 7. The repetition is a Hebraism.

[17] Literally, "onion-beds, onion-beds," that is, "in squares," like a

τῆς ἐρημώσεως,[1] (26) was only natural in Palestine during the period between Herod the Great and the destruction of Jerusalem, and marks the writers for Jews of that time and country. The memory of my hearers will add a multitude of instances from the Gospels and the Acts similar in their general character to those which have been here adduced — indicative, that is, of the semi-Jewish, semi-Roman condition of the Holy Land at the period of the New Testament narrative.

The general tone and temper of the Jews at the time, their feelings towards the Romans and towards their neighbors, their internal divisions and sects, their confident expectation of a deliverer, are represented by Josephus and other writers in a manner which very strikingly accords with the account incidentally given by the Evangelists. The extreme corruption and wickedness, not only of the mass of the people, but even of the rulers and chief men, is asserted by Josephus in the strongest terms; (27) while at the same time he testifies to the existence among them of a species of zeal for religion — a readiness to attend the feasts, (28) a regularity in the offering of sacrifice, (29) an almost superstitious regard for the temple, (30) and a fanatic abhorrence of all who sought to "change the customs which Moses had delivered."[2] The conspiracy against Herod the Great, when ten men bound themselves by an oath to kill him, and having armed themselves with short daggers, which they hid under their clothes, entered into the theatre where they expected Herod to arrive, intending if he

garden-plot; translated "by companies." (Mark vi. 40.) The repetition is Hebraistic, as in the previous instance.

[1] "The abomination of desolation." (Matt. xxiv. 15; Mark xiii. 14.) Borrowed from Dan. xi. 31; xii. 11.

[2] Acts vi. 14.

came to fall upon him and despatch him with their weapons,(31) breathes the identical spirit of that against St. Paul, which the promptness of the chief captain Lysias alone frustrated.[1] Many such close resemblances have been pointed out.(32) We find from Josephus that there was a warm controversy among the Jews themselves as to the lawfulness of "giving tribute to Cæsar;"[2](33) that the Samaritans were so hostile to such of the Galilæans as had their "faces set to go to Jerusalem,"[3] that, on one occasion at least, they fell upon those who were journeying through their land to attend a feast, and murdered a large number;(34) that the Pharisees and Sadducees were noted sects, distinguished by the tenets which in Scripture are assigned to them;(35) that the Pharisees were the more popular, and persuaded the common people as they pleased, while the Sadducees were important chiefly as men of high rank and station;(36) and that a general expectation, founded upon the prophecies of the Old Testament, existed among the Jews during the Roman war, that a great king was about to rise up in the East, of their own race and country.(37) This last fact is confirmed by both Suetonius(38) and Tacitus,(39) and is one which even Strauss does not venture to dispute.(40) Important in many ways, it adds a final touch to that truthful portraiture of the Jewish people at this period of their history, which the Gospels and the Acts furnish — a portraiture alike free from flattery and unfairness, less harsh on the whole than that of Josephus, if less favorable than that of Philo.(41)

It would be easy to point out a further agreement between the Evangelical historians and profane writers with respect to the manners and customs of the Jews at this period. There is scarcely a matter of this kind noted in

[1] Acts xxiii. 12–31. [2] Matt. xxii. 17. [3] Luke ix. 51.

the New Testament which may not be confirmed from Jewish sources, such as Josephus, Philo, and the Mishna. The field, however, is too extensive for our present consideration. To labor in it is the province rather of the Commentator than of the Lecturer, who cannot effectively exhibit arguments which depend for their force upon the accumulation of minute details.

The points of agreement hitherto adduced have had reference to the Holy Land and its inhabitants. It is not, however, in this connection only that the accuracy of the Evangelical writers in their accounts of the general condition of those countries which are the scene of their history, is observable. Their descriptions of the Greek and Roman world, so far as it comes under their cognizance, are most accurate. Nowhere have the character of the Athenians and the general appearance of Athens been more truthfully and skilfully portrayed than in the few verses of the Acts which contain the account of St. Paul's visit.[1] The city "full of idols" (κατείδωλος)[2]—in "gold, and silver, and marble, graven by art and man's device,"[3] recalls the πόλις ὅλη βωμὸς, ὅλη θῦμα θεοῖς καὶ ἀνάθημα[4] of Xenophon,(42) the "Athenæ simulachra deorum hominumque habentes, omni genere et materiæ et artium insignia"[5] of Livy.(43) The people—"Athenians *and strangers*, spending their time in nothing else but hearing or telling of some new thing"[6]—philosophizing and disputing on Mars' Hill and in the market-place,[7] glad to discuss though disinclined to

[1] Acts xvii. 15, et seqq. [2] Ibid. xvii. 16. [3] Ibid. verse 29.

[4] The whole city is an altar—the whole a sacrifice to the gods and an oblation.

[5] Athens, which has famous images of gods and men, of every variety both of material and style of art.

[6] Acts xvii. 21. [7] Ibid. verse 17.

believe,[1] and yet religious withal, standing in honorable contrast with the other Greeks in respect of their reverence for things divine,[2] are put before us with all the vividness of life, just as they present themselves to our view in the pages of their own historians and orators. (44) Again, how striking and how thoroughly classical is the account of the tumult at Ephesus,[3] where almost every word receives illustration from ancient coins and inscriptions, (45) as has been excellently shown in a recent work of great merit on the Life of St. Paul! Or if we turn to Rome and the Roman system, how truly do we find depicted the great and terrible Emperor whom all feared to provoke (46) — the provincial administration by proconsuls and others chiefly anxious that tumults should be prevented (47) — the contemptuous religious tolerance (48) — the noble principles of Roman law, professed, if not always acted on, whereby accusers and accused were brought "face to face," and the latter had free "license to answer for themselves concerning the crimes laid against them" [4] (49) — the privileges of Roman citizenship, sometimes acquired by birth, sometimes by purchase (50) — the right of appeal possessed and exercised by the provincials (51) — the treatment of prisoners (52) — the peculiar manner of chaining them (53) — the employment of soldiers as their guards (54) — the examination by torture (55) — the punishment of condemned persons, not being Roman citizens, by scourging and crucifixion (56) — the manner of this punishment (57) — the practice of bearing the cross, (58) of affixing a title or superscription, (59) of placing soldiers under a centurion to watch the carrying into effect of the sentence, (60) of giving the garments of the sufferer to these persons, (61) of allowing the bodies after

[1] Acts xvii. 32, 33.
[2] Ibid. verse 22.
[3] Ibid. xix. 23, et seqq.
[4] Ibid. xxv. 16.

death to be buried by the friends (62) — and the like! The sacred historians are as familiar, not only with the general character, but even with some of the obscurer customs of Greece and Rome, as with those of their own country. Fairly observant, and always faithful in their accounts, they continually bring before us little points which accord minutely with notices in profane writers nearly contemporary with them, while occasionally they increase our knowledge of classic antiquity by touches harmonious with its spirit, but additional to the information which we derive from the native authorities. (63)

Again, it has been with reason remarked, (64) that the condition of the Jews beyond the limits of Palestine is represented by the Evangelical writers very agreeably to what may be gathered of it from Jewish and Heathen sources. The wide dispersion of the chosen race is one of the facts most evident upon the surface of the New Testament history. "Parthians, and Medes, and Elamites, and dwellers in Mesopotamia and Judæa and Cappadocia, Pontus and Asia, Phrygia and Pamphylia, Egypt, and the parts of Libya about Cyrene, strangers of Rome, Cretes, and Arabians,"[1] are said to have been witnesses at Jerusalem of the first outpouring of the Holy Ghost. In the travels of St. Paul through Asia Minor and Greece there is scarcely a city to which he comes but has a large body of Jewish residents. (65) Compare with these representations the statements of Agrippa the First in his letter to Caligula, as reported by the Jewish writer, Philo. "The holy city, the place of my nativity," he says, "is the metropolis, not of Judæa only, but of most other countries, by means of the colonies which have been sent out of it from time to time — some to the neighboring countries of

[1] Acts ii. 9–11.

Egypt, Phœnicia, Syria, and Cœlesyria — some to more distant regions, as Pamphylia, Cilicia, Asia as far as Bithynia and the recesses of Pontus; and in Europe, Thessaly, Bœotia, Macedonia, Ætolia, Attica, Argos, Corinth, together with the most famous of the islands, Eubœa, Cyprus, and Crete; to say nothing of those who dwell beyond the Euphrates. For, excepting a small part of the Babylonian and other satrapies, all the countries which have a fertile territory possess Jewish inhabitants; so that if thou shalt show this kindness to my native place, thou wilt benefit not one city only, but thousands in every region of the world, in Europe, in Asia, in Africa — on the continents, and in the islands — on the shores of the sea, and in the interior." (66) In a similar strain Philo himself boasts, that "one region does not contain the Jewish people, since it is exceedingly numerous; but there are of them in almost all the flourishing countries of Europe and Asia, both continental and insular." (67) And the customs of these dispersed Jews are accurately represented in the New Testament. That they consisted in part of native Jews, in part of converts or proselytes, is evident from Josephus; (68) that they had places of worship, called synagogues or oratories, in the towns where they lived, appears from Philo; that these were commonly by the sea-side, or by a river-side, as represented in the Acts,[1] is plain from many authors; (69) that they had also — at least sometimes — a synagogue belonging to them at Jerusalem, whither they resorted at the time of the feasts, is certain from the Talmudical writers; (70) that at Rome they consisted in great part of freedmen or "Libertines" — whence "the synagogue of the Libertines"[2] — may be gathered from Philo (71) and Tacitus. (72) Their feelings towards the apostolic preachers

[1] Acts xvi. 13. [2] Ibid. vi. 9.

are such as we should expect from persons whose close contact with those of a different religion made them all the more zealous for their own; and their tumultuous proceedings are in accordance with all that we learn from profane authors of the tone and temper of the Jews generally at this period. (73)

II. I proceed now to consider the second of the three heads under which I proposed to collect the chief incidental allusions to the civil history of the times contained in the New Testament.

The civil governors and administrators distinctly mentioned by the New Testament historians are the following — the Roman Emperors, Augustus, Tiberius, and Claudius — the Jewish kings and princes, Herod the Great, Archelaus, Herod the tetrarch, (or, as he is commonly called, Herod Antipas,) Philip the tetrarch, Herod Agrippa the first, and Herod Agrippa the second — the Roman governors, Cyrenius (or Quirinus,) Pontius Pilate, Sergius Paulus, Gallio, Festus, and Felix — and the Greek tetrarch, Lysanias. It may be shown from profane sources, in almost every case, that these persons existed — that they lived at the time and bore the office assigned to them — that they were related to each other, where any relationship is stated, as Scripture declares — and that the actions ascribed to them are either actually such as they performed, or at least in perfect harmony with what profane history tells us of their characters.

With regard to the Roman Emperors, it is enough to remark, that Augustus, Tiberius, and Claudius occur in their right order, that St. Luke in placing the commencement of our Lord's ministry in the fifteenth year of Tiberius[1] and assigning to its duration a short term — probably

[1] Luke iii. 1.

three years — is in accord with Tacitus, who makes Christ suffer under Tiberius (74) — and that the birth of our Lord under Augustus,[1] and the accession before the second journey of St. Paul of Claudius,[2] are in harmony with the date obtainable from St. Luke for the crucifixion, and sufficiently suit the general scheme of profane chronology, which places the accession of Augustus forty-four years before that of Tiberius, and makes Claudius reign from A. D. 41 to A. D. 54. No very close agreement can be here exhibited on account of the deficiency of an exact chronology, which the Gospels share with many of the most important historical writings; but at any rate the notices are accordant with one another, and present, when compared with the dates furnished by profane writers, no difficulty of any real importance. (75)

The Jewish kings and princes whose names occur in the New Testament narrative, occupy a far more prominent place in it than the Roman Emperors. The Gospel narrative opens "in the days of Herod the king,"[3] who, as the father of Archelaus,[4] may be identified with the first monarch of the name, the son of Antipater, the Idumæan. (76) This monarch is known to have reigned in Palestine contemporaneously with Augustus, who confirmed him in his kingdom, (77) and of whom he held the sovereignty till his decease. (78) Cunning, suspicion, and cruelty are the chief traits of his character as depicted in Scripture, and these are among his most marked characteristics in Josephus. (79) It has been objected to the Scriptural narrative, that Herod would not have been likely to inquire of the Magi at what time they first saw the star, since he expected them to return and give him a full description of the

[1] Luke ii. 1-7.
[2] Acts xviii. 2.
[3] Matt. ii. 1; Luke i. 5.
[4] Ibid. ii. 22.

child; (80) but this keen and suspicious foresight, where his own interests were (as he thought) concerned, is quite in keeping with the representations of Josephus, who makes him continually distrust those with whom he has any dealings. The consistency of the massacre at Bethlehem with his temper and disposition is now acknowledged; (81) scepticism has nothing to urge against it except the silence of the Jewish writers, which is a weak argument, and one outweighed, in my judgment, by the testimony, albeit somewhat late, and perhaps inaccurate, of Macrobius. (82)

At the death of Herod the Great, his kingdom (according to Josephus) was divided, with the consent of Augustus, among three of his sons. Archelaus received Judæa, Samaria, and Idumæa, with the title of ethnarch; Philip and Antipas were made tetrarchs, and received, the latter Galilee and Peræa, the former Trachonitis and the adjoining regions. (83) The notices of the Evangelists are confessedly in complete accordance with these statements. (84) St. Matthew mentions the succession of Archelaus in Judæa, and implies that he did not reign in Galilee;[1] St. Luke records Philip's tetrarchy;[2] while the tetrarchy of Antipas, who is designated by his family name of Herod, is distinctly asserted by both Evangelists.[3] Moreover, St. Matthew implies that Archelaus bore a bad character at the time of his accession or soon afterwards, which is consistent with the account of Josephus, who tells us that he was hated by the other members of his family, (85) and that shortly after his father's death he slew three thousand Jews on occasion of a tumult at Jerusalem. (86) The first three Evangelists agree as to the character of Herod Antipas, which is weak rather than cruel or bloodthirsty; and their portraiture is granted to be "not inconsistent with

[1] Matt. ii. 22. [2] Luke iii. 1. [3] Ibid.; Matt. xiv. 1.

his character, as gathered from other sources." (87) The facts of his adultery with Herodias, the wife of one of his brothers, (88) and of his execution of John the Baptist for no crime that could be alleged against him, (89) are recorded by Josephus; and though in the latter case there is some apparent diversity in the details, yet it is allowed that the different accounts may be reconciled. (90)

The continuance of the tetrarchy of Philip beyond the fifteenth, and that of Antipas beyond the eighteenth of Tiberius, is confirmed by Josephus, (91) who also shows that the ethnarchy of Archelaus came speedily to an end, and that Judæa was then reduced to the condition of a Roman province, and governed for a considerable space by Procurators. (92) However, after a while, the various dominions of Herod the Great were reunited in the person of his grandson, Agrippa, the son of Aristobulus and brother of Herodias; who was allowed the title of king, and was in favor with both Caligula and Claudius. (93) It cannot be doubted that this person is the "Herod the king" of the Acts,[1] whose persecution of the Church, whose impious pride, and whose miserable death are related at length by the sacred historian. My hearers are probably familiar with that remarkable passage of Josephus in which he records with less accuracy of detail than St. Luke the striking circumstances of this monarch's decease — the "set day" — the public assemblage — the "royal dress" — the impious flattery — its complacent reception — the sudden judgment — the excruciating disease — the speedy death. (94) Nowhere does profane history furnish a more striking testimony to the substantial truth of the sacred narrative — nowhere is the superior exactness of the latter over the former more conspicuous.

[1] Acts xii. 1.

On the death of Herod Agrippa, Judæa (as Josephus informs us) became once more a Roman province under Procurators;(95) but the small kingdom of Chalcis was, a few years later, conferred by Claudius on this Herod's son, Agrippa the Second, who afterwards received other territories.(96) This prince is evidently the "king Agrippa" before whom St. Paul pleaded his cause.[1] The Bernice who is mentioned as accompanying him on his visit to Festus,[2] was his sister, who lived with him and commonly accompanied him upon his journeys.(97) Besides his separate sovereignty, he had received from the Emperor a species of ecclesiastical supremacy in Judæa, where he had the superintendence of the temple, the direction of the sacred treasury, and the right of nominating the High Priests.(98) These circumstances account sufficiently for his visit to Judæa, and explain the anxiety of Festus that he should hear St. Paul, and St. Paul's willingness to plead before him.

The Roman Procurators, Pontius Pilate, Felix, and Festus, are prominent personages in the history of Josephus, where they occur in the proper chronological position,(99) and bear characters very agreeable to those which are assigned them by the sacred writers. The vacillation of Pilate, his timidity, and at the same time his occasional violence,(100) the cruelty, injustice, and rapacity of Felix,(101) and the comparatively equitable and mild character of Festus,(102) are apparent in the Jewish historian; and have some sanction from other writers.(103) The character of Gallio, proconsul of Achaia(104) and brother of the philosopher Seneca, is also in close accordance with that which may be gathered from the expressions of Seneca and Statius, who speak of him as "delightful" or "charming."(105)

[1] Acts xxv. 13, et seqq.

[2] Ibid.

Of Quirinus (or Cyrenius) it is enough to say that he was President of Syria shortly after the deposition of Archelaus, and that he was certainly sent to effect a "taxing" or enrolment of all persons within his province, Palestine included.(106) Sergius Paulus is unknown to us except from St. Luke's account of him;[1] but his name is one which was certainly borne by Romans of this period,(107) and his office is designated correctly.(108)

The Greek tetrarch, Lysanias, is the only civil governor mentioned in the New Testament about whom there is any real difficulty. A Lysanias held certainly a government in these parts in the time of Antony;(109) but this person was put to death more than thirty years before the birth of Christ,(110) and therefore cannot be the prince mentioned as ruling over Abilene thirty years after Christ's birth. It is argued that St. Luke "erred," being misled by the circumstance that the region continued to be known as "the Abilene of Lysanias" down to the time of the second Agrippa.(111) But, on the other hand, it is allowed that a second Lysanias might have existed without obtaining mention from profane writers;(112) and the facts, that Abilene was in Agrippa's time connected with the name Lysanias, and that there is no reason to believe that it formed any part of the dominions of the first Lysanias, favor the view, that a second Lysanias, a descendant of the first, obtained from Augustus or Tiberius an investiture of the tract in question.(113)

III. It now only remains to touch briefly on a few of the remarkable facts in the New Testament narrative which might have been expected to attract the attention of profane historians, and of which we should naturally look to have some record. Such facts are the "decree from Cæsar

[1] Acts xiii. 7–12.

Augustus that all the world should be taxed"[1]—the "taxing" of Cyrenius[2]—the preaching and death of John the Baptist—our Lord's execution as a criminal—the adultery of Herod Antipas—the disturbances created by the impostors Theudas and Judas of Galilee[3]—the death of Herod Agrippa—the famine in the days of Claudius[4]—and the "uproar" of the Egyptian who "led out into the wilderness four thousand men that were murderers."[5] Of these events almost one half have been already shown to have been recorded by profane writers whose works are still extant.(114) The remainder will now be considered with the brevity which my limits necessitate.

It has been asserted that no "taxing of all the world"—that is, of the whole Roman Empire—took place in the time of Augustus;(115) but as the opposite view is maintained by Savigny(116)—the best modern authority upon Roman law—this assertion cannot be considered to need examination here. A far more important objection to St. Luke's statement is derived from the time at which this "taxing" is placed by him. Josephus mentions the extension of the Roman census to Judæa under Cyrenius, at least ten years later—after the removal of Archelaus,(117) and *seems* to speak of this as the first occasion on which his countrymen were compelled to submit to this badge of subjection. It is argued that this *must* have been the first occasion; and the words of St. Luke (it is said)—"this taxing was first made when Cyrenius was governor of Syria"—show that he intended the taxing mentioned by Josephus, which he consequently misdated by a decade of years.(118) But the meaning of the passage in St. Luke is doubtful in the extreme; and it admits of several explana-

[1] Luke ii. 1. [2] Ibid. verse 2. [3] Acts v. 36, 37.
[4] Ibid. xi. 28. [5] Ibid. xxi. 38.

tions which reconcile it with all that Josephus says.(119) Perhaps the best explanation is that of Whiston(120) and Prideaux(121)—that the design of Augustus was first *fully executed* (ἐγένετο) when Cyrenius was governor, though the decree went forth and the enrolment commenced ten years earlier.

The taxing of Cyrenius of which St. Luke speaks in this passage, and to which he also alludes in the Acts,[1] is (as we have seen) very fully narrated by Josephus. It caused the rebellion mentioned in Gamaliel's speech, which was headed by Judas of Galilee, who "drew away much people after him," but "perished,"—all, as many as obeyed him, being "*dispersed*."[2] This account harmonizes well with that of Josephus, who regards the followers of Judas as numerous enough to constitute a sect,(122) and notes their reappearance in the course of the last war with Rome, by which it is shown that though scattered they had not ceased to exist.(123)

The disturbance created by a certain Theudas, some time before the rebellion of Judas of Galilee, seems not to be mentioned by any ancient author. The identity of name is a very insufficient ground for assuming this impostor to be the same as the Theudas of Josephus,(124) who raised troubles in the procuratorship of Cuspius Fadus, about ten years after Gamaliel made his speech. There were, as Josephus says,(125) "innumerable disturbances" in Judæa about this time; and it is not at all improbable that within the space of forty years, during which a number of impostors gathered followers and led them to destruction, two should have borne the same name. Nor can it be considered surprising that Josephus has passed over the earlier Theudas, since his followers were only four hundred, and

[1] Acts v. 37. [2] Ibid. verse 36.

since the historian evidently omits all but the most important of the troubles which had afflicted his country.

The "uproar" of the Egyptian who "led out into the wilderness four thousand men that were murderers,"[1] is described at length by the Jewish writer,(126) the only noticeable difference between his account and that of St. Luke being that Josephus in his present text calls the number of this impostor's followers thirty thousand. From internal evidence there is reason to think that τρισμύριοι is a corrupt reading;(127) but even as the text stands, it does not contradict St. Luke; for the four thousand of St. Luke are the number whom the impostor "*led out into* the wilderness," while the thirty thousand of Josephus are the number whom he "*brought from* the wilderness" to attack Jerusalem.

The "famine in the days of Claudius"[2] is mentioned by several writers. Josephus tells us that it was severe in Palestine in the fourth year of this emperor; Dio, Tacitus, and Suetonius, speak of it as raging somewhat later in Rome itself.(128) Helena, queen of Adiabene — the richest portion of the ancient Assyria — brought relief to the Jews on the occasion, as St. Barnabas and St. Paul did to the Christians.[3] The agreement is here complete, even if the words of Agabus's prophecy are pressed — for the scarcity seems to have been general throughout the Empire.

This review — imperfect as it necessarily is — will probably be felt to suffice for our present purpose. We have found that the New Testament, while in its main narrative it treats of events with which heathen writers were not likely to concern themselves, and which they could not represent truly, contains — inextricably interwoven with that main narrative — a vast body of incidental allusions to the civil

[1] Acts xxi. 38. [2] Ibid. xi. 28. [3] Ibid. verses 29, 30.

history of the times, capable of being tested by comparison with the works of profane historians. We have submitted the greater part — or at any rate a great part — of these incidental allusions to the test of such comparison; and we have found, in all but some three or four cases, an entire and striking harmony. In no case have we met with clear and certain disagreement; sometimes, but very rarely, the accounts are difficult to reconcile, and we may suspect them of real disagreement — a result which ought not to cause us any astonishment. Profane writers are not infallible; and Josephus, our chief profane authority for the time, has been shown, in matters where he does not come into any collision with the Christian Scriptures, to "teem with inaccuracies." (129) If in any case it should be thought that we must choose between Josephus and an Evangelist, sound criticism requires that we should prefer the latter to the former. Josephus is not entirely honest: he has his Roman masters to please, and he is prejudiced in favor of his own sect, the Pharisees. He has also been convicted of error, (130) which is not the case with any Evangelist. His authority therefore is, in the eyes of an historical critic, inferior to that of the Gospel writers, and in any instance of contradiction, it would be necessary to disregard it. In fact, however, we are not reduced to this necessity. The Jewish writer nowhere actually contradicts our Scriptures, and in hundreds of instances he confirms them. It is evident that the entire historical framework, in which the Gospel picture is set, is real; that the facts of the civil history, small and great, are true, and the personages correctly depicted. To suppose that there is this minute historical accuracy in all the accessories of the story, and that the story itself is mythic, is absurd; unless we will declare the Apostles and their companions to have sought to palm upon mankind a tale which they knew to be false, and to have aimed at obtaining credit for their fiction by elaborate attention to these minutiæ. From such an avowal even Rationalism itself would shrink; but the only alternative is to accept the entire history as authentic — as, what the Church has always believed it to be, THE TRUTH. "All truth is contained in the Gospel." (131) "It is but just, that he who was worthy of the title of an Evangelist, should be exempt from all suspicion of either negligence or falsehood." (132) "The Evangelists had perfect knowledge, . . . and if any one does not yield his assent to them, he contemns those who were partners of the Lord, he contemns Christ himself, he contemns also the Father."[1] (133) Such has been the uniform teaching of the Church of Christ from the first — and modern Rationalism has failed to show any reason why we should reject it.

[1] "Veritas omnis in Evangelio continetur." "Ab hoc, qui Evangelista esse meruit, vel negligentiæ vel mendacii suspicionem æquum est propulsari." "Evangelistæ habuerunt perfectam agnitionem . . . quibus si quis non assentit, spernit quidem participes Domini, spernit et ipsum Christum, spernit et Patrem."

18

LECTURE VIII.

THE PHARISEES THEREFORE SAID UNTO HIM, THOU BEAREST RECORD OF THYSELF; THY RECORD IS NOT TRUE. JESUS ANSWERED AND SAID UNTO THEM, THOUGH I BEAR RECORD OF MYSELF, YET MY RECORD IS TRUE. — JOHN VIII. 13, 14.

If the evidence from profane sources to the *primary* facts of the New Testament narrative be, as was admitted in the last Lecture, disappointingly scanty, the defect is more than made up to us by the copious abundance of those notices which early Christian writers have left us of the whole series of occurrences forming the basis of our Religion. It has been customary with Christian apologists to dwell more especially on the profane testimony, despite its scantiness — doubtless because it has been felt that a certain amount of suspicion is regarded as attaching to those who "bear record of themselves," and that the evidence of Christian witnesses to the truth of Christianity is in some degree a record of this nature. But our Lord's words teach us that self-witness, however unconvincing to the adversary, may be valid and true; and certainly it is difficult to conceive how the full acceptance of the Christian facts, and conformity of the profession and life thereto, renders a witness unworthy of belief, whose testimony would have been regarded as of the highest value if he had stopped short of such acceptance, and while admitting the facts to a certain extent had remained a Heathen or a Jew. Had Justin Martyr, for instance, when he inquired into Christianity, found the evidence for it such as he could resist, and lived and died a Platonic philosopher, instead of renouncing all for Christ and finally sealing his testimony with his blood, what a value would have been set upon any recognition in his writings of the life and miracles of Christ or the sufferings of the early Christians! It is difficult to see why he deserves less credit, because he found the evidences for the Christian doctrine so strong that he felt compelled to become a believer.(1) At any rate, if for controversial purposes the argument derivable from the testimony of Christians be viewed as weak, it must possess a weight for those who believe far exceeding that of the witness of Jews and Heathens, and must therefore deserve a place in any summary that is made of the Historical Evidences to the truth of the Christian Religion.

It has been sometimes urged that the early Christians were persons of such low rank and station, so wanting in refinement, education, and that critical discernment which is requisite to enable men fairly to judge of the claims of a new religion, that their decision in favor of Christianity is entitled to little respect — since they must have been quite unable to appreciate the true value of its evidences.(2) This objection claims to base itself on certain admissions of the earliest Christian preachers themselves, who remark that "not many wise men after the flesh, not many mighty, not many noble, were called."[1] But such expressions are not to be pressed too far. In their very letter they do but declare the *general* condition of the converts; while they imply that there were, even in the first times, some exceptions — persons to whom the terms, "wise men after the flesh, mighty, and noble," might have been properly ap-

[1] 1 Cor. i. 26.

plied; and the examples of St. Paul himself, of Dionysius the Areopagite, of the Ethiopian eunuch, of "Erastus the chamberlain of the city,"[1] and of the converts from "Cæsar's household,"[2] are sufficient to show that the Gospel found its own in every rank and grade of society, and if it was embraced most readily by the poor and despised, still gathered to it "chosen vessels"[3] from among the educated, and occasionally from among the rich and great. The early Christians furnished, for their number, a considerable body of writers; and these writers will bear comparison in respect of every intellectual qualification with the best Heathen authors of the period. Justin Martyr, Athenagoras, Tertullian, Origen, Clement, would have been reckoned authors of eminence, had they not been "Fathers," and are at least as good evidence for the historical facts of the age immediately preceding their own, as Tacitus, Suetonius, and Dio. It will be my object in the present Lecture to show that these writers, and others of the same age or even earlier, bear copious witness to the facts recorded in the historical books of the New Testament, and are plainly as convinced of their reality as of that of any facts whatever which they have occasion to mention.

The Epistle ascribed to St. Barnabas by Clement of Alexandria (3) and Origen, (4) whether really the work of that person or no, is at any rate one of the most ancient of the uninspired Christian writings, belonging as it does to the first, or to the early part of the second century. (5) The writer's object is to explain the spiritual meaning of the Old Testament; and in the course of his exposition he mentions as undoubted facts the miracles of Christ — his appointment of his apostles — their number, twelve — his scourging — his being smitten on the face — his being set

[1] Rom. xvi. 23. [2] Philipp. iv. 22. [3] Acts ix. 15.

at nought and jested upon — his being arrayed in a scarlet robe — his crucifixion — his receiving gall and vinegar to drink — his death — the casting of lots upon his garment — his resurrection on the first day of the week — and his final ascension into heaven. (6) All these notices moreover occur in a small tract, chiefly concerned with the Old Testament, and extending to no more than ten or twelve ordinary pages.

An Epistle of St. Clement, Bishop of Rome, to the Corinthians, is allowed on all hands to be genuine. (7) This work was certainly composed in the first century, before some of the writings of St. John; and its author, the "fellow-laborer" of St. Paul,[1] must have had frequent communication with those who had witnessed the great events in Judæa which formed the foundation of the new religion. The object of the Epistle is to compose existing dissensions in the Corinthian Church, and its tone is from first to last hortatory and didactic. Historical allusions only find a place in it casually and incidentally. Yet it contains a mention of Christ's descent from Jacob, of his great power and regal dignity, his voluntary humiliation, his sufferings, the character of his teaching, his death for man, his resurrection, the mission of the apostles, their inspiration by the Holy Ghost, their preaching in many lands, their ordination of elders in every city, the special eminence in the Church of Saints Peter and Paul, the sufferings of St. Peter, the hardships endured by St. Paul, his distant travels, his many imprisonments, his flights, his stoning, his bonds, his testimony before rulers. (8) The fact of St. Paul's having written an Epistle to the Corinthians is also asserted; (9) and an allusion is made, in connection with that Epistle, to the early troubles and divisions which the great Apostle

[1] Philipp. iv. 3.

had composed, when the several sections of the newly-planted Church strove together in a jealous spirit, affirming themselves to be "of Paul," or "of Apollos," or "of Cephas," or even "of Christ."

Ignatius, second Bishop of Antioch, who succeeded to that see in about the year of the destruction of Jerusalem,(10) and was martyred nearly forty years later, A. D. 107,(11) left behind him certain writings, which are quoted with great respect by subsequent Fathers, but the existence of which at the present day is questioned. Writings under the name of Ignatius have come down to us in various shapes. Three Epistles, universally regarded as spurious,(12) exist only in Latin. Twelve others are found in Greek, and also in two ancient Latin versions; and of these, seven exist in two different forms — a longer, and a shorter one. Most modern critics accept these seven, in their shorter form, as genuine.(13) They are identical with the seven mentioned by Eusebius and Jerome,(14) and they are thought to be free from the internal difficulties, which cause suspicion to attach to the longer recension, as well as to the Epistles which those writers do not name. Doubts have, however, been recently started even with respect to these seven. The discovery in a very ancient MS. of a Syriac version of three Epistles only out of the seven, and these three in a still briefer form than that of the shorter Greek recension, together with the remarkable fact that the few early references which we possess to the writings of Ignatius are to passages in exactly these three compositions — has induced some learned men of our own day to adopt the view, that even the shorter Greek recension is largely interpolated, and that nothing beyond the three Epistles of the Syriac version can be depended upon as certainly written by the Antiochian Bishop.(15) If we adopt this opinion, the testimony of Ignatius to the historical truth of the New Testament narrative will be somewhat scanty — if we abide by the views generally prevalent before the Syriac version was discovered, and still maintained since that discovery by some divines of great learning and excellent judgment,(16) it will be as full and satisfactory as that borne by St. Clement. In the seven Epistles we find notices of the descent of Christ from David — his conception by the Holy Ghost — his birth of a virgin — her name, Mary — his manifestation by a star — his baptism by John — its motive, "that he might fulfil all righteousness"[1] — his appeals to the Prophets — the anointing of his head with ointment — his sufferings and crucifixion under Pontius Pilate and Herod the tetrarch — his resurrection, not on the Sabbath, but on the "Lord's day" — the resurrection through his power of some of the old prophets — his appearance to his disciples and command to them to "handle him and see"[2] that he was not a spirit — his eating and drinking with them after he had risen — the mission of the Apostles — their obedience to Christ — their authority over the Church — the inclusion of Saints Peter and Paul in their number.(17) If, on the contrary, we confine ourselves to the Syriac version — by which the entire writings of St. Ignatius are comprised in about five pages(18) — we lose the greater portion of these testimonies, but we still retain those to the birth of Christ from the Virgin Mary — his manifestation by a star — his many sufferings — his crucifixion — and the apostolic mission of Saints Peter and Paul.

Polycarp, Bishop of Smyrna, a disciple of St. John, and a younger contemporary of Ignatius, left behind him a single Epistle, addressed to the Philippians, which we possess in the original Greek, with the exception of three or four

[1] Matt. iii. 15. [2] Luke xxiv. 39.

sections, where the Greek text is wanting, and we have only a Latin version.(19) In this Epistle, which is a short composition, and, like the other remains of early Christian antiquity, of a hortatory character, we find allusions to the humble life of Christ, his ministering to those about him, the character of his preaching, his sufferings, death upon the cross, resurrection, and ascension to heaven; his promise to "raise up his disciples at the last day"[1]—the sufferings of St. Paul and the other Apostles, the preaching of St. Paul at Philippi, and the fact of his having written an Epistle to the Philippians.(20) We also learn from Irenæus that this Father used to relate his conversations with St. John and others, who had seen the Lord, and to repeat what they had told him both of the teaching *and miracles* of Jesus.(21)

A work of the first or earlier half of the second century has come down to us under the name of "The Shepherd of Hermas." Eusebius and Jerome ascribe it to the Hermas who is saluted by St. Paul at the end of his Epistle to the Romans;(22) but there are reasons for assigning it to a later Hermas—the brother of Pius, who was the ninth bishop of Rome.(23) This work is an allegory on a large scale, and consequently cannot contain any direct historical testimony. Its tone is consonant with the Christian story, and it contains some allusions to the mission of the Apostles, their travels for the purpose of spreading the truth over the world, and the sufferings to which they were exposed in consequence;(24) but on the whole it is of little service towards establishing the truth of any facts.

It was not until the Christian writers addressed themselves to the world without—and either undertook the task of refuting the adversaries of the truth, or sought by Apolo-

[1] John vi. 40.

gies to recommend the new religion to their acceptance—that the facts of the Christian story came naturally to occupy a prominent place in their compositions. Quadratus, Bishop of Athens in the early part of the second century, was, so far as we know, the first to write a defence of Christianity addressed to the Heathen, which he seems to have presented to the Emperor Adrian (25) about the year A. D. 122. This work is unfortunately lost, but a passage preserved by Eusebius gives us an indication of the sort of evidence which it would probably have furnished in abundance. "The works of our Saviour," says Quadratus, "were always conspicuous, for they were real; both they which were healed and they which were raised from the dead; who were seen not only when they were healed or raised, but for a long time afterwards; not only while he dwelt on this earth, but also after his departure, and for a good while after it; insomuch that some of them have reached to our times." (26)

About twenty-five years after Quadratus had presented his "Apology" to Adrian, his younger contemporary, Justin, produced a similar composition, which he presented to the first Antonine, probably about A. D. 148. (27) Soon afterwards he published his "Dialogue with Tryphon"—an elaborate controversial work, defensive of Christianity from the attacks of Judaism. Finally, about A. D. 165, or a little earlier, he wrote a second "Apology," which he presented to Marcus Aurelius and the Roman Senate. (28) It has been truly observed, that from the writings of this Father—"the earliest, of whose works we possess any considerable remains" (29)—there "might be collected a tolerably complete account of Christ's life, in all points agreeing with that which is delivered in our Scriptures." (30) Justin declares the marriage of Mary and Joseph—their descent from David—the miraculous conception of Christ—the intention of Joseph to put away his wife privily — the appearance to him of an angel which forbade him — the angelic determination of the name Jesus, with the reason assigned for it — the journey from Nazareth to Bethlehem — the birth of our Lord there — his lying in a manger — his circumcision — the extraordinary appearance of a star — the coming of the Wise Men — their application to Herod — their adoration and gifts — the warning to them not to return to Herod — the descent into Egypt — the massacre of the Innocents — the death of Herod and accession of Archelaus — the return from Egypt — the obscure early life of Christ, and his occupation as a carpenter — his baptism by St. John the Baptist in Jordan — the descent of the Spirit upon him in the form of a dove — the testimony borne to his greatness by John — his temptation by the devil — the character of his teaching — his confutation of his opponents — his miracles — his prophecies of the sufferings which should befall his disciples — his changing Simon's name to Peter, and the occasion of it — his naming the sons of Zebedee, Boanerges — his triumphal entry into Jerusalem riding upon an ass — his institution of the Eucharist — his singing a hymn with his disciples — his visit to the Mount of Olives on the eve of his crucifixion, accompanied by the three favored apostles, and the prayer there offered to the Father — his silence before Pilate — his being sent by Pilate to Herod — his sufferings and crucifixion — the mockery of those who stood by — the casting of lots for the garment — the flight of the apostles — the words on giving up the ghost — the burial at eventide — the resurrection on the third day — the appearances to the apostles — the explanation to them of the prophecies — the ascension into heaven as they were looking on — the preaching of the apostles afterwards — the descent of the Holy Ghost

— the conversion of the Gentiles — the rapid spread of the Gospel through all lands.[31] No one can pretend to doubt but that in Justin's time the facts of the New Testament History were received as simple truth — not only by himself, but by Christians generally, in whose name his Apologies were written and presented to the Roman Emperors.

It is needless to carry this demonstration further, or to produce similar lists from Athenagoras, Tertullian, Irenæus, Origen, and others. From the time of Justin the Church of Christ can show a series of writers, who not only exhibit incidentally their belief of the facts which form the basis of the Christian Religion, but who also testify explicitly to the universal reception among Christians of that narrative of the facts which we possess in the New Testament — a narrative which, as was shown in the last Lecture,[32] they maintain to be absolutely and in all respects true. Those who assert the mythic character of the New Testament history, must admit as certain that its mythic character was unsuspected by the Christians of the second century, who received with the most entire and simple faith the whole mass of facts put forth in the Gospels and the Acts, regarding them as real and actual occurrences, and appealing to profane history for their confirmation in various most important particulars. To fair and candid minds the evidence adduced from uninspired writers of the first century, though comparatively scanty, is (I think) sufficient to show that their belief was the same as that of Christians in the second, and that it was just as firm and undoubting.

The arguments hitherto adduced have been drawn from the literary compositions of the first ages of Christianity. Till recently these have been generally regarded as presenting the whole existing proof of the faith and practice of the early Church: and sceptics have therefore been eager to throw every possible doubt upon them, and to maintain that forgery and interpolation have so vitiated this source of knowledge as to render it altogether untrustworthy.[(33)] The efforts made, weak and contemptible as they are felt to be by scholars and critics, have nevertheless had a certain influence over the general tone of thought on the subject, and have caused many to regard the early infancy of Christianity as a dim and shadowy cloud-land, in which nothing is to be seen, except a few figures of bishops and martyrs moving uncertainly amid the general darkness. Under these circumstances it is well that attention should be called — as it has been called recently by several publications of greater or less research[(34)] — to the *monumental remains* of early Christian times which are still extant, and which take us back in the most lively way to the first ages of the Church, exhibiting before our eyes those primitive communities, which Apostles founded, over which Apostolic men presided, and in which Confessors and Martyrs were almost as numerous as ordinary Christians. As when we tread the streets of Pompeii, we have the life of the old Pagan world brought before us with a vividness which makes all other representations appear dull and tame, so when we descend into the Catacombs of Rome we seem to *see* the struggling persecuted community, which there, "in dens and caves of the earth,"[1] wrought itself a hidden home, whence it went forth at last conquering and to conquer, triumphantly establishing itself on the ruins of the old religion, and bending its heathen persecutors to the yoke of Christ. Time was when the guiding spirits of our Church not only neglected the study of these precious remnants of an antiquity which ought to be far dearer to us than that of Greece or Pagan Rome, of Egypt, Assyria, or Babylon —

[1] Heb. xi. 38.

but even ventured to speak of them with contempt, as the recent creations of Papal forgers, who had placed among the *arenariæ* or sandpits of heathen times the pretended memorials of saints who were never born, and of martyrs who never suffered.(35) But with increased learning and improved candor modern Anglicanism has renounced this shallow and untenable theory; and it is at length admitted universally, alike by the Protestant and the Romanist, that the Catacombs themselves, their present contents, and the series of inscriptions which have been taken from them and placed in the Papal galleries, are genuine remains of primitive Christian antiquity, and exhibit to us — imperfectly, no doubt, but so far as their evidence extends, truly — the condition and belief of the Church of Christ in the first ages.

For it is impossible to doubt that the Catacombs belong to the earliest times of Christianity. It was only during the ages of persecution that the Christians were content to hide away the memorials of their dead in gloomy galleries deep below the earth's surface, where few eyes could ever rest on them. With liberty and security came the practice of burying within, and around, the churches, which grew up on all sides; and though undoubtedly the ancient burial places would not have been deserted all at once, since habit and affection would combine to prevent such disuse, yet still from the time of Constantine burying in the Catacombs must have been on the decline, and the bulk of the tombs in them must be regarded as belonging to the first three centuries. The fixed dates obtainable from a certain number of the tombs confirm this view; and the style of ornamentation and form of the letters used in the inscriptions, are thought to be additional evidence of its correctness.

What then is the evidence of the Catacombs? In the first place, it is conclusive as to the vast number of the Christians in these early ages, when there was nothing to tempt men, and every thing to disincline them, towards embracing the persecuted faith. The Catacombs are calculated to extend over nine hundred miles of streets, and to contain almost seven millions of graves! (36) The Roman Christians, it will be remembered, are called by Tacitus "a vast multitude" — (ingens multitudo) — in the time of Nero; (37) by the age of Valerian they are reckoned at one half the population of the city; (38) but the historical records of the past have never been thought to indicate that their number approached at all near to what this calculation — which seems fairly made (39) — would indicate. Seven millions of deaths in (say) four hundred years would, under ordinary circumstances, imply an average population of from five hundred thousand to seven hundred thousand — an amount immensely beyond any estimate that has hitherto been made of the number of Roman Christians at any portion of the period. Perhaps the calculation of the number of graves may be exaggerated, and probably the proportion of deaths to population was, under the peculiar circumstances, unusually large; but still the evidence of vast numbers which the Catacombs furnish cannot wholly mislead; and we may regard it as established beyond all reasonable doubt, that in spite of the general contempt and hatred, in spite of the constant ill-usage to which they were exposed, and the occasional "fiery trials" which proved them, the Christians, as early as the second century, formed one of the chief elements in the population of Rome.

In the next place, the Catacombs afford proof of the dangers and sufferings to which the early Christians were exposed. Without assuming that the phials which have contained a red liquid, found in so many of the tombs, must have held blood, and that therefore they are certain signs of martyrdom, and without regarding the palm-branch as unmistakable evidence of the same (40) — we may find in the Catacombs a good deal of testimony confirmatory of those writers who estimate at the highest the number of Christians who suffered death in the great persecutions. The number of graves, if we place it at the lowest, compared with the highest estimate of the Christian population that is at all probable, would give a proportion of deaths to population enormously above the average — a result which at any rate lends support to those who assert that in the persecutions of Aurelius, Decius, Diocletian, and others, vast multitudes of Christians were massacred. Further, the word Martyr is frequent upon the tombs; and often where it is absent, the inscription otherwise shows that the deceased lost his life on account of his religion. (41) Sometimes the view opens on us, and we see, besides the individual buried, a long vista of similar sufferers — as when one of Aurelius's victims exclaims — "O unhappy times, in which amid our sacred rites and prayers, — in the very caverns, — we are not safe! What is more wretched than our life? What more wretched than a death, when it is impossible to obtain burial at the hands of friends or relatives? Still at the end they shine like stars in Heaven. A poor life is his, who has lived in Christian times!"[1] (42)

Again, the Catacombs furnish a certain amount of evidence with respect to the belief of the early Christians.

[1] "O tempora infausta! quibus inter sacra et vota ne in cavernis quidem salvari possimus. Quid miserius vita? Sed quid miserius in morte, cum ab amicis et parentibus sepeliri nequeant? Tandem in cœlo coruscant! Parum vixit qui vixit in Christianis temporibus."

The doctrine of the resurrection is implied or expressed on almost every tombstone which has been discovered. The Christian is not dead — he "rests" or "sleeps" — he is not buried, but "*deposited*" in his grave (43) — and he is always "at peace," (*in pace.*) The survivors do not mourn his loss despairingly, but express trust, resignation, or moderate grief. (44) The Anchor, indicative of the Christian's "sure and certain hope," is a common emblem; and the Phœnix and Peacock are used as more speaking signs of the Resurrection. The Cross appears, though not the Crucifix; and other emblems are employed, as the Dove and the Cock, which indicate belief in the sacred narrative as we possess it. There are also a certain number of pictures in the Catacombs; and these represent ordinarily historical scenes from the Old or New Testament, treated in a uniform and conventional way, but clearly expressive of belief in the facts thus represented. The Temptation of Eve — Moses striking the rock — Noah welcoming the return of the Dove — Elijah ascending to heaven — Daniel among the lions — Shadrach, Meshech, and Abednego in the fiery furnace — Jonah under the gourd — Jonah swallowed by the whale — and Jonah vomited out on the dry land, are the favorite subjects from the Old Testament; while from the New Testament we find the Adoration of the Wise Men — their interview with Herod — the Baptism of Christ by John the Baptist — the healing of the Paralytic — the turning of the water into wine — the feeding of the five thousand — the raising of Lazarus — the Last Supper — Peter walking on the sea — and Pilate washing his hands before the people. (45) St. Peter and St. Paul are also frequently represented, and St. Peter sometimes bears the Keys, in plain allusion to the gracious promise of his Master.[1]

[1] Matt. xiv. 19.

The parabolic teaching of our Lord is sometimes embodied by the artists, who never tire of repeating the type of the "Good Shepherd"—and who occasionally represent the Sower going out to sow, and the parable of the Wise and Foolish Virgins. In this way indirect evidence is borne to the historic belief of the early Church, which does not appear to have differed at all from that of orthodox Christendom at the present day.

If it be still said—Why are we to believe as they?—why are we in this enlightened nineteenth century to receive as facts, what Greeks and Romans in an uncritical and credulous age accepted without inquiry, or at least without any searching investigation?—the answer is twofold. Allowing that the bulk of men in the first and second centuries were uncritical and credulous with respect to remote times, and to such tales as did not concern action or involve any alteration of conduct, we may remark that it is untrue to represent them as credulous where their worldly interests were at stake, or where any practical result was to follow upon their belief of what they heard. They are not found to have offered themselves a ready prey to impostors, or to have allowed themselves to be carried away by the arts of pretenders, where such weakness would have brought them into trouble. We do not find that Simon Magus or Apollonius of Tyana had many followers. When the slave Clemens gave himself out to be Posthumus Agrippa, though the wishes of most men must have been in favor of his claims, very few appear to have really believed in them.(46) The Romans, and still more the Greeks, had plenty of shrewdness; and there was no people less likely than they to accept on slight grounds a religion involving such obligations as the Christian. It is important to bear in mind what conversion really meant in the early times. It meant the severing of family and social ties — the renunciation of worldly prospects — abstinence from all gayeties and amusements — perpetual exposure to insults — cold looks, contemptuous gestures, abusive words, injurious suspicions, a perpetual sense of danger, a life to lead which was to "die daily."[1] "The early Christians," it has been well said, "were separate from other men. Their religion snapped asunder the ties of a common intercourse. It called them to a new life; it gave them new sentiments, hopes, and desires, a new character; it demanded of them such a conscientious and steady performance of duty as had hardly before been conceived of; it subjected them to privations and insults, to uncertainty and danger; it required them to prepare for torments and death. Every day of their lives they were strongly reminded of it by the duties which it enforced and the sacrifices which it cost them."(47) Before accepting such a position, we may be well assured that each convert scanned narrowly the evidence upon which he was invited to make a change in every way so momentous. When they first heard the doctrine of the resurrection, the Athenians "mocked."[2] Yet after a while Dionysius and others "clave to Paul and believed"[3] — surely because they found the evidence of the resurrection of Christ such as could not be resisted. It must be remembered that the prospect of his own resurrection was all that the new convert had to sustain him. "If in this life only we have hope, we are of all men most miserable," says St. Paul.[4] And the prospect of his own resurrection was bound up inseparably with the fact of Christ's having risen. If Christ were not risen, preaching was vain, and faith was vain[5] — then all who fell asleep in

[1] 1 Cor. xv. 31. [2] Acts xvii. 32. [3] Ibid. verse 34.
[4] 1 Cor. xv. 19. [5] Ibid. verse 14.

Christ perished.[1] The Christian was taught to base his hope of a happy future for himself solely and entirely upon the resurrection and ascent to heaven of Jesus. Surely the evidence for these facts must have been thousands of times closely sifted by converts who could fairly demand to have the assurances on the point of eye-witnesses.

Further, we must not forget that the early converts had a second ground of belief, besides and beyond their conviction of the honesty and trustworthiness of those who came forward to preach the Gospel, declaring themselves witnesses of the "mighty works"[2] which Christ had wrought, and preëminently of his resurrection. These preachers persuaded, not merely by their evident truthfulness and sincerity, but by the miraculous powers which they wielded. There is good evidence that the ability to work miracles was not confined to the apostolic age. The bishops and others who pressed to see Ignatius on his way to martyrdom, "expected that he would communicate to them some spiritual gift." (48) Papias related various miracles as having happened in his own lifetime—among others that a dead man had been restored to life. (49) Justin Martyr declares very simply that in his day both men and women were found who possessed miraculous powers. (50) Quadratus, the Apologist, is mentioned by a writer of the second century as exercising them. (51) Irenæus speaks of miracles as still common in Gaul when he wrote, (52) which was nearly at the close of the second century. Tertullian, Theophilus of Antioch, and Minucius Felix, authors of about the same period, are witnesses to the continuance to their day of at least one class of miracles. (53) Thus the existence of these powers was contemporaneous with the great spread of the Gospel; and it accounts for that speedy conversion of

[1] 1 Cor. xv. 18. [2] Mark vi. 2.

thousands upon thousands — that rapid growth of the Church in all quarters — which would be otherwise so astonishing. The vast number of the early converts and the possession of miraculous powers — which are both asserted by the primitive writers (54) — have the relation of effect to cause, and lend countenance to one another. The evidence of the Catacombs, and the testimony of Pagans, confirm the truth of the representations made in the one case. Unless we hold miracles to be impossible, we cannot reasonably doubt them in the other.

But the possession of miraculous powers by those who spread the Gospel abroad in the first ages, would alone and by itself prove the divinity of the Christian Religion. God would not have given supernatural aid to persons engaged in propagating a lie, nor have assisted them to palm a deceit upon the world in His name. If then there be good evidence of this fact — if it be plain from the ecclesiastical writers that miracles were common in the Christian Church for above two centuries — we have herein an argument of an historical character, which is of no small weight and importance, *additional* to that arising from the mere confirmation by early uninspired writers of the Sacred Narrative. We find in their statements with respect to these contemporary facts, to which they are unexceptionable witnesses, a further evidence of the truth of the Religion whereof they were the ministers — a further proof that Christianity was not of man, but of God.

And here let me notice that in judging of the value which is to be attached to the testimony of the early Christians, we should constantly bear in mind that all in will, and most in fact, sealed that testimony with their blood. If civil justice acts upon a sound principle, when it assigns special weight to the depositions of those who have the prospect of immediate death before their eyes, Christians must be right to value highly the witness of the first ages. The early converts knew that they might at any time be called upon to undergo death for their religion. They preached and taught with the sword, the cross, the beasts, and the stake ever before their eyes. Most of those in eminent positions — and to this class belong almost all our witnesses — *were* martyred. Ignatius, Polycarp, Papias, Quadratus, Justin, Irenæus, certainly suffered death on account of their religion; and every early writer advocating Christianity, by the fact of his advocacy, braved the civil power, and rendered himself liable to a similar fate. When faith is a matter of life and death, men do not lightly take up with the first creed which happens to hit their fancy; nor do they place themselves openly in the ranks of a persecuted sect, unless they have well weighed the claims of the religion which it professes, and convinced themselves of its being the truth. It is clear that the early converts had means of ascertaining the historic accuracy of the Christian narrative very much beyond ourselves; they could examine and cross-question the witnesses — compare their several accounts — inquire how their statements were met by their adversaries — consult Heathen documents of the time — thoroughly and completely sift the evidence. To assume that they did not do so, when the issue was of such vast importance — when, in accepting the religion, they set their all upon the cast, embracing as their certain portion in this life, shame, contempt, and ignominy, the severance of family ties, exclusion from all festal gatherings, loss of friends, loss of worldly position, loss of character, — and looking forward to probable participation in the cruelest sufferings — the rack, the scourge, the pincing-irons, the cross, the stake, the ravening beasts of the amphitheatre — to assume this, is to deny them that average common sense and instinctive regard for their own interests which the mass of mankind possess in all times and countries — to look upon them as under the influence of an infatuation, such as cannot be shown to have at any time affected large bodies of civilized men. If we grant to the early converts an average amount of sense and intellect, we must accord to their witness all the weight that is due to those, who, having ample means of investigating a matter in which they are deeply concerned, have done so, and determined it in a particular way.

The inquiry in which we have been engaged here terminates. We have found that the historical Books of the New Testament are the productions of contemporaries and eye-witnesses — that two at least of those who wrote lives of Christ were his close and intimate friends, while the account of the early Church delivered in the Acts was written by a companion of the Apostles — that the truth of the narrative contained in these writings is evidenced by their sober, simple, and unexaggerated tone, and by their agreement, often undesigned, with each other — that it is further confirmed by the incidental allusions to it which are found in the speeches of the Apostles and in their epistolary correspondence with their converts — that its main facts are noticed, so far as it was to be expected that they would be noticed, by profane writers, while a comparison of its secondary or incidental facts with the civil history of the times, as otherwise known to us, reveals an agreement which is at once so multitudinous and so minute as to constitute, in the eyes of all those who are capable of weighing historical evidence, an overwhelming argument in proof of the authenticity of the whole story — that the narrative was accepted as simple truth, soon after it was published, in most parts of the civilized world, and not by the vulgar only, but by men of education and refinement, and of good worldly position—that it was received and believed, at the time when the truth of every part of it could be readily tested, by many hundreds of thousands, notwithstanding the prejudices of education, and the sacrifices which its acceptance involved—and finally, that the sincerity of these persons' belief was in many cases tested in the most searching of all possible ways, by persecutions of the cruelest kind, and triumphantly stood the test—so that the Church counted her Martyrs by thousands. We have further seen, that there is reason to believe that not only our Lord Himself and His Apostles, but many (if not most) of the first propagators of Christianity had the power of working miracles; and that this, and this only, will account for the remarkable facts, which none can deny, of the rapid spread of the Gospel and the vast numbers of the early converts. All this together—and it must be remembered that the evidence is *cumulative*—constitutes a body of proof such as is seldom producible with respect to any events belonging to remote times; and establishes beyond all reasonable doubt the truth of the Christian Story. In no single respect—if we except the fact that it is miraculous—has that story a mythic character. It is a single story, told without variation,(55) whereas myths are fluctuating and multiform; it is blended inextricably with the civil history of the times, which it every where represents with extraordinary accuracy, whereas myths distort or supersede civil history; it is full of prosaic detail, which myths studiously eschew; it abounds with practical instruction of the plainest and simplest kind, whereas myths teach by allegory. Even in its miraculous element, it stands to some extent in contrast with all known mythologies—where the marvellous has ever a predominant character of grotesqueness, which is entirely absent from the New Testament miracles.(56) Simple earnestness, fidelity, painstaking accuracy, pure love of truth, are the most patent characteristics of the New Testament writers, who evidently deal with facts, not with fancies, and are employed in relating a history, not in developing an idea. They write "that we may know the certainty of those things"[1] which were "most surely believed"[2] in their day. They bear record of what they have seen,[3] and assure us that their "testimony is true."[4] "That which they have heard, which they have seen with their eyes, which they have looked upon, which their hands have handled of the Word of Life, that was manifested unto them—that which they have seen and heard" declare they unto us.[5] And such as were not eye-witnesses, deliver only "that which they also received."[6] I know not how stronger words could have been used to preclude the notion of that plastic growing myth which Strauss conceives Christianity to have been in Apostolic times, and to convince us of its Historic character. And the declarations of the Sacred writers are confirmed by modern research. In spite of all the efforts of an "audacious criticism"—as ignorant as bold—the truth of the Sacred Narrative stands firm, the stronger for the shocks that it has resisted; "the boundless store of truth and life which for eighteen centuries has been the aliment of humanity" is not (as Rationalism boasts) "dissipated."(57) God is not "divested of his grace, or man of his dignity"—nor is the "tie between heaven and earth broken." The "foundation of God"—the "Everlasting Gospel"[7]—still "standeth sure"[8]—and every effort that is made to overthrow, does but more firmly establish it.

[1] Luke i. 4. [2] Ibid. verse 1. [3] John xix. 35.
[4] Ibid. xxi. 24. [5] 1 John i. 1–3. [6] 1 Cor. xv. 3.
[7] Rev. xiv. 6. [8] 2 Tim. ii. 19.

NOTES.

NOTES.

LECTURE I.

Note I., p. 26.

Herodotus, whose easy faith would naturally lead him to accept the Greek myths without difficulty, still makes a marked distinction between Mythology and History Proper. See b. iii. ch. 122, where the dominion of the sea of Polycrates is spoken of as something different in kind from that of the mythical Minos; and compare a somewhat similar distinction between the mythic and the historical in b. i. ch. 5, and again in b. ii. ch. 44, ad fin. A difference of the same kind seems to have been made by the Egyptian and Babylonian writers. See Lecture II., page 64.

Note II., p. 26.

This distinction was, I believe, first taken by George in his work *Mythus und Sage; Versuch einer wissenschaftlichen Entwicklung dieser Begriffe und ihres Verhältnisses zum christlichen Glauben.* It is adopted by Strauss, (*Leben Jesu, Einleitung,* § 10; vol. i. pp. 41–3, Chapman's Translation,) who thus distinguishes the two: "*Mythus* is the creation of a fact out of an idea; *legend* the seeing of an idea in a fact, or arising out of it." The myth is therefore pure and absolute imagination; the legend has a basis of fact, but amplifies, abridges, or modifies that basis at its pleasure. De Wette thus expresses the difference: "The myth is an idea in a vestment of facts; the legend contains facts pervaded and transformed by ideas." (*Einleitung in das alt. Test.* § 136, d.) Compare Professor Powell's *Third Series of Essays,* Essay iii. p. 340. "A myth is a doctrine expressed in a narrative form; an abstract moral or spiritual truth dramatized in action and personification, where the object is to enforce faith, not in the parable, but in the moral."

NOTE III., p. 26.

"The mission of the ancient prophets," says Gibbon, "of Moses and of Jesus, had been confirmed by many splendid prodigies; and Mahomet was repeatedly urged by the inhabitants of Mecca and Medina to produce a similar evidence of his divine legation; to call down from heaven the angel or the volume of his revelation, to create a garden in the desert, or to kindle a conflagration in the unbelieving city. As often as he is pressed by the demands of the Koreish, he involves himself in the *obscure* boast of vision and prophecy, appeals to the *internal* proofs of his doctrine, and shields himself behind the Providence of God, who refuses those signs and wonders that would depreciate the merit of faith, and aggravate the guilt of infidelity. But *the modest or angry tone of his apologies betrays his weakness and vexation;* and these passages of scandal establish beyond suspicion the integrity of the Koran. The votaries of Mahomet are more assured than himself of his miraculous gifts, and *their confidence and credulity increase as they are further removed from the time and place of his spiritual exploits.*" *Decline and Fall*, vol. v. ch. l. p. 210. Compare with this acknowledgment on the part of an enemy of Christianity, the similar statements of its defenders. (Butler, *Analogy*, Part II. ch. vii.; Paley, *Evidences*, Part II. ch. ix. § 3; White, *Bampton Lectures*, Sermon vi. p. 254; Forster, *Mahometanism Unveiled*, vol. i. p. 32; and Dr. Macbride, *Mohammedan Religion Explained*, pp. 28–9.) Ockley, a very unprejudiced writer, observes, that "when the impostor was called upon, as he often was, to work miracles in proof of his divine mission, he excused himself by various pretences, and appealed to the Koran as a standing miracle." (*Life of Mohammed*, pp. 65–6, Bohn's Ed.) He also remarks, that there was no proof of his visions or intercourse with angels beyond his own assertions; and that, on the occasion of the pretended night-journey to heaven, Ayesha testified that he did not leave his bed. (Ibid. p. 20, note.)

NOTE IV., p. 26.

See Butler's *Analogy*, Part II. ch. vii.; Paley's *Evidences*, Part III. ch. viii.; and Rev. R. Michell's Bampton Lectures, Lecture iv. pp. 124–129. Dr. Stanley tersely expresses the contrast between the

Christian and other religions in this respect, when he says of Christianity, that it "alone, of all religions, claims to be founded not on fancy or feeling, but on Fact and Truth." (*Sinai and Palestine*, ch. ii. p. 155.)

NOTE V., p. 27.

Butler's *Analogy*, Part II. ch. vii. p. 311.

NOTE VI., p. 28.

See Sir G. C. Lewis's *Inquiry into the Credibility of the Early Roman History*, vol. i. Introduction, p. 2.

NOTE VII., p. 28.

M. de Pouilly's *Dissertation sur l'incertitude et l'histoire des quatre premiers siècles de Rome*, which was published in the ninth volume of the *Mémoires de l'Académie des Inscriptions*, constitutes an era in the study of ancient history. Earlier scholars had doubted this or that narrative of an ancient author; but M. de Pouilly seems to have been the first to "lay down with clearness and accuracy the principles" by which the historic value of an author's accounts of early times is to be tested. His "Dissertation" was read in December, 1722; and a second Memoir on the same subject was furnished by him to the *Mémoires* soon afterwards, and forms a part of the same volume. (See Sir G. C. Lewis's *Inquiry*, vol. i. ch. i. p. 5, note 11.)

M. de Beaufort, who has generally been regarded as the founder of the modern Historical Criticism, did not publish his "*Dissertation sur l'incertitude des cinq premiers siècles de l'histoire Romaine*" till sixteen years after Pouilly, as this work first appeared at Utrecht in 1738. His merits are recognized to some extent by Niebuhr, (Hist. of Rome, vol. i. pref. of 1826, p. vii. E. T.; and Lectures on Roman History, vol. i. p. 148, E. T.)

NOTE VIII., p. 28.

Niebuhr's views are most fully developed in his "*Roman History*," (first published in 1811–1812, and afterwards reprinted with large additions and alterations in 1827–1832,) and in his *Lectures on the*

History of Rome, delivered at Bonn, and published in 1846. They also appear in many of his *Kleine Schriften*, and in his *Lectures on Ancient History*, delivered at Bonn in 1826, and again in 1829–1830, which were published after his decease by his son. Most of these works have received an English dress, and are well known to students.

Note IX., p. 28.

So early as 1817, Karl Otfried Müller, in a little tract, called *Æginetica*, gave promise of excellence as an historical critic. His *Orchomenus und die Minyer* soon followed, and established his reputation. He is perhaps best known in England by his *Dorians*, (published in 1824, and translated into English by Mr. H. Tufnell and Sir G. C. Lewis in 1830,) a work of great value, but not free from minor blemishes. (See Mr. Grote's *History of Greece*, vol. ii. p. 530, &c.)

Note X., p. 28.

Böckh is best known in England by his book on the *Public Economy of Athens*, (*Staatshaushaltung der Athener*,) published in Berlin in the year 1817, and translated into English in 1828, (London, Murray.) But his great work is the *Corpus Inscriptionum Græcarum*, in four large folio volumes, published at Berlin between 1825 and 1832. In this he shows himself an historical critic of the first order.

Note XI., p. 28.

I refer especially to Bishop Thirlwall, Mr. Grote, Colonel Mure, Mr. Merivale, and Sir G. C. Lewis. The name of Dr. Arnold should also be mentioned as that of one to whom historical criticism in England owes much.

Note XII. p. 29.

See Colonel Mure's *Remarks on Two Appendices to Mr. Grote's History of Greece*, (London, Longman, 1851;) and an excellent article in the Edinburgh Review for July, 1856, (No. 211, Art. I.,) in which the extreme conclusions of Sir G. C. Lewis on the subject of early Roman History are ably combated.

NOTE XIII., p. 30.

The subjoined extract from the correspondence of Niebuhr has been already given in the work of my immediate predecessor in the office of Bampton Lecturer, (see the notes to Mr. Mansel's *Lectures*, pp. 321–2;) but its importance is so great, that I cannot forbear to cite it here. "In my opinion," wrote Niebuhr in the year 1818, "he is not a Protestant Christian who does not receive the historical facts of Christ's early life, in their literal acceptation, with all their miracles, as equally authentic with any event recorded in history, and whose belief in them is not as firm and tranquil as his belief in the latter; who has not the most absolute faith in the articles of the Apostles' Creed, taken in their grammatical sense; who does not consider every doctrine and every precept of the New Testament as undoubted divine revelation, in the sense of the Christians of the first century, who knew nothing of a Theopneustia. Moreover, a Christianity after the fashion of the modern philosophers and pantheists, without a personal God, without immortality, without human individuality, without historical faith, is no Christianity at all to me; though it may be a very intellectual, very ingenious philosophy. I have often said that I do not know what to do with a metaphysical God, and that I will have none but the God of the Bible, who is heart to heart with us."[1] The *general* orthodoxy of Niebuhr with respect to the Old Testament History is plain from his *Lectures on Ancient History*, (vol. i. p. 20, 37, 128, 132, &c.;) though, as will be noticed hereafter, he is not always quite consistent on the point. See below, Notes XXXIV. and XXXVI.

NOTE XIV., p. 31.

Eichhorn, in his examination of the Wolfenbüttel Fragments, (*Recension der übrigen, noch ungedruckten Werke des Wolfenbüttlischen Fragmentisten*, in Eichhorn's *Allgemeiner Bibliothek* for 1787, vol. i. parts i. and ii.,) was, I believe, the first to draw this comparison. "Divine interpositions," he argued, "must be alike admitted, or alike denied, in the primitive histories of all people. It was the practice of all

[1] *Life and Letters of B. G. Niebuhr*, vol. ii. p. 123. Compare Letter ccxxxi. vol. ii. pp. 103–5, and Letter cccxxix. vol. ii. p. 315.

nations, of the Grecians as well as the Orientals, to refer every unexpected or inexplicable occurrence immediately to the Deity. The sages of antiquity lived in continual communion with superior intelligences. Whilst these representations were commonly understood, in reference to the Hebrew legends, verbally and literally, it had been customary to explain similar representations in the Pagan histories by presupposing either deception and gross falsehood, or the misinterpretation and corruption of tradition. But justice evidently required that Hebrew and Pagan history should be treated in the same way." See the summary of Eichhorn's views and reasonings in Strauss's *Leben Jesu*, § 6, (vol. i. pp. 15–18, E. T.) The views thus broached were further carried out by Gabler, Schelling, and Bauer. The last-named author remarked, that "the earliest records of all nations were mythical: why should the writings of the Hebrews form a solitary exception?—whereas in point of fact a cursory glance at their sacred books proved that they also contain mythical elements." See his *Hebraische Mythologie des alten und neuen Testaments*, published in 1820.

Note XV., p. 31.

See the works above cited, and compare an article in Bertholdt's *Kritische Journal*, vol. v. § 235. See also Theodore Parker's De Wette, vol. ii. p. 198.

Note XVI., p. 31.

So Vatke (*Religion des Alten Testamentes*, § 23, p. 289 et seqq.) and De Wette, *Archäologie*, § 30–34. Baron Bunsen takes the same view. See below, Notes XXXIX. and XLIV.

Note XVII., p. 31.

Vatke (l. s. c.) regards the "significant names" of Saul, David, and Solomon, as proof of the legendary character which attaches to the Books of Samuel. Von Bohlen argues similarly with respect to the ancestors of Abraham. (*Alte Indien*, p. 155.)

Note XVIII., p. 31.

Semler, towards the close of the last century, pronounced the histories of Samson and Esther to be myths; Eichhorn, early in the present, assigned the same character to the Mosaic accounts of the Creation and the Fall. (See Strauss's Introduction; *Leben Jesu*, vol. i. pp. 21 and 24, E. T.)

Note XIX. p. 32.

"Tradition," says De Wette, "is uncritical and partial; its tendency is not historical, but rather patriotic and poetical. And since the patriotic sentiment is gratified by all that flatters national pride, the more splendid, the more honorable, the more wonderful the narrative, the more acceptable it is; and *where tradition has left any blanks, imagination at once steps in and fills them up*. And since," he continues, "a great part of the historical books of the Old Testament bears this stamp, it has hitherto been believed possible," &c. (*Kritik der Israelitischen Geschichte*, Einleitung, § 10.) Compare Vater's *Abhandlung über Moses und die Verfasser des Pentateuchs* in the third volume of his *Comment. über den Pentateuch*, § 660.

Note XX., p. 32.

This was the aim of the School, called technically Rationalists, in Germany, of which Eichhorn and Paulus were the chief leaders. See Eichhorn's *Einleitung in das Alte Testament*, and Paulus's *Commentar über das neue Testament*, and also his *Leben Jesu*, in which his views are more fully developed. More recently Ewald, in his *Geschichte Volkes Israels*, has composed on the same principle a complete history of the Jewish people.

Note XXI., p. 32.

See Strauss, *Leben Jesu*, § 8, vol. i. p. 29, E. T. This same view was taken by De Wette, Krug, Gabler, Horst, and others.

Note XXII., p. 32.

An anonymous writer in Bertholdt's *Journal* (vol. v. § 235) objects to the rationalistic method of Paulus, that it "evaporates all sacredness and divinity from the Scriptures;" while the mythical view, of which he is an advocate, "leaves the substance of the narrative unassailed," and "accepts the whole, not indeed as true history, but as a sacred legend." Strauss evidently approves of this reasoning. (*Leben Jesu*, § 8, vol. i. p. 32, E. T.)

Note XXIII., p. 32.

Strauss, *Leben Jesu*, Einleitung, § 4. The weakness of this argument from authority is indeed allowed by Strauss himself, who admits that Origen "does not speak out freely," (p. 9,) and that "his *rule* was to retain the literal together with the allegorical sense," (p. 6) — a rule which he only broke in "a few instances," (p. 12.) He also allows that "after Origen, that kind of allegory only which left the historical sense unimpaired was retained in the Church; and where, subsequently, a giving up of the verbal meaning is spoken of, this refers merely to a trope or simile," (p. 9, note 14.) It is doubtful whether Origen himself ever really gave up the literal and historical sense. That the heretics who sheltered themselves under his name (Origenists) did so is certain; but they are accused of interpolating his writings. (See Mosheim's *Ecclesiastical History*, b. i. ch. iii., note [t] ad fin. vol. i. p. 288, E. T.)

Since the above was in type, I have observed that Professor Powell, relying (as it would seem) on the bold assertions of the infidel Woolston,[1] taxes not Origen only, but the Fathers generally, with an abandonment of the historical sense of Scripture. "The idea," he says, "of the mythic origin of the Gospel narrative had confessedly been applied by some writers, as Rosenmüller and Anton, to certain portions of the Gospels; and so limited, *was acknowledged to possess the sanction of the Fathers*." (*Third Series of Essays*, Essay iii. p. 338.) But the opposite view of Strauss is far more consonant with the facts. The whole subject was elaborately, and, I believe, honestly discussed in one of the celebrated *Tracts for the Times*, (Tract 89, § 3; vol. vi. pp. 38–70;) and the Fathers generally were completely exonerated from the false charge so commonly preferred against them.

Note XXIV., p. 32.

The more recent writers of the mythical School, as De Wette, Strauss, and Theodore Parker, assume that the mythological character of great part of the Old Testament history is fully established. (See De Wette's *Einleitung in das Alt. Test.* § 136; Strauss, *Leben Jesu*, Einleitung, § 9, et seqq.; Theodore Parker's Enlarged Transla-

1 *Six Discourses on the Miracles of our Saviour*, published in 1727, 1728, and 1729.

tion of De Wette, vol. ii., pp. 23–7, et passim.) German orthodox writers bear striking witness to the effect which the repeated attacks on the historical character of the Old Testament narrative have had upon the popular belief in their country. "If," says Keil, "the scientific theology of the Evangelical Church is anxious to strengthen its foundations again, it must force rationalism away from the Old Testament, where till the present time it has planted its foot so firmly, that many an acute theologian has doubted whether it is possible to rescue again the *fides humana et divina* of the historical writings of the ancient covenant." (*Commentar über das Buch Josua*, Vorwort, p. ii. "Will daher die wissenschaftliche Theologie der evangelischen Kirche sich wieder fest gründen, so muss sie den Rationalismus aus dem Alten Testamente verdrängen, in welchem derselbe bis jetzt so festen Fuss gefasst hat, dass nicht wenige tüchtige Theologen daran verzweifeln, die *fides humana et divina* der historischen Schriften des altes Bundes noch retten zu können.") And he complains that the Rationalistic "mode of treating the Old Testament History has been very disadvantageous to the believing theological science, *inasmuch as it can now find no objective ground or stand-point free from uncertainty;*" (dass sie keinen objectiv sichern Grund und Standpunkt gewinnen kann. Ibid. l. c.)

NOTE XXV., p. 32.

Strauss evidently feels this difficulty, (*Leben Jesu*, Einleitung, § 13; vol. i. p. 64, E. T.) He endeavors to meet it by suggesting that "the sun does not shine on all parts of the earth at once. There was enlightenment in Italy and Greece about the time of the establishment of Christianity, but none in the remote Judæa, where the real nature of history had never even been rightly apprehended." In this there is, no doubt, some truth; but Strauss forgets that, though Judæa was the scene of the Gospel story, the Evangelical writings were composed chiefly in Greece and Italy; and he omits to notice, that being written in Greek — the literary language of the time — they addressed themselves to the enlightened circles of Athens, Corinth, Ephesus, and Rome itself, far more than to the rude provincials of Palestine. The miracles, too, by which Christianity was spread, were not alone those which occurred in Judæa; many had been wrought in Rome and in the various cities of Greece; where they challenged the attention of the most civilized and enlightened classes. In Judæa itself, if the Jews generally were not "enlightened," in the modern sense of the word, the Roman Governors, and their courts, were. And among the Jews, it must be remembered, the sect which had most power was that of the Sadducees — sceptics and materialists.

Note XXVI., p. 32.

The subjoined passage from Strauss seems to show something of this feeling: "The results of the inquiry which we have now brought to a close, have apparently annihilated the greatest and most valuable part of that which the Christian has been wont to believe concerning his Saviour Jesus, have uprooted all the animating motives which he has gathered from his faith, and withered all his consolations. The boundless store of truth and life which for eighteen centuries has been the aliment of humanity, seems irretrievably dissipated; the most sublime levelled with the dust, God divested of his grace, man of his dignity, and the tie between Heaven and Earth broken. *Piety turns away with horror from so fearful an act of desecration*, and, strong in the impregnable self-evidence of its faith, pronounces that, let an audacious criticism attempt what it will, all which the Scriptures declare and the Church believes of Christ, will still subsist as eternal truth, nor needs one iota of it to be renounced." (*Leben Jesu*, § 144, vol. iii. p. 396, E. T.)

Note XXVII., p. 33.

See Bauer's *Hebraische Mythologie des alten und neuen Testaments*, Erste Theil, Einleitung, § 3, with Gabler's criticism of it in his *Journal für auserlesene theolog. Literatur*, ii. 1, § 58. Compare Strauss, *Leben Jesu*, §§ 33–43.

Note XXVIII., p. 33.

Eichhorn, *Einleitung in das neue Testament*, § 422; Theile, *Zur Biographie Jesu*, § 23.

Note XXIX., p. 33.

See the account which Strauss gives of the "Development of the Mythical point of view," in his *Leben Jesu*, §§ 9–11. "The mythus," he observes, "when once admitted into the New Testament, was long detained at the threshold, namely, the history of the infancy of Jesus, every farther advance being contested. Ammon, the anonymous E. F.

in Henke's Magazine, and others, maintained a marked distinction between the historical worth of the narratives of the public life and those of the infancy of Jesus. . . . Soon, however, some of the theologians who had conceded the commencement of the history to the province of *mythus*, perceived that the conclusion, the history of the ascension, must likewise be regarded as mythical. Thus the two extremities were cut off by the pruning-knife of criticism," (§ 11, pp. 44–5.) Finally the essential body of the history was assailed, and the Gospels — especially the first three — were "found to contain a continually increasing number of *mythi* and mythical embellishments." (§ 9, p. 86.)

NOTE XXX., p. 33.

Leben Jesu, § 151; vol. iii. p. 437, E. T.

NOTE XXXI., p. 34.

Ibid. pp. 437–8.

NOTE XXXII., p. 34.

Eth. Nic. vi. 7, § 4: "For it is absurd that any one should regard the science of politics, or prudence, as the most important, unless man is the noblest being in the universe."

NOTE XXXIII., p. 34.

See above, Note XIII.

NOTE XXXIV., p. 35.

Vorträge über alte Geschichte, vol. i. pp. 158–9. "Dass das Buch Esther *nicht als ein historisches* zu betrachten sei, davon bin ich überzeugt, und ich stehe nicht im Mindesten an dies hiermit öffentlich auszusprechen; Viele sind derselben Meinung. Schon die Kirchenväter haben sie daran geplagt, und der heilige Hieronymus, wie er klar andeutet, in der grössten Verlegenheit befunden, wenn er es als historisch betrachten wollte. Gegenwärtig wird Niemand die Geschichte in Buche Judith fur historisch ansehen, und weder Origenes noch Hieronymus haben dies gethan; *eben so verhält es sich mit dem Buche Esther; es ist ein Gedicht über diese verhältnisse.*"

NOTE XXXV., p. 35.

On the weight of the external testimonies to the authenticity of the Book of Esther, see Lecture V., Note LXIX.

NOTE XXXVI., p. 36.

There is reason to suspect that Niebuhr would have surrendered the Book of Daniel, as well as the Book of Esther, to the assailants of Scripture, since he nowhere refers to it as an historical document in his Lectures. Such reference would have been natural in several places.

NOTE XXXVII., p. 37.

See M. Bunsen's *Philosophy of Universal History*, vol. i., pp. 190–191, E. T.

NOTE XXXVIII., p. 37.

See the same author's *Egypt*, vol. i., p. 182, E. T.

NOTE XXXIX., p. 37.

Ibid. p. 173.

NOTE XL., p. 37.

Ibid. p. 174.

NOTE XLI., p. 37.

Ibid. p. 173.

NOTE XLII., p. 37.

Ibid. p. 181.

NOTE XLIII., p. 37.

Ibid. p. 180.

NOTE XLIV. p. 38.

Ibid. p. 179; and compare p. 170.

NOTE XLV., p. 38.

German scepticism commenced with the school called the *Naturalists*, who undertook to resolve all the Scripture miracles into natural occurrences. The *mythical* School, which soon followed, very effectually demolished the *natural* theory, and clearly demonstrated its "unnaturalness." (See Strauss, *Leben Jesu*, Einleitung, § 9 and § 12.) The mythical writers themselves oppose one another. Strauss frequently condemns the explanations of Gabler and Weisse; and Theodore Parker often argues against De Wette. That the Scripture History is a collection of myths, all of them are agreed; when and how the myths grew up, at what time they took a written form, when they came into their present shape, what amount of fact they have as their basis, on these and all similar points, it is difficult to find two of them who hold the same opinion. (See below, Lecture II., Note XXXVII.)

NOTE XLVI., p. 39.

"Historical evidence," says Sir G. C. Lewis, "like judicial evidence, is founded on the testimony of credible witnesses. Unless these witnesses had personal and immediate perception of the facts which they report, unless they saw and heard what they undertake to relate as having happened, their evidence is not entitled to credit. As all original witnesses must be contemporary with the events which they attest, it is a necessary condition for the credibility of a witness that he be a contemporary; though a contemporary is not necessarily a credible witness. Unless therefore an historical account can be traced, by probable proof, to the testimony of contemporaries, the first condition of historical credibility fails." (*Credibility of Early Roman History*, Introduction, vol. i. p. 16.) Allowing for a little rhetorical overstating of the case, this is a just estimate of the *primary* value of the testimony borne by contemporaries and eye-witnesses.

NOTE XLVII., p. 39.

It is evident that an historian can rarely have witnessed one half the events which he puts on record. Even writers of commentaries, like Cæsar and Xenophon, record many facts which they had not seen, and which they knew only by information from others. Ordinary historians, who have not had the advantage of playing the chief part in the events which they relate, are still more indebted to inquiry. Hence History seems to have received its name, (ἱστορία.) When the inquiry appears to have been carefully conducted, and the judgment of the writer seems sound, we give very nearly as full credence to his statements founded upon inquiry, as to those of an eye-witness. We trust Thucydides almost as implicitly as Xenophon, and Tacitus almost as entirely as Cæsar. Sir G. C. Lewis allows that accounts . . . derived, directly *or indirectly*, from the reports of original witnesses . . . may be considered as presumptively entitled to credit." (*Credibility*, &c., ch. ii. § 1; vol. i. p. 19. Compare p. 25, and pp. 81–2; and see also his *Methods of Observation and Reasoning in Politics*, ch. vii. § 2; vol. i. pp. 181–5.)

NOTE XLVIII., p. 40.

The tendency of the modern Historical Criticism has been to diminish greatly the value formerly attached to this sort of evidence. Mr. Grote in some places seems to deny it all weight. (*History of Greece*, vol. i. pp. 572–577.) Practically, however, as Col. Mure has shown, (*Remarks on Two Appendices*, &c., pp. 3–6,) he admits it as sufficiently establishing a number of very important facts. Sir G. C. Lewis regards oral tradition as a tolerably safe guide for the general outline of a nation's history "for a period reaching back nearly 150 years." (*Credibility*, &c., ch. iv. § 2; vol. i. p. 100.) Special circumstances might, he thinks, give to an event a still longer hold on the popular memory. Among such special circumstances he notices "commemorative festivals, and other periodical observances," as in certain cases serving to perpetuate a true tradition of a national event, (ibid. p. 101.)

NOTE XLIX., p. 40.

The modern historical critics have not laid much stress on this head of evidence in their discussions of the abstract principles of their science; but practically they often show their sense of its importance. Thus Niebuhr urges against the theory of the Etruscans being colonists from Lydia, the fact that it had no Lydian tradition to rest upon. (*History of Rome*, vol. i. p. 109, E. T.) Mr. Kenrick and others regard it as decisive of the question, whether the Phœnicians migrated from the Persian Gulf, that there was a double tradition in its favor, (Kenrick's *Phœnicia*, ch. iii. p. 46, et seqq.,) both the Phœnicians themselves and the inhabitants of the islands lying in the Gulf agreeing as to the fact of the emigration. The ground of the high value of such evidence lies in the extreme improbability of an accidental harmony, and in the impossibility of collusion.

NOTE L., p. 41.

Ezra i. 1; v. 17; vi. 1–12. Esther ii. 23; iii. 14; vi. 1.

NOTE LI., p. 42.

Analogy, Part II. ch. vii. p. 329.

NOTE LII., p. 42.

Let it be ten to one that a certain fact is true upon the testimony of one witness, and likewise ten to one that the same fact is true upon the evidence of another, then it is not twenty to one that the fact is true on the evidence of both, but 130 to one. And the evidence to the same point of a third independent witness of equal credibility with the others would raise the probability to 1330 to one.

NOTE LIII., p. 42.

See Strauss, *Leben Jesu*, § 13, (vol. i. p. 64, E. T.) For a complete refutation of this view — "the shallowest and crudest of all the assumptions of unbelief"[1] — see the *Bampton Lectures* of my predecessor, Lecture VI. pp. 170–181, [Am. Ed.]

NOTE LIV., p. 43.

See Bauer's *Hebraische Mythologie des Alten und Neuen Testaments*, quoted by Strauss, *Leben Jesu*, § 8, (vol. i. p. 25, E. T.)

NOTE LV., p. 44.

Ecclesiastical Polity, Book I., ch. 3, § 4. "Those things which Nature is said to do, are by Divine art performed, using nature as an instrument; nor is there any such art or knowledge divine in nature herself working, but only in the Guide of Nature's work. . . . Unto us there is one only guide of all agents natural, and He both the Creator and *Worker of all in all*, alone to be blessed, adored, and honored by all forever." Compare Dean Trench, *Notes on the Miracles of our Lord*, ch. ii. pp. 9–10.

1 Mansel's *Bampton Lectures*, Lecture VI. p. 177, [Am. Ed.]

Note LVI., p. 45.

Plato's Phædo, § 46–7. "Now when I once heard a person reading from a book, as he said, of Anaxagoras, and affirming that there is a *mind* which disposes all things, and is the cause of all, I was delighted with this view of the cause of things; and it commended itself to my judgment, &c. Indeed, my expectations were raised to the highest pitch; and having with great pains obtained the book, I improved the very first opportunity to read it, that I might know as soon as possible the best and the worst. But my wonderful expectations, O my friend, met with a woful disappointment; for as I read on I saw that the man made no mention of this *mind*, even when he was assigning certain causes for the disposition of things, but assigned as causes air, and ether, and water, and many other absurd things." The "*Vestiges of Creation*," and other works of the same stamp, are the modern counterparts of these Anaxagorean treatises.

Note LVII., p. 46.

On the latter subject see Mr. J. H. Newman's *Essay* prefixed to a portion of Fleury's Ecclesiastical History, and also published in a separate form, (Oxford, Parker, 1843;) and compare the views of Dodwell, (*Dissertat. in Irenæum*, ii. 28, et seqq.,) Burton, (*Ecclesiastical History of the First Three Centuries*, vol. ii. pp. 5, 230–3, &c.,) and Kaye (*Tertullian*, p. 104; *Justin Martyr*, p. 121.) On the supernatural element in Heathenism, see Mr. Newman's *Arians*, (ch. i. § 3, pp. 87–91;) and compare Trench, *Notes on the Miracles*, ch. iii. pp. 21–3; Alford's *Greek Testament*, vol. ii. p. 164; Huc's *Voyage dans la Tartarie*, vol. i. pp. 295–6; and Hävernick, *Handbuch der Historisch-kritischen Einleitung in das Alte Testament*, § 23, p. 244, E. T.

LECTURE II.

NOTE I., p. 51.

See Horne's *Introduction to the Critical Study and Knowledge of Holy Scriptures*, ch. ii. § 1; vol. i pp. 51–6, sixth edition; Graves, *Lectures on the Pentateuch*, Lecture I.; Hävernick, *Handbuch der Historisch-kritischen Einleitung in das Alte Testament*, vol. i. ch. ii. § 108; Stuart's *Defence of the Old Testament Canon*, § 3, p. 42, &c. This fact is not denied by those who oppose the Mosaic authorship. (See De Wette's *Einleitung in das Alte Testament*, § 163 and § 164, pp. 203–5.)

NOTE II., p. 51.

The history of the controversy concerning the authorship of the Iliad will illustrate what is stated in the text. It cannot but be allowed that arguments of very considerable weight have been adduced by Wolf and others in disproof of the Homeric authorship. Yet the opposite belief maintains its ground in spite of them, and is regarded by the latest Critic as fully and finally established. (See Gladstone's *Homer and the Homeric Age*, vol. i. pp. 3, 4.) The reason is, that the opposing arguments, though strong, are pronounced on the whole *not strong enough to overcome the force of a unanimous tradition.*

NOTE III., p. 51.

For instance, De Wette repeats the old objection of Spinoza, that the author of the Pentateuch cannot be Moses, since he uses the expression "beyond Jordan" as a dweller in Palestine would, whereas Moses never entered Palestine. (*Einleitung*, &c., § 147, *a* 4.) But all tolerable Hebraists are aware that the term בְּעֵבֶר is ambiguous, and may mean on either side of a river. Buxtorf translates it, "*cis, ultra,* trans." (*Lexicon Hebraicum et Chaldaicum*, p. 527, ad voc. עֵבֶר.) So Gesenius and others. Even De Wette admits *in a note* that the expression has the two senses; but the objection maintains its place in his text notwithstanding.

De Wette's translator and commentator, Mr. Theodore Parker, repeats the objection, and amplifies it. He remarks, that in the Pentateuch the expression "beyond Jordan" means "on the east side of that river," while "this side Jordan" means "to the west of that river." (Vol. ii. p. 41.) Apparently he is not aware that in the original it is one and the same expression (בְּעֵבֶר) which has been rendered in the two different ways.

NOTE IV., p. 51.

Examples of interpolations, or insertions into the text by another hand, are, I think, the following: Gen. xxxvi. 31–9; Exod. xvi. 35–6, and perhaps Deut. iii. 14.) (See Graves, *Lectures on the Pentateuch*, vol. i. p. 342, pp. 345–6, and p. 349.) The first of these cannot have been, and the others probably were not, written by Moses. They are supplementary notes of a similar character to the supplementary chapter of Deuteronomy, (ch. xxxiv.,) in which every commentator recognizes an addition to the original document. (Graves, vol. i. pp. 349, 350; Hävernick, *Handbuch*, &c., § 134, sub fin. vol. i. p. 549; Horne's *Introduction*, &c., vol. i. p. 62; &c.)

The other passages, which have been regarded as interpolations, such as Gen. xiii. 8, xxii. 14; Deut. ii. 10–12, 20–23, iii. 9, 11, &c., may (I think) have all been written by Moses. Hävernick (l. s. c.) maintains, that even the passages mentioned in the last paragraph are from the pen of the Lawgiver, and holds that the Pentateuch is altogether "free from interpolation" — the last chapter of Deuteronomy alone being from another hand, and constituting an Appendix to the Pentateuch, or even an Introduction to Joshua. He seems to think that if interpolation be once admitted, all is rendered uncertain. "From interpolation to revision," he says, "is so short a step, especially if we conceive of the latter according to the sense and spirit of the East, that we should find it impossible to oppose any barrier to the latter supposition, if the former could be proved." But it is our business to be guided not by the exigencies of controversy, but by the demands of Reason and Truth. It would be strange if in a book as old as the Pentateuch there were not some interpolations. And all reasonable men will readily see that a few interpolations, whether made by authority, or glosses which have crept in from the margin, do not in the slightest degree affect the genuineness of the work as a whole. (See Horne's *Introduction*, vol. i. ch. ii. p. 62; Graves's *Lectures*, Appendix, § 1, p. 346, and pp. 355–361; Rosenmüller's *Prolegomena*,

p. 36; Eichhorn's *Einleitung in das Alte Testament*, § 434, &c.; Jahn's *Einleitung und Beiträge zur Vertheid. der Aechtheit des Pentateuchs*, p. 60; and Fritzsche's *Prufung der Gründe*, &c., p. 135.)

NOTE V., p. 51.

De Wette, *Einleitung*, § 145; pp. 168, 16–9.

NOTE VI., p. 51.

Ibid. § 163, p. 204. "Against the authorship by Moses the entire analogy of the language and literary history of the Hebrews bears witness. . . . It is folly to suppose that one man could have created in advance the epic-historical, the rhetorical, and the poetical styles in their fullest compass, and also these three departments of Hebrew literature in their contents and spirit, and have left nothing but imitation to all succeeding writers."

NOTE VII., p. 51.

Hartmann, *Historisch-kritische Forschungen über d. Bildung, &c. des Pentateuchs*, p. 545, et alibi. Norton, *Genuineness of the Gospels*, vol. ii. p. 444, second edition. The objection is as old as Spinoza. (See his *Tractatus Theologico-Politicus*, ch. viii. p. 154.)

NOTE VIII., p. 51.

De Wette, *Einleitung*, § 144, p. 167.

NOTE IX., p. 52.

Hartmann, l. s. c. So Spinoza, *Tractatus Theologico-Politicus*, ch. viii. pp. 154–5.

NOTE X., p. 52.

Leben Jesu, Einleitung, § 13, vol. i. p. 60, E. T. The genuineness of the First Epistle to the Corinthians, which contains so many references to miracles,[1] is specially acknowledged, § 140; vol. vii. p. 367, E. T.

[1] See especially ch. xii. verses 9, 10, and 28–30, ch. xiv. 2, 5, 6, 13, &c., and ch. xv. 3.

NOTE XI., p. 52.

Strauss allows, though with evident reluctance, that the Acts are, or at least may be, the work of St. Luke (*Leben Jesu*, § 13, vol. i. p. 60, E. T.) He regards it as "not a little remarkable, that the author makes no distinct allusion to his connection with the most distinguished of the Apostles." It is certainly very remarkable how completely St. Luke keeps himself, and his own actions, in the background, while engaged in recording the history of events in which he himself took part. But this reticence is a feature of that humility which characterizes the Sacred Writers generally.

NOTE XII., p. 52.

It was the existence of considerable remains of Greek literature, earlier in date than the latter half of the sixth century B. C., and an exact acquaintance with it, which enabled Bentley so thoroughly to establish the spuriousness of the alleged Epistles of Phalaris. In the Homeric controversy, on the other hand, the want of any contemporary literature has rendered the argument, that a single man in such early times could not possibly have composed both the Iliad and the Odyssey, so weak and inconclusive that the opposite opinion still maintains its ground, and on the whole seems tending to become the established one. (See above, Note II.)

NOTE XIII., p. 52.

The only remains of ancient literature which are even supposed to reach as high as the age of Moses, are certain Hieratic Papyri found in Egypt, belonging to the nineteenth or even to earlier dynasties. Two of these have been translated by the Vicomte de Rougé,[1] and several others by the Rev. J. D. Heath.[2] But it is very doubtful whether these translations give much real insight into the originals. As Mr. Goodwin observes, (*Cambridge Essays*, 1858, p. 229,) "Egyptian philology is yet in its infancy. Champollion got little farther than the accidence of the language; and since his time not much has been done

[1] See the *Révue Archéologique* for May 1852, and the *Révue Contemporaine* for 1856.

[2] *The Exodus Papyri*, London, 1855.

in the investigation of the syntax. . . . With an incomplete knowledge of the syntax, and a slender vocabulary, *translation becomes guesswork*, and the misconception of a single word or phrase may completely confound the sense." Hence Mr. Goodwin and Mr. Heath often differ as to the entire subject and bearing of a document. (See Mr. Goodwin's *Essay*, pp. 249, 259, 261, &c.)

NOTE XIV., p. 53.

The antiquity of the diction of the Pentateuch has been denied by some critics,[1] among others by Gesenius. (See his *Geschichte der Hebräischen Sprache und Schrift*, § 8.) But Jahn seems to have established the point beyond any real controversy. (See Jahn's contributions to Bengel's *Archiv.*, vol. ii. p. 578, et seqq.; vol. iii. p. 168, et seqq. Compare Fritzsche, *Prufung der Gründe*, &c., p. 104, et seqq.; and see also Marsh's *Authenticity of the Five Books of Moses*, p. 6, et seqq.; and Stuart's *History and Defence of the Old Testament Canon*, pp. 12–13.) At least De Wette, writing after both Jahn and Gesenius, is constrained to admit that archaisms exist in considerable number, and has to account for them by supposing that they were adopted from the ancient documents of which the Compiler, who lived later than Solomon, made use. (*Einleitung*, § 157. See also § 163, where he allows that the *linguistic*, as distinct from the *literary* argument, against the Mosaic authorship, is weak.)

NOTE XV., p. 53.

This is abundantly shown by Hävernich, (*Handbuch*, &c., § 136; pp. 554–564.)

NOTE XVI., p. 53.

See Lecture III., pp. 80 and 81.

NOTE XVII., p. 53.

Mr. Norton is the writer who in recent times has urged this point with the greatest distinctness, and has given it the most prominent

[1] Vater, *Abhandlung über Moses*, &c., § 393; Norton, *Authenticity of the Gospels*, vol. ii. pp. 441, 442.

position. In his section, headed "Some general considerations respecting the Authorship of the Pentateuch," he begins his argument against the genuineness with this objection. Moses, he says, lived probably in the fifteenth century before Christ; certainly not much later. "*There is no satisfactory evidence that alphabetical writing was known at this time.* If known to others, it is *improbable that it was known to the Hebrews. They could not, during their residence in Egypt, have learnt alphabetical writing from the Egyptians;* for the mode of representing ideas to the eye, which the Egyptians employed till a period long subsequent, was widely(?) different from the alphabetical writing of the Hebrews. If they were acquainted with the art, they must have brought it with them into the country. But we can hardly suppose that it was invented, or acquired except by tradition, in the family of Isaac, or in that of Jacob before his residence in Egypt, engaged as they both were in agriculture and the care of cattle. We must then go back to Abraham at least for what traditionary knowledge of it his descendants in Egypt may be supposed to have possessed. But *it would be idle to argue against the supposition that alphabetical writing was known in the time of Abraham.*" [1]

That writing was unknown to the Hebrews till the time of the Judges, was, at one period of their lives, maintained by Gesenius and De Wette. (See Gesenius, *Geschichte der Hebräischen Sprache und Schrift*, § 140, et seqq., and De Wette's *Archäologie*, § 277.) Both, however, saw reason to change their opinion, and admitted subsequently that it must have dated at least from Moses. See Gesenius' *Hebrew Grammar*, Excursus I. p. 290, (English Translation, 13th edition,) and De Wette's *Einleitung*, § 12, p. 13. The bulk of modern German critics, whether rationalist or orthodox, acquiesce in this latter opinion. See Ewald, *Geschichte Volkes Israel*, pp. 64–69, Von Lengerke, *Känaan*, p. xxxv., Hävernick, *Einleitung in das Alte Testament*, § 44, &c.; and compare the American writer, Stuart, *Old Testament Canon*, § 3, pp. 40, 41.

NOTE XVIII., p. 53.

See the statements of Sir Gardner Wilkinson in the author's *Herodotus*, vol. ii. p. 311, and pp. 43–4. The date assigned to the fourth dynasty rests upon the same authority.

[1] *Genuineness of the Gospels*, vol. ii., Appendix, Note D., § 3; pp. 439–441.

NOTE XIX., p. 53.

Sir Henry Rawlinson regards the earliest inscribed bricks in the Babylonian series as dating from about B. C. 2200. (See the author's *Herodotus*, vol. i. pp. 435 and 440.)

NOTE XX., p. 53.

See Wilkinson's statements on this subject in the author's *Herodotus*, vol. i. pp. 306, 321, &c. He regards the hieratic character as having come into use "at least as early as the 9th dynasty," (p. 306,) which he places about B. C. 2240. A considerable number of hieratic papyri belonging to the 19th dynasty, and one or two of a still earlier date, are now in the British Museum. (See *Cambridge Essays* for 1858, pp. 229, 230.)

Some writers urge, that the Jews could not have learnt *alphabetic* writing from the Egyptians, since "the mode of representing ideas to the eye, which the Egyptians employed till a period long subsequent, was *widely different* from the alphabetical writing of the Hebrews." (Norton, l. s. c. Compare Hävernick, *Einleitung*, § 42–43.) But the difference was really not very great. It is a mistake to suppose that the Egyptian writing was, except to a small extent, symbolical. Both in the hieroglyphic and the hieratic, as a general rule, *the words are spelt phonetically first*, and are then followed by a symbol or symbols. (See Mr. Goodwin's Essay, p. 227, and compare Wilkinson, *Herodotus*, vol. ii. p. 317.)

NOTE XXI., p. 53.

Ur, or Hur (אוּר), the modern *Mugheir*, has furnished some of the most ancient of the Babylonian inscriptions. (See the author's *Herodotus*, vol. i. p. 435; and compare Loftus's *Chaldæa and Susiana*, ch. xii. p. 130.) It seems to have been the primeval capital of Chaldæa. The inscriptions, which are either on bricks or on clay cylinders, and which are somewhat rudely executed, have been assigned to about the 22d century before Christ, (see the *Herodotus*, vol. i. p. 440,) which is at least three centuries before Abraham.

Attempts have sometimes been made to determine the questions, whence exactly and when exactly the Hebrews obtained their alphabetic system. (See Hävernick's *Einleitung*, § 44.) It is considerably different both from that of Egypt and that of Babylon, while it is almost identical with that of Phœnicia; whence it is inferred that the Hebrews learnt it from the Phœnicians. Of this, however, there is no evidence, since the Phœnicians may equally as well have learnt of them. (See the statement of Eupolemus, quoted in Note XXV.) The probability seems to be, that the family of Abraham brought an alphabetic system from Ur, which may have been modified in Canaan and again in Egypt,[1] and which may not have assumed a settled shape until the writings of Moses fixed it for after ages. The system which they brought may have been either originally common to them with the Aramaic, Phœnician, and other cognate races; or it may have gradually spread from them to those people.

Note XXII., p. 54.

Hecatæus of Abdera lived in the fourth century before Christ. He was a friend of Alexander the Great, and wrote a work upon the history and religious antiquities of the Jews. The following is his testimony to Moses: —

"When in ancient times Egypt was visited with a pestilence, most of the people referred the cause of the calamity to the divinity. For since many foreigners and strangers dwelt in the country, who used diverse customs in regard to rites and sacrifices, it came to pass that the worship of the gods was very much neglected among them. Therefore the native inhabitants of the country conceived the idea, that there would be no end to their calamities, unless they should rid themselves of the foreigners. They accordingly banished them without delay. The most illustrious and energetic of them betook themselves, as some say, into Greece; . . . but the mass of the people fled into what is now called Judea, a country which is situated not far from Egypt, and which was at that time nothing but a desert. The colony was led by a man named Moses, who was distinguished for his great prudence and courage. This man, having taken possession of the country, founded, among other cities, that one called Jerusalem, which is now very celebrated. He built also

[1] It seems scarcely possible that the resemblance between the Hebrew *shin* and the Egyptian *sh* can be accidental. A fainter similarity may be traced in some other letters.

the temple which is so greatly honored by them, and appointed the sacred rites in honor of the divinity, and organized and regulated their civil affairs." After giving an account of the chief points of the law, Hecatæus adds, "It is also written at the end of the laws, that Moses heard these things from God, and spake them to the Jews." (See the fragments of Hecatæus in Mons. C. Müller's *Fragmenta Historicorum Græcorum*, vol. ii. p. 392, Fr. 13.)

NOTE XXIII., p. 54.

Manetho, the Egyptian, was also contemporary with Alexander, and wrote his Egyptian History under the first Ptolemy. His words, as reported by Josephus, are, "Now it is said that their state was organized, and their laws established by a priest, a Heliopolitan by birth, named Osarsiph, from Osiris, a god who was worshipped in Heliopolis; and that when he joined himself to this people, his name was changed, and he was called Moses." (*Fragmenta Hist. Græc.* vol. ii. p. 580, Fr. 54.)

NOTE XXIV., p. 54.

Lysimachus of Alexandria, a writer (probably) of the Augustan age, abused Moses and his laws. See Josephus, (contr. Apion. ii. 14:) "Lysimachus and some others, partly through ignorance, but more from ill-will, have discoursed concerning our lawgiver, Moses, and concerning his laws, in a manner which is neither just nor true, calumniating him as a juggler and impostor, and affirming that his laws teach us lessons of vice, and not of virtue."

NOTE XXV., p. 54.

Eupolemus is by some thought to have been a Jew; but the liberties which he takes with Scripture seem to mark him for a heathen. Josephus evidently considers him such, since he couples him with Demetrius Phalereus, and speaks of him as unable to follow exactly the sense of the Jewish Scriptures. (Contr. Apion. i. 23.) He lived in the latter half of the second century before Christ, and wrote a work in Greek on the history of the Jews, which was largely quoted by Alexander Polyhistor, the contemporary of Sylla. (See Eusebius,

Præparatio Evangelica, vol. ii. pp. 370–3, 394, 423–433, &c.) Polyhistor thus reported his testimony concerning Moses: —

"Eupolemus says that Moses was the first wise man, and that he first taught the Jews letters; — that the Phœnicians received them from the Jews, and the Greeks from the Phœnicians; and also that Moses was the first who wrote laws for the Jews." (*Fragmenta Hist. Græc.* vol. ii. p. 220, Fr. 13.)

Note XXVI., p. 54.

Histor. v. 4: "Moses, in order that he might firmly attach the people to himself for the time to come, gave them new rites, contrary to those of the rest of mankind."

Note XXVII., p. 54.

"Some, having descended from a father who reverenced the Sabbaths, worship nothing but the clouds and the divinity of heaven, and think that the swine's flesh, from which their father abstained, is no different from human flesh. Besides, they also remove the foreskin. And they are accustomed to despise the Roman laws, while they commit to memory, and observe and reverence, the Jewish law, whatever it be, which Moses delivered to them in a secret volume." *Satir.* xiv. 9–1026.

Note XXVIII., p. 54.

Longinus does not mention Moses by name, but it cannot be doubted that he intends him in the famous passage where he speaks of "the Jewish legislator" as a person historically known, and as the writer of Genesis. "Thus also the legislator of the Jews, who was no ordinary man, since he worthily comprehended and declared the power of the gods, writing thus at the very introduction to his laws, says, 'And God said'— what? 'Let the light be; and it was; let the earth be; and it was.'" *De Sublimitate*, § 9.

Note XXIX., p. 54.

Hecatæus, Eupolemus, Juvenal, and Longinus. See above, Notes XXII., XXV., XXVII., and XXVIII. Nicolas of Damascus may be added as a witness to the composition of the Pentateuch by Moses.

Speaking of a certain man as saved in the Ark at the time of the Great Deluge, he says, "This may also have been he whose history is narrated by Moses, the lawgiver of the Jews." (See Josephus, *Antiq. Jud.* i. 3, § 6.)

NOTE XXX., p. 54.

According to some writers, Hellanicus, the contemporary of Herodotus, mentioned Moses. (Justin Martyr, *Cohortatio ad Gentes*, § 8, p. 13, D. "Those who have written the annals of the Athenians, Hellanicus, and Philochorus, the Atthidæ, Castor, and Thallus, and Alexander Polyhistor, . . . have mentioned Moses as a very early and ancient ruler of the Jews." Cyrillus Alexandrinus, *Contra Julianum*, i. p. 15, D. "Now that Moses was well known to the Greek historians, may be easily seen from those things which they have written. For Polemon has mentioned him in the first book of his Grecian History, and Ptolemy the Mendesian,[1] and also Hellanicus, and Philochorus, and Castor, and others besides these.") As he wrote a work entitled Concerning the Nations, or Barbaric Customs, there is no improbability in this statement. It is less easy to see what could have led Philochorus (B. C. 300) to speak of him, but we are scarcely entitled on this ground to pronounce (as Mons. C. Müller does, *Fr. Hist. Gr.* vol. i. p. 385) that Justin misunderstood his author. Polemon of Ilium (ab. B. C. 200) seems to have spoken of Moses leading the Israelites out of Egypt. (Africanus ap. Euseb. *Præp. Ev.* x. 10; vol. ii. p. 512: "Now some of the Greeks also relate, that Moses lived at the same time. Polemon, in the first book of his Grecian History, says, 'In the reign of Apis, the son of Phoroneus, a division of the army of the Egyptians deserted Egypt, and settled in what is called Syrian Palestine, not far from Arabia; these were they who were with Moses.'" Comp. Cyril. Alex. l. s. c.; Justin Martyr, *Cohort. ad Gentes*, p. 11; Syncellus, vol. i. p. 116.) Apollonius Molo, Cicero's instructor in rhetoric, (about B. C. 80) called Moses a juggler and an impostor, and gave a very incorrect account of his legislation. (Josephus, *Contra Apionem*, ii. 14. Vide supra, note 24.) Trogus Pompeius (ab. B. C. 20) spoke of him at some length, but he did not give his readers very correct information, if we may judge by the epitome of Justin. Justin says, "His

[1] Mendes was a city of Egypt, situated in the Delta. It gave its name to one of the mouths of the Nile.

son (i. e. Joseph's) was Moses, who, besides inheriting his father's knowledge, was recommended also by the beauty of his person. But the Egyptians, when they were suffering from the itch and tetter, in obedience to the response of an oracle, in order that the disease might not become general, drove him, together with those affected by the disease, out of the Egyptian territory. Being made therefore the leader of the exiles, he carried off by stealth the sacred images of the Egyptians. The Egyptians attempted to recover these by force, but were compelled by storms to return home. Moses, therefore, seeking again his ancient country Damascus, took possession of Mount Sinai. When he came thither at length, with his people, wearied with a seven days' journey through the desert of Arabia without food, he consecrated as a day of perpetual fasting the seventh day, called, in the language of that people, Sabbath, because that day had put an end to their famine and their wanderings. . . . After Moses his son Aruas, who had been a priest of the Egyptian worship, was next made king." (Hist. xxxvi. 2.) The Egyptian historians Apion, (B. C. 30,) Cæremon (A. D. 50,) and Ptolemy of Mendes — the last an author of uncertain date, probably of the first century after Christ — noticed the fact of his leading the Jews out of Egypt. (See Tatian, *Oratio adversus Græcos*, § 37, p. 273: "Now there are accurate records of the Egyptian chronicles. And Ptolemy, who was an interpreter of their literature, — not the king of that name, but the priest of Mendes, — in setting forth the acts of their kings, says that in the time of Amosis, king of Egypt, the Jews marched out of Egypt, and went into whatsoever countries they chose, under the command of Moses." Compare Clem. Alex. *Stromata*, i. p. 379; Cyril. Alex. l. s. c.; Euseb. *Præp. Ev.* x. 11; vol. ii. p. 519, &c. And for the testimonies of Chæremon and Apion, which will be adduced in Note LXXXI., see Joseph. *c. Apion.* i. 32, and ii. 2.) It is also probable that Moses was mentioned by Castor the chronologer, (about B. C. 160,) and by Thallus, the freedman of Tiberius. (See the passages from Justin Martyr and Cyril quoted at the beginning of this note.) Numenius, the Pythagorean philosopher, who lived in the age of the Antonines, called Moses "a man very powerful with God through prayer," and mentioned his contest with the Egyptian magicians, Jannes and Jambres. (See Euseb. *Præp. Ev.* ix. 8; vol. ii. p. 358: "Afterwards, at the time when the Jews were driven out of Egypt, there flourished Jannes and Jambres, the Egyptian sacred scribes, men who were reputed inferior to none in magical arts. These were the persons who were judged worthy by the Egyptian populace to withstand even Mousæus, the leader of the Jews, a man who was very powerful with God in prayer; and they were found able to remove the heaviest of the calamities which Mousæus brought upon Egypt.") (Compare Pliny, *Hist. Nat.*, xxx. 1, § 2.) Nicolas of Damascus also mentioned Moses, and called him "the Jewish lawgiver." (See the passage quoted in Note XXIX.)

NOTE XXXI., p. 54.

The only classical writer, so far as I am aware, who expresses any doubt with respect to the Mosaic origin of the Jewish law is Strabo, a very untrustworthy authority in the field of ancient history. Strabo ascribes the establishment of Monotheism and of the moral law to Moses, but believes the ceremonial law to have been added by his successor. (*Geographica*, xvi. 2, § 35–37: "For Moses, one of the Egyptian priests, dissatisfied with the established order of things, made great innovations in every direction; and many of those who honored the divinity joined his secession. Now this man said and taught that the Egyptians, and likewise the Libyans, were in error in likening the divinity to beasts and cattle. He also censured the Greeks as well, for representing their gods in human form. For he maintained that God was nothing else but that which comprehends us all, and the earth and the sea — that which we are wont to call heaven, and the world, and the nature of things; and that those who live virtuously and justly may always expect good gifts from God, and tokens of his favor; but that others could have no such expectation. Thus this man became popular, and established his authority very firmly; for all those who were about him were easily induced, by his personal influence, and by the benefits proposed, to fall in with his views. Now those who came after him continued for a time in the same course, practising justice and showing true piety; but afterwards there were introduced into the priesthood, first superstitious, and then tyrannical men. The former established the prohibitions from food, which they are accustomed to observe at the present day, and the circumcisions and excisions, and whatever else of this kind has been instituted among them; and the latter introduced oppressive exactions.") It is to be remarked that

Strabo quotes no authority, whence it may be suspected that his account is based rather on his own views of probability, and of the natural sequence of events in such cases, than on the statements of any earlier writers. (See his words at the opening of the next section.)

NOTE XXXII., p. 55.

See Exod. xvii. 14; xxiv. 4, 7; Numb. xxxiii. 2; Deut. xvii. 18, et seqq.; xxviii. 58, et seqq.; xxix. 20, 27; and xxxi. 9, 24, et seqq.

NOTE XXXIII., p. 55.

Strauss, *Leben Jesu*, § 6; vol. i. p. 20, E. T.

NOTE XXXIV., p. 55.

See particularly Deuteronomy xxviii. 58, and xxix. 20, 27. Hävernick's comment on these and other kindred passages deserves the attention of the student. (See his *Handbuch des Historisch-critischen Einleitung in das Alte Testament*, § 108; § 4, pp. 14–19, Clark's Translation.[1])

NOTE XXXV., p. 56.

"The Deuteronomist," says De Wette, "will, as it appears, have his whole book regarded as the composition of Moses." (*Einleitung in das Alte Testament*, § 162, d, p. 203.) Hartman makes a similar assertion with respect to "the author of the last four books." (*Forschungen über d. Pentateuch*, p. 538.)

NOTE XXXVI., p. 56.

The earliest writers whom De Wette can quote as doubting the genuineness of the Pentateuch, are Celsus the Neo-Platonist, (A. D. 130,) and Ptolemy, the Valentinian Gnostic, a writer of the third century. (See his *Einleitung*, § 164, a; p. 205; and for the passages to which he refers see Origen, *Contra Celsum*, iv. 42, and Epiphanius, *Adversus Hæreses*, xxxiii. 4, p. 207.) Apion, and the other adversaries whom Josephus answers, all admitted the Pentateuch to be the work of Moses.

1 *Historico-Critical Introduction to the Pentateuch*, Edinburgh, Clark, 1850.

NOTE XXXVII., p. 56.

The differences in the rationalistic views of the time when the Pentateuch was composed, are thus summed up by Professor Stuart,[1] "Almost every marked period from Joshua down to the return from the Babylonish exile, has been fixed upon by different writers, as a period appropriate to the production of the work. To Ezra some have assigned the task of producing it; in which, if we may hearken to them, he engaged in order that he might confirm and perpetuate the ritual introduced by him. To Hilkiah the priest, with the connivance of Josiah, Mr. Norton and others have felt inclined to attribute it, at the period when a copy of the Law is said to have been discovered in the Temple. Somewhere near this period, Gesenius and De Wette once placed it; but both of them, in later times, have been rather inclined to recede from this, and to look to an earlier period. The subject has been through almost boundless discussion, and a great variety of opinions has been broached respecting the matter, until recently it has taken a turn somewhat new. The *haut ton* of criticism in Germany now compounds between the old opinions and the new theories. Ewald and Lengerke both admit a *groundwork* of the Pentateuch. But as to the extent of this they differ, each one deciding according to his subjective feelings. The leading laws and ordinances of the Pentateuch are admitted to belong to the time of Moses. Ewald supposes that they were written down at that period. Then we have, secondly, historical portions of the Pentateuch, written, as Ewald judges, not by prophets, but before this order of men appeared among the Hebrews. . . . Then came next, according to him, a *prophetic* order of historical writers, about the time of Solomon. . . . Next comes a narrator . . . who is to be placed somewhere near the period of Elijah. . . . Then comes a fourth narrator, whom we cannot place earlier than about the middle of the eighth century B. C. He was followed by the Deuteronomist . . . some time during the latter half of Manasseh's reign. . . . Then just before the Babylonish exile the great *Collectaneum* or *Corpus Auctorum omnium*, was brought to a close.

Lengerke . . . admits a *groundwork;* but, with the exception of some laws, it was not composed till the time of Solomon. Next comes a

[1] *Critical History and Defence of the Old Testament Canon,* § 3, pp. 43, 44.

supplementarist, who must have lived some time in the eighth century. Then comes the Deuteronomist, as in Ewald; but he is assigned by Lengerke to the time of Josiah, about B. C. 624.

Each of these writers is confident in his critical power of discrimination. . . . Each is sure that he can appreciate all the niceties and slight diversities of style and diction, and therefore cannot be mistaken. Each knows, in his own view with certainty, how many authors of the Pentateuch there are; while one still reckons *six* and the other *three*. . . . I will not now ask, Who shall decide when Doctors disagree?"

Compare also Hävernick, *Handbuch*, &c., § 145; § 41, pp. 442–444, E. T.

Note XXXVII. *b*, p. 57.

Leben Jesu, § 13; pp. 55–56, E. T.

Note XXXVIII., p. 58.

The purpose of Moses is to write not his own history, nor even the *civil* history of his nation, but the *theocratic* history of the world up to his own time. This is the clew to all those curious insertions and omissions which have astonished and perplexed mere historians. (See Hävernick, *Handbuch*, &c., § 106; § 2, pp. 1–7, E. T.; and compare Lecture VII., p. 178.) Still, his own history to a certain extent, and the public history of his nation, up to his time, do in fact form the staple of his narrative.

Note XXXIX., p. 58.

Sir G. C. Lewis says, "The infidelity of oral tradition, with respect to past occurrences, has been so generally recognized, that it would be a superfluous labor to dwell upon it. For our present purpose, it is more material to fix the time during which *an accurate memory of historical events* may be perpetuated by oral tradition alone. Newton, in his work on Chronology,[1] fixes it at eighty or a hundred years for a time anterior to the use of writing; and Volney says that, among the Red Indians of North America, there was no accurate tradition of facts which were a century old. Mallet, in his work on Northern Anti-

[1] *Chronology of Ancient Kingdoms amended*, (1728, 4to,) Introduction, p. 7.

quities,[1] remarks that, among the common class of mankind, *a son remembers his father, knows something about his grandfather*, but never bestows a thought on his more remote progenitors. This would carry back a man's knowledge of his own family for about a hundred years; and it is not likely that his knowledge of public affairs, founded on a similar oral tradition, could reach to an earlier date." (*Credibility of Early Roman History*, vol. i. pp. 98, 99.)

NOTE XL., p. 58.

See Horne's *Introduction to the Critical Study and Knowledge of the Holy Scriptures*, ch. ii. § 1, vol. i. p. 54. "In the antediluvian world, when the life of man was so protracted, there was comparatively little need for writing. Tradition answered every purpose to which writing, in any kind of characters, could be subservient; and the necessity of erecting monuments to perpetuate public events could scarcely have suggested itself; as, during those times, there could be little danger apprehended of any important fact becoming obsolete, its history having to pass through very few hands, and all these friends and relatives in the most proper sense of the terms; for they lived in an insulated state, under a patriarchal government. Thus it was easy for Moses to be satisfied of the truth of all he relates in the Book of Genesis, as the accounts came to him through the medium of very few persons. From Adam to Noah there was but *one* man necessary to the transmission of the history of this period of 1656 years. Adam died in the year of the world 930, and Lamech, the father of Noah, was born in the year 874; so that Adam and Lamech were contemporaries for fifty-six years. Methusaleh, the grandfather of Noah, was born in the year of the world 687, and died in the year 1656, so that he lived to see both Adam and Lamech — from whom (Adam?) doubtless he acquired the knowledge of this history, and was likewise contemporary with Noah for 600 years. In like manner Shem connected Noah and Abraham, having lived to converse with both; as Isaac did with Abraham and Joseph, from whom these things might be easily conveyed to Moses by Amram, who was contemporary with Joseph. Supposing then all the curious facts recorded in the Book of Genesis to have had no other authority than the tradition already referred to, they would stand upon

[1] Ch. ii.

a foundation of credibility superior to any that the most reputable of the ancient Greek and Latin historians can boast."

NOTE XLI., p. 59.

See Sir G. C. Lewis's *Credibility*, &c., vol. i. p. 101. "In a nation which has no consecutive written history, leading events would be perhaps preserved, in their general outlines, for about a hundred years. Special circumstances might, however, give to an event a larger hold on the popular memory." He instances, 1. The attempt of Cylon at Athens, the circumstances of which were remembered in B. C. 432, *one hundred and eighty* years after, (Thucydid. i. 126;) and 2. The battle of the Allia, the memory of which continued (he thinks) among the common people at Rome to the time of the earliest annalists, or one hundred and fifty years.

NOTE XLII., p. 59.

The force of this argument is, no doubt, weakened, but it is not destroyed, by a preference of the Septuagint or of the Samaritan numbers to those of the Hebrew text. The Septuagint numbers, which are the most unfavorable to the argument, would make the chain between Adam and Moses consist of eight links — viz. Mahalaleel, Noah, Salah, Reu, Nahor, Abraham, Jacob, and Jochebed.

NOTE XLIII., p. 59.

See above, Note XXXVII.; and compare Hävernick, *Handbuch*, &c., § 111, (§ 7, pp. 45–48, E. T.,) and Horne, *Introduction*, &c., ch. ii. § 1, vol. i. pp. 64–56.

NOTE XLIV., p. 59.

Having argued that the Patriarchs were almost sure to have committed to writing the chief facts of the early history, especially those of the Creation, the Fall of Man, the promise of Redemption, and the various revelations which they received from God, Vitringa says — "We believe, indeed, that Moses collected these writings and papers of the patriarchs, preserved among the Israelites, arranged them, prepared them, filled up their deficiencies, and out of them made up the first of his own books." (*Observationes Sacræ*, i. 4, § 2; p. 36.)

NOTE XLV., p. 59.

Commentaire Littérale, Préface, vol. i. p. xiii. "Although, strictly speaking, it is not *impossible* that Moses might have learned from oral tradition all that he has told us concerning the Creation of the World, the Deluge, and the times of the Patriarchs, . . . yet it is highly probable that this Lawgiver had access to records and documents which had been preserved in the families of the Jews. The detailed account of genealogies, the dates of events, and their circumstances, the number of the years of the lives of the Patriarchs, — all these things could hardly be learned in a manner so precise and exact, except from written documents." Compare Hävernick, (*Handbuch*, &c., § 115; § 11, pp. 81–2, E. T.,) who, while he maintains that the narrative of Genesis "has its origin primarily in oral tradition," still allows it to be probable "that in the time of the writer a part of the oral tradition had been already committed to writing," and that "the author makes use of certain older monuments."

NOTE XLVI., p. 59.

See above, Notes XIX., XX., and XXI. In estimating the antiquity of alphabetic writing, we must remember, that the earliest extant specimens of the Babylonian (which have been assigned to about the 22d century B. C.) present indications of previous stages having been passed through, which must have each occupied some considerable period. It is certain that the Babylonians, like the Egyptians, began with picture-writing.[1] But in the most ancient remains this stage has been long past: a few letters only still bear a resemblance to the objects: while the bulk have lost all trace of their original form. The writing too has ceased altogether to be symbolical, and (with the exception of certain *determinatives*) is purely phonetic, having thus passed the second stage of the art. In Egypt, the hieroglyphics of the Pyramid period, (B. C. 2450–2300,) sometimes "written in the cursive character, prove that writing had been long in use." (See Wilkinson's *Appendix* to Book ii. of the author's *Herodotus*, ch. viii. § 9; vol. ii. p. 344.)

[1] See Sir H. Rawlinson's Essay, "*On the Early History of Babylonia*," in the first volume of the author's *Herodotus*, Essay vi. pp. 443, 444.

NOTE XLVII., p. 60.

See Bishop Gleig's *Introduction*, in his edition of Stackhouse's *History of the Bible*, vol. i. p. 20. Compare the article on WRITING in Kitto's *Biblical Cyclopædia*, vol. ii. pp. 971, 972.

NOTE XLVIII., p. 61.

The Armenian History of Moses of Chorene commences from Adam. Taking the Hebrew Scriptures for his basis, he endeavors to blend and harmonize with them the traditions of primeval times recorded by Berosus, Abydenus, and especially by a certain Mar Ibas, or Mar Àbas, a learned Syrian, said to have lived about B. C. 150. He identifies Adam with the Babylonian Alorus, (i. 3,) Noah with Xisuthrus, (ibid.,) Shem with Zervan, who (he says) is the same as Zoroaster, (i. 5. ;) Ham with Titan, whence the Titans are the descendants of Ham, (ibid.,) and Nimrod with Belus, (i. 6.) Armenian history is regarded as commencing from this time. Haïcus or Haïg, the fifth descendant of Japhet, son of Thaclath or Togarmah, revolts from Belus, or Nimrod, and withdraws from Babylon to Armenia, where he establishes himself. War follows: Haïcus is attacked by Belus, but makes a successful resistance, and Belus falls in the battle, (i. 9, 10.) From this point Moses seems in the main to follow native traditions, which do not appear to have possessed much historical value. It has been conjectured with good reason that "the earliest literature of Armenia was a series of national poems," and that these compositions furnished Moses of Chorene with a great part of his materials. (See Prichard's *Physical History of Mankind*, vol. iv. p. 255; and compare Neumann's *Versuch einer Geschichte der Armenischen Literatur*, published at Leipsic in 1836.) Michael Chamich and other Armenian writers have chiefly copied from Moses.

NOTE XLIX., p. 61.

The two Epic poems, the Râmâyana and the Mahâbhârata, profess to be historical, but are not thought by the best modern authorities to contain more than some "shadow of truth." They are assigned to about the third century B. C. (See Professor H. H. Wilson's Introduction to his translation of the *Rig-Veda-Sanhita*, pp. xlvi., xlvii.) The attempt to construct from them, and from other Sanscritic sources of even worse character, by the aid of Megasthenes and of a large amount of conjecture, a chronological scheme reaching to B. C. 3120, which M. Bunsen has made in the third volume of his *Egypt*, (pp. 518–564,) appears to me a singular instance of misplaced ingenuity.

NOTE L., p. 61.

The Chinese, like the Hindus, carry back the history of the world for *several hundred thousand* years. Their own history, however, as a nation, does not profess to commence till about B. C. 2600; and authentic accounts, according to the views of those who regard their early literature with most favor, go back only to the 22d century B. C. (See Rémusat, *Nouveaux Mélanges Asiatiques*, vol. i. p. 65. "The history of China runs back with certainty to the twenty-second century before our era, and some respectable traditions permit us to carry back the point of departure four centuries earlier, to the year 2637 before Jesus Christ." Compare Mailla, *Histoire Générale de la Chine*, vol. i.; Grosier's Discours Préliminaire prefixed to his *Description de la Chine*, published at Paris in 1818–1820; and M. Bunsen's *Egypt*, vol. iii. pp. 379–407.) The entire isolation of China, and the absence of any points of contact between it and the nations of Western Asia, would render this early history, even if authentic, useless for the purposes of the present Lectures. I confess, however, that I put little faith in the conclusions of modern French antiquarians; and that I incline to look with suspicion on all Chinese history earlier than the time of Confucius, B. C. 550–480, when it is admitted that contemporary records commence. (See Prichard's *Physical History of Mankind*, vol. iv. pp. 475–9; and compare *Asiatic Researches*, vol. ii. p. 370.)

NOTE LI., p. 61.

The evidences on this head were carefully collected by Mr. Stanley Faber in his *Bampton Lectures* for the year 1801, afterwards published as *Horæ Mosaicæ*, ch. iv. pp. 130–184. The most remarkable tradition is that of the Hindus. In the *Bhagavat* it is related that in the reign of Satiavrata, the seventh king of the Hindus, mankind became almost universally wicked, only Satiavrata and *seven* saints continuing pious. The lord of the universe, therefore, loving the pious man, and intending to preserve him from the sea of destruction caused by the depravity of, the age, thus told him how he was to act. "In seven days from the present time, O thou tamer of enemies, the three worlds will be plunged in an ocean of death; but in the midst of the destroying waves, *a large vessel*, sent by me for thy use, shall stand before thee. Then shalt thou take all medicinal herbs, all the variety of seeds; and accompanied by seven saints, encircled by *pairs of all brute animals*, thou shalt enter the spacious ark and continue in it, secure from the flood on one immense ocean without light, except the radiance of thy holy companions. . . . Then shalt thou know my true greatness, rightly named the supreme Godhead; by my favor all thy questions shall be answered, and thy mind abundantly instructed." After seven days, the sea overwhelming its shores, deluged the whole earth; while the flood was augmented by showers from immense clouds; when Satiavrata saw the vessel advancing, and entered it with his companions, having executed the commands of God. After a while the deluge abated, and Satiavrata, having been instructed in all divine and human knowledge, was appointed the seventh Menu, and named Vaivaswata by the Supreme Being. From this Manu the earth was repeopled, and from him mankind received their name Manudsha. (See an Article by Sir W. Jones in the 1st volume of the *Asiatic Researches*, pp. 230–4. Compare Faber's *Horæ Mosaicæ*, ch. iv. pp. 139, 140; Carwithen's *Bampton Lectures*, III. pp. 87, 88; and Kalisch's *Historical and Critical Commentary on the Old Testament*, vol. i. p. 138, E. T.)

The Chinese traditions are said to be less clear and decisive. They speak of a "first heaven"—an age of innocence, when "the whole creation enjoyed a state of happiness; when every thing was beautiful, every thing was good; all beings were perfect in their kind;" whereto succeeded a "second heaven," introduced by a great couvulsion. "The pillars of Heaven were broken — the earth shook to its foundations — the heavens sunk lower towards the north — the sun, the moon, and the stars changed their motions — the earth fell to pieces; and *the waters enclosed within its bosom burst forth with violence, and overflowed it.* Man having rebelled against heaven, the system of the Universe was totally disordered. The sun was eclipsed, the planets altered their course, and the grand harmony of nature was disturbed." (Faber, *Horæ Mosaicæ*, ch. iv. pp. 147, 148.)

The Armenians accept the Scriptural account, which they identify with the Chaldæan. They can scarcely be said to possess any special national tradition on the subject, except that which continues to the present day — the belief that the timbers of the ark are still to be seen on the top of Ararat. The Greek tradition concerning the flood of Deucalion needs only to be mentioned. Curiously enough it takes the form most closely resembling the Mosaic account in the pages of Lucian,[1] the professed scoffer. Traditions of a great deluge were also found in all parts of the new world, and in some of the islands of the Pacific. (Faber, *Horæ Mosaicæ*, ch. iv.; Kalisch, vol. i. p. 140, E. T.)

NOTE LII., p. 62.

See Gen. x. 10; xi. 2–5; xxxix., et seqq. Compare Herod. i. 7; ii. 2, 109–142; Plat. Tim. p. 22, B.; Diod. Sic., books i. and ii.; Justin, i. 1; &c. Josephus well expresses the grounds on which the Egyptian and Babylonian annals are to be preferred to those of all other heathen nations. He ranks the Phœnician histories decidedly below them. (See his work *Contra Apionem*, i. 6: "Now that among the Egyptians and the Babylonians, from the most ancient times the charge of preparing the public records was committed, among the former people, to the priests, who were skilled in this business, and among the Babylonians to the Chaldeans; and that of the nations which held intercourse with the Greeks, the Phœnicians were the most familiar with letters; — all this, I think, will be granted to me, since it is conceded by all.")

NOTE LIII., p. 63.

Scaliger was the first to draw the attention of scholars to the writings of Berosus and Manetho. In his work *De Emendatione Temporum* he collected their fragments and supported their authority. The value of Manetho was acknowledged by Heeren, (*Handbuch der Geschichte der Staaten des Alterthums*, i. 2, p. 54, E. T.,) Marsham, (*Canon Chronicus*, Pref. p. 2, &c.,) and others, before much progress had been made in deciphering the inscriptions of Egypt. Berosus, always quoted with respect by our Divines, did not find much favor with German historical critics till his claims were advocated by Niebuhr. (See the *Vorträge über Alte Geschichte*, vol. i. pp. 16–19.)

[1] *De Deâ Syriâ*, § 12.

NOTE LIV., p. 63.

One other ancient writer, had his work come down to us in a complete form, or had we even possessed a fragment or two of its earlier portion, might have deserved to be placed nearly on a level with Berosus and Manetho: viz., Menander of Ephesus; who living probably about the same time with them, and having access to the archives of the only nation which could dispute with Egypt and Babylon the palm of antiquity and the claim of inventing letters, composed in Greek a Phœnician history; which seems, from the few fragments of it that remain, to have been a work of the very highest character. Of these fragments, however, none touch the period between the Creation and the death of Moses; and it may even be suspected that Menander's history did not go back so far. At any rate, if it did, we are completely ignorant what representation he gave of the early times. (See the Fragments of Menander in Mons. C. Müller's *Fragmenta Historicorum Græcorum*, vol. iv. pp. 445–8, and the testimony to his value borne by Niebuhr, *Vorträge über Alte Geschichte*, vol. i. p. 17, and p. 93, note [1].)

Nothing has been said here of Sanchoniathon, in the first place because it seems more than probable that the work ascribed to him was the mere forgery of Philo Byblius; and secondly, because, though called a "Phœnician History," the fragments of the work which remain show it to have been mainly, if not entirely, *mythological*. (See Movers, *Jahrbücher für Theologisch. und Christlich. Philosophie*, 1836, vol. i. pp. 51–91; Lobeck, *Aglaoph.*, p. 1264, et seqq.; Niebuhr, *Vorträge über alte Geschichte*, vol. i. p. 93, note [1]; and C. Müller, *Fragmenta His. Gr.*, vol. iii. pp. 560–1.)

NOTE LV., p. 63.

M. Bunsen, speaking of the Egyptian monuments, says, "Such documents cannot indeed compensate for the want of written History. Even Chronology, its external framework, cannot be elicited from them." (*Egypt's Place in Universal History*, vol. i. p. 32, E. T.) This may be said with at least as much truth of the Babylonian and Assyrian records.

NOTE LVI., p. 64.

The following is Manetho's chronological scheme, according to Eusebius, (*Chronica*, i. 20, pp. 93–107, ed. Mai. :) —

	Years.
Reign of Gods	13,900
Reign of Heroes	1,255
Reign of Kings	1,817
Reign of 30 Memphite Kings	1,790
Reign of 10 Thinite Kings	350
Reign of Manes and Heroes	5,813
	24,925
Thirty dynasties of Kings (about)	5,000[1]
	29,925

NOTE LVII., p. 64.

The following was the scheme of Berosus, if we may trust Eusebius. (See his *Chronica*, i. 1, and 4 ; p. 5, and p. 18 :) —

	Years.
1. Ten kings from Alorus to Xisuthrus reigned	432,000
2. Eighty-six kings from Xisuthrus to the Median conquest	33,080[2]
3. Eight Median kings	224
4. Eleven kings	[48][3]
5. Forty-nine Chaldæan kings	458
6. Nine Arabian kings	245
7. Forty-five kings down to Pul	526
	466,581

NOTE LVIII., p. 64.

Vide supra, Note LVI. M. Bunsen (*Egypt's Place*, &c., vol. i. p. 70, E. T.) accuses Eusebius of having changed the order of Manetho's numbers, and by a dexterous transposition he seeks to transfer to the

1 Baron Bunsen gives the sum of the years of the 30 dynasties as 4922, 4954, or 5329, according to variations of reading or statement. (Egypt, vol. i. p. 82, E. T.)

2 In the Armenian the number here is 33,091, but this may be corrected from Syncellus. (*Fragm. Hist. Gr.*, vol. ii. p. 503.)

3 This number is only given in the margin, and is very doubtful.

human period a space of nearly 4000 years. He would make the divine period consist of the following: —

	Years.
1. Reign of Gods	13,900
2. Reign of Heroes	1,255
3. Reign of Heroes and Manes together	5,813
	20,968

The human period he represents thus: —

1. Kings (no capital mentioned)	1,817
2. Thirty Memphite kings	1,790
3. Ten Thinite kings	350
4. Thirty Dynasties (say)	5,000
	8,957

But there is absolutely no ground, beyond gratuitous conjecture, for making this change; which involves Manetho in the contradiction, that *Manes*, the Ghosts of Mortals, exist before there have been any mortals. (See the *Fragmenta Historicorum Græcorum* of Mons. C. Müller, vol. ii. p. 528, where M. Bunsen's theory is rejected.)

NOTE LIX., p. 64.

Chronographia, p. 52, D. M. Bunsen was the first to call attention to this passage. (*Egypt's Place*, &c., vol. i. p. 86.) If sound, it is of very great importance, as indicating that Manetho knew and allowed that his kings and dynasties were not always consecutive. It has been recently denied that Manetho did this, and it has been proposed to amend the passage of Syncellus by introducing into it the name of another writer, Anianus, who (it is supposed) made the reduction in question. (See an Article in the *Quarterly Review* for April, 1859; Art. IV. pp. 395–6.) But this emendation is quite inadmissible; for the clear object of Syncellus in the passage is to show that *Manetho's own numbers* were at variance with Scripture. Whether Syncellus rightly reports Manetho or no, is another question. If he does not, the argument in the text, so far, falls to the ground; and we must admit that Egyptian Chronology — as represented by Manetho — was about 2000 years in excess of the Chronology of Scripture. Still we must bear in mind, that, whether Manetho allowed it or not, his dynasties *were in fact* sometimes contemporary, as is proved by the Egyptian monuments. (Wilkinson in the author's *Herodotus*, vol. ii. pp. 343, 349, &c. Stuart Poole, *Horæ Ægyptiacæ*, pp. 110, 112, 123, &c.) If therefore he did not in his chronology make any allowance on this account, he could not fail to be in considerable excess of the truth.

NOTE LX., p. 65.

See the latest conclusions of Sir Gardner Wilkinson in the author's *Herodotus*, vol. ii. pp. 342–3; and compare Mr. Stuart Poole's *Horæ Ægyptiacæ*, p. 97. See also the extracts from Professor Rask's *Egyptian Chronology*, contained in Dr. Prichard's *Historical Records of Ancient Egypt*, § 6, pp. 91–111.

A slight error has crept into the calculation on which the date given in the text (B. C. 2660) is founded. Sir G. Wilkinson places the accession of the 4th dynasty about B. C. 2450, and allows to the 1st, on which he considers the 4th to have followed, 241 years. The date of Menes, according to his views, should therefore have been given as B. C. 2690, instead of B. C. 2660.

NOTE LXI., p. 66.

See the fragments of Berosus in Mons. C. Müller's *Fragmenta Historicorum Græcorum*, vol. ii. p. 496, Frs. 1, and 5. "He says there was a time when the universe was but darkness and water, and in these were generated monstrous animals, of strange forms. . . . And besides these there were fishes and reptiles, and a vast number of other wonderful animals. . . . And over all these ruled a woman, whose name was Homoroka: now this word in the language of the Chaldees is translated Thalath, but in Greek Thalassa, (i. e. the Sea.) Now, while all things were in this condition, Belus returned, and cutting the woman asunder in the midst, made of the one half of her the earth, and of the other half the heaven, and destroyed the animals. He says that this is an allegorical cosmogony. For when the universe was in a fluid state, and animals were generated in it, this god cut off his own head, and the other gods mixed the blood which flowed from it with the earth, and so formed men; whence it came to pass that they are intelligent, and partake of the divine wisdom. Then Belus, divining the darkness, separated the earth and the heaven from each other, and brought the world into order; and the animals that could not endure the power of the light were destroyed. Then Belus, seeing that the place was desolate, though fruitful, commanded one of the gods to cut off his own head, and to mix the flowing blood with the earth, and to form [men and] beasts able to breathe the air. Belus also formed the stars, and the sun, and the moon, and the seven planets." (Ap. Syncell. *Chronograph.* pp. 29, 30.)

"After saying these things, he proceeds to enumerate the kings of Assyria, individually and in order, — namely, ten from Alorus, who was the first, down to Xisuthrus, in whose reign occurred that first great deluge which Moses also mentions." (Ap. Euseb. *Chronica,* i. 1, p. 5, ed. Mai.)

Note LXII., p. 66.

See Niebuhr's *Vorträge über Alte Geschichte,* (vol. i. p. 20, note,) where he notices the abuse of the parallel made by some, who maintained that the Mosaical account of the Creation was derived from the Babylonian.

Note LXIII., p. 67.

See the well-known passage of Josephus, where, after remarking on the longevity of the Patriarchs, he says, "All those who have written on the subject of antiquities, both among the Greeks and among the Barbarians, bear witness to the truth of my words. For Manetho, who wrote the chronicles of the Egyptians, and Berosus, who collected those of the Chaldeans, and Molus [read *Molon*] and Hestiæus, and besides these Hieronymus the Egyptian, and those who composed the Phœnician annals, agree with what I have said. Hesiod also, and Hecatæus, Hellanicus and Acusilaus, and besides these Ephorus and Nicolaus, relate that the ancients used to live a thousand years." (*Antiq. Jud.* i. 3.)

Note LXIV., p. 67.

See Faber's *Horæ Mosaïcæ,* ch. iii. pp. 119, 120; and Horne's *Introduction,* vol. i. p. 158.

NOTE LXV., p. 68.

Fragmenta Historicorum Græcorum, vol. ii. p. 501, Fr. 7. "In the reign of Xisuthrus there was a great deluge. The account is given as follows: 'Kronos, appearing to him in his sleep, declared that on the 15th day of the month Dæsius, men would be destroyed by a flood. He commanded the king therefore to commit to writing an account of the principles and progress and issues of all things, and to bury it in Sippara, the city of the sun; and then to construct a vessel, and to embark in it with his kindred and his intimate friends; also to deposit therein food and drink, and to take in birds and quadrupeds; and having put all things in order to set sail. . . . He therefore, obeying the command, constructed a vessel, whose length was five stadia, and its breadth two stadia; and after he had gathered into it all things as directed, he embarked with his wife and children and intimate friends. But when the flood came, and forthwith ceased, Xisuthrus let go some of the birds. Not finding, however, any food, or any place to alight, they came again to the ship. After some days, Xisuthrus let loose the birds again; but they again came back to the ship, having their feet covered with mud. But being let go a third time, they returned no more to the ship. Xisuthrus then understood that the land had appeared, and passing through a certain part of the seams of the ship, and seeing that it had grounded on a certain mountain, he went forth, with his wife and daughter, and the pilot, and saluted the ground; and when he had built an altar, and sacrificed to the gods, he and those who came out of the ship with him disappeared. Now those who remained in the ship, when Xisuthrus and his companions did not return, went forth to seek him, calling his name aloud. But Xisuthrus himself was never more seen by them; there came, however, a voice from the air, which commanded them to be dutiful worshippers of the gods, since he, in consequence of his piety, had gone to live with the gods. . . . It also directed them to go again to Babylon, and, according as it had been decreed, to take up the letters from Sippara, and communicate them to men whom they would find in the country of Armenia. . . . They accordingly came to Babylon, dug up the letters which had been buried at Sippara, restored the temples, and rebuilt Babylon." (Ap. Syncell. *Chron.*, pp. 30, 31. Compare Euseb. *Chronica*, i. 3, pp. 14–16.)

NOTE LXVI., p. 68.

Fragment. Hist. Gr., vol. iv. p. 280, Fr. 1. "After Euedoreschus, several others reigned, among whom was Sisithrus, whom Kronos forewarned that there would be a great abundance of rain on the 15th of Dæsius. And he commanded him to hide every thing which pertained to letters in Heliopolis, in Sippara. Sisithrus, having performed all these things, immediately sailed towards Armenia. And what the god had foretold straightway came to pass. Now on the third day, when the rain had ceased, he let loose some birds, to try whether they could find any land above the water. But finding nothing save a wide-yawning sea, where there was no place for them to rest, they came back to Sisithrus. He sent forth others afterwards, with the same result. But when on the third trial he succeeded, (for the birds returned with their feet covered with mud,) the gods snatched him from the view of men, and the vessel, from the fragments of its planks used as amulets, furnished to the inhabitants of Armenia effectual antidotes against poison." (Ap. Syncell. *Chronograph.*, p. 70, A.; compare Euseb. *Chronica*, i. 7; p. 22, ed. Mai.)

But little is known of Abydenus. He is first quoted by Eusebius in the fourth century after Christ; on which account it has been generally supposed that he did not write till the second or third century of our era. (See Niebuhr's *Kleine Schriften*, p. 187, note 4; and C. Müller's *Fragm. Hist. Gr.*, vol. iv. p. 279.) Some, however, regard him as a contemporary and pupil of Berosus, and therefore as not much later than the time of Alexander, (Bauer in Ersch and Gruber's *Encyclopædia*, s. v. Abydenus; C. O. Müller, *History of Greek Literature*, vol. ii. p. 490, E. T.) His use of the Ionic dialect favors the earlier date.

NOTE LXVII. p. 68.

Buttmann, (*Mythologus*, i. pp. 190, 200, &c.,) Von Bohlen, (*Alte Indien*, p. 78, et seqq.,) and Hartmann (*Forschungen über d. Pentateuch*, p. 795, et seqq.) maintain that the story of the flood "sprang up in the soil of India, whence it was brought to the Hebrews through Babylon, after having first received a new coloring there." (See Hävernick's *Einleitung*, § 120, pp. 266, 267; § 16, p. 112, E. T.) But the absence of exaggeration and of grotesqueness from the Hebrew account sufficiently disproves this theory. It might be argued with much more plausibility that the Babylonians obtained their knowledge from the Jews.

Note LXVI. b., p. 69.

See Niebuhr's *Vorträge über Alte Geschichte*, vol. i. p. 23. "This account differs from the Noachian, so far as it allows to be saved not only the family of Xisuthrus, but all pious persons, and supposes *not a universal, but only a Babylonian* deluge."

Note LXVII. b., p. 70.

Antiq. Jud. i. 7, § 2: Berosus mentions our father Abraham, not by name, but after this manner: "In the tenth generation after the flood, there was among the Chaldeans a righteous and great man, who was also skilled in the knowledge of the heavens."

Note LXVIII., p. 70.

It has been acutely suggested that the actual scheme of Berosus was probably the following: —

	Years.	B. C.	
1. Antediluvian dynasty of 10 kings	432,000	466,618 to 34,618	Mythical
2. Dynasty of 86 kings (Chaldæans ?) .	34,080	34,618 to 2,458	Mythical
3. Dynasty of 8 Median kings . . .	224	2,458 to 2,234	Historical
4. Dynasty of 11 kings (Chaldæans ?) .	[258][1]	2,234 to 1,976	Historical
5. Dynasty of 49 Chaldæan kings . .	458	1,976 to 1,518	Historical
6. Dynasty of 9 Arabian kings . . .	245	1,518 to 1,273	Historical
7. Dynasty of 45 kings (Assyrians ?) .	526	1,273 to 747	Historical
8. Dynasty of 8 (?) Assyrian kings . .	122	747 to 625	Historical
9. Dynasty of 6 Chaldæan kings . . .	87	625 to 538	Historical
	36,000		

[1] This number fills up the blank in Euseb. *Chron.* i. 4, p. 18, where 48 is absurdly suggested in the margin. See above, Note LVII. It is conjectural, but it seems required by the native tradition that Babylon was founded 1903 before Alexander's capture of it, or B. C. 2234.

(See Gutschmidt in the *Rheinisches Museum*, vol. viii. p. 252; who is followed by Brandis, *Rerum Assyriarum Tempora Emendata*, p. 17; and Sir H. Rawlinson in the *Journal of the Asiatic Society*, vol. xv. part 2; p. 218.) If this be a true representation, it would follow that the number 34,080 is purely artificial, being simply the number required to make up the great Babylonian year or cycle of 36,000 years, in conjunction with the years of the real historical dynasties. The first number, 432,000, is made up of 12 such cycles, ($36,000 \times 12 = 432,000$.)

NOTE LXIX., p. 70.

See the Fragments of Abydenus in Müller's *Fragm. Hist. Gr.*, vol. iv. p. 282, Fr. 6: "At that time the men of antiquity are said to have been so puffed up with strength and haughtiness, that they despised even the gods, and undertook to build that lofty obelisk which is now called Babylon. And when they had already built it up into the heavens almost as high as the gods, the gods, by the help of the winds, smote the well-contrived but futile work, and prostrated it to the ground. And that rubbish took the name of Babel. For up to that time men relied upon the use of one language; but then a various and discordant confusion of tongues was sent by the gods upon those who had heretofore used but one language." (Ap. Euseb. *Chronica*, i. 8, p. 24.) Compare also the subjoined passage, which Syncellus quotes from Polyhistor: "Now the Sibyl says, that when all men were of one speech, some of them built a huge tower, that they might ascend up to heaven. But God caused a wind to blow, and overthrew their design, and gave to each a different language; wherefore the city was called Babylon. (*Chronograph.*, p. 81, C.)

NOTE LXX., p. 71.

The affinity of the Sanskrit with the Persian, Greek, Latin, and German languages was first remarked by our own countryman, Sir W. Jones; but it remained for F. Schlegel in Germany and for Dr. Prichard in England to make a scientific use of the material thus provided for them. Schlegel's "Essay on the Language and Philosophy of the Hindoos," and Dr. Prichard's inaugural "Dissertation on the Varieties of the Human Race," were published almost simultaneously; but Schlegel's work is regarded as the more advanced production. (See Bunsen's *Philosophy of Universal History*, vol. ii. p. 50.)

NOTE LXXI., p. 71.

In 1854 M. Bunsen wrote: "Geographically then, and historically, it is true that Canaan was the son of Egypt; for the Canaanitic tribes which inhabited historical Canaan came from Egypt. *In the same sense*, Nimrod is called a Kushite, which means a man of the land of Kush. The Bible mentions but one Kush, Æthiopia; *an Asiatic Kush exists only in the imagination of the interpreters*, and is the child of their despair. Now, *Nimrod was no more a Kushite by blood* than Canaan was an Egyptian; but the Turanian (Transoxanian) tribe, represented by him, came as a devastating people, which had previously conquered that part of Africa, back into Asia, and there established the first great empire." (*Philosophy of Univ. History*, vol. i. p. 191.) But in 1858, Sir Henry Rawlinson, having obtained a number of Babylonian documents more ancient than any previously discovered, was able to declare authoritatively, that the early inhabitants of Southern Babylonia "were of a cognate race with the primitive colonists both of Arabia and of the African Ethiopia." (See the author's *Herodotus*, vol. i. p. 442.) He found their vocabulary to be "*undoubtedly Cushite* or Ethiopian," belonging to that stock of tongues which in the sequel were every where more or less mixed up with the Semitic languages, but of which we have the purest modern specimens in the *Mahra* of Southern Arabia, *and the Galla of Abyssinia*." (Ibid. note 9.) He found also that "the traditions both of Babylonia and Assyria pointed to a connection in very early times between Ethiopia, Southern Arabia, and the cities on the Lower Euphrates." (Ibid.) He therefore adopted the term Cushite as the most proper title by which to distinguish the earlier from the later Babylonians; and reëstablished beyond all doubt or question the fact of "an Asiatic Ethiopia," which probably no one now would be hardy enough to deny. (See, besides the Essay referred to above, Essay xi. of the same volume, p. 655, and an elaborate Article in the *Journal of the Asiatic Society*, vol. xv. part 2, pp. 215–259.)

NOTE LXXII., p. 71.

The monuments give distinct evidence of the early predominance of Babylonia over Assyria, of the spread of population and civilization northwards, and of the comparatively late founding of Nineveh. (See the author's *Herodotus*, vol. i. pp. 448, 455, 456, &c.) They do not exactly *prove* the colonization of Assyria by Semites from Babylonia, but they favor it. (Ibid. pp. 447 and 647.)

NOTE LXXIII., p. 71.

The Hamitic descent of the Canaanites is energetically denied by M. Bunsen, (*Philosophy of Univ. Hist.*, vol. i. pp. 190 and 244,) who identifies them with the Phœnicians, and regards their Semitic character as established. But the researches of Sir H. Rawlinson have convinced him, that the Canaanites proper were not Semites. He holds that they had a "common origin" with the Egyptians, Ethiopians, and Libyans, — an origin which he calls indifferently Scythic or Hamite. "All the Canaanites," he says, "were, I am satisfied, Scyths; and the inhabitants of Syria retained their distinctive ethnic character until quite a late period of history. According to the inscriptions the *Khatta*, or Hittites, were the dominant Scythic race from the earliest times, and they gave way very slowly before the Aramæans, Jews, and Phœnicians, who were the only extensive Semitic immigrants." (*Journal of Asiatic Society*, vol. xv. part 2, p. 230, note.)

NOTE LXXIV., p. 72.

See M. Bunsen's *Philosophy of Univ. Hist.*, vol. i. pp. 221–230, where, though classing the Himyaric with the Semitic languages, he admits its close resemblance, both in vocabulary and in grammatical forms, to the Ethiopic; and compare the author's *Herodotus*, vol. i. p. 447, note 4, and pp. 659, 660.

NOTE LXXV., p. 72.

See Sir H. Rawlinson, in the *Asiatic Society's Journal*, l. s. c. "The Toldoth Beni Noah is undoubtedly *the most authentic record we possess* for the affiliation of those branches of the human race which sprung from the triple stock of the Noachidæ." And again, p. 215, note 3: "The fragment which forms the tenth chapter of Genesis bears the Hebrew title of Toldoth Beni Noah, or the Genealogies of the Noachidæ, and is probably *of the very greatest antiquity*." Compare also the author's *Herodotus*, (vol. i. p. 445,) where the same ethnologist remarks: "We must be cautious in drawing direct ethnological inferences from the linguistic indications of a very early age. It will be far *safer*, at any rate, in these early times to follow the general scheme of ethnic affiliation which is given in the tenth chapter of Genesis."

NOTE LXXVI., p. 72.

The passages to which reference is here made will all be found in the second volume of Dr. Gaisford's edition of the work of Eusebius, pp. 370–392. They were derived by Eusebius from the "Jewish History" of Alexander Polyhistor, a heathen writer. It is thought that some of Polyhistor's authorities, as Artapanus, Cleodemus, Demetrius, and Eupolemus, were Jews. (See the remarks of C. Müller in his preface to the fragments of Polyhistor, *Fragment. Hist. Gr.*, vol. iii. p. 207.) If this be allowed, the weight of heathen testimony is of course *pro tanto* diminished. But reasons have been already given for regarding Eupolemus as a heathen. (See above, Note XXV.) And the religious character of the other three is at least doubtful.

To the writers mentioned in the text may be added, Nicolas of Damascus, who spoke of Abraham's emigration from Chaldæa and settlement in Canaan. (See the *Frag. Hist. Gr.*, vol. iii. p. 373.)

NOTE LXXVII., p. 72.

See especially Faber's *Horæ Mosaicæ*, ch. v. pp. 225–228; and compare Patrick's *Commentary on the Historical Books of the Old Testament*, vol. i. p. 58; Horne's *Introduction to the Critical Study and Knowledge of Holy Scripture*, vol. i. p. 174, &c.

NOTE LXXVIII., p. 73.

Sir H. Rawlinson, in the author's *Herodotus*, vol. i. Essay vi. p. 446.

NOTE LXXIX., p. 73.

The name of the king whom Sir H. Rawlinson identifies with Chedor-laomer is, in the native (Hamitic) Babylonian, *Kudur-Mabuk*. *Mabuk* in Hamitic is found to be the exact equivalent of *Laomer* in Semitic. This is a very recent discovery.

NOTE LXXX., p. 73.

By means of certain monumental notices it has been proved, with a near approach to certainty, that a Babylonian monarch, whose name is read as *Ismi-dagon*, reigned about B. C. 1860. *Kudur-Mabuk* is evidently, by the type of writing which he uses, and the position in which his bricks are found, considerably earlier. Now in the year B. C. 1976 — a century before *Ismi-dagon* — occurs one of the breaks in Berosus' list; and this break moreover occurs within 60 years of the date (B. C. 1917) commonly assigned to the expedition of Chedor-laomer. These chronological coincidences strongly confirm the argument from the identity of name.

NOTE LXXXI., p. 74.

This passage is probably known to most students, but as it is too important to be omitted from the present review of the historical evidences, I subjoin it entire.

"Manetho . . . introducing a supposititious king, Amenophis, says that he desired to see the gods, as Orus had done, one of those who reigned before him. He expressed this desire to his namesake Amenophis, the son of Paapis, who had the reputation of being a partaker of the divine nature, on account of his wisdom and knowledge of the future. His namesake accordingly told him that he would be able to see the gods, if he should purge the whole country of lepers, and all other polluted men. Delighted with this promise, the king gathered out of Egypt all who had any bodily defect, and placed them in the quarries, on the east side of the Nile, that they might work in them, and be separate from the rest of the Egyptians. He says also that there were among them some of the learned priests afflicted with the leprosy; but that Amenophis, the wise man and prophet, feared the anger of the gods towards himself and the king, if they should see the gods without their consent. He also declared, that certain men would form an alliance with these polluted persons, and would get possession of Egypt, and hold it for thirteen years. But not daring to tell these things to the king, he committed them all to writing, and then destroyed himself, to the great grief of the king. After this he writes thus, word for word. 'But when those who were sent to the mines had endured their misery for a long time, the king consented to assign to them, for their abode and protection, the city Avaris, which had then been abandoned by the shepherds. Now this city, according to the ancient theology, is the city of Typhon. Entering into this city, and having it for a centre of their rebellion, they appointed as their prince one of the priests of the Heliopolitans, named Hosarsiphus, and they took an oath to obey him in all things. He gave them, first of all, this law, not to worship the gods, nor to abstain from any of those animals esteemed most sacred in Egypt, but to kill and destroy them all; and not to have intercourse with any but those who had taken the oath. Having established these laws, and many others exceedingly contrary to the Egyptian customs, he commanded that many hands should be employed in repairing the walls of the city, and that they should make themselves ready for war with King Amenophis. Then, joining with him the other priests and polluted persons, he sent ambassadors to the shepherds who had been driven out by Tethmosis, to the city called Jerusalem. He declared to them the treatment which he, and those who shared in his dishonor, had received, and asked them to join all their forces in an expedition against Egypt. He promised first of all to lead them back to Avaris, their ancestral city, to furnish their army abundantly with all things necessary, to fight for them, if need should require, and easily to make the country subject to them. The shepherds were overjoyed, and all eagerly sallied forth, to the number of 200,000, and soon came to Avaris. But Amenophis, the king of Egypt, when he was apprised of their invasion, was not a little troubled, remembering the prediction of Amenophis the son of Paapis. And in the first place gathering the multitude of the Egyptians, and taking counsel with their rulers, he sent for the sacred animals that were chiefly worshipped in their temples to be brought to him, and commanded the priests in different places to hide the images of the gods as securely as possible. His son Sethos, called also Rameses, from his father Rhampses, being a child of five years old, he consigned to his friend. He then passed on with the rest of the Egyptians, amounting to 300,000 men skilled in war. When he met the enemy, however, he did not engage in battle with them, but, thinking that this would be to fight against the gods, he turned back, and came to Memphis. Then taking Apis, and the other sacred animals which had been sent thither, he immediately departed into Ethiopia. For the king of the Ethiopians was under obligations to him; wherefore he received the whole multitude, and furnished them with such necessaries of life as the country afforded, and gave them cities and villages sufficient for them to dwell in during the predetermined period of thirteen years while Amenophis was expelled from his kingdom. He moreover put the Ethiopian army at the service of King Amenophis, for the defence of the frontiers of Egypt. Thus far concerning the Ethiopians. But the Jerusalemites came down with the polluted Egyptians, and treated men with such impious cruelty, that their rule seemed to them who beheld their impieties the very worst possible. For they not only burned cities and villages, and sacrilegiously abused the images of the gods, but, not content with this, they used these images in roasting the animals that were reverenced as sacred, and compelled the priests to be the sacrificers and slaughterers of these animals, and then drove them naked out of the country. It is said also that the priest who gave them their laws, and ordered their civil officers, who was by birth a Heliopolitan, named Osarsiph, from Osiris, the god of Heliopolis, when he had joined himself to this race of men, changed his name, and was called Moses.'

"Such things the Egyptians relate concerning the Jews, and many more which I pass over for the sake of brevity. And Manetho says again, that after these things Amenophis came from Ethiopia with a great force, and his son Rhampses with him, he also having an army; and the two together, engaging in battle with the shepherds and the polluted men, defeated them, and having slain many, drove them *even to the borders of Syria*." (Joseph. *Contra Apionem*, i. 26, 27.)

Compare with this the briefer account of Chæremon, who said, —

"Isis appeared to Amenophis in his sleep, and blamed him because her temple had been destroyed in the war. But Phritiphantes, the sacred scribe, told him that all cause of alarm would be removed, if he should purify Egypt from men who were polluted. Whereupon he gathered 250,000 of these obnoxious persons, and banished them. Over these were the scribes, Moses and Joseph, who was also a sacred scribe. Their Egyptian names were, of Moses, Tisithen, and of Joseph, Peteseph. These came to Pelusium, and found there 380,000 persons, who had been left by Amenophis, because he did not wish to bring them into Egypt. Forming an alliance with these, they marched against Egypt. But Amenophis, without awaiting their attack, fled into Ethiopia, leaving his wife, who was pregnant. She hid herself in a certain cave, where she brought forth a son, whose name was

Messenes. He, after he grew up to manhood, drove the Jews, who were about 200,000, into Syria, and brought back his father from Ethiopia." (Joseph., l. s. c. ch. 32.)

NOTE LXXXII., p. 74.

The name Osarsiph, which, according to Manetho, was the Egyptian appellation of Moses, seems to be a corruption of Joseph, whom Chæremon made Moses' companion and fellow-helper. The statement that Moses was "a priest of Heliopolis" — which was also made by Apion (Josephus, *Contra Apionem*, ii. 2) — is either a perversion of the Scriptural fact of Joseph's marriage with "the daughter of Potipherah, priest of On,"[1] or possibly an indication of a fact not recorded in Scripture, that Moses gained his knowledge of the Egyptian wisdom at that seat of learning. The fear of Amenophis for his son's safety recalls to our thoughts the last of the plagues: the forced labor of the Jews in the stone quarries is not very different from the compulsory brick-making; the cry of pollution is probably connected with the earlier plagues, or perhaps it is only an exaggeration of the feeling which viewed "every shepherd" as "an abomination." (Gen. xlvi. 34.) The mention of Jerusalem, or rather Salem, (the Salemites,) at this time, confirms Gen. xiv. 18; and the occurrence of Rameses as a family name in the dynasty harmonizes with its use as a local designation. (Gen. xlvii. 11; Exod. i. 11, and xii. 37.)

NOTE LXXXIII., p. 75.

See Sir Charles Lyell's *Principles of Geology*, vol. i. p. 240. "I need not dwell," he says, "on the proofs of the low antiquity of our species, for *it is not controverted by any experienced geologist;* indeed, the real difficulty consists in tracing back the signs of man's existence on the earth to that comparatively modern period when species, now his contemporaries, began to predominate. If there be a difference of opinion respecting the occurrence in certain deposits of the remains of man and his works, *it is always in reference to strata confessedly of the most modern order;* and it is never pretended that our race co-existed with assemblages of animals and plants, of which all or even a great part of the species are extinct."

This remark will, I conceive, hold good, whatever judgment is ulti-

[1] Gen. xli. 45.

mately formed by science of the results which have been recently obtained by Mr. Horner in Egypt,[1] by M. Boucher de Perthes in France,[2] and by Mr. Prestwich and others in our own country. The strata examined and said to contain the most ancient human remains hitherto found, are the *alluvium* of Egypt, and the *diluvium* or "drift" of Europe; which are both, geologically, strata of a comparatively modern origin. The rashness of the conclusions as to the *minimum* antiquity of our race in Egypt, which Mr. Horner drew from his researches, has been ably exposed by a writer in the *Quarterly Review*, (April, 1859, No. 210, pp. 419–421.)

Note LXXXIV., p. 75.

The researches and arguments of Blumenbach, Haller, Cuvier, and, above all, of Dr. Prichard, (*Physical History of Mankind*, vol. i. pp. 114–376,) have established this point beyond all reasonable doubt. Even the author of the *Vestiges of Creation* admits "the result, on the whole, of inquiries into what are called the physical history of man," to be, "that conditions such as climate and food, domestication, and perhaps an inward tendency to progress under tolerably favorable circumstances, are sufficient to account for all the outward peculiarities of form and color" observable among mankind. (*Vestiges*, p. 262, tenth edition.)

Note LXXXV., p. 75.

"Physiological Ethnology," says Professor Max Müller, "has accounted for the varieties of the human race, and removed the barriers which formerly prevented us from viewing all mankind as the members of one family, the offspring of one parent. The problem of the variety of language is more difficult, and has still to be solved, as we must include in our survey the nations of America and Africa. But over the languages of the primitive Asiatic Continent of Asia and Europe a new light begins to dawn, which, in spite of perplexing appearances, *reveals more and more clearly the possibility of their common origin.*" (See M. Bunsen's *Philosophy of Universal History*, vol. i. p. 474; and compare pp. 478, 479.)

1 *Account of some recent Researches near Cairo*, (first published in the *Philosophical Transactions*,) by Leonard Horner, Esq., Parts i. and ii. London, 1855 and 1858.

2 *Antiquités Celtiques et Ante-diluviennes*, par M. Boucher de Perthes, Paris, 1847.

NOTE LXXXVI., p. 75.

"It is pleasing to remark," says Sir H. Rawlinson, speaking of the different races in Western Asia, "that if we were to be guided by the mere intersection of linguistic paths, and independently of all reference to the Scriptural record, *we should still be led to fix on the plains of Shinar, as the focus from which the various lines had radiated.*" (*Journal of Royal Asiatic Society*, vol. xv. part 2, p. 232. Compare the statements of the same writer in the author's *Herodotus*, vol. i. p. 586.)

NOTE LXXXVII., p. 75.

The only case in which we can form a judgment of the *linguistic* accuracy of the Pentateuch is that of the Egyptian terms, since here only have we any sufficient knowledge of the language spoken in the country at the time. Under this head come the following: —

1. *Pharaoh*, (פַּרְעֹה,) as the title of Egyptian kings (Gen. xii. 15, xl. 2; Ex. i. 11,) which has been explained as *Ph-ouro*, "the king;" but which is more probably *Ph-rah*, "the Sun," a title borne by the Egyptian monarchs from very early times. (Wilkinson, in the author's *Herodotus*, vol. ii. p. 182, note 1.)

2. *Potiphar*, (פּוֹטִיפַר,) or *Potipherah*, (פּוֹטִי־פֶרַע,) which is *Pete-ph-re*, "belonging to the Sun" — a name common upon the monuments, (Rosellini, *Monumenti Storici*, i. 117; Champollion, *Précis*, Table Générale, p. 23,) and specially appropriate to a Priest of On, or *Heliopolis*. Compare the name *Peteseph*, "belonging to Seb, (Chronos,)" which, according to Chæremon, was the Egyptian name of Joseph. (Supra, Note LXXXI.)

3. *Asenath*, (אָסְנַת,) which is, according to Jablonsky, (*Opuscula*, ii. 208,) *Asshe-neith*, "worshipper of Neith," or more probably, as Gesenius observes, (*Thesaurus*, ad voc.,) *As-neith*, "quæ Neithæ (est,)" "belonging to Neith." It has been doubted whether Neith was worshipped at this early date; but she seems to have been really one of the primitive deities of Lower Egypt. (Bunsen, *Egypt's Place*, vol. i. p. 389.) Her name forms an element in that of Nitocris, (*Neith-akri*,) a queen of the sixth dynasty. (Wilkinson, *Herodotus*, vol. ii. p. 165, note 2.)

4. *Zaphnath-Paaneah*, (צָפְנַת־פַּעְנֵחַ,) the name which Pharaoh gave

to Joseph, is best explained through the Septuagint Psontho-mphanech, which closely corresponds to the Coptic *Psont-mfuneh*, "sustainer of the age," or as Jerome says, a little freely, "salvator mundi." (See Gesenius, *Thesaurus*, p. 1181.) The first two letters have been transposed in the Hebrew, either by accident, or to suit Jewish articulation, and at the same time to produce a name significant to Jewish ears.

5. *Moses* (מֹשֶׁה) was undoubtedly an Egyptian name, since it was selected by Pharaoh's daughter, (Ex. ii. 10.) We are told that it was significant, being chosen "because she drew him out of the water." The real etymology was long since given fully by Josephus, (*Ant. Jud.* ii. 9, § 6,) partially by Philo, (*De vita Mosis*, i. Op. vol. ii. p. 83,) and Clemens Alexandrinus, (*Strom.* i. p. 412.) Josephus — "The Egyptians call water *mo*, and those who are rescued from the water *uses*." Philo — "The Egyptians call water *mos*." Clem. Alex. — "The Egyptians call water *moū*." The last of these forms is the best. *Moū* is still "water" in Coptic, and the old Egyptian word — given by Bunsen as *muau*[1] — was similar. According to Jablonsky (*Opuscula*, i. 152) *oushe* in Coptic is "to save." I am not aware whether this root has been found yet in the ancient Egyptian.

6. Besides these names, a certain number of Egyptian words have been detected in the language of the Pentateuch. Such are אָחוּ, (or אָחֻר; LXX. ἄχει,) which Jablonsky found to signify in Coptic "every green thing which is produced in a pool," (*Opuscula*, vol. i. p. 45;) perhaps תֵּבָה, (LXX. θίβη,) the word used both for Noah's Ark, and for the small ark in which Moses was placed, (La Croze, *Lexicon Egyptiacum*, sub voc.;) and אַבְרֵךְ, which is explained from the Coptic as *au-rek*, "bow every one," or *ape-rek*, "bow the head." (See Gesenius, *Hebräisches und Chaldäisches Handwörterbuch*, ad voc., p. 10, E. T., and compare de Rossi, *Etym. Egypt.*, p. 1.)

The *geographic* accuracy of the Pentateuch has been illustrated by a number of writers. Dr. Stanley, one of the most recent and most calm-judging of modern Oriental travellers, observes with respect to the Mosaic accounts of the Sinaitic desert — "Even if the precise route of the Israelites were unknown, yet the peculiar features of the country have so much in common that the history would still receive *many remarkable illustrations*. . . . The occasional springs, and wells, and

[1] Bunsen's *Egypt*, vol. i. p. 471, No. 313.

brooks, are in accordance with the notices of the 'waters' of Marah, the 'springs' of Elim, the 'brook' of Horeb; the 'well' of Jethro's daughters, with its 'troughs' or tanks. The vegetation is still that which we should infer from the Mosaic history," &c. (*Sinai and Palestine*, pp. 20, 21; compare pp. 22, 24, 129, &c.) In the account of Egypt the accuracy is seen not only in the general description of the territory — its rich meadows and corn-lands; its abounding river, edged with flags and bulrushes, (Ex. ii. 3;) its wealth of waters derived therefrom, "streams and rivers, and ponds, and pools of water," (Ex. vii. 19;) its wheat, and rye, and barley, and flax, (ib. ix. 31, 32,) and green trees (palm-trees?) yielding fruit, (ib. x. 15;) but also in the names and sometimes in the sites of towns. On, (אֹן,) Pithom, (פִּתֹם,) Ramesses, (רַעְמְסֵס,) Zoan, (צֹעַן,) and Migdol, (מִגְדֹּל,) which are among the few Egyptian towns mentioned by Moses, are all well-known places. Of On, the Greek Heliopolis, it is unnecessary to speak. Pithom is the Patumus of Herodotus, (ii. 158,) the city of *Thmei*, (Justice,) called "Thmuin" in the *Itinerary* of Antonine, (p. 9.) Ramesses is *Beth-Rameses*, a city of which we have a description in a hieratic papyrus of the 18th or 19th dynasty. (See *Cambridge Essays*, 1858, Art. VI. p. 254.) Zoan, the Tanis of the LXX. — whence the "Tanitic nome" of Herodotus, (ii. 166,) and the "Tanitic mouth" of later authors, is the modern *San* or *Zan*, evidently a great town in the time of the Rameside monarchs. (Wilkinson, *Ancient Egypt*, i. p. 449.) Migdol, the Magdolus of Hecatæus, (Fr. 282,) retains its name in the *Itinerary* of Antonine, (p. 10,) and appears in the position assigned by Moses, on the north-east frontier, near Pelusium. Again, the name by which Egypt itself is designated, Mizraim, (מִצְרַיִם,) has a peculiar geographical significancy. The dual form marks the *two* Egypts — "the upper and the lower country"— as they are termed in the inscriptions.[1] Equally significant is *Padan*-aram, (פַּדַּן־אֲרָם,) "the *plain* Syria"— the country stretching away from the foot of the hills, (Stanley's *Palestine*, p. 128, note 1,) where Harran stood, which was so different a tract from the mountainous Syria west of the Euphrates. Again, the expression, "the entrance of Hamath," (Numb. xiii. 21,) shows a conversance with the geography of Upper Palestine, whereof this "entrance" is so

[1] The common hieroglyphic signs for the whole of Egypt are *two* crowns, *two* water-plants, or *two* layers of earth. (Lepsius, *Sur l'Alphabet Hiéroglyphique*, Planche I. Groupe vii. col. C.

striking a feature, (Stanley, p. 399,) and with the existence of Hamath at the time, which may be proved from the hieratic papyri of the period. (See *Cambridge Essays*, 1858, p. 268.) Some further geographical points will be touched in Note LXXXIX.

The *ethological* accuracy of the Pentateuch as respects Oriental manners and customs generally, has never been questioned. The life of the Patriarchs in Canaan, the habits of those who dwell in the desert, the chiefs and followers, the tents, the wealth in cattle, the "sitting in the door," the salutations and obeisances, the constant migrations, the quarrels for pasture and water, the marriages with near relatives, the drawing of water from the wells by the young maidens, the troughs for the camels, the stone on the well's mouth, the camels kneeling with their burdens and waiting patiently till the troughs are full, the purchase by weight of silver, the oaths accompanied by peculiar ceremonies, the ox unmuzzled as he treads out the corn, — these and ten thousand similar traits are so true to nature and to fact, even at the present day, (for the East changes but little,) that travellers universally come back from Syria deeply and abidingly impressed with the reality and truthfulness of the Pentateuch in all that respects Eastern manners. Rationalism, in order to meet in any degree the weight of this argument, is forced to betake itself to Egypt, where an artificial system existed in the time of Moses which has now completely passed away. Von Bohlen maintains that in many respects the author of the Pentateuch shows a want of acquaintance with the customs of Egypt, e. g., in his mention of eunuchs at the Egyptian court, (*Commentar*, p. 360,) in his representation of Pharaoh's daughter as bathing in the Nile, (ibid.,) and in his making wine a product of Egypt, (p. 374.) The objections taken are not particularly happy. (See Rosellini as quoted by Hengstenberg, *Ægypten und Mose*, p. 23; and Wilkinson, *Ancient Egyptians*, vol. iii. p. 389; *Herodotus*, vol. ii. p. 126.) Were they more important, they would be greatly outweighed by the multitude of passages where an intimate acquaintance with Ancient Egypt may be discerned. The position of the Egyptians with respect to foreigners — their separation from them, yet their allowance of them in their country, their special hatred of *shepherds*, the suspicion of strangers from Palestine as *spies* — their internal government, its settled character, the power of the King, the influence of the Priests, the great works, the employment of foreigners in their construction, the use of bricks, (cf. *Herod.* ii. 136, with

Wilkinson's note ad loc.,) and of bricks with straw in them, (Wilkinson, l. s. c. and *Camb. Essays*, 1858, p. 259,) the taskmasters, the embalming of dead bodies, the consequent importation of spices, (Gen. xxxvii. 25,) the violent mournings, (Herod. ii. 85,) the dissoluteness of the women, (ibid. ii. 111 ; *Camb. Essays*, 1858, p. 234,) the fighting with horses and chariots, (Wilkinson on Herod. ii. 108 ; *Camb. Essays*, 1858, pp. 240, 241,) — these are a few out of the many points which might be noted marking an intimate knowledge of Egyptian manners and customs on the part of the author of the Pentateuch. (For a full treatment of the question, see the work of Hengstenberg quoted above, which exhibits a very good acquaintance with the works of modern Egyptologers.)

NOTE LXXXVIII., p. 76.

The uncertainty of geographers as to the sites of these cities, and the weak grounds upon which identifications of them were attempted, will be seen by reference even to works so recent as Winer's *Realwörterbuch* (1848) and Kitto's *Biblical Cyclopædia*, (1856.) Ur was thought by some (Ritter, Kitto) to be Orfa or Edessa (so even Bunsen, *Egypt*, vol. iii. p. 366 ;) which according to others (Winer) was Erech : Calneh was supposed to be Ctesiphon, Calah to be Holwan ; Ellasar, which should have been in Lower Babylonia, was thought to be the Larissa of Xenophon, on the middle Tigris ; while Accad was either Sacada or Nisibis. Any slight resemblance of name — any late authority of a Talmudical or Arabic writer — was caught at, in order to fix what the scanty remains of primeval geography left completely unsettled.

NOTE LXXXIX., p. 76.

The following sites seem to have been determined beyond all reasonable doubt by the Babylonian and Assyrian Inscriptions : —

1. Ur of the Chaldees, at *Mugheir*, on the right bank of the Euphrates, not very far above its junction with the *Shat-el-Hie*. This is the true Chaldæa of Scripture and of History, an Armenian Chaldæa being a fiction of the Greeks.

2. Calah at *Nimrúd*, on the left bank of the Tigris, a little above its junction with the Greater Zab. (The Halah of 2 Kings xvii. 6, is a

different place.) The province in which it stands long continued to be called Calachene, (Strab. xvi. 1, § 1; Ptol. vi. 1.)

3. Erech at *Warka*, (the Greek Ὀρχόη,) on the left bank of the Euphrates, and at some distance from the river, about 35 miles N. W. of Ur.

The following identifications, if not certain, are at least highly probable: — 1. Resen with *Kileh-Sherghát*, on the right bank of the Tigris, not very far from its junction with the Lesser Zab. 2. Accad with a town in Lower Babylonia, called *Kinzi Accad* in the Inscriptions, the site of which is not yet determined. 3. Ellasar with *Senkereh*, 15 miles S. E. of *Warka*, on the same side of the Euphrates. 4. Calneh with *Niffer*, in the same tract with *Senkereh* and *Warka*, but much nearer Babylon, and about midway between the two streams. (See the author's *Herodotus*, vol. i. pp. 313, 447, 592, &c.)

For a description of the ruins of Ur and Erech, see Mr. Loftus's *Chaldæa and Susiana*, pp. 128–134, and 162 et seqq.; for those of Calah, see Mr. Layard's *Nineveh and its Remains*, ch. ii. et seqq.; some account is given of Resen (*Kileh-Sherghát*) in the same work, ch. xii.; and of Calneh (*Niffer*) in the same writer's *Nineveh and Babylon*, ch. xxiv.

Note XC., p. 76.

See the account which Mr. Cyril Graham has given of his travels in this region in the *Cambridge Essays* for 1858, pp. 157–162. Compare Dr. Stanley's *Sinai and Palestine*, p. 118.

Note XCI., p. 76.

See Commander Lynch's *Narrative of the United States Expedition to the River Jordan*, and also his *Official Report*. Compare the *Journal* of the Geographical Society, vol. xviii. Artt. 8, 9, and 10, and vol. xx. Art. 15. For a summary of the facts, see Stanley's *Sinai and Palestine*, pp. 276–279, and the *Essays* appended to the first volume of the author's *Herodotus*, Essay ix. pp. 548, 549. Commander Lynch gives the following account of the impression made upon himself and his friends by their careful examination of the River and of the Lake in which it ends: — "It is for the learned to comment on the facts which we have laboriously collected. Upon ourselves, the result is a decided one. We entered upon this sea with conflicting opinions. One of the party was sceptical, and another, I think, a professed unbeliever of the Mosaic account. After twenty-two days' close investigation, if I am not mistaken, *we were unanimous in the conviction of the truth of the Scriptural account* of the destruction of the cities of the plain." (*Narrative*, ch. xvii. p. 253.)

LECTURE III.

Note I., p. 79.

See König, *Alttestament. Studien*, p. 63, et seqq.; Jahn, *Einleitung*, ii. 1, p. 160; and Horne's *Introduction*, vol. v. p. 35.

Note II., p. 79.

See Carpzov, *Introductio ad libros Canonicos Veteris Testamenti*, part i. p. 213, who gives the following list of writers by whom this view has been taken: Theodoret, Procopius, Gregory the Great, Isidore, Eucherius, among the ancients; among the moderns, Walther, Calovius, Hugo, De Lyra, Cajetan, Vatablé, Sixtus Sinensis, Sanctius, Serarius, and Cornelius a Lapide."

Note III., p. 79.

There is no reference to the Book of Joshua *as the work of Joshua* in Scripture. It is first assigned to him in the Talmud. The Fathers are divided in opinion as to its authorship. Athanasius, for instance, includes it among the books "not written by the persons whose names they bear and of whom they treat." (Synops. S. S. § 10; *Opera*, vol. ii. p. 139, B.)

Note IV., p. 79.

See the summary of the arguments in Keil's *Commentar über d. Buch Josua*, Einleitung, § 3, p. xlvii. Keil's conclusion is, "that the historical references and the peculiarity of style completely disprove the supposition that the Book of Joshua was written during the captivity; that they do not point to the times of Samuel, or Saul, or David, as the date of its composition, but rather to those after Joshua, and *within a generation of his death*. Who then," he asks, "was the author? Most probably one of the elders, who lived for some time after Joshua, and who had seen all the works of Jehovah which he did for Israel, occupied himself at the close of his life with writing down, partly from recollection, partly from contemporary documents and other written notices, the things which he had himself witnessed, and thus composed the work which we possess under the name of Joshua."[1] I should be disposed to acquiesce in this view.

NOTE V., p. 81.

De Wette boldly denies this. "The book," he says, "nowhere contains any separate contemporary documents," (nicht einmal einzelne gleichzeitige Bestandtheile enthält es. *Einleitung*, § 169, p. 213.) But Rosenmüller, Jahn, and others, seem to have reason on their side when they urge, that the accounts of the boundaries of the tribes, (xv. 21–62; xviii. 21–28; xix. 1–48,) and of the cities of the Levites, (xxi. 13–40,) have all the appearance of such documents. Such a document is also, as it seems to me, the list of slaughtered kings in chapter xii., (verses 9–24.) It appears by ch. xviii. 1–10, and xxiv. 26, that such records were in use at the time; and it is a reasonable supposition that they formed the basis upon which the author, who quotes them, composed his work. Eichhorn observed long ago — "The account of the division of the land bears in many places the marks of a *protocol*, which from its very nature never gives at once a brief sketch of the whole arrangement, but describes its gradual progress, and relates, one after another, all the alterations, improvements, and additions, that were made from time to time." (*Einleitung*, vol. iii. p. 365.) Keil remarks recently — "When we come to the second part of the book, and observe the things of which it particularly treats; how the history which it contains of the division of Canaan amongst the tribes is accompanied with full descriptions of the boundaries of the territory of each tribe, with catalogues of cities, and so on, we are necessarily led to the

[1] In the quotations from Professor Keil's learned and sensible work, I follow the Translation of Mr. J. Martin, which forms the fourteenth volume of Clark's *Foreign Theological Library*, New Series, (Edinburgh, 1857.)

conclusion, that the writer availed himself of *written records*, if not of *official documents*." (*Commentar*, Einleitung, § 4; p. 47, E. T.) Compare Horne, *Introduction*, vol. v. pp. 36, 37.

NOTE VI., p. 81.

See Carpzov, *Introductio ad Libros Canonicos Veteris Testamenti*, p. 172, et seqq.; and compare the quotation from Baba-Bathra in Theodore Parker's *Translation of De Wette*, vol. i. p. 31. See also Horne's *Introduction*, vol. v. p. 42.

NOTE VII., p. 81.

Compare Judges i. 21 with 2 Sam. v. 6–9. This passage, it is admitted, "*seems* to belong to the time of David." (Parker's *De Wette*, vol. i. p. 206.)

NOTE VIII., p. 81.

The chronology of the Book of Judges is involved in great uncertainty. Several periods are unestimated, as the time between the death of Joshua and the first servitude, the judgeship of Shamgar, and some portion of the reign of Abimelech. The servitudes added together occupy 111 years, and the periods during which the land was at rest or under Judges occupy apparently 299 years, or if Samson's judgeship be included in the last servitude, (Jud. xv. 20,) 279 years. The total is thus 410, or 390.[1] But in 2 Kings vi. 1, the entire period between the Exodus and the Dedication of the Temple is declared to have been no more than 480 years. Now if we take the lower of the two numbers derivable from Judges, and add the sojourn in the wilderness, (40 years,) the time of Joshua's judgeship, (say 20 years,) the interval between Joshua's death and the 1st servitude, (say 5 years,) the judgeships of Eli, (40 years,) and of Samuel, (more than 20 years, 1 Sam. vii. 2,) the reigns of Saul, (40 years,) of David, (40 years,) and the three years of Solomon's reign before the Dedication, we obtain the result of $(390 + 40 + 20 + 5 + 40 + 20 + 40 + 40 + 3 =)$ 598 years, or more than a century beyond the estimate in Kings. It is therefore

[1] With this nearly agrees St. Paul's estimate of 450 years from the division of the land by lot to Samuel the prophet, (Acts xiii. 20;) for $390 + 40$ (the time of Eli's judgeship) $+ 20$ (a not improbable estimate for the time between the death of Moses and the 1st Servitude) $= 450$ years.

thought that the period of the Judges must be reduced; and the term ordinarily assigned to them, exclusive of Eli and Samuel, is from 300 to 350 years. (See the marginal dates in the English Bible, and compare Clinton, *Fasti Hellenici*, vol. i. p. 313, note [n].) M. Bunsen, with his usual boldness, reduces the time still further, making the period from the death of Joshua to that of Samson no more than 173 years. (See his *Egypt*, vol. iii. p. 288.) This is effected by giving Othniel and Deborah 8 years each instead of 40, by reducing the time between the 2d and 3d servitudes from 80 years to 7, by shortening Gideon's presidency from 40 years to 10, and by regarding the line of Judges from Tola to Abdon as double, whereby 94 years are compressed into 48! If chronology be treated in this spirit, it is to be feared that it will shortly come to be regarded pretty nearly in the same light as the etymology of the last century, in which, it was said, "Vowels are good for nothing, and consonants of small account." —

NOTE IX., p. 82.

Jahn, *Einleitung*, § 46, vol. ii. p. 232, et seqq. Herbst, *Einleitung*, vol. ii. p. 139, et seqq.; Graf, *Dissertatio de librorum Samuelis et Regum compositione*, &c. A good refutation of Jahn's theory will be found in Kitto's *Cyclopædia*, in the article on the "Books of Samuel," vol. ii. p. 685.)

NOTE X., p. 82.

See Carpzov, *Introductio*, &c., p. 213. Modern critics mostly take the view that the Books of Samuel were merely *founded* on these documents. (See Hävernick, *Einleitung*, § 161; Stuart, *History of the Old Testament Canon*, § 6, p. 134; Rev. J. Eadie in Kitto's *Cyclopædia*, vol. ii. p. 684; &c.) Horne, however, with Carpzov (p. 215) and Spanheim, (*Opera*, vol. i. p. 367,) holds to the ancient view. (See his *Introduction*, vol. v. p. 48.) The difference between the two views is not great.

NOTE XI., p. 83.

Ahijah the Shilonite is mentioned as a contemporary of Solomon in 1 Kings xi. 29. As the visions of Iddo the seer were "against Jeroboam the son of Nebat," he must have been, at the latest, contemporary with Solomon's successor.

NOTE XII., p. 84.

De Wette says correctly — "The history of David, contained in 1 Chron. x.–xxix., is in parts entirely consistent with that in the books of Samuel; but it is distinguished from that by having *several accounts peculiar to itself*, and especially by its Levitical accounts." (Einleitung, § 188, p. 241; vol. ii. p. 261, of Parker's *Translation*.) Such accounts are particularly the following — 1. The lists of those who joined David at Ziklag and at Hebron, (ch. xii.) 2. David's imstructions to Solomon and the princes with regard to the temple, (ch. xxii. and ch. xxviii.) 3. His offerings and those of the people, (ch. xxix. 1–9.) 4. His thanksgiving, and prayer, (ibid. 10–19.) 5. His great sacrifice and installing of Solomon as king for the second time, (ibid. 20–25.) And, 6. The lists of the Levites, Priests, singers, porters, captains, &c., as made out or appointed by David, (chs. xxii.–xxvii.) The remainder of the first book of Chronicles follows Samuel closely, in most passages almost to the letter; e. g.

1 CHRON. x. 1–10.	1 SAM. xxxi. 1–10.
Now the Philistines fought against Israel; and the men of Israel fled from before the Philistines, and fell down slain in mount Gilboa. And the Philistines followed hard *after* Saul, and *after* his sons; and the Philistines slew Jonathan, and Abinadab, and Malchi-shua, the sons of Saul. And the battle went sore against Saul, and the archers hit him, and he was wounded of the archers, &c., &c.	Now the Philistines fought against Israel: and the men of Israel fled from before the Philistines, and fell down slain in mount Gilboa. And the Philistines followed hard *upon* Saul and *upon* his sons; and the Philistines slew Jonathan, and Abinadab, and Melchi-shua, Saul's sons. And the battle went sore against Saul, and the archers hit him; and he was *sore* wounded of the archers, &c., &c.

NOTE XIII., p. 84.

That the seventy-eighth Psalm is a work of David's time, is apparent from its bringing the history down to him, and then closing abruptly. The title, "Maschil of Asaph," is an external confirmation of this view.

Even De Wette appears to allow that Asaph was the author. (*Einleitung*, § 271, p. 366.) In this Psalm are mentioned the following historical facts: (1.) The giving of the law by Jehovah, (verse 5;) (2.) The command that it should be made known by fathers to their children, (verses 5, 6; compare Deut. iv. 9, &c.;) (3.) the miracles wrought in Egypt, (verse 12;) (4.) the turning of the rivers, and (5.) other waters, into blood, (verse 44;) (6.) the plague of flies, (v. 45;) (7.) of frogs, (ib.;) (8.) of locusts, (v. 46;) (9.) of hail, (v. 47;) (10.) the destruction by the hail of cattle as well as trees, (v. 48;) (11.) the death of the first-born, (v. 51;) (12.) the employment of *angels* in this destruction, (v. 49;) (13.) the divine leading of the Israelites out of Egypt, (v. 52;) (14.) the pillar of cloud (15.) by day, (v. 14;) (16.) the pillar of fire (17.) by night, (ibid.;) (18.) the division of the Red Sea, (v. 13;) (19.) the standing of the water *in a heap*, (ibid.; compare Ex. xv. 8;) (20.) the divine guidance of the Israelites through the sea, (v. 53;) (21.) the overwhelming of the Egyptians, (ib.;) (22.) the frequent murmuring in the wilderness, (verses 17–20;) (23.) the bringing forth of water from the rock, (v. 15;) (24.) in vast abundance, (v. 16;) (25.) the asking for meat, (v. 18;) (26.) the kindling of a fire against the people, (v. 21; compare Numb. xi. 1;) (27.) the manna, (v. 24;) (28.) its coming down from heaven, (v. 23; compare Ex. xvi. 4;) (29.) the ampleness of the supply, (v. 25;) (30.) the giving of quails, (v. 27;) (31.) which were brought by a wind, (v. 26; compare Numb. xi. 30,) (32.) and let fall "round about their habitation," (v. 28; compare Numb. xi. 31;) (33.) the destructive plague which followed, (v. 31,) (34.) "while the meat was yet in their mouths," (v. 30; compare Numb. xi. 33;) (35.) the various further provocations, (vv. 32, 37, &c.;) (36.) the punishment by "consuming their days" in the wilderness, (v. 33;) (37.) the mercy of God in "not stirring up all his wrath," (v. 38;) (38.) the frequent repentances after punishment, and frequent relapses, (vv. 34–42;) (39.) the divine conduct to the border of the Holy Land, (v. 54;) (40.) the casting out of the Heathen before them, (v. 55;) (41.) the division of the inheritances, (ib.;) (42.) the cowardice of Ephraim, (v. 9; compare Josh. xvi. 10; Judges i. 29;) (43.) the backsliding and idolatry in Canaan, (vv. 56–58;) (44.) the placing of the tabernacle at Shiloh, (v. 60;) (45.) its capture, (v. 61;) (46.) the great slaughter at the same time, (v. 62;) (47.) the slaughter of priests in the battle, (v. 64;) (48.) the punishment of the captors by emerods, (v. 66;) (49.) the choice of the territory of Judah for the final resting-place of the tabernacle, (v. 68;) (50.) the choice of Mount Zion as the place where it should be set up, (ib.;) (51.) the selection of David to be king, (v. 70;) (52.) his being taken "from the sheep-folds," (ibid.;) and (53.) the integrity and excellence of his rule, (v. 72.)

NOTE XIV., p. 85.

Stanley's *Sinai and Palestine*, pp. 132, 133.

NOTE XV., p. 85.

M. Bunsen supposes that Assyria, from the commencement of its independence in B. C. 1273, was not only a powerful kingdom, but a great empire, holding Syria, Palestine, and even occasionally Egypt in subjection, (*Egypt*, vol. iii. pp. 269, 289, &c.) But this view rests entirely upon Ctesias, a writer (as M. Bunsen confesses[1]) of very low authority; or rather it rests upon an odd jumble between the facts (?) of Ctesias and the dates of Herodotus and Berosus. Nothing is more plain from the Assyrian inscriptions, the authority of which M. Bunsen admits,[2] than the *gradual* rise of Assyria to power during the 520 (526) years assigned by Herodotus to the Empire. Tiglath-Pileser I., whose date is fixed, with a near approach to certainty, in the latter part of the eleventh century B. C., gives a list of his four ancestors and predecessors which must reach back at least to B. C. 1200, wherein he calls the first of them "the king who first organized the country of Assyria;" the second and third kings who were "established in the government of Assyria;" and the fourth, his father, "the subduer of foreign countries;" while he calls himself "the illustrious prince who has pursued after the enemies of Asshur and has subjugated *all the earth*." Yet his campaigns are only in the Kurdish mountains, in Armenia, Cappadocia, and upper Syria about Carchemish. He does not penetrate to Hamath, to Phœnicia, or to Damascus, much less to Palestine; while he constantly declares that he is engaged with tribes and countries which none of the Assyrian kings had ever before reached. (See the Great

[1] *Egypt*, vol. iii. p. 433. [2] Ibid. p. 436.

Inscription, published by the Royal Asiatic Society,[1] pp. 22, 24, 34, 42, &c.)

Note XVI., p. 85.

See Wilkinson in the author's *Herodotus*, vol. ii. pp. 374–376. Compare Bunsen, *Egypt*, vol. iii. pp. 210, 211, 219–221, &c.

Note XVII., p. 86.

See above, Note XV. Chushan-Rishathaim is placed by most Biblical chronologists between B. C. 1400, and B. C. 1350. M. Bunsen puts him a century later. (*Egypt*, vol. iii. p. 272.) Even according to this latter view, he preceded Tiglath-Pileser I. by above a century.

It is quite a gratuitous supposition of M. Bunsen's, that Chushan-Rishathaim was "a Mesopotamian satrap," (l. s. c.,) — "the Assyrian satrap of Mesopotamia," (p. 289.) Scripture calls him "king;" and besides, the cuneiform monuments make it perfectly clear that Assyria did not extend her dominion to Aram-Naharaim (the Aramaic portion of Mesopotamia, or the country between the Khabour and the Euphrates) till the middle of the twelfth century. M. Bunsen says, "There *can never have been* an empire in Eastern Syria coexistent with Assyria and Babylonia," (p. 293.) Why can there not? If the Assyrian and Babylonian kingdoms of the early period be rightly apprehended, there is no more difficulty in supposing a powerful Aramæan state in Western Mesopotamia, than in imagining the country divided up, as we must otherwise regard it, among a number of petty principalities. Chushan-Rishathaim, however, it is to be observed, reigned probably *before* the Assyrian independence was established.

Note XVIII., p. 86.

Moses says, "When he (i. e. Joshua) was destroying the Canaanites, some fled to Agra, and sought Tharsis in ships. This appears from an inscription, carved on pillars in Africa, which is extant even in our own time, and is of this purport: 'We, the chiefs of the Canaanites, fleeing from Joshua the Robber, have come hither to dwell.'" *Hist. Armen.*, i. 18.

[1] Printed by J. W. Parker, West Strand, London, 1857.

NOTE XIX., p. 86.

Procopius expresses himself as follows. Having mentioned Tigisis, (Tangiers,) a city of Numidia, he proceeds — "Where there are two columns, made of white stone, near the great fountain, having carved upon them Phœnician letters, which read thus in the language of the Phœnicians: — 'We are they who fled from the face of Joshua the Robber, the son of Nun.'" (*De Bello Vandalico*, ii. 10.) This is clearly the language of an eye-witness. Procopius, it must be remembered, had accompanied Belisarius to Africa.

NOTE XX., p. 86.

(Suidas ad voc. *Χαναάν* — Canaan.) "And there are up to the present time such slabs in Numidia, containing the following inscription: —'We are Canaanites, whom Joshua the Robber drove out.'"

NOTE XXI. p. 87.

Keil, *Commentar über d. Buch Josua*, Einleitung, § 4, p. li.; p. 51, E. T.

NOTE XXII., p. 87.

Mr. Kenrick, who admits the existence of an inscription supposed to have the meaning given to it by the writers above quoted, decides that the inscription must have been *mistranslated*. (*Phœnicia*, p. 68.) He remarks that the explanations of the hieroglyphical and cuneiform inscriptions which were furnished by those who professed to understand them to the inquisitive Greeks, read us a lesson of distrust; and suggests that a monument of the time of Joshua would have been unintelligible even to learned archæologists in the days of Justinian. But the monument may have been national and genuine without its dating from within a thousand years of the time of Joshua; and if the cuneiform and hieroglyphical inscriptions were not accurately rendered to the Greeks, it was less through ignorance than through malice that they were perverted. In this case the translation given by the natives is clearly an honest one; and its peculiarities seem to me in its favor. The Aramaism, "ἐκ προσώπου,"[1] is admitted to be "a plausible argument for the

[1] From the face.

correctness of the interpretation," (Kenrick, l. s. c.) The form of the inscription, in which certain persons, not named or described, speak in the first person plural, which is said to be "wholly unlike that of genuine lapidary documents," (Kenrick, p. 67,) is no doubt unusual; but as certainly it is not impossible. The early cuneiform documents are commonly in the first person. And if the inscription were set up in a public place in Tingis, it would be sufficiently evident that by "we" was meant the people of the city. Besides, we are not sure that this was the whole of the inscription. The authors who report it are only concerned with a particular passage. There may have been a context, which would have taken away all appearance of harshness and abruptness from the record.

Note XXIII. p. 87.

Very few Phœnician inscriptions have been found in Africa of a later date than the age of Augustus. (See Gesenius's *Monumenta Scripturæ Linguæque Phœniciæ*, pp. 13, 313–328.) The Latin language appears to have by that time almost entirely superseded the Carthaginian for all public purposes.

Note XXIV., p. 88.

Herod. ii. 142. "Within this period, they say that the sun has four times departed from his usual course, rising twice where he now sets, and setting twice where he now rises."

Note XXV., p. 88.

"When Herodotus, the father of profane history, tells us, from the priests of Egypt, that their traditions had informed them, that in very remote ages the sun had four times departed from his regular course, having twice set where he ought to have risen, and twice risen where he ought to have set, — it is impossible to read this most singular tradition without recollecting the narrative in the book of Joshua, which relates, 'that the sun stood still in the midst of heaven, and hastened not to go down about a whole day;' and the fact related in the history of Hezekiah, 'that the sun went back ten degrees on the dial of Ahaz.'" (Horne, *Introduction to the Critical Study and Knowledge of Holy Scripture*, vol. i. p. 176. Compare Goguet, *Origines Legum et Artium*, vol. iii. p. 300.)

NOTE XXVI., p. 88.

Three other explanations of the narrative in Joshua have been suggested. Grotius, Isaac Peyrerius, Spinoza, and others, conjecture that a miracle was wrought, but not an astronomical one. Divine power caused, they think, an extraordinary refraction of the sun's rays, by which it continued to light up the field of battle long after its disk had sunk below the horizon. Michaelis, Schultz, Hess, and Dathe believe that nothing strange took place with regard to the sun, but that it continued to lighten all night, in consequence of which the Israelites were able to continue the pursuit. Finally, Keil has suggested that nothing marvellous or out of the common course is intended in the narrative. The words of Joshua, "Sun, stand thou still," &c., (or "Sun, wait thou," as he translates it,) were, he thinks, spoken *in the morning;* and the prayer was simply that the sun might not set till the people had avenged themselves upon their enemies. The whole passage from verse 12 to verse 15 inclusive, he considers to be quoted from the poem known as "the book of Jasher;" and therefore he feels justified in explaining its language poetically: "If we had had before us simple prose or the words of the historian himself," it would have been necessary to admit that the day was miraculously lengthened. But the words of a poet must be understood poetically. He remarks, that there is no reference to the miracle in the rest of Scripture (for he fairly enough questions whether Hab. iii. 11 is such a reference) — a strange silence, if so great a miracle as that commonly understood at the present day, was really wrought on the occasion. These views on the part of a learned Hebraist, and of one who has no prejudice against miracles, seem to deserve attention. (See Keil's *Commentar über d. Buch Josua,* ch. x. pp. 177-193; pp. 251-269, E. T.)

NOTE XXVII., p. 89.

Ap. Euseb. *Præp. Ev.* ix. 30. "After this arose the prophet Samuel. Then, by the will of God, through the agency of Samuel, Saul was chosen king; and he died after having reigned twenty-one years. Then David, his son, took possession of the kingdom, and discomfited *the Syrians, who dwell by the river Euphrates,* and subdued Commagene, and the Assyrians and Phœnicians of Galadene."

Note XXVIII., p. 89.

Fragmenta Hist. Græc., vol. iii. pp. 373, 374, Fr. 31: "Now a great while after this, one of the inhabitants of the country, whose name was Adad, reigned over Damascus, and the rest of Syria except Phœnice. He made war with David, king of Judæa, and contended with him in many battles: but in the last, fought on the banks of the Euphrates, in which he was defeated, he showed himself the foremost of kings in strength and valor. It may be said that Nicolas, being the friend of Herod the Great, would have ready access to the sacred books of the Jews, and may have drawn his narrative thence. But the fragments of Nicolas do not indicate this. In the very few places where he touches ancient Jewish history, it is always in connection with his own country, and from a Damascene point of view. It is also to be remarked, that while he omits main features of the Jewish narrative, as the fact that the Syrians took part in the war against David as allies of the king of Zobah, he adds features not contained in that narrative; as the name of the Syrian king, the extent of his dominions, and the occurrence of several battles before the last disaster. These points are quite compatible with the Jewish narrative, but they could not be drawn from it."

Note XXIX., p. 90.

Eupolemus said, in continuation of the passage above quoted: "He also made expeditions against the Idumeans, and Ammonites, and Moabites, and Ituræans, and Nabatæans, and Nabdæans." (Euseb. *Præp. Ev.* l. s. c.)

Note XXX., p. 90.

See Dr. Stanley's *Sinai and Palestine*, pp. 262–264.

Note XXXI., p. 90.

See Heeren's *Asiatic Nations*, vol. ii. pp. 119–126; and Kenrick's *Phœnicia*, pp. 201–205.

Note XXXII., p. 91.

The superior antiquity and preëminence in early times of Sidon over Tyre has been disputed. Niebuhr in his Lectures (*Vorträge über Alte*

Geschichte, vol. i. p. 94; p. 78, E. T.) speaks of it as doubtful. And the writer of the article on Phœnicia, in Dr. Smith's *Dictionary of Greek and Roman Geography*, endeavors to prove the contrary, (vol. ii. p. 609.) But his arguments do not appear to me very cogent. It is easy to understand how Tyre, which in later times completely eclipsed her neighbor, should have assertors of her superior antiquity in the days of her glory, without supposing that her claim was founded in justice; but is inexplicable that Sidon should in her lowest depression have succeeded in maintaining her claim against Tyre, unless there had been truth on her side. Mr. Kenrick appears to me to decide the controversy aright, when he concludes, that "Tyre was probably at first only a dependency of Sidon." (See his *Phœnicia*, pp. 340–342.)

There is one important argument in favor of the early preëminence of Sidon, which is not noticed either by Mr. Kenrick, or the writer in Smith's Dictionary. *Sidon takes precedence of Tyre in the early Egyptian lists.* (See M. Bunsen's *Egypt*, vol. iii. p. 214; and *Cambridge Essays* for 1858, Art. vi. p. 257.)

NOTE XXXIII., p. 91.

Homer makes no mention at all of Tyre or the Tyrians, while he speaks of Sidon and the Sidonians repeatedly. (See Hom. Il. vii. 289, 290; xxiii. 741–744; Od. iv. 618; xv. 117, and 425.) He also in one passage uses "Sidonia" as the name of Phœnicia in general.[1] It has been suggested that he preferred "Sidon" and "Sidonian" to "Tyre" and "Tyrian," because the words are more "sonorous." (See *Dict. of Greek and Roman Geography*, l. s. c.) But he would scarcely on that account have so determinedly excluded Tyre, the more important city of the two at the time when he wrote, from all mention in either of his poems.

NOTE XXXIV., p. 91.

Strabo in one place (xvi. 2, § 22) speaks somewhat obscurely on the subject; but in another (i. 2, § 33) he distinctly calls Sidon the mother city (τὴν μητρόπολιν) of all Phœnicia.

[1] "They have embarked and gone away to populous Sidonia, but I am left behind with an aching heart." (*Od.* xiii. 285, 286.)

Note XXXV., p. 91.

Justin says, "The nation of the Tyrians was founded by the Phœnicians, who, being annoyed by earthquakes, left their native country, and dwelt first in the Assyrian marsh, but afterwards on the sea-coast. Here they built a city, which they named Sidon, from the abundance of fish; for *Sidon* is the Phœnician name for *fish*. Many years afterwards, being overcome by the king of the Ascalonians, (i. e. the inhabitants of Ashkelon,) they took to their ships, and landing at Tyre founded a city there, a year before the overthrow of Troy." (*Historiæ*, xviii. 3.) Tyre is here made an actual colony from Sidon. (Compare Isaiah xxiii. 12, where Tyre is addressed as "daughter of Sidon.")

Note XXXVI., p. 91.

Josephus calls Dius "a man who is believed to have been very exact in Phœnician history." (*Contra Apion.* i. 17.) He probably lived soon after the time of Alexander.

Note XXXVII., p. 91.

Josephus distinctly states that Menander drew his Phœnician history from native sources. See his treatise *Contra Apion.*, i. 18: "Now this man wrote an account of the acts performed among the Greeks and the Barbarians, under each of their kings, taking great pains to learn the history from the national literature of each people." (Compare *Ant. Jud.* ix. 14.)

Dius and Menander appear to have been silent about Sidon, and to have made their Phœnician histories little more than histories of Tyre. (See their fragments in C. Müller's *Fragm. Hist. Gr.*, vol. iv. pp. 398 and 445–447.)

Note XXXVIII., p. 91.

The preëminence of Tyre over the other Phœnician cities from the time of David to the close of Phœnician history, has never, I believe, been denied. It is indicated in Scripture by the uniform tenor of the prophecies, (Is. xxiii. 1–18; Jer. xxv. 22, xlvii. 4; Ez. xxvi.–xxviii., &c.;) on the monuments by the precedency assigned to Tyre in the lists of Phœnician towns, (Layard, *Nineveh and Babylon*, p. 356; Sir

H. Rawlinson's *Commentary on the Inscriptions of Babylonia and Assyria*, p. 30; compare the author's *Herodotus*, vol. i. p. 470,) and in profane history by the constant mention which is made of Tyre, and the few and scattered notices of Sidon which occur during this period. The only remarkable exception to this *consensus* is Herodotus, who seems impressed with the superiority of Sidon. (See book vii. ch. 98, where the Sidonian king is given the post of honor; and chaps. 44, 96, 99, 100, &c., where the Sidonian ships are represented as excelling all the rest.) Perhaps he is unconsciously biassed by his Homeric learning; or perhaps Sidon did temporarily recover the preëminence from about B. C. 580 to B. C. 480, in consequence of Nebuchadnezzar's siege and destruction of Tyre. Tyre, however, was manifestly once more the leading city at the time of the invasion of Alexander. (Arrian, *Exped. Alex.*, ii. 15, et seqq.)

NOTE XXXIX., p. 91.

See Kenrick's *Phœnicia*, p. 58.

NOTE XL., p. 92.

A "Hiram, king of Tyre," is mentioned in an inscription of Tiglath-Pileser II. (See the author's *Herodotus*, vol. i. p. 470.)

NOTE XLI., p. 92.

"Mapen, the son of Sirom," (or Hirom,) was king of Tyre at the time of Xerxes's expedition against Greece, (Herodot. vii. 98.) The name also occurs among the Phœnicians of Cyprus, (ib. v. 104.)

NOTE XLII., p. 92.

The following is the passage of Menander concerning Hiram which Josephus has preserved to us: — "Now when Abibalus died, his son Hiram succeeded to the kingdom. He lived fifty-three years, and reigned thirty-four. He raised a bank on what was called 'the broad place,' and set up the golden pillar in the temple of Jupiter. *Moreover he went and cut timber from the mountain called Lebanon*, for cedar beams for the roofs of the temples; and tearing down the ancient temples he built new ones, and consecrated the groves of Hercules and Astarte, and built the temple of Hercules first in the month Peritius, and afterwards that of Astarte, when he had marched against the Tityans, who refused to pay tribute. Having subdued them, he returned. In his reign there was one Abdemon, a very young man, who solved the problems which Solomon, King of Jerusalem, proposed." (*Contra Apion.*, i. 18.)

Note XLIII., p. 92.

The words of Dius, as reported by Josephus, are — "On the death of Abibalus, his son Hiram became king. This man raised banks in the eastern part of the city, and made it larger, and united to it the temple of Olympian Jupiter, which before stood on an island by itself. He built a causeway between, and adorned this temple with golden offerings. Moreover, *he went up into Lebanon, and cut timber* to build temples. Now they say that *Solomon*, who ruled over Jerusalem, *sent riddles to Hiram*, and asked to receive riddles from him; on the condition that the one who could not solve them should pay a sum of money to the one who solved them. When Hiram had agreed to this, and was not able to solve the riddles, he paid a large sum of money as a forfeit. The account states, moreover, that one Abdemon, a man of Tyre, solved the riddles proposed, and proposed others himself, which Solomon being unable to solve, he forfeited a large sum to Hiram. (*Contra Apion.*, i. 17.)

Note XLIV., p. 93.

See Clem. Alex. *Stromata*, i. p. 386: "Hiram gave his own daughter to Solomon . . . as Menander of Pergamus says." Compare Tatian, *Adversus Græcos*, 37, p. 273. Mr. Kenrick thinks this was a mere "popular tradition," to which the intimate friendship between the two kings gave rise. He argues that Hiram would not have married his daughter to Solomon, "since she could only have been a secondary wife," and he further urges the silence of Scripture. (See his *Phœnicia*, p. 356.) The latter is always a weak ground, and in the present instance is not fully sustained, since among Solomon's secondary wives are mentioned "Sidonian (i. e. Phœnician) princesses." The force of the former argument will depend on the relative greatness which we assign to the two princes. I should be inclined to regard the power of Solomon as greater, and that of Hiram as less, than Mr. Kenrick imagines.

NOTE XLV., p. 93.

Wilkinson, in the author's *Herodotus*, vol. ii. p. 375; Bunsen, *Egypt*, vol. iii. pp. 206, 207.

NOTE XLVI., p. 93.

See Euseb. *Præp. Ev.*, ix. 31–34. The passage is also given among the fragments of Polyhistor, in Müller's *Fragmenta Historicorum Græcorum*, vol. iii. pp. 225, 226, Fr. 18.

NOTE XLVII., p. 94.

Egyptian chronology has been made out with tolerable certainty from the Apis stelæ discovered by M. Mariette, as far as the accession of Tirhakah, which appears to have been in B. C. 690. (Wilkinson, in the author's *Herodotus*, vol. ii. pp. 380, 381.) Manetho's dynasties place between Tirhakah and the commencement of the 22d dynasty a space of about 275 years. This would give B. C. 965 as the date of Shishak's (or Sesonchis') accession. Assuming from the Canon of Ptolemy B. C. 651 as the date of Evil-merodach's accession, we obtain, by following the line of the kings of Judah, B. C. 976 for the accession of Rehoboam, and B. C. 1016 for that of Solomon. This is as near an agreement as we could reasonably expect, between two chronologies both of which are somewhat uncertain.[1]

NOTE XLVIII., p. 94.

Sesonchis is the form used by Africanus, Sesonchosis that adopted by Eusebius. (See the Fragments of Manetho, collected by Mons. C. Müller, in his *Fragmenta Hist. Gr.*, vol. ii. p. 590, Frs. 60 and 61.)

NOTE XLIX., p. 94.

See Wilkinson, in the author's *Herodotus*, vol. ii. p. 377, and Bunsen, *Egypt*, vol. iii. p. 241.

[1] The dates furnished by the Apis *stelæ* prove that Manetho's lists, as we have them, are not wholly to be depended on. In the Scripture chronology of the time, one element of doubt is furnished by the difference which sometimes exists between the LXX. and the Hebrew text. Another arises from the want of exact agreement between the chronology of the Israelite and of the Jewish kings.

The 21st, or first Tanite dynasty, belonged to the sacerdotal caste, and in various respects bore a peculiar character. With Sheshonk, the first king of the 22d, or first Bubastite, dynasty, we have a return to the old character of Egyptian monarchs. (Wilkinson, in the author's *Herodotus*, vol. ii. pp. 375, 376; Bunsen, *Egypt*, vol. iii. pp. 220, 221, and 241.)

NOTE L., p. 94.

See Euseb. *Præp. Ev.*, ix. 34.

NOTE LI., p. 94.

Ibid. l. s. c. "Now Theophilus says, that Solomon sent the surplus of gold to the king of the Tyrians, and that this last made a life-like statue of his daughter, of full length, and for a covering to the statue a hollow pillar of gold."

NOTE LII., p. 95.

See the author's *Herodotus*, vol. i. Essay vii. pp. 490, 491. Compare Layard's *Nineveh and Babylon*, pp. 634, 635.

NOTE LIII., p. 96.

Nineveh and Babylon, ch. xxvi. pp. 650 and 655. For an account of the structures at Susa and Persepolis, see Mr. Loftus's *Chaldæa and Susiana*, ch. xxviii. pp. 364–380, and Mr. Fergusson's elaborate work, *The Palaces of Nineveh restored*, pp. 95–190.

NOTE LIV., p. 96.

Fergusson's *Palaces of Nineveh restored*, pp. 272–276; compare Layard's *Nineveh and Babylon*, ch. xxvi. pp. 649, 650.

NOTE LV., p. 96.

Ker Porter says, "The total height of each column is 60 feet; the circumference of the shaft is sixteen; the length from the capital to the tor, *forty-four* feet." (*Travels*, vol. i. p. 633.) In another part of the ruins, he measured two pillars, the total height of which, including capital and tor, was *forty-five* feet. (Ibid. p. 590.) The measurements adopted by Mr. Fergusson are, for the palace of Darius, 20 feet; for the hall of the Hundred Columns, 25 feet; for the Propylæum of Xerxes 46 feet, 9 inches; and for the Hall of Xerxes, 64 feet. (*The Palaces of Nineveh restored*, pp. 108, 125, 158, and 177.)

NOTE LVI., p. 96.

See Kugler's *Handbuch der Kunstgeschichte*, p. 81.

NOTE LVII., p. 97.

Even Mr. Layard, while admitting that "some of the Assyrian sphinxes may have been overlaid with gold, like the cherubim in Solomon's temple," adds in a note, "I cannot, however, but express my conviction that much of the metal called gold both in the sacred writings and in profane authors of antiquity, was *really copper*, the orichalchum of the Greeks, such as was used in the bowls and plates discovered at Nimroud." (*Nineveh and Babylon*, p. 652.) But metal of this slight value would hardly have been torn with violence from a sacred building, as the plating appears to have been from the fourth stage of the *Birs Nimrud*. It is further to be remarked, that in the classical accounts the golden beams, &c., are distinctly said to have been far less numerous than the silver ones. Polybius says of the palace at Ecbatana — for although it was built entirely of cedar-wood and cypress, yet none of the wood work was exposed, but the beams, and the panels, and the columns in the porches and peristyles were plated, *some with silver and some with gold*, and the tiles *were all of silver*. And again, the temple . . . had columns covered with gilding, and there were very many silver titles in it, and there were *a few golden plinths*, but *a great many silver ones remained*. (Bk. x. ch. 27, § 10 and § 12.)

NOTE LVIII., p. 97.

For the use of gold in ornamentation by the Phœnicians, see above, Notes XLIII. and LI.; and compare Kenrick's *Phœnicia*, p. 252, and O. Müller's *Handbuch der Archäologie der Kunst*, p. 273, 2d edition.

For its use by the Assyrians, see Mr. Layard's *Nineveh and Babylon*, pp. 651, 652. For its use by the Babylonians, see the last Note, and compare the author's *Herodotus*, vol. i. p. 243, note [5].

NOTE LIX., p. 97.

Menander, Fr. 1: "This man (i. e. Hiram) raised a bank on what was called 'the broad place,' and set up a golden pillar in the temple of Jupiter." Compare Theophilus, as quoted in Note LI.

NOTE LX., p. 97.

See Mr. Kenrick's *Phœnicia*, p. 252.

NOTE LXI., p. 97.

Layard's *Nineveh and Babylon*, pp. 195, 196.

NOTE LXII., p. 97.

Ibid. p. 150.

NOTE LXII. *b*, p. 98.

See Mr. Kenrick's *Phœnicia*, p. 354.

NOTE LXIII., p. 98.

The geographic accuracy of this portion of Scripture is even more striking than that of the Pentateuch. Dr. Stanley says, "It is impossible not to be struck by the constant agreement between the recorded history and the natural geography both of the Old and New Testament. To find a marked correspondence between the scenes of the Sinaitic mountains and the events of the Israelite wanderings is not much, perhaps, but it is certainly something towards a proof of the truth of the whole narrative. . . . The *detailed harmony* between the life of Joshua and the various scenes of his battles, is a slight but true indication that we are dealing not with shadows, but with realities of flesh and blood. Such coincidences are not usually found in fables, least of all in fables of Eastern origin." (*Sinai and Palestine*, Preface, p. xviii.) And this detailed harmony he exhibits in his fourth, seventh, and eleventh chapters.

Among minute points of agreement brought to light by recent researches may be mentioned (1.) the position of the Hagarites or Hagarenes to the east of the land of Gilead, towards or upon the Euphrates, (1 Chron. v. 9, 10 ;) which is the exact locality where they are found three or four centuries later, in an inscription of Sennacherib. (See the author's *Herodotus*, vol. i. p. 476.) (2.) The existence of female sovereigns among the Arabs about this period, which is shown by the mention of certain "Queens of the Arabs" in the inscriptions of Tiglath-Pileser and others. (Ibid. pp. 470 and 473.) (3.) The continued importance of the Moabites and Ammonites which appears by the occurrence of their names[1] in the inscriptions among the enemies of Assyria.

NOTE LXIV., p. 99.

The great Assyrian Empire of Ctesias, which was said to have extended from Egypt to India, and to have lasted about 1300 years, from about B. C. 2182 to B. C. 876, is one of the most palpable contradictions of Scripture which profane history furnishes. Hence it was generally accepted and maintained by the French historians of the last century. Equally opposed to Scripture is the Median Empire of Ctesias, commencing in B. C. 876 with the destruction of Nineveh, and continuing to the time of Cyrus. It was for a long time considered doubtful among historical critics whether the authority of Ctesias or that of Herodotus was to prevail; but as time went on, as the importance of Berosus's history came to be recognized, and more especially when the cuneiform monuments began to be deciphered, the star of Ctesias began to pale and his credit to sink. Niebuhr long ago remarked, that his Assyrian history was "wholly to be rejected." (*Vorträge über Alt. Geschicht.*, vol. i. p. 16 ; p. 12, E. T.) M. Bunsen, even while making use of him, allows that he was "a confused and uncritical writer." (*Egypt*, vol. iii. p. 432.) Col. Mure (*Language and Literature of Ancient Greece*, vol. v. p. 484) calls him "an author of proverbially doubtful veracity." Even his apologists can now say

1 Moab appears as *Mahab*, (Heb. מוֹאָב,) Ammon as *Beth-Ammon*, which is probably the chief city, the Rabbah or Rabbath-Ammon of Scripture.

little more in his defence, than that "there is no positive evidence for charging him with *wilfully* falsifying history." (See the article on Ctesias in Dr. Smith's *Dictionary of Greek and Roman Biography*, vol. i. p. 899.)

NOTE LXV., p. 100.

See Norton's Disquisition on the Old Testament in his *Genuineness of the Gospels*, vol. ii. p. 498. De Wette, after objecting to the miracles and prophecies recorded in Samuel, says, "Elsewhere the narrative *bears the marks of a genuine history*, and where it is not partly derived from contemporary documents — as it is in some places — it is yet drawn from an oral tradition, very lively and true, and is only disturbed and confused here and there." (*Einleitung*, § 178, p. 222; Parker's *Translation*, vol. ii. p. 210.) He also finds "*authentic historical accounts*" in the books of Kings. (Ibid. § 183, p. 232; vol. ii. p. 230, E. T.)

LECTURE IV.

NOTE I., p. 102.

See Lecture III., page 80.

NOTE II., p. 103.

Ibid. p. 83.

NOTE III., p. 103.

The author of Chronicles refers us either to "the book of the Kings," (2 Chr. xxiv. 27,) or more explicitly to "the book of the Kings of Israel and Judah," (2 Chr. xxvii. 7; xxviii. 26; xxxii. 32; xxxv. 27.) But the author of Kings throughout distinguishes between "the book of the Chronicles of the Kings of Judah," (1 Kings xiv. 19; xv. 7, 23; xxii. 46; 2 Kings viii. 23; xii. 19; xiv. 18, &c.,) and "the book of the Chronicles of the Kings of Israel, (1 Kings xiv. 19; xv. 31; xvi. 5, 14, 20, 27; xii. 39; 2 Kings i. 18; x. 34; xiii. 8,

12; &c.) The most probable explanation of this difference is, that the two documents were originally separate, having been drawn up in and for the two different kingdoms; but that by the time of the writer of our books of Chronicles they had been united in one, and were known to the Jews under the title which he uses. (See Keil, *Apologetischer Versuch über die Bücher der Chronik*, p. 252, et seqq. And compare his *Commentar über die Bücher der Könige*, Einleitung, § 3; p. 18, E. T.[1])

NOTE IV., p. 104.

This seems to be the real meaning of the difficult passage in Chronicles, (2 Chr. xx. 34,) which our translators have rendered incorrectly in the text, but correctly, so far as the letter goes, in the margin; — "Now the rest of the acts of Jehoshaphat, first and last, behold, they are written in the words of Jehu, the son of Hanani, who *was made to ascend into* the book of the kings of Israel" — אֲשֶׁר הֹעֲלָה עַל־סֵפֶר מַלְכֵי יִשְׂרָאֵל — i. e. who (the author being identified with his work) was transferred or removed to the book of the Kings of Israel. The LXX. interpreters paraphrase rather than translate when they say, "who wrote a book of the Kings of Israel" (*ὃς κατέγραψε βίβλιον βασιλέων Ἰσραήλ.*) Compare Keil, l. s. c.

NOTE V., p. 104.

See 2 Chron. xxxii. 32. Our translators have destroyed the force of the passage by following the LXX. and interpolating the word "and." "The rest of the acts of Hezekiah," they say, "and his goodness, behold, they are written in the vision of Isaiah the prophet, the son of Amos, *and* in the book of the kings of Judah and Israel." But in the original there is no "and:" the passage runs, "the rest of the acts of Hezekiah, and his goodness, behold, they are written in the vision of Isaiah the prophet, the son of Amos, *in the book* of the kings of Judah and Israel."

NOTE VI., p. 104.

The 36th, 37th, and 38th chapters of Isaiah are almost identical with a part of the 18th, the 19th, and the 20th chapters of the second Book

[1] Commentary on the Books of Kings, by Karl Friedrich Keil, D. D., translated by James Murphy, LL. D. Edinburgh, Clark, 1857.

of Kings. The slightness of their differences will best be seen by placing an extract or two in parallel columns: —

2 KINGS.

Chap. xviii. 17–20. And the King of Assyria sent *Tartan and Rabsaris and* Rab-shakeh from Lachish *to* King Hezekiah, with a great host *against* Jerusalem. *And they went up and came to Jerusalem. And when they were come up, they came and* stood by the conduit of the upper pool, which is in the highway of the fuller's field. *And when they had called to the king*, there came out to *them* Eliakim, the son of Hilkiah, which was over the household, and Shebna the scribe, and Joah the son of Asaph the recorder. And Rab-shakeh said unto them, Speak ye now to Hezekiah, Thus saith the great king, the King of Assyria, What confidence is this wherein thou trustest? *Thou sayest* — but they are but vain words — I have counsel and strength for *the* war. Now on whom dost thou trust, that thou rebellest against me?

Chap. xix. 15–19. And Hezekiah prayed *before* the Lord, *and said*, O Lord God of Israel, which dwellest between the cherubims, thou art the God, even thou alone, of all the kingdoms of the earth: thou hast made heaven and earth. Lord, bow down thine ear and

ISAIAH.

Chap. xxxvi. 2–5. And the King of Assyria sent Rab-shakeh from Lachish *to* Jerusalem *unto* King Hezekiah with a great army. And he stood by the conduit of the upper pool in the highway of the fuller's field. Then came forth unto *him* Eliakim, Hilkiah's son, which was over the house, and Shebna the scribe, and Joah, Asaph's son, the recorder. And Rab-shakeh said unto them, Say ye now to Hezekiah, Thus saith the great king, the King of Assyria, What confidence is this wherein thou trustest? *I say*, [sayest thou,] but they are but vain words, I have counsel and strength for war: now on whom dost thou trust, that thou rebellest against me?

Chap. xxxvii. 15–20. And Hezekiah prayed *unto* the Lord, *saying*, O Lord *of hosts*, God of Israel, that dwellest between the cherubims, thou art the God, even thou alone, of all the kingdoms of the earth; thou hast made heaven and earth. Incline thine ear, O Lord, hear; open, Lord, thine eyes, and see; and hear the word of Sennacherib, which hath sent *him* to reproach the living God. Of a truth, Lord, the kings of Assyria have destroyed the *nations* and their lands, and have cast their gods into the fire, for they were no gods, but the work of men's hands, wood and stone: therefore they have destroyed them. Now, therefore, O Lord our God, *I beseech thee*, save thou us out of his hand, that all the kingdoms of the earth may know that thou art the Lord God, even thou only.

and hear; open thine eyes, O Lord, and see; and hear all the words of Sennacherib, which hath sent to reproach the living God. Of a truth, Lord, the kings of Assyria have laid waste *all the lands* and their countries, and have cast their gods into the fire, for they were no gods, but the work of men's hands, wood and stone; therefore they have destroyed them. Now, therefore, O Lord our God, save us from his hand, that all the kingdoms of the earth may know that thou art the Lord, even thou only.

NOTE VII., p. 104.

This agreement is chiefly between the last chapter of Jeremiah and the 24th and 25th chapters of the second Book of Kings. It is fully equal to that above exhibited between Kings and Isaiah.

NOTE VIII., p. 104.

Keil, *Commentar über die Bücher der Könige*, Einleitung, § 3; p. 19, E. T.

NOTE IX., p. 105.

De Wette, *Einleitung*, § 184, p. 234; vol. ii. p. 241, Parker's Translation; Bertholdt, *Einleitung*, vol. iii. p. 154, et seqq.

NOTE X., p. 106.

This has been well shown by Hävernick, (*Einleitung*, § 176, vol. ii. p. 201, et seqq.,) and Keil, (*Versuch über die Bücher der Chronik*, p. 199, et seqq.) Keil, however, appears to me to go too far when he denies that the author of Chronicles made any use at all of Kings,

(*Commentar über die Bücher der Könige*, Einleitung, § 3; p. 17, note 1, E. T.) Such passages as the subjoined show something more than the mere use of a common authority: —

2 Chron. i. 14–17.

And Solomon gathered chariots and horsemen: and he had a thousand and four hundred chariots, and twelve thousand horsemen, which he *placed* in the chariot cities, and with the king at Jerusalem. And the king made silver *and gold* at Jerusalem as plenteous as stones, and cedar trees made he as the sycamore trees that are in the vale for abundance. And Solomon had horses brought out of Egypt, and linen yarn: the king's merchants received the linen yarn at a price. And *they fetched up and brought forth* out of Egypt a chariot for six hundred shekels of silver, and a horse for a hundred and fifty: and so brought they out [horses] for all the kings of the Hittites, and for the kings of Syria, by their means.

1 Kings x. 26–29.

And Solomon gathered together chariots and horsemen: and he had a thousand and four hundred chariots, and twelve thousand horsemen, whom he *bestowed* in the cities for chariots, and with the king at Jerusalem. And the king made silver to be in Jerusalem as plenteous as stones, and cedars made he to be as the sycamore trees that are in the vale for abundance. And Solomon had horses brought out of Egypt, and linen yarn: the king's merchants received the linen yarn at a price. And a chariot *came up and went out* of Egypt for six hundred shekels of silver, and a horse for a hundred and fifty: and so for all the kings of the Hittites, and for the kings of Syria, did they bring *them* out by their means.[1]

Compare also 2 Chron. xiv. 1–4 with 1 Kings xv. 11, 12; 2 Chron. xvi. 11–14 with 1 Kings xv. 23, 24; 2 Chron. xxii. 10–12 with 2 Kings xi. 1–3; 2 Chron. xxiii. 1–21 with 2 Kings xi. 4–20; and 2 Chron. xxxiv. 8–33 with 2 Kings xxiii. 5–20. In almost all these passages, however, the Chronicler introduces points not mentioned by the author of Kings, so that he evidently does not trust to him as his sole authority; e. g.

[1] In the original the resemblance is even closer than in our translation. It is the same word which is translated as "placed," and as "bestowed," and the same *roots* are used where we have to say in the one case "fetched up and brought forth," in the other "came up and went out."

2 CHRON. xvi. 11–14.

And, behold, the acts of Asa, first and last, lo, they are written in the book of the kings of Judah *and Israel.* And Asa *in the thirty and ninth year of his reign* was diseased in his feet, *until his disease was exceeding great; yet in his disease he sought not to the Lord, but to the physicians.* And Asa slept with his fathers, and died in the one and fortieth year of his reign; and they buried him in his own sepulchres *which he had made for himself* in the city of David, *and laid him in the bed which was filled with sweet odors and divers kinds of spices prepared by the apothecaries' art; and they made a very great burning for him.* And Jehoshaphat, &c.

1 KINGS xv. 23, 24.

The rest of the acts of Asa, and all his might, and all that he did, and the cities which he built, are they not written in the book of the Chronicles of the kings of Judah? Nevertheless, in the time of his old age he was diseased in his feet. And Asa slept with his fathers, and was buried with his fathers in the city of David his father; and Jehoshaphat his son reigned in his stead.

NOTE XI., p. 106.

See the remarks of Mons. C. Müller, prefixed to his collection of the fragments of Manetho in the *Fragmenta Historicorum Græcorum*, vol. ii. pp. 514, 515.

NOTE XII., p. 106.

The discrepancies between the books of Chronicles, on the one hand, and the books of Samuel and Kings, on the other, have been largely, if not forcibly, stated by De Wette, (*Einleitung*, § 190, p. 244, et seqq.,) and his commentator, Mr. Theodore Parker, (vol. ii. pp. 266–305.) A satisfactory explanation of the greater number will be found in Keil's *Apologetischer Versuch*, to which the student is referred, as well as to Bertheau's *Commentar*, of which a translation has recently appeared.[1] Some, however, as the difference of numbers and names, cannot but

[1] This translation forms the latter portion of the 16th volume of Clark's *Foreign Theological Library*, New Series, Edinburgh, 1857.

remain discrepancies; in these we may be allowed to suspect corruptions of the original text, by carelessness in transcription, or by the insertion of marginal addenda. (See the excellent remarks of Professor Stuart, *Defence of the Old Testament Canon*, § 6, pp. 143–145; and compare the article on Chronicles, in Kitto's *Cyclopædia.*)

NOTE XIII., p. 107.

See Mr. Vance Smith's *Prophecies relating to Nineveh and the Assyrians*, p. 76. The special object of this work is to elucidate a certain portion of the prophecies by the light thrown upon them from the connected histories of the Assyrians and the Hebrews. Similar efforts have been made in Germany by Hitzig,[1] Otto Strauss,[2] and others.

NOTE XIV., p. 107.

Jonah is commonly placed somewhat earlier; but his work (if it be his, which is doubtful) belongs rather to the historical than the prophetical Scriptures.

NOTE XV., p. 108.

By Paley, in his *Horæ Paulinæ*, a work which for closeness, clearness, and cogency of reasoning, has never been surpassed, and rarely equalled.

NOTE XVI., p. 109.

The kings of Israel and Judah mentioned in the Assyrian Inscriptions are, Jehu, Menahem, Hezekiah, and Manasseh. Jehu's name appears on the Black Obelisk in the British Museum, a monument of the Old Empire, dating probably from about B. C. 870; Menahem is mentioned by Tiglath-Pileser II., the first monarch of the New Empire, who began to reign in B. C. 747; Hezekiah occurs among the enemies of Sennacherib, who did not ascend the throne till about B. C. 700; and Manasseh is found among the tributaries of Sennacherib's son, Esarhaddon. No doubt the Scriptural names have helped to determine the date of the monuments; but putting these names aside, and look-

1 Zwölf Kleinen Propheten erklärt, Leipsic, 1838.

2 Nahumi de Nino Vaticinium, Berlin, 1853.

ing merely to forms of language, style of writing, character of sculpture, and position of the monuments when *in situ*, I believe no cuneiform scholar would hesitate as to the relative antiquity to be assigned to them.

Note XVII., p. 109.

The practice of calling cities after the names of their founders has always prevailed in the East. Perhaps the earliest known instance is that of Ramesses — the Beth-Rameses of the Hieratic Papyri. (See Note LXXXVII., on Lecture II., p. 287.) That the Assyrians were acquainted with the practice we know from the case of Sargon, who called the city which he built a little to the north of Nineveh, *Beth-Sargina*, or *Dur-Sargina*, "the abode of Sargon." Esarhaddon too, in one of his Inscriptions, says, "A city I built. City of Esarhaddon I called its name."[1] In more recent times the names Ahmed-abad, Shereef-abad, Hyder-abad, &c., have had a similar origin.

Samaria is only called *Beth-Khumri* in the earlier inscriptions. From the time of Tiglath-Pileser II., the term used is *Tsamirin*.

Note XVIII., p. 110.

So Wilkinson, in the author's *Herodotus*, vol. ii. p. 376. M. Bunsen reads the legend *Jutah Malk*, and translates (not very intelligibly) "Judah, King." (See his *Egypt*, vol. iii. p. 242.) He agrees, however, as to its intention, and views it as a proof of Sheshonk's having made an expedition to Jerusalem.

Note XIX., p. 110.

There were three Osorkons in the 21st dynasty, according to the monuments, though Manetho mentioned but one. Osorkon I. was the son and successor of Shishak. It is just possible that he may have been the assailant of Asa.[2] Sir G. Wilkinson, however, regards Osorkon II., who married the great granddaughter of Shishak, as more naturally the contemporary of Asa, the great grandson of Solomon, since Solomon and Shishak were contemporaries. (See the author's *Herodotus*, vol. ii. p. 378.)

1 See Mr. Fox Talbot's *Assyrian Texts translated*, p. 11.

2 This is M. Bunsen's view, *Egypt*, vol. iii. p. 308.

Note XX., p. 111.

Menander said — "On the death of Hiram, his son Baleazar (read Balthazar) succeeded to the kingdom. He lived 43 years, and reigned 7. After him came his son Abdastratus, (read Abdastartus,) who lived 29 years, and reigned 9. Against this man the four sons of his nurse conspired, and slew him, whereupon the eldest of these brothers reigned 12 years. After these came Astartus, the son of Deleastartus, who lived 54 years, and reigned 12. His brother Aserymus succeeded him, living 54 years, and reigning 9. He was slain by his brother Pheles, who took possession of the kingdom, but reigned only 8 months, when he was murdered, in the 50th year of his age, by Ithobalus, (i. e. Ethbaal,) the priest of Astarte, who reigned 32 years, and lived 68." (Ap. Joseph. *Contra Apionem*, i. 18.) We have thus from the death of Hiram, which cannot have taken place till the 26th year of Solomon's reign (1 Kings ix. 10–14,) the following series — Balthazar, 7 years; Abdastartus, 9 years; his successor, 12 years; Astartus, 12 years; Aserymus, 9 years; Pheles, eight months; total 49 years and eight months. In Ahab's case we have Jeroboam, 22 years; Nadab, 2 years; Baasha, 24 years; Elah, 2 years; Omri, 12 years; total 62 years; to which must be added some 10 or 12 years for the excess of Solomon's reign over Hiram's. It thus appears that Ahab ascended the throne about 20 or 25 years after Eth-baal.

Note XXI., p. 111.

See Kenrick's *Phœnicia*, p. 362; Bunsen's *Egypt*, vol. iii. p. 428; Keil's *Commentar*, (p. 259, E. T.,) &c.

Note XXII., p. 111.

The term "Zidonians" seems to bear the generic sense in 1 Kings xi. 1 and 5; and 2 Kings xxiii. 13; but the specific in Judges x. 12, and xviii. 7. The early preëminence of Sidon (see Note XXXII. to Lecture III.) sufficiently accounts for the generic use, which was well known to the Greek and Latin poets, (Hom. Od. xiii. 285; Soph. Fr. lxxxii.; Eurip. Hel. 1429; Virg. Æn. i. 446, &c.)

NOTE XXIII., p. 112.

See Josephus, *Ant. Jud.* viii. 13: "Menander also mentions this drought, writing thus in the Acts of Ithobalus, king of the Tyrians: 'Under this man there was a want of rain from the month Hyperberetæus to the same month of the following year. But when he made supplication, there was a violent thunder storm.'" May we connect the "supplication" in the last clause with that of Elijah on Mount Carmel, (1 Kings xviii. 42, 43,) which overhung the Tyrian territory?

NOTE XXIV., p. 112.

No continuous history of Syria has come down to us. Nicolas of Damascus, whose influence with Herod the Great and with Augustus must have given him access to any archives that Damascus or the other Syrian towns may have possessed, appears to have introduced a short sketch of ancient Syrian history into the fourth book of his great work, which treated mainly of the early Lydian kings. (See Müller's preface to the fragments of Nicolas, in his *Fragm. Hist. Gr.*, vol. iii. p. 345.) Of this sketch, however, we unfortunately possess but three short fragments, preserved to us by Josephus.[1] The first of these relates the sojourn of Abraham at Damascus, on his way from Chaldæa to Canaan — a sojourn deriving some support from the fact that Abraham's steward was a Damascene (Gen. xv. 2) — but absurdly makes Abraham "king of Damascus" during his stay, (Fr. 30.) The second has been given at length in the notes on Lecture III. (Note XXVIII.). The third is interpreted by Josephus as bearing upon the Syrian war of Ahab; but its true reference is to that of Baasha. It runs thus: "Now when he died (i. e. Hadad I.) his posterity reigned for ten generations, each one inheriting from his father, together with the royal authority, the same name also, like the Pharaohs in Egypt. But the third, who was the mightiest of all these, wishing to avenge his grandfather's defeat, marched against the Jews, and took the city now called Samaria." (Fr. 31.) It is evident that Hadad III., who was the grandson of David's antagonist, cannot have contended against Ahab, 140 years afterwards. Nicolas undoubtedly intends the antagonist of Baasha, half a century earlier, whose inroad was completely suc-

[1] *Ant. Jud.* vii. 5.

cessful, and who reduced Samaria to a sort of subjection, (1 Kings xv. 20; xx. 34.) With respect to the continuance of the name and family of Hadad on the Damascene throne for ten generations, Nicolas appears to be at variance with Scripture. Seemingly he takes no account of the break in the line caused by the usurpation of Hazael. Perhaps in Syrian history this was glossed over, and Hazael regarded as having had a claim of blood. At any rate it is remarkable that he adopted the family name of the preceding dynasty for his son, who is called Ben-hadad in 2 Kings xiii. 3.

NOTE XXV., p. 113.

See the Black Obelisk inscription, which has been very accurately translated by Dr. Hincks, in the *Dublin University Magazine* for October, 1853. Compare the author's *Herodotus*, vol. i. pp. 464, 465.

NOTE XXVI., p. 113.

"Benhadad, the king of Syria, gathered all his host together; and there were *thirty and two kings* with him, and *horses*, and *chariots*." (1 Kings xx. 1.) "Number thee an army like the army which thou hast lost, *horse for horse*, and *chariot for chariot*." (Ibid. verse 25.) The Syrian armies appear in the Black Obelisk inscription to be composed to a very large extent of *chariots*. As many as 1100 are taken on one occasion. The multitude of petty princes mentioned is also in accordance with the inscriptions generally, which represents the whole country between the Euphrates and Egypt as divided up among a number of tribes and nations, each under its own king or chief.

NOTE XXVII., p. 113.

The Black Obelisk king, in his 6th, 11th, and 14th years, contends with Benhadad, but in his 18th his adversary is Hazael. (*Dublin Univ. Mag.*, October, 1853, pp. 422, 423, and 424.)

NOTE XXVIII., p. 113.

The Obelisk contains no account of any war with Jehu; but mentions him among those who paid tribute to the Assyrian monarch. He is styled "*Yahua*, the son of *Khumri*"—Jehu, the son of Omri, which causes some difficulty. Jehu is said in Scripture to have been the son of Jehoshaphat, and grandson of Nimshi, (2 Kings ix. 2, 14.) It is possible, however, that he may have been *on the mother's side* descended from Omri. Or the story of his being so descended may have been invented by the Samaritans, and believed by foreign nations. Or, finally, the Assyrians may merely have assumed that he was a descendant of Omri, since he sat on his throne, and ruled in the city known to them by his name. (See above, Note XVII.) His tribute consisted of silver, gold, and articles of various kinds manufactured from gold.

NOTE XXIX., p. 114.

The only remains of this period are an inscription set up by the son of the Black Obelisk king, relating his military exploits during the first four years of his reign, and two or three brief inscriptions of the time of his successor, the most important of which is that noticed below, (Note XXXIII.) The campaigns of the earlier king are in Babylonia, Media, Armenia, and along the flanks of Taurus, but do not touch Syria or Palestine.

NOTE XXX., p. 114.

See Kenrick's *Phœnicia*, p. 367 : "Our knowledge of the history of Tyre ceases with Dido's flight, at the end of the ninth century, B. C., and we hear nothing of its internal state till the reign of Elulæus, the contemporary of Shalmaneser." In fact we have nothing authentic for the early period but the fragments of Menander, and these fail us entirely from the reign of Pygmalion to that of Elulæus.

NOTE XXXI., p. 114.

See Euseb. *Chronica*, i. 4 ; p. 18, ed. Mai. "After these, he says there was a king of the Chaldæans whose name was Pul."

NOTE XXXII., p. 114.

In 2 Kings xv. 19, the LXX. interpreters render Pul by *Phua*, (Φουά,) where the terminal *a* is probably a false reading arising out of the resemblance of *Λ* to *A*. In 1 Chron. v. 26, the reading of the Vatican and most MSS. is Φαλὼχ, but some copies have Φαλώς.

Note XXXIII., p. 115.

A full account of this inscription, first deciphered by Sir H. Rawlinson, will be found in the *Athenæum*, No. 1476, p. 174. A general summary of its contents is given in the author's *Herodotus*, vol. i. p. 467.

Note XXXIV., p. 115.

See Sir H. Rawlinson's letter in the *Athenæum*, l. s. c.

Note XXXV., p. 116.

The conjunction of Rezin with Pekah, and the capture *and destruction* of Damascus, which are noted in the inscription, seem to prove that it is the second expedition that is intended. Whether it be the first, however, or the second, the name of Menahem must equally be rejected. (See 2 Kings xv. 29, and xvi. 9.) It is easily conceivable, that, if the sculptor had been accustomed to engrave the royal annals, and had often before entered the name of Menahem as that of the Samaritan king, he might engrave it here in his haste, without consulting his copy. Or possibly, Pekah may have taken the name of Menahem, to connect himself with the dynasty which he had displaced.

Note XXXVI., p. 117.

The older interpreters, as Keil remarks,[1] proceeding on the supposition that the altar was Syrian, and dedicated to the Syrian gods, endeavored to answer the question why Ahaz chose the gods, not of the victorious Assyrians, but of the vanquished Syrians — a question to which it was very difficult to give a satisfactory reply. Among recent writers, Bertheau, (*Commentar über d. Büch. d. Chronik*, p. 421, E. T.,) Ewald, (*Geschichte des Volkes Israel*, vol. iii. pp. 325, 326,) and Vance Smith, (*Prophecies concerning Assyria*, p. 27,) follow the old view. Keil himself regards the question as unimportant, since he supposes that no idolatrous rites or ideas were connected with the altar. Ahaz, according to his view, having seen a pattern which he fancied better

1 *Commentar über d. Büch. d. Könige*, § 2; vol. ii. p. 45, E. T.

than that of Solomon's altar, adopted it; and his sin was "a silly will-worship." (So Buddæus, *Hist. Eccles.*, vol. ii. p. 428.)

NOTE XXXVII., p. 117.

See the great inscription of Tiglath-Pileser I., pp. 30, 38, 40, 44, 48, &c.; and compare the author's *Herodotus*, vol. i. p. 495.

NOTE XXXVIII., p. 117.

Josephus says of Shalmaneser: "The name of this king is inscribed in the archives of the Tyrians. For he made an expedition against Tyre, when Eluleus was king over them. To this we have the testimony of Menander, who wrote an account of their chronicles, and translated their archives into the Greek language." (*Antiq. Jud.*, ix. 14.)

NOTE XXXIX., p. 117.

See the author's *Herodotus*, vol. i. p. 471, note [7].

NOTE XL., p. 117.

Ibid. p. 472.

NOTE XLI., p. 118.

Scripture states that Shalmaneser "came up against Hoshea," and besieged Samaria, (2 Kings xviii. 9;) but Scripture nowhere expressly states that Shalmaneser took the city. "The king of Assyria," it is said in one place, "took it," (ib. xvii. 6;) in another, "they (i. e. the Assyrians) took it," (ib. xviii. 10.) That Shalmaneser was the captor is only an *inference* from Scripture — a natural inference undoubtedly, but not a necessary one.

NOTE XLII., p. 118.

Sargon has been identified with Shalmaneser by Vitringa, Offenhaus, Prideaux, Eichhorn, Hupfeld, Gumpach, and M. Niebuhr;[1] with Sennacherib by Grotius, Lowth, Keil, and Schröer; with Esarhaddon by Perizonius, Kalinsky, and Michaëlis. (See Winer's *Realwörterbuch*, ad

1 *Geschichte Assurs und Babels seit Phul*, p. 160.

voc. Sargon.) His separate personality is now generally admitted. (See Brandis, *Rerum Assyriarum Tempora Emendata*, p. 64, and Tab. Chron. ad fin. Oppert, *Rapport d'une Mission Scientifique en Angleterre*, p. 38; Vance Smith, *Prophecies*, &c., pp. 31, 32; Ewald, *Geschichte des Volkes Israel*, vol. iii. pp. 333, 334; Layard, *Nineveh and Babylon*, pp. 618–620, &c.)

NOTE XLIII., p. 118.

See Sir H. Rawlinson's *Commentary on the Inscriptions of Babylonia and Assyria*, p. 19, note [2], where a passage proving this is quoted from Yacút, the famous Arabian geographer.

NOTE XLIV., p. 118.

See the author's *Herodotus*, vol. i. p. 473, note [4]; and compare Vance Smith's *Prophecies*, &c., p. 35.

NOTE XLV., p. 119.

When Sargon took Ashdod, its king (he tells us) fled to *Muzr*, (Mizraim or Egypt,) which was subject to *Mirukha*, (Meroë or Ethiopia.) See the author's *Herodotus*, vol. i. p. 474.

NOTE XLVI., p. 119.

Ibid. p. 473.

NOTE XLVII., p. 120.

The translation in the text has been read by Sir H. Rawlinson before various Societies and Public Meetings; but it has remained, I believe, hitherto unpublished. It will be found to agree in all important points with Dr. Hincks's version, as given by Mr. Layard, (*Nineveh and Babylon*, pp. 143, 144.)

NOTE XLVIII., p. 121.

Mr. Layard gives a slightly different explanation, (*Nin. and Bab.*, p. 145:) "There is a difference of 500 talents, as it will be observed, in the amount of silver. It is probable that Hezekiah was much pressed by Sennacherib, and compelled to give him all the wealth that he could collect, as we find him actually taking the silver from the house of the Lord, as well as from his own treasury, and cutting off the gold from the doors and pillars of the temple to satisfy the demands of the Assyrian king. The Bible may therefore only include the actual amount of *money* in the 300 talents of silver, whilst the Assyrian records comprise *all the precious metal* taken away."

NOTE XLIX., p. 121.

Herodot. ii. 141. This testimony was first adduced by Josephus, (*Ant. Jud.* x. 1,) from whom it passed on to the Christian commentators generally. The "chief difficulty" in reconciling Herodotus with Scripture has been generally said to be the *scene* of the destruction. (See Joseph. l. s. c., Prideaux's *Connection of Sacred and Profane History*, vol. i. p. 18; M. Niebuhr's *Geschichte Assurs und Babels*, p. 179; Vance Smith's *Prophecies relating to Assyria*, Introduction, p. 43.) It has been commonly assumed that the scene was the immediate neighborhood of Jerusalem; but this assumption is not only, as Mr. Vance Smith has shown, (*Prophecies*, &c., p. 213,) without warrant from Scripture, but it is actually contradictory to Scripture. God's promise to Hezekiah through Isaiah was: "He (Sennacherib) shall not come into this city, nor shoot an arrow there, *nor come before it* with shield, nor cast a bank against it. *By the way that he came, by the same* shall he return, and shall not come into this city, saith the Lord." (2 Kings, xix. 32, 33; compare Is. xxxvii. 33, 34.)

NOTE XLIX. *b.*, p. 121.

Eusebius says of Polyhistor — "Having already described the rest of the acts of Senecherim, he adds, that he lived [as king] 18 years. . . . until *he was destroyed by a plot formed against him by his son* Ardumazan." (*Chronica*, i. 5; p. 19, ed. Mai.)

Abydenus gives the name of one of the murderers more correctly, but represents the murder as committed, not on Sennacherib, but on his successor. "Next after him (i. e. Sennacherib) reigned Nergil, whom his son Adramelech slew; and he in his turn was slain by his brother Axerdis." (Esar-haddon?) (Ap. Euseb. *Chronica*, i. 9, p. 25.)

Note L., p. 122.

Both Sennacherib and Esarhaddon led hostile expeditions into Armenia, which appears to have been at no time thoroughly subjected by the Assyrian monarchs. (See the author's *Herodotus*, vol. i. pp. 478–481.)

Note LI., p. 122.

Mos. Choren. i. 22: "When his sons, Adrammelech and Sanasar, had slain him, (i. e. Senacharim,) they fled to us. One of whom, Sanasar, our most illustrious ancestor Sacordius placed near the borders of Assyria, in that part of our country which lies between the west and south; and his descendants . . . filled . . . that mountain." But Argamozan obtained a settlement in the same region, between the East and the South. From him this historian (Mar-Abas) reports that the Arzerunii and the Genunii were descended.

Note LII., p. 122.

Esarhaddon in his inscriptions frequently speaks of Sennacherib as his father. (See Fox Talbot, *Assyrian Texts translated*, p. 13, and elsewhere.) The relationship is also witnessed to by Polyhistor, following Berosus. (Ap. Euseb. *Chron.* i. v. p. 19; compare p. 20, where Eusebius says, "Having gone through with all this, Polyhistor proceeds anew to relate some of the acts of Senecherib also; and concerning his son *he writes in quite the same manner as the books of the Hebrews.*"

Note LIII., p. 122.

Abydenus interpolates a reign between Sennacherib and Esarhaddon, which he assigns to a certain *Nergilus*, of whom no other trace is to be found. *Nergal* was one of the Assyrian deities, (2 Kings xvii. 30; and see the author's *Herodotus*, vol. i. pp. 631–633; compare also *Dublin Univ. Mag.*, (Oct. 1853, p. 420,) and cannot therefore have been a king's name. The Assyrian royal names *contain* most commonly a god's name as an element, but are never identical with the names of deities. It was otherwise in Phœnicia, where Baal and Astartus were monarchs. The account of Abydenus seems therefore unworthy of credit.

Note LIV., p. 122.

"Manasseh, King of Judah," is mentioned among the subject princes, who lent Esarhaddon workmen for the building and ornamentation of his palaces. (See the author's *Herodotus*, vol. i. p. 483.) It is not surprising that we have no account of the expedition against Manasseh, since we do not possess the *annals* of Esarhaddon, but only some occasional inscriptions.

NOTE LV., p. 123.

The Assyrians ordinarily governed Babylon through native viceroys. (See Berosus, Fr. 12; and the inscriptions, *passim.*) But Esarhaddon appears to have reigned there in his own person. Bricks found on the site of Babylon show that he repaired temples and built himself a palace there. Consequently in the authentic list of Babylonian kings preserved by Ptolemy, (*Magn. Syntax.* v. 14,) his name occurs, under the Grecized form of Asaridinus. A Babylonian tablet has been found, dated by the year of his reign — a sure indication that he was the actual ruler of the country. No similar facts can be proved of any other Assyrian monarch.[1] (See the author's *Herodotus*, vol. i. p. 482.)

NOTE LVI., p. 123.

There is one only mention of Assyria in the historical Scriptures later than the reign of Manasseh, namely, the statement in 2 Kings xxiii. 29, that in the days of Josiah "Pharaoh-Necho, king of Egypt, went up against the *king of Assyria* to the river Euphrates." If this expression is to be taken strictly, we must consider that Assyria maintained her existence so late as B. C. 610. I believe, however, that the word "Assyria" is here used, somewhat negligently, for "Babylonia." (Cf. Keil, ad loc., p. 154, E. T.,) and that the Assyrian empire was destroyed in B. C. 625. (See Niebhur, *Vorträge über Alte Geschichte*, vol. i. p. 47.) The first *clear* indication which Scripture gives of the destruction is found in Ezekiel xxxi. 3–17 — a passage written B. C. 585. A more obscure notification of the event is perhaps contained in Jeremiah xxv. 15–26, where the omission of Assyria from the general list of the idolatrous nations would seem to imply that she had ceased to exist. This passage was written about B. C. 605.

[1] It has been suggested by Dr. Hincks and others that the "Arceanus" of Ptolemy's list is Sargon. But this is a mere conjecture grounded upon a certain degree of resemblance in the names. No traces of Sargon have been found in Babylonia.

NOTE LVII., p. 123.

Compare Herod. i. 106 and 178; Ctesias ap. Diod. Sic. ii. 26–28; Abydenus ap. Euseb. *Chronica*, i. 9, p. 25; Joseph. *Ant. Jud.* x. 5. See also Tobit xiv. 15.

NOTE LVIII., p. 124.

The slight authority of the present "pointing" of the Hebrew text is generally admitted. The pointing from which our translators took their rendering of "So" is סוֹא; if the word were pointed thus — סֶוֶא — it would have to be rendered by "Seveh." (See Keil on 2 Kings xvi. 4–6, pp. 52, 52, E. T.; and compare the author's *Herodotus*, vol. i. p. 472, note [2].)

NOTE LIX., p. 124.

See Mr. Birch's note in Layard's *Nineveh and Babylon*, ch. vi. pp. 156–159. Compare Wilkinson, in the author's *Herodotus*, vol. ii. pp. 217, 218, and 379; and Bunsen, *Egypt's Place*, &c., vol. ii. p. 597.

NOTE LX., p. 124.

Herod. ii. 137. Most moderns incline to the view that the second Shebek is the So of Scripture. (See Winer's *Realwörterbuch*, ad voc. So; Keil, *Commentar über die Bücher der Könige*, l. s. c.; Layard, *Nineveh and Babylon*, p. 157; Gesenius, *Comment. in Jes.*, vol. i. p. 696, &c.) The question is one of exact chronology. Tirhakah, it is argued, came against Sennacherib in the 14th year of Hezekiah, and So made a league with Hoshea in Hezekiah's third or fourth year. This then must have been in the reign of the second Shebek, to whom Manetho gave not less than 12 years. (See Keil, l. s. c.) But, in the first place, So's league cannot be fixed to Hezekiah's third or fourth year. A space of several years may intervene between the 4th and 5th verses of 2 Kings xvii. And, secondly, Manetho's numbers (as they have come down to us) cannot be trusted absolutely. According to them Tirhakah reigned 18 or 20 years. (Frs. 64 and 65.) But the monuments distinctly assign him 26 years. (See Wilkinson, in the author's *Herodotus*, vol. ii. p. 381.) They also appear to fix his accession to the year B. C. 690. The reign of Hoshea was from B. C. 729 to B. C. 721, and his league with the Egyptians cannot have been later than B. C. 724. This is 34 years before the accession of Tirhakah, which is certainly too long a time to assign to the second Shebek. I therefore regard the So of Kings as Shebek I.

The difficulty with respect to Tirhakah's chronology will be considered in Note LXIV.

NOTE LXI., p. 125.

See Mr. Layard's *Nineveh and Babylon*, pp. 156–159.

NOTE LXII., p. 125.

Tarcus is the form given as Manetho's by Africanus, Taracus that given by Eusebius. See the fragments of Manetho, in Müller's *Fr. Hist. Gr.*, vol. ii. p. 593; Frs. 64 and 65.) The Hebrew word is תִּרְהָקָה; the LXX. give Θαρακά.

NOTE LXIII., p. 125.

Strabo, *Geograph.*, i. 3, § 21; xv. i. § 6.

NOTE LXIV., p. 125.

This is the reading of Sir Gardner Wilkinson. (See the author's *Herodotus*, vol. ii. p. 380.) Bunsen reads Taharuka, (*Egypt*, vol. ii. p. 598;) Rosellini, Tahraka. The consonants, T, H, R, K, are certain, but the vowels doubtful.

If Tirhakah did not ascend the Egyptian throne till B. C. 690, how (it may be asked) could he be contemporary with Hezekiah, whose last year was about B. C. 697, or B. C. 696? And how, especially, could he oppose Sennacherib, about the middle of Hezekiah's reign, or B. C. 703? I venture to suggest that Tirhakah, when he marched against Sennacherib, may not yet have been king of Egypt. He is called "king of Ethiopia;" and he may have ruled in Ethiopia, while the Shebeks, under his protection, held Egypt. I venture further to doubt whether we can fix the year of Sennacherib's contact with Tirhakah from Scripture. His first invasion of Judæa is said to have been in Hezekiah's 14th year, (2 Kings xix. 13;) but it seems to be a second invasion, falling some years later, which is described in verses

17 to 36. In the marginal notes to our Bible, the two invasions are made to be three years apart. But the number three is purely conjectural; and perhaps thirteen or fourteen is as likely. (See the author's *Herodotus*, p. 479, notes 1, 2, and 9.)

NOTE. LXV., p. 125.

Fragmenta Hist. Gr., vol. ii. pp. 593, 594; Frs. 66 and 67. The form used is Νεχαώ.

NOTE LXVI., p. 125.

Herodotus (ii. 158) uses the form Νεκῶς, where the ς is the Greek nominative, and may therefore be cancelled.

NOTE LXVII., p. 125.

Rosellini expressed the monumental name by *Neko*, but M. Bunsen reads it *Nekau* or *Neku*. (Egypt, vol. ii. pp. 604, 605.)

NOTE LXVIII., p. 125.

On the frequent confusion between the names Migdol (מִגְדֹּל, Μαγδαλά, Μάγδολον) and Megiddo (מְגִדּוֹ, Μαγεδδώ, Μαγεδών,) see Dr. Stanley's *Sinai and Palestine*, p. 375, note [1]. Herodotus was not acquainted with the interior of Palestine, or he would have seen how much more suited for the site of a great battle was Megiddo in the plain of Esdraelon, than Magdolum on the shores of the Sea of Galilee.

NOTE LXIX., p. 125.

See Prideaux's *Connection*, &c., vol. i. pp. 56, 57; Rennell's *Geography of Herodotus*, pp. 245 and 683; Heeren's *Asiatic Nations*, vol. ii. ch. 4, p. 109, note 2, E. T.; Dahlmann's *Life of Herodotus*, ch. iv. p. 55, E. T.; Bähr's *Excursus* on Herod. ii. 159, vol. i. pp. 922, 923; Smith's *Dict. of Greek and Roman Geography*, vol. ii. p. 17; Keil's *Commentar über d. Büch. d. Könige*, ch. xxiii. p. 159, E. T.; Horne's *Introduction*, vol. i. p. 208; and Kenrick's *Ancient Egypt*, vol. ii. p. 406.

NOTE LXX., p. 125.

That the Cadytis of Herodotus was not Jerusalem, but a town upon the Syrian *coast*, is now generally admitted by scholars, and seems to follow necessarily from Herod. iii. 5. The best authorities incline to identify it with Gaza, or *Ghuzzeh*, called in the Assyrian Inscriptions *Khazita*. (See Hitzig, *Disputatio de Cadyte urbe Herodotea;* and compare Wilkinson, in the author's *Herodotus*, vol. ii. p. 246, note [2]; Ewald, *Geschichte des Volkes Israel*, vol. iii. p. 418, note [1]; Sir H. Rawlinson, *Outlines of Assyrian History*, &c.; and Bertheau, *Commentar über d. Büch. d. Chronik*, § 17, ad fin.; p. 457, E. T.

NOTE LXXI., p. 125.

Africanus and Eusebius both report Manetho to have said of Necho, "This man took Jerusalem, and carried Jehoahaz the king captive into Egypt. (See the fragments of Manetho in the *Fragm. Hist. Gr.*, vol. ii. pp. 593, 594; Frs. 66 and 67.)

NOTE LXXII., p. 125.

So Sir Gardner Wilkinson reads the name on the monuments, (*Herodotus*, vol. ii. p. 248, note [8].) Rosellini read it as *Hophre*. M. Bunsen gives the strange form, *Ra-uah-hat*, (*Egypt*, vol. ii. pp. 604, 605.)

NOTE LXXIII., p. 125.

Egyptian chronology placed the accession of Amasis 48 years before that of Darius Hystaspis; for Amasis, according to the consentient testimony of Herodotus, (iii. 10,) Manetho, (ap. Syncell. p. 141, C.,) and the monuments, (Wilkinson, in the author's *Herodotus*, vol. ii. p. 387,) reigned 44 years, Psammetichus his son, half a year; Cambyses, (in Egypt,) 3 years,[1] and the Pseudo-Smerdis a little more than half a year. The last year of Apries would thus be the 49th before Darius. Babylonian chronology made Nebuchadnezzar's last year the 41st before that king. (See the Canon.) As Nebuchadnezzar reigned 43 years,

[1] Or six years. (See Bunsen's *Egypt*, vol. ii. pp. 610, 611.)

and Apries only 19, (or at the utmost 25,) the reign of the latter must have been entirely included within that of the former. Nebuchadnezzar reigned from B. C. 604 to B. C. 561; Apries, probably from B. C. 588 to B. C. 569.

Note LXXIV., p. 126.

Manetho is reported to have said of Hophra, (Uaphris,) that he was the king "with whom the remnant of the Jews took refuge, after Jerusalem was captured by the Assyrians." (*Fragm. Hist. Gr.*, vol. ii. pp. 593, 594; Frs. 66 and 67.)

Note LXXV., p. 126.

Herodotus was altogether misinformed about the rank and position of Amasis, who (according to him) deposed Apries and put him to death. (See Wilkinson, in the author's *Herodotus*, vol. ii. pp. 386, 387.) It is therefore less surprising that he should have been kept in ignorance of the part which, it is probable, Nebuchadnezzar played in the transaction. The Egyptians would naturally seek to conceal from him the fact, that the change of sovereigns was brought about by foreign influence. But nothing is more unlikely than that they should have invented the deposition and execution of one of their monarchs. Thus the passage, "I will deliver Pharaoh-Hophra into the hands of his enemies, and into the hands of those *who seek his life*," (Jer. xliv. 30,) is confirmed by an unimpeachable testimony.

Note LXXVI., p. 126.

M. Bunsen was, I believe, the first to suggest that the *d* in this name had taken the place of *l*, through the resemblance of Λ to Δ. (See his *Egypt*, vol. i. p. 726.) The restoration of the *l* brings the two names into close accordance, the only difference then being that in the Greek form one of the original elements of the name, *adan* or *iddan*, is suppressed. Such suppression is not uncommon. It may be traced in Pul for Phaloch, in Bupalussor for Nabopolassar, (Abyden.,) in Asaridanus for Assur-*akh*-iddan or Esar-*h*addon, and probably in Saracus for *Assur-akh-uzur*, or some similar word.

The identity of the Mardocempadus of the Canon with the *Marduk-bal-iddan* of the Inscriptions is certain; and no reasonable doubt can be entertained of the identity of the latter with the Merodach-Baladan of Scripture. These views are now generally accepted. (See Brandis, *Rerum Assyr. Temp. emend.*, p. 45; Oppert, *Rapport*, &c., pp. 48, 49; Hincks in *Dubl. Univ. Mag.*, No. 250, p. 421; Layard, *Nineveh and Babylon*, p. 140; Keil on 2 Kings xx. 12–19; p. 118, E. T.; &c.)

NOTE LXXVII., p. 126.

Merodach-Baladan had two reigns, both noted in the Inscriptions. One of them is marked in Ptolemy's Canon, where it occupies the years B. C. 721–709. His other reign does not appear, since it lasted but six months, and the Canon marks no period short of a year. Polyhistor says (ap. Euseb. *Chronica*, i. 5) that it immediately preceded the reign of Elibus or Belibus, and the Inscriptions show that it was in the earlier part of the same year. This was the year B. C. 702, according to the Canon. As Hezekiah appears to have reigned from about B. C. 726 to B. C. 697, both reigns of Merodach-Baladan would have fallen within the time of his rule. (See the author's *Herodotus*, vol. i. pp. 502–504.)

NOTE LXXVIII., p. 126.

Fragm. Hist. Gr., vol. ii. p. 504; Fr. 12.

NOTE LXXIX., p. 126.

Sargon relates, that in his twelfth year he made war upon Merodach-Baladan, who had been for twelve years king of Babylon, defeated him, and drove him out of the country. The expelled monarch took refuge in Susiana, with a number of his partisans; and Sargon continued to contend against him and his allies for three years more at the least. (See the author's *Herodotus*, vol. i. pp. 474 and 503.) Sennacherib says, that immediately after his accession he invaded Babylonia, defeated and expelled Merodach-Baladan, and placed Belib over the land as ruler. (Ibid. p. 476; Fox Talbot's *Assyrian Texts*, pp. 1–2.)

NOTE LXXX., p. 127.

The Babylonian Gods may be to a great extent identified with the heavenly bodies. *San* or *Sansi* is the Sun; *Hurki*, the Moon; *Nebo* is Mercury; *Ishtar*, Venus; *Nergal*, Mars; *Merodach*, Jupiter; and probably *Nin* (or *Bar*) Saturn. (See the Essay of Sir H. Rawlinson on the Assyrian and Babylonian religious systems, in the first volume of the author's *Herodotus*, Essay x. pp. 584–642.) The dedication of the great temple at Borsippa to the Seven Spheres shows a similar spirit. Mr. Loftus has found that the temple platforms are so placed that their angles *exactly* face the four cardinal points, which seems to be a sufficient proof that they were used for astronomical purposes. (See his *Chaldæa and Susiana*, ch. xii. p. 128.) On the astronomical skill of the Babylonians, see Herod. ii. 109; Simplicius ad Aristot. *De Cœlo*, ii. p. 123; Pliny, *Hist. Nat.* vii. 56; Vitruvius, ix. 9, &c.

Note LXXXI., p. 127.

Berosus said: "When Nabopolassar his father (i. e. the father of Nebuchadnezzar) heard that the Satrap appointed over Egypt and the regions of Cœle-Syria and Phœnice had rebelled against him, being no longer able himself to endure hardship, he intrusted a certain portion of his army to his son Nebuchadnezzar, who was of age, and sent him against the rebel. Nebuchadnezzar, meeting the rebel, and engaging in battle with him, was victorious, and reduced the rebellious country into subjection to himself. . . . Not long after, Nebuchadnezzar, having heard of the death of his father, when he *had settled the affairs of Egypt* and the adjacent region, and had arranged with certain of his friends to bring to Babylon *the captives of the Jews*, and Phœnicians and Syrians and nations near Egypt, came himself, with great haste and with a small company, through the wilderness to Babylon." (Ap. Joseph. *Ant. Jud.* x. 11.)

Note LXXXII., p. 127.

See Josephus, *Contra Apion.*, i. 21: "I will add also the records of the Phœnicians; for even the superabundance of proofs ought not to be omitted. This is the reckoning of the time. 'Under the king Ithobalus, Nebuchadnezzar besieged Tyre for thirteen years.'"

Note LXXXIII., p. 127.

In continuation of the passage cited in Note LXXXI., Berosus said: "Assuming the administration of affairs, which had been under the management of the Chaldæans, and the kingdom which had been kept for him by the most eminent one among them, he succeeded to all his father's dominion; and when the captives arrived, he appointed colonies for them in the most suitable parts of Babylonia."

NOTE LXXXIV., p. 128.

The chief chronological difficulty which meets us is connected with the reign of Hezekiah. Scripture places no more than eight years between the fall of Samaria and the first invasion of Judæa by Sennacherib, (2 Kings xviii. 9 and 13.) The monuments place *at least* eighteen years between the two events; for Sargon says he took Samaria in his first year, and then gives his annals for fifteen years, while Sennacherib says that he attacked Hezekiah and took his fenced cities in his third year. Ptolemy's Canon, taken in conjunction with the monuments, raises the interval to twenty-two years. According to this, if the capture of Samaria was in Hezekiah's sixth year, the accession of Sennacherib must have fallen in his twenty-fifth, and the first attack of Sennacherib in his 27th year. But our present text of Kings (2 Kings xviii. 9) and of Isaiah (xxxvi. 1) calls it his 14th year. I have suggested elsewhere that the original number may have been altered under the idea that the invasion of Sennacherib and the illness of Hezekiah were synchronous, whereas the expression "in those days" was used by the sacred writers with a good deal of latitude. (See the author's *Herodotus*, vol. i. p. 479, note [2].)

Minor difficulties are the synchronism of Tirhakah with Hezekiah, and of So with Hoshea, of which I have already spoken. See Notes LIX. and LXIV.

NOTE LXXXV., p. 128.

Vorträge über Alte Geschichte, vol. i. p. 126; p. 106, E. T.

NOTE LXXXVI., p. 128.

A few instances may be noted under each head, as *specimens* of the sort of agreement.

1. Geographic. (*a*) In 2 Kings xvii. 6 (compare xviii. 11) it is said that the captive Israelites were placed by the conqueror "at Halah and

Habor, the river of Gozan, and in the cities of the Medes." Misled by the last clause, various commentators have struggled vainly to find Habor, Halah, and Gozan in or near Media. (See Bochart, *Geograph. Sac.*, iii. 14; Kitto, *Bibl. Cyclopædia*, ad voc. Gozan; Keil on 2 Kings xvii. 6; pp. 54–58, E. T., &c.) But this attempt is quite unnecessary. The true position of Gozan may be gathered from 2 Kings xix. 12, where it is coupled with Haran, the well-known city of Mesopotamia. In this locality all the names may be found, not only in old geographers, but even at the present day. The whole tract east of Harran about Nisibis, was anciently called *Gauzanitis* or Gozan, (Ptolemy, v. 18,) of which the better known name Mygdonia is a corruption;[1] the great river of this tract was the *Aborrhas* or *Chaboras*, (Habor;) and adjoining it (Ptol. l. s. c.) was a district called *Chalcitis*, (Halah.) Of this district a probable trace remains in the modern *Gla*, a large mound in these parts marking a ruined city, (Layard, *Nin. and Bab.*, p. 312, note;) while the river is still known as the *Khabour*, and the country as *Kaushan*.[2] The author of Chronicles (1 Chron. v. 26) adds Hara to the places mentioned in Kings, which is clearly Haran, or *Harran*, known to the Romans as *Carrhæ*. Undoubtedly the bulk of the Israelites were settled in this country, while Sargon selected a certain number to colonize his new cities in Media. (*b*) In 2 Kings xvii. 24, Cuthah, Ava, Hamath, and Sepharvaim are mentioned together as cities under the Assyrian dominion, and as furnishing the colonists who replaced the transplanted Israelites. Of these Hamath is familiar to us, but of the other cities little has been known till recently. "The site of Cutha," says Winer,[3] "is wholly uncertain." And so Keil:[4] "The situation of Cuthah cannot be determined with certainty" The discovery, however, of an ancient Babylonian city of the name, at the distance of about 15 miles from Babylon itself, where, moreover, Nergal was especially worshipped, (2 Kings xvii. 30,) seems to remove all doubt on the subject. Cuthah was most certainly the city, whose ruins

1 Mygdonia represents Gozan, with the adjectival or participial מ prefixed. The Greek writers always substituted their δ for the Semitic z. Hence Gaza became Ca*d*ytis, Achzib became Ec*d*ippa, the river Zab became the *D*iaba; and so M'gozan became Myg*d*on.

2 So at least Winer says, but I do not know on what authority. (*Realwörterbuch*, ad voc. *Gosan*.)

3 *Realwörterbuch*, vol. i. p. 237.

4 See Keil on 2 Kings xvii. 24; vol. ii. p. 67, E. T.

are now called *Ibrahim.* (See the author's *Herodotus*, vol. i. p. 632, and vol. ii. p. 587.) With almost equal confidence may we pronounce on the position of Ava, of which Winer says, that it is most probably a Mesopotamian town, "of which no trace remains in ancient authors or in modern Oriental topography."[1] Ava, (עַוָּא,) or Ivah, (עִוָּא,) is a city dedicated to the god Hea, (Neptune,) which was on the Euphrates at the extreme northern limit of Babylonia. It is called by the Talmudical writers *Ihi*, (יהי,) or with an epithet *Ihi-dakira*, (יהידקירא,) by Herodotus *Is*, (Ἴς,) by the Egyptians *Ist*, by the Turks and Arabs of the present day *Hit.* The first corruption of the name may be traced in the Ahava (אַהֲוָא) of Ezra, (viii. 15, 21; compare the *river* Is of Herodotus,) where the Jews encamped on their way from Babylon to Jerusalem. (See the remarks of Sir H. Rawlinson in the author's *Herodotus*, vol. i. p. 602.) Sepharvaim has less completely baffled the geographers, who have seen that it must be identical with the Sippara or Sipphara of Ptolemy (v. 18) and the city of the Sipparenes of Abydenus, (Fr. 9.) See Winer and Kitto ad voc. They have not, however, been able to fix the site; which the Inscriptions show to have been at *Mosaib*, a town on the Euphrates between *Hit* and Babylon. Nor have they given any account of the *dual* form, Sepharv*aim*, (סְפַרְוַיִם;) which is explained by the fact, noted in the Inscriptions, that the city was partly on the right, partly on the left bank of the Euphrates. (*c*) With Sepharvaim are connected, in 2 Kings xix. 13, the two cities of Hena and Ivah. It is implied that they had recently been united under one king: we must seek them therefore in the same neighborhood. As Ivah, like Sepharvaim, was upon the Euphrates above Babylon, and as the towns in this tract have always been clustered along the banks of the streams, we must look for Hena (Heb. הֵנַע; LXX. Ἀνά) in a similar position. Now on the Euphrates in this region is found in the Inscriptions an important town, *Anah* or *Anat;* which has always borne nearly the same name, and which is even now known as *Anah.* Hena is thus identified almost to a certainty.

2. Religious. (*a*) The worship of Baal and Astarte by the Phœnicians, almost to the exclusion of other gods, is strongly suggested by the whole history from Judges to Ahaz. (See Jud. x. 6; 1 Kings xi.

[1] *Realwörterbuch*, vol. i. p. 118.

5; xvi. 31, &c.) A marked confirmation of this exclusive, or nearly exclusive, worship is found in the names of the Tyrian kings and judges, which, like those of the Assyrian and Babylonian monarchs, comprehend almost always a divine element. Their names, so far as they are known, run as follows: Abi*baal*, Hiram, *Bal*eazar, Abd*astartus*, *Astartus*, Aserymus, Pheles, Eth*baal*, *Bal*ezar, Matgen, Pygmalion, Elulæus, Eth-*baal* II., *Baal*, Ecni*baal*, Chelbes, Abbarus, Mytgon, *Bal*-ator, Ger*astartus*, Mer*bal*, and Hiram II. Farther confirmation is derivable from the few authentic notices of the religion which remain, as from the fragments of Dius and Menander, where these two are the only deities mentioned.[1] (*b*) It has been already noticed that Nergal, who is said to have been worshipped by the Cuthites in Samaria, (2 Kings xvii. 30,) is found in the inscriptions to have been the special god of Cutha. (*c*) So too it appears from them that the city of Sepharvaim was under the special protection of two deities, conjointly worshipped, *Shamas* or *San*, the Sun, and his wife *Gula* or *Anunit*. Here we have evidently the Adrammelech and Anammelech of 2 Kings xvii. 31; Adrammelech, "the Fire-king," and Anammelech, "Queen Anunit" — the latter name being assimilated to the former with insolent carelessness. (See Sir H. Rawlinson in the author's *Herodotus*, vol. i. pp. 611, 612.) (*d*) If a satisfactory explanation cannot be given from Babylonian mythology of Succoth-Benoth, Nibhaz, and Tartak, (2 Kings xvii. 30, 31,) it is probably because they are not really the names of Babylonian gods. The first seems to mean "tents of daughters," or small tabernacles in which were contained images of female deities. The second and third are most likely scornful modifications of certain Babylonian names, which I should suspect to have been Nebo and *Tir* — the latter a title by which Nebo was sometimes called. Or they may possibly be gods which have yet to be discovered.

3. Manners, customs, &c. (*a*) The whole character of the Assyrian wars, as represented in Kings and Chronicles, is in close accordance with what we gather from the Inscriptions. The numerical force of their armies, the direction of them by the monarch in person, the multitude of their chariots, (2 Kings xix. 23,) their abundant cavalry,

[1] Mr. Kenrick gives the Phœnicians three "national deities," Astarte, Belus, Hercules. (*Phœnicia*, p. 345.) But Movers has shown satisfactorily that Melcarth (the Tyrian Hercules) was only another name for Baal.

(2 Kings xviii. 23,) their preference of the bow as a weapon,[1] (ib. xix. 32,) the manner of their sieges by "casting banks" against the walls of cities,[2] (ibid.,) and again the religious enthusiasm with which the wars were carried on, the antagonism maintained between the Assyrian gods and those of the invaded countries, (2 Kings xviii. 33, 34, &c.,) and the practice of carrying off as plunder, and therefore probably of melting down, the idols of the various nations, (2 Kings xix. 18,) are all distinctly marked in the sacred history, and might be abundantly illustrated from the monuments.[3] (*b*) No less harmonious with Scripture is the representation which the monuments give of the Assyrian political system. Something has been already said on this point. (Lecture III., pp. 94–96.) The empire is one made up of a number of petty kingdoms. ("Are not my princes altogether kings?" Is. x. 8.) Absorption of the conquered districts is not aimed at, but only the extension of suzerainty, and government through native tributary monarchs. Rebellion is promptly punished, and increased tribute is its natural consequence. (2 Kings xviii. 14.) Finally, transplantation is made use of when other means fail — sometimes on a larger, sometimes on a smaller scale, as the occasion requires.[4] (*c*) The continued power of the Hittites, the number of their princes, and their strength in chariots, which appears from 1 Kings x. 29, and again remarkably from 2 Kings vii. 6, is strikingly confirmed by the Black Obelisk inscription, where we find twelve kings of the *Khatti*, allied with Syria and Hamath, and fighting against the Assyrians with a force whose chief strength seems to be chariots. Many similar points of *minute* agreement might be adduced, but this note has, I fear, already extended itself beyond the patience of most readers.

1 This appears sufficiently on the sculptures; but it is even more strikingly evinced in the language of the Inscriptions where the phrase which has to be translated, "killed in battle," is constantly "killed *with arrows*." (See *Dubl. Univ. Mag.*, No. 250, p. 423.)

2 See Layard's *Nineveh and Babylon*, p. 149. Describing a bass-relief of Sennacherib's, he says, "Against the fortifications had been thrown up *as many as ten banks or mounds*, compactly built of stones, bricks, earth, and branches of trees."

3 See the Great *Inscription of Tiglath-Pileser I.*, pp. 23, 30, 38, &c.; *Dubl. Univ. Mag.*, No. 250, pp. 423, 424; Fox Talbot's *Assyrian Texts*, pp. 1, 3, 4, 11, 22, &c. Compare the author's *Herodotus*, vol. i. p. 495.

4 See the author's *Herodotus*, vol. i. p. 493.

LECTURE V.

NOTE I., p. 131.

So Ewald, *Die Propheten des Alten Bundes*, p. 560.

NOTE II., p. 131.

This is the theory of De Wette (*Einleitung*, § 253, p. 342; vol. ii. p. 485, E. T.,) who bases the view on the passages of Ezekiel, where Daniel is so highly commended. See below, Note X.

NOTE III., p. 131.

See the statements of Jerome concerning Porphyry in the preface to his *Comment. in Daniel.* (*Op.*, vol. iii. pp. 1073, 1074.)

NOTE IV., p. 131.

It is urged by Ewald, (*Propheten des Alt. Bundes*, p. 565;) by Knobel, *Prophetismus der Hebräer*, ii. p. 401; by Strauss, (*Leben Jesu*, § 13; vol. i. p. 56, E. T.;) by De Wette, (*Einleitung*, § 255 b, p. 346;) and by Mr. Theodore Parker, (*Translation of De Wette*, vol. ii. pp. 491 and 501.) Hence Auberlen observes with justice, "The *true argument of all others*, even in modern criticism, lies in the dogmatic doubt of the reality of miracles and predictions." (*Prophecies of Daniel*, Introduction, p. 10, E. T.[1]) And Stuart, "Nearly all the arguments employed to disprove the genuineness of Daniel, have their basis, more or less directly, in the assumption, that miraculous events are impossibilities. Of course, all the extraordinary occurrences related in the book of Daniel, and all the graphic predictions of events, are, under the guidance of this assumption, stricken from the list of probabilities, and even of possibilities." (*History and Defence of the Canon*, § 4, pp. 110, 111.)

[1] The Prophecies of Daniel and the Revelation of St. John viewed in their mutual relation by C. A. Auberlen, Ph. D. Translated by the Rev. A. Saphir; Edinburgh, Clark, 1856.

Note V., p. 132.

Undoubtedly a peculiar character attaches to the prophecies of Daniel, if they are compared with those of the other prophets. As Auberlen observes, "his prophecies abound, above all the rest, in historical and political detail." (*Prophecies of Daniel*, Introduction, p. 3, E. T.) But to make this an objection to the authenticity of the Book is to assume, either that we have an *a priori* knowledge of the nature and limits of prophetical inspiration, or else that the law of such inspiration may be gathered inductively from the other Scriptures, and then applied to exclude the claims of a Book which has as much external sanction as any other. But induction should be from all the instances; and to exclude the Book of Daniel by a law drawn from the rest of Scripture, is first to assume that it is not Scripture, and then to prove that it is not by means of that assumption. We are quite ignorant beforehand to what extent it might please the Omniscient to communicate to any of his creatures the knowledge of the future, which He possesses in perfection; and we have no means of determining the question but by a careful study of all the facts which the Bible sets before us. We have no right to assume that there will be a uniform law, much less that we shall be able to discover it. It is a principle of the Divine Economy that "there is a time for every thing;" and the minute exactness which characterizes some of the Prophecies of Daniel may have been adapted to peculiar circumstances in the history of God's people at some particular time,[1] or have otherwise had some special object which we cannot fathom.

Note VI., p. 132.

See Hengstenberg, *Authentie des Daniel*, p. 303, et seqq. The *alternate* use of Hebrew and Chaldee, which is the main linguistic peculiarity of Daniel, is only natural at a time when both languages were currently spoken by the Jews; and is only found in writings of about this period, as in Ezra and Jeremiah. De Wette's answer to this argument, that both languages were known to the learned Jews at a later date,

[1] Auberlen thinks that the minuteness, which is chiefly in chs. viii. and xi., was "necessary to prepare the people for the attacks and artful machinations of Antiochus," and that "the glorious struggle of the Maccabees, so far as it was a pure and righteous one, was a fruit of this book." (pp. 54, 55.)

(*Einleitung*, § 255 c, p. 349,) is a specimen of the weak grounds on which men are content to rest a foregone conclusion. The Hebrew Scriptures were not written *for* the learned; and *no instances at all* can be found of the *alternate* use, (as distinct from the occurrence of Chaldaisms in Hebrew, or Hebraisms in Chaldee,) excepting at the time of the Captivity.

NOTE VII., p. 132.

I have here followed the ordinary tradition, which rests on the authority of Aristeas, Philo, Justin Martyr, Josephus, Epiphanius, &c. It is questioned, however, if the Greek version of Daniel was made so early. The book of Esther, according to the subscription to it, was not translated till the fourth year of Ptolemy Philometor, B. C. 178 or 177, a year or two before the accession of Epiphanes. And it is possible that Daniel may have been translated still later. (See Horne's *Introduction*, &c., vol. iii. p. 44.)

If the argument in the text is weakened by this admission, it may receive the following important accessions: — 1. Passages of Daniel are referred to by Jesus the son of Sirach, who must have written as early as B. C. 180, or before the time of Epiphanes.[1] (See Ecclus. xvii. 17, compared with Dan. x. 20, 21; xii. 1; and Ecclus. x. 8, compared with Dan. viii. 23, &c.) And, 2. Daniel's prophecies were shown to Alexander the Great in the year B. C. 332, and inclined him to treat the Jews with special favor. (Joseph. *Ant. Jud.* xi. 8.) The authority of Josephus as to the main fact is not discredited by the circumstance, that "the narrative of Josephus is not credible in all of its particulars." (De Wette, *Einleitung*, § 255 c, p. 349.)

NOTE VIII., p. 132.

The fundamental arguments in favor of this are, 1. The constant representation of Daniel as the author from ch. vii. to the end; and, 2. Our Lord's words, "the abomination of desolation, *spoken of by Daniel the Prophet*," (Matt. xxiv. 15.) De Wette's arguments to the contrary, besides those noted in the text, seem to be the following, — 1. The miracles are grotesque. 2. The apocalyptic tone is unlike that of the proph-

1 Even De Wette admits this. (*Einleitung*, § 316, p. 419, "As we maintain at the time of its composition., d. J. 180, v. Chr.")

ets belonging to this period. 3. Honorable mention is made of Daniel himself in the book. 4. The language is corrupt, containing Persian and Greek words. 5. The book is placed by the Jews among the Hagiographa, and is therefore later than Malachi. 6. The angelology, christology, and asceticism, mark a late date.[1] Of these the first and last may be simply denied; the second is reduced to a shadow by De Wette himself when he admits that the style of Ezekiel's and Zechariah's prophesying is not very unlike ("nicht ganz fremd") Daniel's; the third is an objection equally to the Pentateuch, the Gospel of St. John, and some of St. Paul's Epistles, and rests merely upon an *a priori* conception of how prophets should write, not borne out by experience; the fourth is not urged with any confidence, since it is allowed to be "certainly possible that the Greek words may have been known to the Babylonians at the time," (p. 347;) and if so, *a fortiori*, the Persian words; and the fifth argument, if it has any weight at all, would make the Book of Job, and the Proverbs of Solomon, later than Malachi! No wonder Professor Stuart should say—"Beyond the objections founded on the assumption, that miracles and predictions are impossibilities, there is little to convince an enlightened and well-balanced critical reader, that the book is supposititious." (*History and Defence of the Canon*, p. 111.)

NOTE IX., p. 132.

See Dan. i. 3. Josephus says that Daniel was of the seed of Zedekiah. *Ant. Jud.* x. 10.)

NOTE X., p. 132.

Ewald contends, that the Daniel commended by Ezekiel must have been an ancient hero, like Job and Noah, (*Propheten des Alt. Bundes*, p. 560,) of whose wisdom and righteousness he knew from some sacred book, with which both himself and the Jews of his time were well acquainted. We are not told what has become of this book, or what proof there is of its existence. Nor is it explained how this "ancient hero" comes not to be mentioned in the historical Scriptures at all, or by any writer earlier than Ezekiel. Doubtless if we had no means of knowing to the contrary, we should naturally have supposed from Ezek. xiv. 14 and 20, that Daniel was an ancient historical personage

[1] *Einleitung*, § 255, pp. 346, 347.

in Ezekiel's time, having lived between Noah and Job; but as this is impossible from the absolute silence of the historical books, Ezekiel's mention of him at all can only be accounted for by the fact that he was the great Jew of the day, and that his wisdom and virtue were known to those for whom Ezekiel wrote, — the *Chaldæan* Jews,[1] be it remembered, (Ezek. i. 2, 3,) — not historically, or from any book, but from personal acquaintance and common rumor. Why Daniel *precedes* Job, is still a question. Perhaps, because Daniel and Noah are actual men, while Job is not? Or because the two former are viewed as Jews, Job as a Gentile?

NOTE XI., p. 132.

Einleitung, § 255 a, p. 344; "full of improbabilities, and even of historical errors, such as no other prophetical book of the Old Testament contains." Compare p. 349.

NOTE XII., p. 132.

See above, Note LXXXVI. on Lecture IV. Sargon seems to have been the first king who introduced this practice *on a large scale.* He was followed by Sennacherib, (Fox Talbot's *Assyrian Texts*, pp. 3, 4, 7, &c.;) and Esarhaddon, (ibid. pp. 11 and 17.)

NOTE XIII., p. 132.

See Herod. iv. 181; v. 15; vi. 20 and 119; Ctes. *Pers.*, § 9; Arrian. *Exp. Alex.*, iii. 48; and compare the author's *Herodotus*, vol. ii. pp. 563, 564. The practice continues to modern times. (See Chardin's *Voyage en Perse*, vol. iii. p. 292; and Ferrier's *Caravan Journeys*, p. 395.)

NOTE XIV., p. 133.

Lee Lecture IV., Note LXXXIII.

[1] It has been usual to regard Ezekiel as writing in Mesopotamia, the Chebar being supposed to be the Khabour. But we have no right to assume the identity of the words כְּבָר and חָבוֹר. The Chebar is probably the Nahr Malcha, or Royal Canal, the *great* (כַּבִּר) cutting of Nebuchadnezzar. See the article on CHEBAR in Smith's (forthcoming) *Biblical Dictionary*.

NOTE XV., p. 133.

See the fragments of these writers in the *Fragmenta Hist. Gr.*, vol. ii. pp. 506, 507; and vol. iv. p. 284. Compare with the expression in Daniel, "Is not this great Babylon which I have built?" (Dan. iv. 30,) the statement of Berosus. Nebuchadnezzar . . . repaired the city which had existed from the first, and added another to it; and in order that besiegers might not again be able, by turning aside the course of the river, to get possession of the city, he built three courses of walls around the inner city, and as many around the outer. Both statements are confirmed by the fact that nine tenths of the inscribed bricks from the site of Babylon are stamped with Nebuchadnezzar's name.

NOTE XVI., p. 133.

Ap. Euseb. *Præp. Ev.* ix. 41, pp. 441, 442. "Afterwards, as is said by the Chaldæans, he went up into his palace, where he was seized by some divine influence, and uttered these words: 'O Babylonians, I Nebuchadnezzar announce to you this future calamity. . . . There shall come a Persian mule, using our divinities as allies: he shall bring us into bondage: leagued with him shall be the Mede, the boast of Assyria.' Having uttered these predictions, he immediately disappeared."

NOTE XVII., p. 133.

Beros. ap. Joseph. *Contr. Apionem*, i. 20; Polyhist. ap. Euseb. *Chronica*, i. 5, § 3, p. 21; Ptol. *Mag. Syntax.*, v. 14.

NOTE XVIII., p. 134.

These tablets are commonly orders on the imperial treasury, dated in the current year of the reigning monarch, like modern Acts of Parliament. They give a *minimum* for the length of each monarch's reign, but of course by the nature of the case they cannot furnish a *maximum*. Still, where they are abundant, as in Nebuchadnezzar's case, they raise a strong probability that the highest number found was not much exceeded.

NOTE XIX., p. 134.

The eighth year of Nebuchadnezzar being the first of Jehoiachin's captivity, (2 Kings xxiv. 12,) we must place the beginning of Nebuchadnezzar's reign *seven* years earlier; and the 37th of the captivity being the first of Evil-Merodach, (Ibid. xxv. 27,) the 36th would be Nebuchadnezzar's last *complete* year. Now $36 + 7 = 43$.

NOTE XX., p. 134.

So De Wette, (*Einleitung*, § 255 a; p. 345 c.,) who quotes von Lengerke, Hitzig, and others, as agreeing with him. Ewald also compares Daniel to Judith, on account of its confusing together various times and countries. (*Propheten des Alt. Bundes*, p. 562.)

NOTE XXI., p. 134.

De Wette gives the first place among his "historical inaccuracies," to the "erroneous representations concerning the wise men of Babylon," and the "inexplicable admission of Daniel among the same;" the second to the "mention of the Persian arrangement of Satrapies under Nebuchadnezzar and Darius the Mede." (*Einleitung*, l. s. c.)

NOTE XXII., p. 134.

The word which we translate "magicians" in Dan. i. 20, ii. 2, 10, &c., is *chartummim*, or *khartummim*, (חַרְטֻמִּים,) which is derived from *cheret*, or *kheret*, (חֶרֶט,) "a graving-tool." (See Buxtorf's *Lexicon Hebraicum et Chaldaicum*, ad voc.) Babylonian documents are sometimes written on clay, where the character has been impressed, before the clay was baked, by a tool with a triangular point; but they are also frequently on stone — large pebbles from the Euphrates's bed — in which case they have been engraved with a fine chisel.

NOTE XXIII., p. 135.

The Chaldæans in Kings, Chronicles, Isaiah, Jeremiah, and even Ezekiel, are simply the inhabitants of Chaldæa, which is the name applied to the whole country whereof Babylon is the capital. But in

Daniel the Chaldæans are a special set of persons at Babylon, having a "learning" and a "tongue" of their own, (Dan. i. 4,) and classed with the magicians, astrologers, &c. Strabo notes both senses of the term, (xvi. i. § 6 ;) and Berosus seems to use the narrower and less common one, when he speaks of Nebuchadnezzar as finding on his arrival at Babylon after his father's death, that affairs were being conducted by the Chaldæans, and that their chief was keeping the throne vacant for him, ("assuming the administration of affairs, which had been under the management of the Chaldæans, and the kingdom which had been kept for him by the most eminent one among them, he succeeded," &c., Fr. 14,) while elsewhere (as in Frs. 1, § 1 ; 5, 6, 11, &c.) he employs the generic and more usual sense. Compare Herod. i. 181, and vii. 63. The inscriptions show that the Chaldæans (*Kaldi*) belonged to the primitive Scythic inhabitants, and that the old astronomical and other learning of the Babylonians continued to be in this language during the later Semitic times. (See Sir H. Rawlinson's note in the author's *Herodotus*, vol. i. p. 319, note [8].)

Note XXIV., p. 135.

Compare an article on the Chaldæans in Smith's (forthcoming) *Biblical Dictionary*.

Note XXV., p. 135.

See above, Lecture IV., Note LXXXI.

Note XXVI., p. 136.

I do not intend to assert that this *was* the case. We have no satisfactory proof that the Babylonians ever approached more nearly to the Satrapial system than by the appointment in exceptional cases of a native "governor" in lieu of an hereditary king, as in the case of Gedaliah. The maintenance of Jehoiakim, Jehoiachin, and Zedekiah on the throne of Judæa seems to indicate the *general* character of their government. It may even be suspected that Berosus's "Satrap of Egypt and Syria" was really Pharaoh-Necho, whose position Babylonian vanity represented in that light. The LXX. translate Daniel's "princes" (אֲחַשְׁדַּרְפְּנַיָּא) by σατράπαι, but this cannot be regarded as an argument of much weight. Babylonian *historical* inscriptions are so scanty that we can derive little assistance from them towards determining the question.

NOTE XXVII., p. 136.

The extent of the kingdom, (Dan. iv. 22,) the absolute power of the king, (ib. ii. 5, 13, 48; iii. 29, &c.,) the influence of the Chaldæans, (ib. ii. 2; iii. 8, &c.,) the idolatrous character of the religion, the use of images of gold, (ib. iii. 1; compare Herod. i. 183,) are borne out by profane writers, and (so far as their testimony can be brought to bear) by the monuments. The building (rebuilding) of Babylon (Dan. iv. 30) by Nebuchadnezzar, is confirmed in every way. (See above, Note XV.) Again, there is a curious notice in Daniel of a certain peculiarity which may be remarked in Nebuchadnezzar's religion, viz., his special devotion to a particular god. Nebuchadnezzar throughout his inscriptions presents himself to us as a devotee of Merodach. "Merodach, his lord," is the chief — almost the sole object of his worship and praise — invocations, prayers, and thanksgivings are addressed to him, and him only. (See Sir H. Rawlinson's remarks in the author's *Herodotus*, vol. i. pp. 628, 629, and compare the Inscription of Nebuchadnezzar in the same work, vol. ii. pp. 585–587.) This peculiarity is casually and incidentally noticed by Daniel, when he says that Nebuchadnezzar carried the sacred vessels of the temple "into the land of Shinar, to the house of *his god;* and brought the vessels into the treasure-house of *his god.*" (i. 2.)

NOTE XXVIII., p. 136.

See his *Beiträge zur Einleitung in das Alt. Test.*, p. 105. Hengstenberg has on his side the authority of Eusebius, who so understood the passage, (*Chronica*, i. 10, p. 21;) but Eusebius's arguments appear to me very weak.

NOTE XXIX., p. 137.

See Sir H. Rawlinson's translation of the Standard Inscription in the author's *Herodotus*, vol. ii. pp. 585–587. The passage to which reference is made in the text runs as follows — "Four years (?) . . . the seat of my kingdom in the city . . . which . . . did not rejoice my heart. In all my dominions I did not build a high place of power; the precious treasures of my kingdom I did not lay up. In Babylon, buildings for myself and for the honor of my kingdom I did not lay out. In the worship of Merodach my lord, the joy of my heart, (?) in Babylon the city of his sovereignty and the seat of my empire, I did not sing his praises, (?) and I did not furnish his altars (with victims), nor did I clear out the canals." Other negative clauses follow. From this literal rendering of the passage, only one or two words of which are at all doubtful, the reader may judge for himself to what event in his life it is likely that the monarch alludes. He should perhaps bear in mind that the whole range of cuneiform literature presents no similar instance of a king putting on record his own inaction.

NOTE XXX., p. 137.

Berosus ap. Joseph. *Contr. Ap.*, i. 20: "Now Nebuchadnezzar, just as he began to build the aforesaid wall, fell sick, and died, after having reigned 43 years. His son, Evil-Merodach, became master of the kingdom." Compare Abyden. ap. Euseb. *Chron.*, i. 10, p. 28; and Polyhist. ap. eund. i. 5, § 3; p. 21.

NOTE XXXI., p. 137.

Berosus continues after the passage above quoted—"This man, having used his authority in a lawless and dissolute manner, was slain by conspirators."

NOTE XXXII., p. 138.

The Babylonian name is read as *Nergal-shar-uzur;* the Hebrew form (נֵרְגַל־שַׂרְאֶצֶר) is exactly expressed by our authorized version, which gives Nergal-shar-ezer. The Greek renderings are far inferior to the Hebrew. Berosus, as reported by Josephus, (l. s. c.,) called the king Neriglissoor; Polyhistor called him Neglissar, (Euseb. *Chron.*, i. 5; p. 21;) Abydenus, Niglissar, (Armen. Euseb.,) or Neriglissar, (Euseb. *Præp. Ev.*, ix. 41;) Ptolemy, (*Mag. Synt.*, l. s. c.,) Nerigassolassar.

NOTE XXXIII., p. 138.

The Babylonian vocalization somewhat modifies the word, which is read as in the Inscriptions as *Rubu-emga.* (See Sir H. Rawlinson's note in the author's *Herodotus*, vol. i. p. 518, note[3].) With this the

Hebrew *Rub-mag* (רַב־מָג) is identical in all its consonants; and there can be no reasonable doubt that it is the same term. Gesenius has translated the title as "Chief of the Magi," (Lexicon, p. 388, E. T.;) but the Babylonian word which represents the Persian Magi in the Behistun Inscription bears no resemblance at all to the *emga* of this title. Sir H. Rawlinson believes the signification to be "Chief Priest," but holds that there is no reference in it to Magism.

Note XXXIV., p. 138.

Abydenus has the form Nabannidochus, (ap. Euseb. *Chron.* i. 10, p. 28,) with which may be compared the Naboandelus (probably to be read Naboandechus,) of Josephus, (*Ant. Jud.* x. 11.) Berosus wrote Nabonnedus (Joseph. *Contr. Ap.* i. 20;) Herodotus, Labynetus, (i. 77, 188.) The actual name seems to have been *Nabu-nahit* in Semitic, *Nabu-induk* in the Cushite Babylonian.

Note XXXV. p. 139.

So Josephus, (*Ant. Jud.* l. s. c.;) Perizonius, (*Orig. Babylon.* p. 359;) Heeren, *Manual of Ancient History*, p. 28, E. T.; Des Vignoles, *Œuvres*, vol. ii. p. 510, et seqq.; Clinton, *F. H.* vol. ii. pp. 369–371; the author of *L'Art de Vérifier les Dates*, vol. ii. p. 69; Winer, *Realwörterbuch* ad voc. Belshazzar; Kitto, *Biblical Cyclopædia* ad voc. eand.; &c.

Note XXXVI., p. 139.

It has been almost universally concluded, by those who have regarded the book of Daniel as authentic, that the Belshazzar of that book must be identical with one or other of the native monarchs known from Berosus and Abydenus to have occupied the throne between Nebuchadnezzar and Cyrus. Each monarch has been preferred in his turn. Conringius, Bouhier, Larcher, Marsham, Hupfeld, Hävernick, and others, have identified Belshazzar with Evil-Merodach; Eusebius, Syncellus, and Hales, with Neriglissar; Jackson and Gatterer, with Laborosoarchod; but the bulk of commentators and historians with Nabonadius. (See the last note.) In every case there was the same difficulty in explaining the diversity of name, as well as in reconciling the historical facts recorded of the monarch preferred with what Scripture tells us of Belshazzar. On the whole, perhaps the hypothesis of Conringius was the least objectionable.

NOTE XXXVII., p. 139.

So De Wette, *Einleitung*, § 255 a, p. 345.

NOTE XXXVIII., p. 139.

This view was maintained by Sir Isaac Newton. (See his *Chronology*, pp. 323–330.)

NOTE XXXIX., p. 139.

Sir H. Rawlinson made this important discovery in the year 1854, from documents obtained at *Mugheir*, the ancient Ur. (See Mr. Loftus's *Chaldæa and Susiana*, ch. xii. pp. 132, 133; and compare the author's *Herodotus*, vol. i. p. 525.)

NOTE XL., p. 140.

Jehu, though ordinarily called "the son of Nimshi," was really his grandson, (2 Kings ix. 2.) Merodach-Baladan, "the son of Baladan," according to Isaiah, (xxxix. 1,) is in the Inscriptions the son of *Yagina*. Baladan was probably one of his more remote ancestors. In Matt. i. 1, our Blessed Lord is called "the Son of David, (who was) the son of Abraham."

NOTE XLI., p. 140.

Such marriages formed a part of the state policy of the time, and were sought with the utmost avidity. When Zedekiah's daughters were committed to Gedaliah, (Jerem. xli. 10,) it was undoubtedly that he might marry them, in order (as Mr. F. Newman justly observes [1]) "to establish for his descendants an hereditary claim on Jewish allegiance." So Amasis married a daughter of Psammetik III.; [2] and Atossa was taken to wife both by the Pseudo-Smerdis and by Darius, the son of Hystaspes, (Herod. iii. 68 and 88.) On the same grounds

[1] *Hebrew Monarchy*, p. 361.

[2] Wilkinson in the author's *Herodotus*, vol. ii. p. 387.

Herod the Great married Mariamné. (See Joseph. *De Bell. Jud.* i. 12, § 3.) An additional reason for suspecting that such a marriage as that suggested in the text was actually contracted by Nabonadius, is to be found in the fact, which may be regarded as certain, that he adopted the name of Nebuchadnezzar among his own family names. That he had a son so called, is proved by the rise of two pretenders in the reign of Darius, who each proclaimed himself to be "Nebuchadnezzar, the son of Nabonadius." (*Behistun Inscr.* Col. i. Par. 16; and Col. iii. Par. 13.)

NOTE XLII., p. 140.

Syncellus, *Chronograph.* p. 438, B; Apoc. Dan. xiii. ad fin.; Jackson, *Chronolog. Antiq.* vol. i. p. 416; Marsham, *Can. Chron.* p. 604, et seqq.; Winer, *Realwörterbuch* ad voc. *Darius;* &c.

NOTE XLIII., p. 140.

This was the view of Josephus, (*Ant. Jud.* x. 11, § 4;) and from him it has been adopted very generally. See Prideaux's *Connection*, &c., vol. i. p. 95; Hales's *Analysis of Chronology*, vol. ii. p. 508; Offerhaus, *Spicileg. Hist. Chron.*, p. 265; Bertholdt, *Exc. zum Daniel*, p. 483; Hengstenberg, *Authentie des Daniel*, § 48; Von Lengerke, *Das Buch Daniel*, § 92; Hooper's *Palmoni*, pp. 278–283; and Kitto's *Biblical Cyclopædia*, ad voc. *Darius.* But Xenophon is the sole authority for the existence of this personage; and Herodotus may be quoted against his existence, since he positively declares that Astyages "had no male offspring." (Herod. i. 109.)

NOTE XLIV., p. 140.

By Larcher, (*Hérodote*, vol. vii. p. 175,) Conringius, *Adversar. Chron.* c. 13,) and Bouhier, (*Dissertations sur Hérodote*, ch. iii. p. 29.)

NOTE XLV., p. 140.

Syncellus regarded Darius the Mede as at once identical with Astyages and Nabonadius. (*Chronograph.* pp. 437, 438.)

NOTE XLVI., p. 140.

That Cyrus placed Medes in situations of high trust, is evident from Herodotus, (i. 156 and 162.) He may therefore very possibly have established Astyages, his grandfather (?), as vice-king of Babylon, where the latter may have been known to the Jews as Darius the Mede. The diversity of name is no real objection here; for Astyages (Asdahages = *Aj-dahak*) is not a name, but (like Pharaoh) a title. And if it be said that Darius the Mede was the son of Ahasuerus or Xerxes, (Dan. ix. 1,) while Astyages was the son of Cyaxares, it may be answered that, according to one explanation, Cyaxares is equivalent to *Kei-Axares*, or King Xerxes. There is still an objection in the age of Darius Medus, who was only 62 in B. C. 538, (Dan. v. 31,) whereas Astyages (it would seem) must have been 75 at that time. (See the author's *Herodotus*, vol. i. pp. 417, 418.) But as the numbers depend here on the single authority of Herodotus, whose knowledge of Median history was not very great, perhaps they are not greatly entitled to consideration.

If, however, it be thought that, for this or any other reason, Darius Medus cannot be Astyages, we may regard him as a Median noble, intrusted by Cyrus with the government of Babylon. Scripture makes it plain that his true position was that of a subordinate king, holding his crown of a superior. Darius the Mede, we are told, (Dan. v. 30,) "*took* the kingdom" — קַבֵּל מַלְכוּתָא — that is, "accepit regnum," (Buxtorf. ad voc. קְבַל,) "received the kingdom at the hand of another." And again we read in another place, (Dan. ix. 1,) that he "*was made king* over the realm of the Chaldæans;" where the word used is הָמְלַךְ, the Hophil of מָלַךְ, the Hiphal of which is used when David appoints Solomon king, and which thus means distinctly, "was appointed king by another."

NOTE XLVII., p. 141.

Herod. i. 191; Xen. *Instit. Cyr.* vii. 5, § 15.

NOTE XLVIII., p. 141.

See the author's *Herodotus*, vol. i. pp. 401–403.

Note XLIX., p. 141.

Even the tyrant Cambyses, when he wished to marry his sister, because he was intending to do an unusual thing, called together the royal judges, and asked them *if there was any law which allowed* one who wished, to marry his sister. (Herod. iii. 31.) And Xerxes, when he had been entrapped, like Herod Antipas, into making a rash promise, feels compelled to keep it, being restrained by the law, namely, that *it is not allowable* that one who makes a request at the time of a royal feast should be denied. (Ibid. ix. 111.)

Note L., p. 141.

See De Wette, *Einleitung*, § 255 a, p. 345. Compare Mr. Parker's *Translation*, (vol. ii. p. 490,) where it is suggested that the author has copied and exaggerated what Herodotus ascribes to Darius Hystaspis.

Note LI., p. 141.

See Clinton's *Fasti Hellenici*, vol. ii. p. 372: "The one hundred and twenty princes appointed by Darius (Dan. vi. 1) correspond to the one hundred and twenty-seven provinces of Ahasuerus, (Esth. i. 1,) and to the enlarged extent of the empire."

Note LII., p. 142.

Nebuchadnezzar's first conquest of Judæa in the reign of Jehoiakim — which was the occasion on which Daniel became a captive (Dan. i. 1) — fell, as appears from the fragment of Berosus quoted in Note LXXXI. to Lecture IV., in his father's last year, which, according to Ptolemy's Canon, was B. C. 605. Nebuchadnezzar then reigned himself 43 years, Evil-Merodach, his son, reigned two years, Neriglissar three years and some months, Laborosoarchod three quarters of a year, Nabonadius 17 years, and Darius the Mede one year. Consequently Daniel's prayer "in the first year of Darius the Mede" (Dan. ix. 1–3) fell into the year B. C. 538, or 68 years after the first conquest of Judæa by Nebuchadnezzar in B. C. 605.

NOTE LIII., p. 142.

See Clinton's *Fasti Hellenici*, vol. ii. pp. 366–368; and Mr. Hooper's *Palmoni*, p. 390.

NOTE LIV., p. 143.

In Daniel's prophecy of the weeks, we have (I think) the term of seventy years used first (Dan. ix. 24) as a round number, and afterwards explained — accuracy being of especial importance in this prophecy — as 68½ weeks, (ibid. 25–27.) In Ezekiel, the forty years' desolation of Egypt (Ez. xxix. 11–13) can scarcely be understood to extend really to the full term. Prophecy is, as Bacon says, "a kind of historiography;" but it does not ordinarily affect the minuteness and strict accuracy of human history.

NOTE LV., p. 143.

Einleitung, § 196, 197, pp. 260–265. It is obvious that the insertion of documents, such as the proclamation of Cyrus, (Ez. i. 24,) the list of those who came up with Zerubbabel, (ib. ii. 3–67; Neh. viii. 7–69;) the letters of the Samaritans, the Jews, the Persian kings, (ib. iv. 11–22, &c.,) and the like, does not in the slightest degree affect the unity and integrity of the works. But De Wette does not appear to see this, (§ 196 a, p. 260.)

NOTE LVI., p. 143.

The number of generations from Joshua to Jaddua, which is six, (Neh. xii. 10–12,) should cover a space of about 200 years. This would bring Jaddua to the latter half of the fourth century B. C. Exactly at this time there lived the well-known high priest Jaddua, who received Alexander at Jerusalem, and showed him the prophecies of Daniel. (Joseph. *Ant. Jud.* xi. 8.) At this time too there was a Darius (Darius Codomannus) upon the Persian throne, as noted in verse 22. The Jaddua of Nehemiah must therefore be regarded as the contemporary of Alexander.

Hävernick allows this, but still thinks that Nehemiah may have written the whole book, since he may have lived to the time of Jaddua! But as Nehemiah was old enough to be sent on an important mission in

B. C. 445, (Neh. ii. 1–8,) he would have been considerably above a hundred before Jaddua can have been priest, and 130 or 140 before the accession of Codomannus.

NOTE LVII., p. 144.

Eight Dukes or Kings are mentioned in Genesis xxxvi. 31–39, as having reigned over Edom, "*before there reigned any king in Israel.*" This last clause must have been written after the time of Saul, the first Israelite king; and it has commonly been regarded as an interpolation. (Graves's *Lectures on the Pentateuch*, vol. i. p. 346; Horne, *Introduction*, vol. i. p. 64; &c.) But the real interpolation seems to be from verse 31 to verse 39 inclusive. These kings, whose reigns are likely to have covered a space of 200 years, *must* come down later than Moses, and probably reach nearly to the time of Saul. The whole passage seems to have been transferred from 1 Chr. i. 43–50.

In 1 Chronicles iii. 17–24, the genealogy of the descendants of Jechoniah is carried on for nine generations, (Jechoniah, Pedaiah, Zerubbabel, Hananiah, Shekaniah, Shemaiah, Neariah, Elioenai, and Hodaiah,) who must have occupied a period not much short of three centuries. As Jechoniah came to the throne in B. C. 597, this portion of Chronicles can scarcely have been written before B. C. 300. See De Wette, *Einleitung*, § 189, p. 242, whose argument here appears to be sound. He remarks, that the occurrence of a Shemaiah, the son of Shekaniah, among the contemporaries of Nehemiah, (Neh. iii. 29,) confirms the calculation, and indicates that the genealogy is consecutive.

NOTE LVIII., p. 144.

De Wette in one place admits that Ezra may have written a chapter (ch. x.) in which the third person is used, but pronounces against his having written the opening passage of ch. vii., (verses 1–10,) chiefly on this ground. (*Einleitung*, § 196 a, p. 261.) Bertholdt and Zunz go farther, and deny that Ezra can have written ch. x. Professor Stuart concludes, chiefly on account of the alternation of persons, that "some one of Ezra's friends, probably of the prophetic order, compiled the book from various documents," among which were some written by Ezra himself. (*Defence of the Old Testament Canon*, § 6, p. 148.)

NOTE LIX., p. 144.

The third person is used through the first six chapters of Daniel, and at the opening of the seventh. The first then takes its place to the end of ch. ix. The third recurs in the first verse of ch. x.; after which the first is used uninterruptedly.

NOTE LX., p. 144.

Thucydides begins his history in the third person, (i. 1.;) but changes to the first after a few chapters, (i. 20–22.) Further on, in book iv., he resumes the third, chs. 104–106.) In book v. ch. 26, he begins in the third, but runs on into the first, which he again uses in book viii. ch. 97.

NOTE LXI., p. 144.

See Sir H. Rawlinson's *Memoir on the Persian Cuneiform Inscriptions*, vol. i. pp. 279, 286, 287, 292, 293, 324, 327, &c.

NOTE LXII., p. 145.

The "first year of Cyrus," (Ez. i. 1,) by which we must understand his first year in *Babylon*, was B. C. 538. The seventh year of Artaxerxes, when Ezra took the direction of affairs at Jerusalem, (ib. vii. 8,) was B. C. 459 or 458. (See Clinton's *Fasti Hellenici*, vol. ii. p. 378.)

NOTE LXIII., p. 145.

See above, Lecture I. page 39, and compare p. 244, Note XLVIII.

NOTE LXIV., p. 145.

De Wette, *Einleitung*, § 196 a, p. 260; vol. ii. p. 324, Parker's Translation; Stuart, *Defence of the Canon*, § 6, p. 148; Horne, *Introduction*, vol. v. pp. 64, 65.

NOTE LXV., p. 145.

See Lecture IV., p. 104.

NOTE LXVI., p. 145.

See Lecture I., pp. 34, 35 ; and p. 241, Note XXXIV.

NOTE LXVII., p. 145.

"Die Erzählung," says De Wette, "besteht aus einer Reihe geschichtlicher Schweirigkeiten und Unwahrschein-lichkeiten, und enthält mehrere Verstösse gegen die Persischen Sitten." (*Einleitung*, § 198 a, p. 266.)

NOTE LXVIII., p. 145.

Œder, *Freien Untersuchungen über d. Kanon des Alt. Test.*, p. 12, et seqq. ; Michaelis, *Orient. Bibliothek*, vol. ii. p. 35, et seqq. ; Corrodi, *Beleucht. d. Geschicht. d. Jüd. Kanons*, vol. i. p. 66, et seqq. ; and Bertholdt, *Historisch-Kritische Einleitung in sämmt. kanon. und apokr. Schriften d. Alt. und Neuen Testaments*, p. 2425.

NOTE LXIX., p. 145.

See Carpzov's *Introductio*, xx. § 6, pp. 365, 366, where he shows that the Jews place the Book of Esther on a par with the Pentateuch, and above all the rest of Scripture.

NOTE LXX., p. 146.

Even De Wette allows it to be "incontestable (*unstreitig*) that the feast of Purim originated in Persia, and was occasioned by an event similar to that related in Esther." (*Einleitung*, § 198 b, p. 267 ; vol. ii. p. 339, Parker's Translation.) Stuart says very forcibly — "The fact that the feast of Purim has come down to us from time almost immemorial, proves as certainly that the main events related in the Book of Esther happened, as the declaration of independence and the celebration of the fourth of July prove that we (Americans) separated from Great Britain, and became an independent nation." (*History and Defence of the O. T. Canon*, § 21, p. 308.)

NOTE LXXI., p. 146.

It is remarkable that the name of God is not once mentioned in Esther. The only religious ideas introduced with any distinctness are the efficacy of a national humiliation, (Esth. iv. 1–3,) the certainty that punishment will overtake the wicked, (ib. verse 14,) and a feeling of confidence that Israel will not be forsaken, (ibid.) Various reasons have been given for this reticence, (Carpzov, *Introduct.* p. 369 ; Baumgarten, *De Fide Lib. Estheris,* p. 58 ; Horne, *Introduction,* vol. v. p. 69, &c. ;) but they are conjectural, and so uncertain. One thing only is clear, that if a Jew in later times had wished to palm upon his countrymen, as an ancient and authentic narrative, a work which he had composed himself, he would have taken care not to raise suspicion against his work by such an omission. (See the remarks of Professor Stuart, *Defence of the Canon,* p. 311.)

NOTE LXXII., p. 146.

The grounds upon which the historical character of the Book of Esther is questioned, are principally the following : —(1.) The Persian king intended by Ahasuerus seems to be Xerxes. As Esther cannot be identified with Amestris, the daughter of Otanes, who really ruled Xerxes, the whole story of her being made queen, and of her great power and influence, becomes impossible. (2.) Mordecai, having been carried into captivity with Jechoniah, (in B. C. 588,) must have been 120 years old in Xerxes' twelfth year, (B. C. 474,) and Esther must have been "a superannuated beauty." (3.) A Persian king would never have invited his queen to a carousal. (4.) The honors paid to Mordecai are excessive. (5.) The marriage with a Jewess is impossible, since the queens were taken exclusively from the families of the seven conspirators. (6.) Esther's concealment of her Jewish descent, and Haman's ignorance of her relationship to Mordecai, are highly improbable. (7.) The two murderous decrees, the long notice given, and the tameness ascribed to both Jews and Persians, are incredible. (8.) The massacre of more than 75,000 Persians by the Jews in a day, without the loss (so far as appears) of a man, transcends belief, and is an event of such a nature that "no amount of historical evidence would render it credible." (See Mr. Parker's additions to De Wette, vol. ii. pp. 340–345.) It is plain that none of these objections are of very great weight. The first, second, and last are met and refuted in the text. To the third it is enough to answer, in De Wette's own words, (*Einleitung,* § 198 a, p. 267, that such an invitation is "possible on account of the advancing corruption in Xerxes' time, and through the folly of Xerxes himself." To the fourth we may reply, that the honors, being analogous (as De Wette observes) to those paid to Joseph, are thereby shown to be not greater than under some circumstances were assigned to benefactors by Eastern monarchs. Nor would any one acquainted with the East make the objection. The fifth objection is met by observing, that when Cambyses wished to marry his sister, which was as much against the law as marrying a Jewess, and consulted the royal judges on the point, they told him, that there was no law, so far as they knew, which allowed a man to marry his sister, but that there was a law to this effect, that the Persian king *might do what he pleased*. The sixth objection scarcely needs a reply, for its answer is contained in the preceding objection. If it was contrary to Persian law that the king should marry a Jewess, the fact of Esther's nationality would be sure to be studiously concealed. Finally, to the seventh objection we may answer, that the murderous tenor of the decrees is credible (as De Wette confesses) on account of the "base character and disposition of Xerxes" — that the length of notice in the first instance was the consequence of Haman's superstition, while the length of the notice in the second instance followed necessarily upon the first — and that no "tameness" is proved by the mere silence of Scripture as to the number of Jews who fell in the struggle. "The author of the book," as Professor Stuart observes, "is wholly intent upon the victory and the deliverance of the Jews. The result of the encounter he relates, viz., the great loss and humiliation of Persian enemies. But how much it cost to achieve this victory he does not relate. . . . We can scarcely doubt that many Jews were killed or wounded." (*History and Defence of the O. T. Canon*, § 21, pp. 309, 310.)

NOTE LXXIII., p. 146.

Carpzov, *Introductio*, c. xx. § 4, pp. 360, 361.

NOTE LXXIV., p. 146.

Carpzov, § 6, pp. 368, 369. This was probably the ground of Luther's objections to the Canonicity of Esther. (*De Servo Arbitrio*, p. 118, et alibi.) It may also have caused the omission of Esther from some lists of the canonical books in the fathers. (Athanas. *Ep. Festal.*, vol. i. p. 963; *Synops. S. S.*, vol. ii. p. 128; Melito ap. Euseb. *Hist. Eccl.*, iv. 26, &c. In recent times the objection has not been much pressed.

NOTE LXXV., p. 148.

See Sir H. Rawlinson's *Memoir on the Persian Cuneiform Inscriptions*, vol. i. pp. 197–200, 273, 274, 280, 286, 291, 299, 320, 324, 327, 330, 335, 338, and 342.

NOTE LXXVI., p. 148.

Ibid., pp. 285, 291, 319, 323, &c.

NOTE LXXVII., p. 148.

Ewald, *Geschichte d. Volkes Israel*, vol. iii. part ii. p. 118; Winer, *Realwörterbuch*, ad vocc. *Ahasuerus* and *Artachschàschta*; Kitto, *Biblical Cyclopædia*, vol. i. pp. 98 and 229, &c.

NOTE LXXVIII., p. 148.

The Pseudo-Smerdis seems to have been known by several names. According to Darius, (*Behist. Inscr.*, col. i. par. 11,) his true name was Gomates, (*Gaumata*,) and he gave himself out for Smerdis, (*Bardiya*.) According to Justin, (i. 9, § 9,) he was called Oropastes. As Artaxerxes means "Great King, Great Warrior," (see the author's *Herodotus*, vol. iii. p. 552,) it may perhaps have been in common use as an epithet of any Persian monarch. The application to Cambyses of the name Ahasuerus (= Xerxes) is still more curious. Cambyses was known as *Kembath* in Egypt, *Kabujiya* in Persia, Καμβύσης in Greece. It is certainly very remarkable that the Jews should only know him as Xerxes. Perhaps the theory of Mr. Howes (*Pictorial Bible*, ad loc.) with respect to the Ahasuerus of Ezra iv. 6, viz., that Xerxes is intended, might be adopted, without the adoption of his view that the Artaxerxes of the next verse is Artaxerxes Longimanus. The author may go on in verse 6 to a fact subsequent to the time of Darius, whom he has mentioned in verse 5, and then return in verse 7 to a time anterior to Darius. But Mr. Howes's view of the Artaxerxes of verse 7 is incompatible with the *nexus* of verses 23 and 24.

Note LXXIX., p. 148.

The reigns are in each case four — Cyrus, Cambyses, Smerdis the Mage, Darius Hystaspis, in profane history — Cyrus, Ahasuerus, Artaxerxes, Darius, in Ezra. The harmony of the chronology is best seen from Zechariah. That prophet implies that 70 years were not completed from the destruction of Jerusalem in the second year of Darius, (Zech. i. 7 and 12;) but that they were completed two years later, in the fourth year of that prince, (ib. vii. 5.) He therefore, it would seem, placed the completion in Darius's 3d or 4th year; i. e. in B. C. 519 or 518. Taking the latter date, and counting back by the years of the Astronomical Canon, we find the first of the seventy years to fall into B. C. 587. Now this appears by the same Canon to have been the 18th of Nebuchadnezzar, which was the exact year of the destruction of Jerusalem, (Jer. lii. 29.)[1] Thus the two chronologies harmonize *exactly*.

Note LXXX., p. 149.

See the *Behistun Inscript.*, col. i. par. 14.

Note LXXXI., p. 149.

Behist. Inscr., l. s. c.

Note LXXXII., p. 150.

The length of the Persian kings' reigns from the time of Darius Hystaspis to that of Darius Nothus is fixed beyond the possibility of doubt. Besides the Greek contemporary notices, which would form a very fair basis for an exact chronology, we have the consentient testimony on the point of Babylonian and Egyptian tradition, preserved to us in the Astronomical Canon and in Manetho, as reported by Eusebius. From both it appears, that from the sixth year of Darius to the seventh of Artaxerxes (Longimanus) was a period of 58 years.

[1] In 2 Kings xxv. 8, we find the *nineteenth* year mentioned as that of the destruction, instead of the eighteenth. I believe the cause of this difference to be, that some reckoned the reign of Nebuchadnezzar to have commenced in B. C. 605 — the last year of Nabopolassar — when Nebuchadnezzar came into Palestine as his father's representative, defeated Necho, and made Jehoiakim tributary. (See Lecture IV., Note LXXXI.)

NOTE LXXXIII., p. 150.

The Persian word is read as *Khshayarsha*. Ahasuerus (אֲחַשְׁוֵרוֹשׁ) only differs from *Khshayarsha* by the adoption of the prosthetic א, which the Hebrews invariably placed before the Persian *Khsh*, and the substitution of ו for י, a common dialectic variation. Gesenius, (*Thesaurus*, vol. i. p. 75,) and Winer (*Realwörterbuch*, ad voc. *Ahasuerus*) admit the identity of the words.

NOTE LXXXIV., p. 150.

The construction of Esther ii. 5, 6, is ambiguous. The word "who," (אֲשֶׁר,) at the commencement of verse 6, may refer either to Mordecai, the *chief* subject of the narrative, or to Kish, the *last* individual mentioned in verse 5. If Kish was carried off by Nebuchadnezzar about B. C. 597, we should expect to find his great grandson living in B. C. 485–465, four generations or 130 years afterwards.

NOTE LXXXV., p. 151.

See Herod. vii. 19, 20.

NOTE LXXXVI., p. 151.

Ibid. ix. 108.

NOTE LXXXVII., p. 151.

De Wette, *Einleitung*, § 198 a, p. 267; vol. ii. p. 337, Parker's Translation.

NOTE LXXXVIII., p. 151.

Amestris was the daughter of Otanes, according to Herodotus, (vii. 61;) according to Ctesias, of Onophas, or Anaphes, (*Exc. Pers.*, § 20.) It has been maintained, that she was Esther by Scaliger and Jahn; but, besides other objections, the character of Amestris makes this very improbable. (See Herod. vii. 114; ix. 112; Ctes. *Exc. Pers.*, § 40–43.)

NOTE LXXXIX., p. 152.

Einleitung, § 199 ; p. 268. The following points of exact knowledge are noted by De Wette's Translator (vol. ii. p. 346) more distinctly than by De Wette himself: — 1. The unchangeableness of the royal edicts ; 2. The prohibition of all approach to the king without permission ; 3. The manner of publishing decrees ; 4. The employment of eunuchs in the seraglio ; 5. The absence of women at banquets ; 6. The use of lots in divination ; and, 7. The sealing of decrees with the royal signet. (Compare Herod. iii. 128.) To these may be added, 1. The general character of the Persian palaces, (i. 5, 6 ; compare Loftus's *Chaldæa and Susiana*, pp. 373–375 ;) 2. The system of posts, (viii. 10 ; Herod. viii. 98 ;) 3. The law that each wife should go in to the king *in her turn*, (ii. 12 ; Herod. iii. 69 ;) 4. The entry in "the book of records" of the names and acts of royal benefactors, (ii. 23 ; vi. 1, 2 ; Herod. vii. 194 ; viii. 85, 90, &c. ;) and, 5. The principle that all such persons had a right to a reward, (vi. 3 ; Herod. iii. 140 ; viii. 85 ; ix. 107.)

NOTE XC., p. 152.

Herod. iii. 79 ; Ctes. *Exc. Pers.*, § 15.

NOTE XCI., p. 152.

Some writers have supposed that the Artaxerxes who befriended Ezra was really Xerxes. So Josephus, (*Ant. Jud.* xi. 5 ;) who is followed by J. D. Michaelis, (ad loc.,) Jahn, (*Einleitung*, vol. ii. p. 276,) and others. But there seems to be no good reason for supposing him to have been a different person from the Artaxerxes of Nehemiah, who is allowed on all hands to be Longimanus. (See the article on ARTAXERXES in Kitto's *Biblical Cyclopædia*, where the question is ably argued.) That the Artaxerxes of Nehemiah is Longimanus, appears from the length of his reign, (Neh. v. 14,) combined with the fact that he was contemporary with the grandsons or great-grandsons of those who were contemporary with Cyrus.[1]

[1] The length of his reign, 32 years at the least, shows him to have been either Longimanus or Mnemon. But as Eliashib, the grandson of Jeshua, who went from Babylon as high-priest in the first year of Cyrus, (B. C. 538,) is still alive in the 32d year of Nehemiah's Artaxerxes, (Neh. xiii. 6, 7,) it seems quite impossible that he can be Mnemon, whose 32nd year was B. C. 374. (See the author's *Herodotus*, vol. iv. pp. 260, 261, note 13.)

NOTE XCII., p. 152.

Ctesias ap. Phot. *Bibliothec.*, pp. 115–124.

NOTE XCIII., p. 153.

On the non-historical character of the Book of Judith, see the author's *Herodotus*, vol. i. p. 245, note [8].

LECTURE VI.

NOTE I., p. 155.

On the different views entertained as to the exact year of our Lord's birth, see Olshausen's *Biblischer Commentar*, vol. ii. pp. 619–622; vol. iv. pp. 334–337, E. T.[1] On the testimonies which determine the death of Herod the Great to the year of Rome 750, see Clinton's *Fasti Hellenici*, vol. iii. pp. 254 and 256. The Nativity thus falls *at least as early* as A. U. C. 749, and the vision of Zachariah as early as A. U. C. 748. Some important astronomical reasons are assigned by Dean Alford (*Greek Testament*, vol. i. p. 7) for believing that the actual year of the Nativity was A. U. C. 747, or *seven* years before the Christian era. The termination of the history of the Acts has also been variously placed, in A. D. 58, 59, 61, 62, 63, 64, and 65. (See Olshausen, l. s. c.) I prefer the shorter reckoning on the grounds stated by Dr. Burton. (*Ecclesiastical History of the First Three Centuries*, vol. i. pp. 277, 278.)

NOTE II., p. 157.

See Lecture II., p. 51.

NOTE III., p. 157.

Strauss, *Leben Jesu*, § 13; p. 56, E. T.

[1] *Commentary on the Gospels and the Acts*, by Hermann Olshausen, D. D. Translated by the Rev. H. B. Creak, A. M. Third edition. Edinburgh, Clarke, 1857.

NOTE IV., p. 158.

Strauss, *Leben Jesu*, l. s. c.

NOTE V., p. 158.

Ibid. § 14; p. 84, E. T.

NOTE VI., p. 158.

Ibid. § 13; p. 56, E. T.

NOTE VII., p. 158.

Ibid. l. s. c.; pp. 62, 63, E. T.

NOTE VIII., p. 159.

In the Syriac Version of Matthew, which is undoubtedly very old, and which some regard as of nearly equal authority with the Greek Gospel,[1] the title runs, "The Gospel, the Preaching of Matthew." The Persian has, "The Gospel of Matthew;" and the Arabic, "The Gospel of Saint Matthew the Apostle, which he wrote in Hebrew by the inspiration of the Holy Spirit." (See Horne's *Introduction*, vol. i. pp. 260, 261.)

NOTE IX., p. 159.

Herodotus, for example, is quoted but by one author (Ctesias) within this period, (B. C. 450–350.) In the next century (B. C. 350–250) he is also quoted by one author, Aristotle; in the century following (B. C. 250–150) he is not quoted at all; in the fourth century, he for the first time musters two witnesses, Scymnus Chius and Cicero;[2] it is not till the fifth century from the time of his writing his history, that he is largely and commonly cited by writers of the day. (See Mr. Isaac Taylor's recent work on the *Transmission of Ancient Books to*

1 See Dr. Cureton's recent work, *Remains of a very Ancient Recension of the four Gospels in Syriac*, London, 1858.

2 Posidonius should perhaps be added as a third witness belonging to this period. He quoted Herodotus, not very correctly, in his Treatise concerning the Ocean. (*Fr. Hist. Gr.*, vol. iii. p. 279.)

Modern Times, pp. 295–299.) The first distinct quotation[1] of Thucydides seems to be that by Hermippus, *Fragm. Hist. Gr.*, vol. iii. p. 48, Fr. 54,) who lived about B. C. 200, nearly two centuries after him. Posidonius, writing about B. C. 75, first quotes Polybius, who wrote about B. C. 150. Livy is, I believe, only quoted by Quinctilian among writers of the century following him; Tacitus, though mentioned as a writer by the younger Pliny, is first cited — nearly a century after his death — by Tertullian. If the reader will cast his eye over the "Testimonies," as they are called, prefixed to most old editions of the classics, he will easily convince himself of the general truth of the assertion upon which I have ventured in the text. The argument is one advanced, but without proof, by Paley. (*Evidences*, Part i. ch. 10; p. 104.)

NOTE X., p. 160.

Strauss, *Leben Jesu*, § 13; p. 56, E. T.

NOTE XI., p. 160.

See Lecture II., pp. 51–56; and Note VIII. on Lecture V., pp. 346, 347.

NOTE XII., p. 161.

See Horne's *Introduction*, vol. v. p. 113; Kitto, *Biblical Cyclopædia*, vol. ii. p. 582.

NOTE XIII., p. 161.

See Grabe, *Spicilegium Patrum*, vol. ii. p. 225; Pearson, *Vindiciæ Ignatianæ*, Pars i. c. 6; Burton, *Ecclesiastical History*, vol. ii. pp. 29, 30; and p. 152.

NOTE XIV., p. 161.

Constitutiones Apostolicæ, vi. 16; Irenæus, *adv. Hæres.* i. 20; &c.

NOTE XV., p. 162.

Strauss, *Leben Jesu*, § 13; pp. 62, 63; E. T. Some writers have maintained that the expression, "according to Matthew," is exactly equivalent to the genitive of Matthew. (See Horne's *Introduction*, vol. v. p.

[1] Cratippus alluded to the fact that there were no speeches in the last book, and that the work was left unfinished; but he did not (so far as we know) make any quotation. (*Fr. Hist. Gr.*, vol. ii. p. 76.)

260.) Olshausen observes more correctly, that the expression is ambiguous. It may mark actual and complete authorship, as in the passage quoted from 2 Maccab. in the text; or it may mean editorship, as in the phrase "Homer according to Aristarchus." The unanimous testimony of the early Christian writers proves that, as applied to the Gospels, it was used in the former sense. If it be asked why the simple genitive was not used, Olshausen replies, (rightly, as it seems to me,) because the Gospel was known as "the Gospel of Jesus Christ." Piety, therefore, made the use of such phrases as "Gospel of Matthew," "Gospel of Mark," "impossible." (*Biblischer Commentar, Einleitung*, § 4; p. 11, note.)

NOTE XVI., p. 162.

Faustus, the Manichæan, did indeed attempt to prove that the first Gospel was not the work of St. Matthew; but, 1. He wrote late in the fourth century; and, 2. It seems that he could find no flaw in the external evidence, since he based his conclusion on an internal difficulty — the use of the third instead of the first person by the supposed writer, (Matt. ix. 9.) Eichhorn, having ventured on the assertion, that "many ancient writers of the Church doubted the genuineness of many parts of our Gospels," is only able to adduce in proof of it this instance of Faustus. (See his *Einleitung in das N. Test.*, vol. i. p. 145.)

NOTE XVII., p. 162.

Irenæus says — "Now Matthew published his treatise on the Gospel among the Hebrews, in their own dialect, while Peter and Paul were preaching in Rome, and founding the church there. But after their death, Mark, the disciple and interpreter of Peter, also wrote down what Peter had preached, and delivered it to us. And Luke also, the follower of Paul, wrote out in a book the Gospel which was preached by that Apostle. Afterwards John, the disciple of the Lord, who also leaned upon his breast, — he too published a Gospel, while he was living at Ephesus in Asia." (*Advers. Hæres.*, iii. 1.) And again, — "These things are in accordance with the Gospels, in which Christ is enshrined. For that of John relates his princely birth and glorious lineage from the Father, saying, 'In the beginning was the Word,' &c. And that of Luke, as being more of a sacerdotal character, begins with the priest Zacharias, burning incense to God. . . . Matthew declares his human birth, saying, 'The book of the generation of Jesus Christ,' &c. Mark, as partaking more of the prophetic spirit, begins by saying, 'The beginning of the Gospel of Jesus Christ,' &c." (Ibid. iii. 11, § 11.)

Clement — "The digest of the contents of the Gospels should be preceded by an account of their origin. The Gospel of Mark had its origin in this way: When Peter was preaching the word publicly in Rome, and proclaiming the gospel under the inspiration of the Spirit, many of those who heard him besought Mark, as having been his follower for a long time, and as having in remembrance what he had heard, to write out the things spoken by Peter. Having thus composed a Gospel, he gave it to those who had requested it. When Peter knew this, he neither strictly forbade nor positively approved. But John, the last one, perceiving that what related to the outward had been exhibited in the (other) Gospels, in compliance with the solicitations of his friends, and under the promptings of the Divine Spirit, wrote a spiritual Gospel." (Ap. Euseb. *Hist. Eccles.* vi. 14.)

Tertullian writes — "In fine, if it is evident that what is most ancient is truest, that what is from the beginning is most ancient, and that what is from the Apostles is from the beginning, then it will be equally evident, that what has been sanctioned *among the churches of the Apostles* is handed down from the Apostles. Let us see what milk the Corinthians imbibed from Paul; according to what rule were the Galatians corrected; what did the Philippians read, the Thessalonians, the Ephesians; what do the nearer Romans say, to whom both Peter and Paul left a gospel sealed with their blood. We have also churches that were under the tuition of John. . . . I say therefore that among these, — I do not mean the Apostolical churches merely, but *among all* which are united with them in sacramental communion, — this Gospel of Luke, which we regard with the highest reverence, has been received from the time when it was first published. . . . *The same authority of the Apostolical churches supports also the other Gospels* which we have received from them, and which we esteem just as they esteem them; I mean those of John and Matthew; that also which Mark published we may be allowed to call Peter's, for Mark was his interpreter. Indeed Luke's digest also is commonly ascribed to Paul. For what the disciples publish is regarded as coming from the master." (*Adv. Marcion.*, iv. 5.)

Origen — "I learned from tradition about the four Gospels, *which alone are indisputable in the church of God under the whole heaven;* — how that first Matthew, who was originally a tax-gatherer, but afterwards an apostle of Jesus Christ, published his, composed in the Hebrew language, for those who had believed from among the Jews; and secondly, Mark, writing it according to Peter's dictation; and thirdly, Luke, the Gospel which was praised by Paul, composing it for the converts from the Gentiles; and to crown all, that according to John." (Ap. Euseb. *Hist. Eccles.*, vi. 25.)

Of course these passages do not form a hundredth part of the testimony borne by these writers to the authority of the four Gospels. They use them with the same frequency and deference as modern divines. They appeal to them alone in proof of doctrine, making the most marked difference between them and such apocryphal "Lives of Christ" as they mention. The student will find this portion of the Christian evidences drawn out most fully by Lardner, in his great work on the *Credibility of the Gospel History*, vol. i. pp. 283, et seqq. A good selection from the evidence is made by Mr. Norton, (*Genuineness of the Gospels*, vol. i. pp. 83–105.) Paley's Synopsis also deserves the attention of the student. (*Evidences*, part i. ch. 10, § 1.)

NOTE XVIII., p. 162.

Justin's ordinary expression is "the *Memoirs* of the Apostles, (τά ἀπομνημονεύματα τῶν ἀποστόλων;) but in one place he identifies these Memoirs with the Gospels by adding, ἃ καλεῖται εὐαγγέλια, "which are called Gospels." (*Apol.*, i. p. 83, B.) He appears to prefer the former term in addressing the heathen, as more classical. In his Dialogue with Trypho he sometimes uses the term εὐαγγέλιον simply. (*Opera*, p. 195, D.) These Memoirs, or Gospels, he says, were composed "by the Apostles of Christ and their companions," ("the memoirs, I mean those which were composed by his Apostles and their followers.")[1] It has been questioned by Bishop Marsh and others whether the quotations are really from our Gospels; but the doubt, if it deserves the name, has (I think) been wholly set at rest by Bishop Kaye, (*Account of the Life and Opinions of Justin Martyr*, ch. viii. pp. 132–152,) and Mr. Norton, (*Credibility*, &c., vol. i. note E, pp. 316–324.) The careful

1 Compare Luke i. 1: "It seemed good to me also, having had perfect knowledge."

analysis of the latter writer exhausts the subject, and deserves attentive perusal.

NOTE XIX., p. 163.

Papias said — "Now Matthew composed his book in the Hebrew dialect; and each one interpreted it as he was able. And Mark, who was the interpreter of Peter, wrote accurately whatever he remembered, but not an orderly account of what was said and done by Christ." (Ap. Euseb., *Hist. Eccles.* iii. 39.)

It has been questioned whether Papias was really a disciple of the apostle John, (Strauss, *Leben Jesu*, § 13,) or only of a certain John the Presbyter, whom he calls "a disciple of our Lord." It appears from Eusebius (l. s. c.) that he did not himself claim to have received his knowledge of Christianity from the apostles themselves. Still the testimony of Irenæus is express, ("Papias, who was a hearer of John, and a companion of Polycarp," Euseb. l. s. c.,) and cannot without violence be understood of any one but St. John the Evangelist.

NOTE XX., p. 163.

Leben Jesu, § 14. "It is however by no means necessary to attribute this same freedom from all *conscious intention of fiction* to the authors of all those narratives in the Old and New Testament, which must be considered as unhistorical. . . . The authors of the Homeric songs *could not have believed* that every particular which they related of their gods and heroes had really happened; . . . and *exactly as little* may this be said of all the unhistorical narratives of the Gospels, as for example, of the first chapter of the third, and *many parts of the fourth Gospel.*" (pp. 83, 84, E. T.)

NOTE XXI., p. 163.

Ibid. § 13; p. 60, E. T.

NOTE XXII., p. 164.

Ibid. l. s. c.

NOTE XXIII., p. 164.

See above, Note I. The date A. D. 63 is preferred by Bertholdt, Feilmoser, Dean Alford, Mr. Birks, and others.

NOTE XXIV., p. 164.

Leben Jesu, § 13; p. 61, E. T.

NOTE XXV., p. 164.

See above, Note XVII.

NOTE XXVI., p. 165.

This is Burton's conclusion, (*Eccles. Hist.*, vol. i. p. 255,) deduced from the discrepancies in the external evidence. Dean Alford's unanswerable argument in favor of the *independent origin* of the first three Gospels, deduced from their internal character, implies the same. The first three Gospels were probably all written within the space A. D. 58–65.

NOTE XXVII., p. 166.

The Old Testament furnishes us with but one instance of even a *second* record — viz., that of Chronicles; which deals with the period of history already treated in Samuel and Kings. Elsewhere we have throughout but a single narrative.

NOTE XXVIII., p. 166.

Theophylact and Euthymius placed the composition of St. Matthew's Gospel within eight years of the Ascension; Nicephorus placed it 15 years after that event; Cosmas Indicopleustes assigned it to the time of the stoning of Stephen. (See Alford's *Greek Testament*, Prolegomena, vol. i. p. 26.) In modern times Bishop Tomline, Le Clerc, Dr. Owen, Dr. Townson, and others, incline to a date even earlier than that fixed by Theophylact.

NOTE XXIX., p. 167.

On the various theories to which the combined resemblances and differences of the first three Gospels have given birth, see Horne's *Introduction*, vol. v. Appendix, pp. 509–529; Alford's *Greek Testament*, vol. i. Prolegomena, ch. i. § 2, 3; and Norton's *Genuineness of the Gospels*, vol. i. Note D. pp. 239–296. The last-named writer, after having proved that no one of the first three Evangelists copied from another, observes with much force — "If the Evangelists did not copy one from another, it follows, that the first three Gospels must all have been written about the same period; since, if one had preceded another by any considerable length of time, it cannot be supposed that the author of the later Gospel would have been unacquainted with the work of his predecessor, or would have neglected to make use of it; especially when we take into view, that its reputation must have been well established among Christians." And he concludes, "that no one of the first three Gospels was written long before or long after the year 60." (*Genuineness*, &c., vol. i. pp. 297, 298.)

NOTE XXX., p. 167.

See the passage quoted above, Note XVII., page 372. Irenæus, it will be observed, makes St. Matthew write his Gospel *while St. Peter and St. Paul were founding the Church at Rome*, i. e. during the term of St. Paul's imprisonment, (probably A. D. 56–58.) He writes it "among the Hebrews" — i. e. in Palestine. After the two great apostles left Rome, and separated — soon after, he seems to mean — their respective companions, Mark and Luke, are said to have written. At least this is declared positively of Mark; less definitely of Luke, whose Gospel had perhaps been composed a year or two earlier, and sent privately to Theophilus.

NOTE XXXI., p. 167.

It is unnecessary to prove this agreement; which is such, that each of the three writers has been in turn accused of copying from one or both of his fellow-Evangelists. (See Horne's *Introduction*, vol. v. Appendix, pp. 509, 510.)

NOTE XXXII., p. 167.

This is one of the main objects at which Strauss aims in the greater portion of his work. See Sections 21, 24, 39, 46, 53, 57, 59, &c. &c.

NOTE XXXIII., p. 168.

If we take, for example, the second of the sections in which the "disagreements of the Canonical Gospels" are expressly considered, (§ 24,) we find the following enumeration of "discrepancies," in relation to the form of the Annunciation. "1. The individual who appears is called in Matthew *an angel of the Lord;* in Luke, *the angel Gabriel.* 2. The person to whom the angel appears is, according to Matthew, Joseph; according to Luke, Mary. 3. In Matthew, the apparition is seen in a dream, in Luke while awake. 4. There is a disagreement with respect to the time at which the apparition took place. 5. Both the purpose of the apparition, and the effect, are different." In this way five "discrepancies" are created out of the single fact, that St. Matthew does not relate the Annunciation to the Virgin, while St. Luke gives no account of the angelic appearance to Joseph. Similarly in the section where the calling of the first Apostles is examined, (§ 70,) "discrepancies" are seen between the fourth and the first two Evangelists in the following respects — "1. James is absent from St. John's account, and instead of his vocation, we have that of Philip and Nathaniel. 2. In Matthew and Mark the scene is the coast of the Galilæan sea; in John it is the vicinity of the Jordan. 3. In each representation there are two pairs of brothers; but in the one they are Andrew and Peter, James and John; in the other, Andrew and Peter, Philip and Nathaniel. And, 4. In Matthew and Mark all are called by Jesus; in John, Philip only, the others being directed to him by the Baptist." Here again we have four discrepancies made out of the circumstance, that the first two Evangelists relate only the actual call of certain disciples, while St. John informs us what previous acquaintance they had of Jesus. So from the mere silence of Matthew, Strauss concludes positively that he opposes St. Luke, and did not consider Nazareth, but Bethlehem, to have been the original residence of our Lord's parents, (§ 39;) from the omission by the three earlier writers of the journeys into Judæa during our Lord's Ministry, he pronounces that they "contradict" St. John, who speaks of such journeys, (57;) he finds a "discrepancy" between this Evangelist's account of the relations between the Baptist and our Lord, and the account of the others, since he gives, and they do not give, the testimony borne by the former to our Lord's character, (§ 46;) he concludes from St. Luke's *not saying* that St. John was in prison when he sent his two disciples to our Lord, that he considered him as not yet cast into prison, (ibid.;) he finds St. Luke's and St. Matthew's acccounts of the death of Judas "irreconcilable," because St. Luke *says nothing* of remorse, or of suicide, but relates what has the appearance of a death by accident, (§ 130;) he regards the presence of Nicodemus at our Lord's interment as a "fabrication of the fourth Evangelist," simply because it is unnoticed by the others, (§ 80;) he concludes from their silence as to the raising of Lazarus that "it cannot have been known to them," and therefore that it cannot be true, (§ 100;) and in other instances, too numerous to mention, he makes a similar use of the mere fact of omission.

NOTE XXXIV., p. 169.

See Norton's *Credibility of the Gospels*, vol. i. pp. 74, 75.

NOTE XXXV., p. 169.

In point of fact there is scarcely a difficulty brought forward by Strauss which has not been again and again noticed and explained by biblical commentators. Mr. Norton correctly says of his volumes — "They present *a collection from various authors* of difficulties in the history contained in the Gospels, to which their expositor should particularly direct his attention." The critical portion of them presents little which is novel.

NOTE XXXVI., p. 171.

See Paley's *Horæ Paulinæ*, ch. i. p. 1.

NOTE XXXVII., p. 172.

Leben Jesu, § 13; vol. i. p. 60, E. T.

NOTE XXXVIII., p. 172.

If we take, for example, the earliest of St. Paul's Epistles, the first to the Thessalonians, we shall find that the following little coincidences between it and the Acts are unnoticed by Paley: —

1. The identity in the order of names, "Paul, and Silvanus, and

Timotheus," (1 Thess. i. 1; compare Acts xvii. 10, 15; xviii. 5.) This was the order of dignity at the time, and was therefore naturally used; but had the Epistle been forged after St. Paul's death, Timothy would probably have taken precedence of Silas, since owing to the circumstance of St. Paul addressing two Epistles to him, his became the name of far greater note in the Church.

2. The peculiarly impressive mention of the Thessalonians as objects of the divine *election* (i. 4; "knowing, brethren beloved, your election of God") seems to be an allusion to the fact of the vision which summoned St. Paul into Macedonia, (Acts xvi. 9,) whereby the Macedonians were "chosen out" from the rest of the Western world to be the first European recipients of the Gospel. The term ἐκλογή is a rare one in Scripture, and is absent, except in this instance, from all St. Paul's earlier Epistles. It had been used, however, of St. Paul himself in the vision seen by Ananias, (Acts ix. 15,) with special reference to his similar selection by miraculous means as an object of the Divine favor.

3. The great *success* of the Gospel at Thessalonica is strongly asserted in verse 5, ("our gospel came not unto you in word only, but also in power," &c.) Compare Acts xvii. 4: "And some of them (the Jews) believed, and consorted with Paul and Silas, and of the devout Greeks *a great multitude*, and of the chief women *not a few*."

4. The aorist tenses in ch. i. verses 5 and 6, and elsewhere, (ἐγενήθη,[1] ἐγενήθημεν,[2] ἐγενήθητε,[3] δεξάμενοι,[4] ἐκηρύξαμεν,[5] κ. τ. λ.,) point naturally, but very unobtrusively, to a *single* visit on the part of St. Paul, which by the history of the Acts is exactly what had taken place.

5. The peculiar nature of the Apostolic sufferings at Philippi is hinted at, without being fully expressed, in the term ὑβρισθέντες,[6] (ii. 2.) It was ὕβρις[7] to scourge a Roman citizen.

6. The statement that while at Thessalonica St. Paul toiled and labored, that he might not be chargeable or burdensome to the converts, (ii. 6, 9,) though not directly confirmed by the history of the Acts, is in harmony with the fact that at Corinth, a few months afterwards, he wrought at his craft with Aquila and Priscilla, (Acts xviii. 3,) having the same object in view, (1 Cor. ix. 12; 2 Cor. xi. 9; xii. 13, &c.)

7. The reference to the hinderance offered by the Jews to St. Paul's

[1] Came, v. 5. [2] We were, v. 5. [3] Ye became, v. 6. [4] Having received, v. 6. [5] We preached, ii. 9. [6] Were shamefully treated. [7] Shameful treatment.

preaching the Gospel to the Gentiles, (ii. 16,) accords both with the general conduct of the Jews elsewhere, (Acts xiii. 45, 50, &c.,) and especially with their conduct at Thessalonica, where "being moved with envy" (ζηλώσαντες) at the conversion of the Gentiles, they "set all the city on an uproar." (Acts xvii. 5.)

8. The expression, "we would have come unto you—*even I, Paul*—once and again," derives peculiar force from the circumstance related in the Acts, (xvii. 14–16,) that after leaving Macedonia he was for some time *alone* at Athens, while Silas and Timothy remained at Berœa.

9. The mention of "the brethren throughout all Macedonia," in ch. iv. 10, harmonizes with the account in the Acts that St. Paul had founded churches at Philippi and Berœa as well as at Thessalonica. (Acts xvi. 12–40; xviii. 10–12.)

10. The "affliction and distress" in which St. Paul says he was (iii. 7) at the time of Timothy's return from Macedonia, receive illustration from Acts xviii. 4–6, where we find that just at this period he was striving, but vainly, ("persuaded," Acts xviii. 4,) to convert the Jews of Corinth, "pressed in spirit," and earnestly testifying, but to no purpose, so that shortly afterwards he had to relinquish the attempt. What "affliction" this would cause to St. Paul we may gather from Romans ix. 1–5.

NOTE XXXIX., p. 173.

I was not aware, at the time of delivering my sixth Lecture, that any work professedly on this subject had been published. My attention has since been directed to a very excellent, though very unpretending, treatise, by the Rev. T. R. Birks, entitled, *Horæ Apostolicæ*,[1] and attached to an annotated edition of the *Horæ Paulinæ* of Paley. The first chapter of this treatise contains a supplement to Paley's examination of the Pauline Epistles. It will well repay perusal; though it is still far from exhausting the subject. Chapter ii. is concerned with the internal coincidences in the Acts of the Apostles; and chapter iii. with those in the Gospels. The treatment of this latter point is, unfortunately, but scanty. No more than twenty-five pages are devoted to it, the author remarking, that "in his present supplementary work, this

[1] *Horæ Paulinæ*, by William Paley, D. D., with notes, and a Supplementary Treatise, entitled *Horæ Apostolicæ*, by the Rev. T. R. Birks, A. M., late Fellow of Trinity College, Cambridge: London, Religious Tract Society, 1850.

branch of the subject is confined, of necessity, within narrow limits; since its complete investigation would *demand a distinct treatise*, and the prosecution of some deep and difficult inquiries." (*Horæ Apostolicæ*, p. 188.)

NOTE XL., p. 173.

Leben Jesu, § 13; vol. i. p. 60, E. T.

NOTE XLI., p. 173.

See on these points Horne's *Introduction*, vol. v. pp. 422–435, and pp. 487, 488; Kitto's *Cyclopædia*, vol. i. pp. 163–166, and 826–832; and Alford's *Greek Testament*, vol. iv. part i. Prolegomena, pp. 1–62.

NOTE XLII., p. 174.

Strauss, *Leben Jesu*, § 14, sub fin. vol. i. p. 84, E. T.

NOTE XLIII., p. 176.

Ibid. l. s. c. See above, Note XX.; where a passage to this effect is quoted at length.

LECTURE VII.

NOTE I., p. 178.

The only exception to this general rule, among the strictly historical books, is the Book of Ruth, which is purely biographical. It belongs to the Christology of the Old Testament, but it has no bearing on the history of the nation.

NOTE II., p. 179.

So Lardner — "It is plainly the design of the historians of the New Testament to write of the actions of Jesus Christ, chiefly those of his public Ministry, and to give an account of his death and resurrection, and of some of the first steps by which the doctrine which he had taught, made its way in the world. But though this was their main design, and they have not undertaken to give us the political state or history of the countries in which these things were done; yet in the course of their narration they have been led unavoidably to mention many persons of note; and to make allusions and references to the customs and tenets of the people, whom Jesus Christ and his apostles were concerned with." (*Credibility*, &c., vol. i. p. 7.)

NOTE III., p. 179.

Hence the certainty with which literary forgeries, if historical, are detected, in all cases where we possess a fair knowledge of the time and country to which they profess to belong. The alleged "Epistles of Phalaris," the pretended Manetho, the spurious Letters of Plato and of Chion, were soon exposed by critics, who stamped them indelibly with the brand of forgery, chiefly by reason of their failure in this particular. It is important to bear in mind, in this connection, the fact that there is no period in the whole range of ancient history, whereof we possess a more full and exact knowledge than we do of the first century of our era.

NOTE IV., p. 180.

These testimonies have been adduced by almost all writers on the Evidences of the Christian Religion; but I do not feel justified in omitting them from the present review. They are as follows:—

Tacitus says, speaking of the fire which consumed Rome in Nero's time, and of the general belief that he had caused it, "In order therefore to put a stop to the report, he laid the guilt, and inflicted the severest punishments, upon a set of people who were holden in abhorrence for their crimes, and called by the vulgar, *Christians*. *The founder of that name was Christ, who suffered death in the reign of Tiberius, under his procurator Pontius Pilate.* This pernicious superstition, thus checked for a while, broke out again; and spread not only over *Judea, where the evil originated,* but through Rome also, whither all things that are horrible and shameful find their way, and are practised. Accordingly the first who were apprehended confessed, and then on their information a *vast multitude* were convicted, not so much of the crime of setting (Rome) on fire, as of hatred to mankind. And when they were put to death, mockery was added to their sufferings; for they were either disguised in the skins of wild beasts, and worried to death by dogs, or they were crucified, or they were clothed in some inflammable covering, and when the day closed were burned as lights to illumine the night. Nero lent his own gardens for this exhibition, and also held the shows of the circus, mingling with the people in the dress of a charioteer, or observing the spectacle from his chariot. Wherefore, although those who suffered were guilty, and deserving of some extraordinary punishment, yet they came to be pitied, as victims not so much to the public good, as to the cruelty of one man." (*Annal.* xv. 44.)

Suetonius says briefly in reference to the same occasion, "*The Christians were punished*, a set of men of a *new* and mischievous superstition." (*Vit. Neron.*, § 16.) And with a possible, though not a certain, reference to our Lord, "[Claudius] expelled from Rome the Jews, who were continually exciting disturbances, at the *instigation of Chrestus*." (*Vit. Claud.*, § 25.)

Juvenal, with a meaning which cannot be mistaken,[1] when the passage of Tacitus above quoted has once been read, remarks: —

"Expose Tigellinus; you will blaze in that torch where, with throats confined and emitting froth, they stand and burn; and you do but draw a broad furrow in the midst of the sand." (*Sat.*, i. 155–157.)

Pliny writes to Trajan, "It is my custom, sir, to refer to you all things about which I am in doubt. For who is more capable of directing my hesitancy, or instructing my ignorance? I have never been present at any trials of the Christians; consequently I do not know what is the nature of their crimes, or the usual strictness of their examination, or severity of their punishment. I have moreover hesitated not a little, whether any distinction was to be made in respect to age, or whether those of tender years were to be treated the same as adults; whether repentance entitles them to a pardon, or whether it shall avail nothing for him who has once been a Christian to renounce his error; whether the name itself, even without any crime, should subject them

[1] Compare the observations of the old Scholiast on the passage, "*In the public shows* of Nero living men were burnt; for he ordered them to be covered with wax, that they might give light to the spectators." And again, "He covered certain mischievous men (compare Suetonius' '*mischievous* superstition') with pitch, and paper, and wax, and then commanded fire to be applied to them, that they might burn."

to punishment, or only the crimes connected with the name. In the mean time, I have pursued this course towards those who have been brought before me as Christians. I asked them whether they were Christians; if they confessed, I repeated the question a second and a third time, adding threats of punishment. If they still persevered, I ordered them to be led away to punishment; for I could not doubt, whatever the nature of their profession might be, that a stubborn and unyielding obstinacy certainly deserved to be punished. There were others also under the like infatuation; but as they were Roman citizens, I directed them to be sent to the capital. But the crime spread, as is wont to happen, even while the prosecutions were going on, and numerous instances presented themselves. An information was presented to me without any name subscribed, accusing a large number of persons, who denied that they were Christians, or had ever been. They repeated after me an invocation to the gods, and made offerings with frankincense and wine before your statue, which I had ordered to be brought for this purpose, together with the images of the gods; and moreover they reviled Christ; whereas those who are truly Christians, it is said, cannot be forced to do any of these things. I thought, therefore, that they ought to be discharged. Others, who were accused by a witness, confessed that they were Christians, but afterwards denied it. Some owned that they had been Christians, but said they had renounced their error, some three years before, others more, and a few even as long ago as twenty years. They all did homage to your statue and the images of the gods, and at the same time reviled the name of Christ. They declared that the whole of their guilt or their error was, that they were accustomed to meet on a stated day before it was light, and to sing in concert a hymn of praise to Christ, as God, and to bind themselves by an oath, not for the perpetration of any wickedness, but that they would not commit any theft, robbery, or adultery, nor violate their word, nor refuse, when called upon, to restore any thing committed to their trust. After this they were accustomed to separate, and then to reassemble to eat in common a harmless meal. Even this, however, they ceased to do, after my edict, in which, agreeably to your commands, I forbade the meeting of secret assemblies. After hearing this, I thought it the more necessary to endeavor to find out the truth, by putting to the torture two female slaves, who were called 'deaconesses.' But I could discover nothing but a perverse and extravagant superstition; and therefore I deferred all further proceedings until I should consult with you. For the matter appears to me worthy of such consultation, especially on account of the number of those who are involved in peril. For many of every age, of every rank, and of either sex, are exposed and will be exposed to danger. Nor has the contagion of this superstition been confined to the cities only, but it has extended to the villages, and even to the country. Nevertheless, it still seems possible to arrest the evil, and to apply a remedy. At least it is very evident, that the temples, which had already been almost deserted, begin to be frequented, and the sacred solemnities, so long interrupted, are again revived; and the victims, which heretofore could hardly find a purchaser, are now every where in demand. From this it is easy to imagine what a multitude of men might be reclaimed, if pardon should be offered to those who repent." (*Plin. Epist.*, x. 97.)

Trajan replies, "You have pursued the right course, my dear Pliny, in conducting the case of those Christians who were brought before you. Nor is it possible to adopt one uniform and invariable mode of proceeding. I would not have you seek out these persons; if they are brought before you, and are convicted, they must be punished; yet with this proviso, that he who denies that he is a Christian, and confirms this denial by actually invoking our gods, however he may have been suspected in time past, shall obtain pardon upon his repentance. But informations without the accuser's name subscribed, ought not to be received in prosecutions of any kind; for they are of the worst tendency, and are unworthy of the age in which we live." (Ibid. x. 98.)

Adrian, in his rescript addressed to Minucius Fundanus, the Proconsul of Asia, says,[1] "To Minucius Fundanus: I have read a letter addressed to me by Serenius Granianus, a most illustrious man, and your predecessor in office. The matter seems to me to require examination, in order that peaceable people may not be disturbed, and that occasion of evil-doing may be taken away from calumniators. If, therefore, in accusations of this sort, the people of the province can clearly affirm any thing against the Christians, so as to bring the case before the tribunal, to this only let them have recourse, and not to informal accusations and mere clamors. For it is much more suitable, if any one wishes to bring an accusation,

1 The Latin original is lost, and we possess only Eusebius's translation.

that it should come under your adjudication. If, therefore, any one accuses them, and proves that they have done any thing contrary to the laws, do you determine accordingly, in proportion to the greatness of the offence: but, by Hercules, if any one brings forward such an accusation slanderously, take him and punish him for his impudence." (Ap. Euseb. *Hist. Eccles.*, iv. 9.)

NOTE V., p. 181.

I refer especially to Strauss and his school, who attach no importance at all to the existence of Christ, but still allow it as a fact which is indisputable. (See the *Leben Jesu*, passim.)

NOTE VI., p. 181.

Ch. ii. pp. 24–30.

NOTE VII., p. 182.

One slight reference is found, or rather suspected, in Seneca, (*Epist.* xiv.,) one in Dio Chrysostom, (*Orat. Corinthiac.*, xxxvii. p. 463,) none in Pausanius, one (see the next note) in the Epictetus of Arrian.

NOTE VIII., p. 182.

Epictet. *Dissertat.* iv. 7, §§ 5, 6: "If any one now should so regard his possessions, as this man regards his body, and his children, and his wife, &c., what tyrant would any longer be terrible to him? What soldiers, or what weapons of theirs, would he fear? Under the influence of madness, one may so regard these things; and the *Galilæans* do it under the influence of custom."

NOTE IX., p. 183.

The passage in the second book of the Discourses, (c. 9, § 20,) which has been supposed by some to refer to Christians, seems really to intend only those whom it mentions — viz., the Jews. (See Lardner, *Credibility*, &c., vol. iv. p. 49; Fabricius ad Dion. xxxvii. 17.)

NOTE X., p. 183.

Thi point has been slightly touched by Paley, (*Evidences*, Part i. ch.

5, pp. 70, 71,) and insisted on at some length by Lardner. (*Credibility*, &c. vol. iv. pp. 50, 78, 160, &c.)

Note XI., p. 184.

Josephus was born in A. D. 37, the first year of the reign of Caligula, and the fourth after our Lord's ascension. He was bred up at Jerusalem, where he seems to have continued, with slight interruptions, till he was 26 years of age. He would thus have been, as boy and man, a witness of the principal occurrences at Jerusalem mentioned in the Acts, subsequently to the accession of Herod Agrippa.

Note XII., p. 184.

See Joseph. *Ant. Jud.* xx. 9, § 1. This passage has been much disputed, and its genuineness is disallowed even by Lardner. (*Credibility*, &c., vol. iii. pp. 352–354.) But I agree with Burton, (*Eccles. Hist.*, vol. i. p. 287,) and Paley, (*Evidences*, Part i. ch. 5, p. 69,) that there is no sufficient reason for the suspicions which have attached to the passage.

Note XIII., p. 184.

Josephus went to Rome in his 27th year, A. D. 63, and remained there some time. Probably he witnessed the commencement of the Neronic persecution in A. D. 64, after the great fire which broke out in July of that year. (See above, Note IV., page 383.)

Note XIV., p. 184.

"Ananus . . . called the council of judges, and bringing before them James, the brother of *Jesus who was called Christ*, and certain others, he accused them of transgressing the laws, and delivered them up to be stoned." (*Ant. Jud.* xx. 9, § 1.) According to Eusebius, (*Hist. Eccles.* ii. 23,) Josephus had the following also in another place: "These things came upon the Jews as an avengement of James the Just, who was the brother of Jesus called Christ; for the Jews slew him, although he was the most righteous of men."

I regard the arguments which have been brought against the famous passage in our copies of Josephus concerning our Lord's life and teaching (*Ant. Jud.* xviii. 3, § 3) as having completely established its spuriousness. (See Lardner, *Credibility*, vol. iii. pp. 537–542; and, on the other side, Horne, *Introduction*, vol. i. Appendix, ch. vii.)

NOTE XV., p. 184.

See Paley's *Evidences*, Part i. ch. 7, p. 71; and Dr. Traill's *Essay on the Personal Character of Josephus*, prefixed to his *Translation*, pp. 19, 20.

NOTE XVI., p. 184.

The probable value of these writings may be gathered from the fragments of Celsus, preserved by Origen. Celsus quotes from all the Gospels, allows that they were written by the disciples of Jesus, and confirms all the main facts of our Lord's life, even his miracles, (which he ascribes to magic;) only denying his resurrection, his raising of others, and his being declared to be the Son of God by a voice from heaven. A collection of the "testimonies" which his fragments afford will be found in Lardner. (*Credibility*, &c., vol. iv. pp. 115, et seqq.)

NOTE XVII., p. 184.

See Socrat. *Hist. Eccles.* i. 9, p. 32; Justinian, Nov. 42, c. 1; Mosheim, *De Rebus Christ. ante Constantin. Magn.* p. 561.

NOTE XVIII., p. 185.

Apolog. i. p. 65, and p. 70.

NOTE XIX., p. 185.

So at least Justin believed. (*Apol.* i. p. 70.) Tertullian adds, that they contained an account of our Saviour's resurrection, of his appearances to his disciples, and his ascension into heaven before their eyes. (*Apolog.* c. 21.) Eusebius (*Hist. Eccles.* ii. 2) and Orosius (vii. 4) bear nearly similar testimony. As Dr. Burton remarks, (*Eccles. Hist.* vol. i. p. 34,) "It is almost impossible to suppose that the Fathers were mistaken in believing some such document to be preserved in the archives." Their confident appeals to it show that they believed its substance not to be unfavorable to our Lord's character. Whether they exactly *knew* its contents, or no, must depend primarily on the question, whether the documents of this class, preserved in the State Archives, were generally accessible to the public. They were certainly not published; and as they were of the nature of secret communications to the Emperor, it may be doubted whether it was easy to obtain a sight of them. Still, perhaps, the Christians may have learnt the contents of Pilate's "Acts," from some of those members of the Imperial household (Phil. iv. 22) or family, (Burton, *Eccl. Hist.*, vol. i. p. 367,) who became converts at an early period.

NOTE XX., p. 187.

On the extent of the dominions of Herod the Great, see Joseph. *Ant. Jud.* xiv. 14–18. He died, as we have already seen, (supra, Lecture VI. Note I.,) in the year of Rome 750. On his death, there was a division of his territories among his sons, Archelaus receiving Judæa, Samaria, and Idumæa; Antipas, Galilee and Peræa; Philip, Trachonitis and the adjoining countries. (Joseph. *De Bell. Jud.* i. 33, § 8, and ii. 6, § 3.) Ten years later (A. D. 8) Archelaus was removed, and his dominions annexed to the Roman Empire, being placed under a Procurator, (Coponius,) who was subordinate to the President of Syria, (Joseph. *Ant. Jud.* xviii. 1, § 1,) while Philip and Antipas continued to rule their principalities. Thirty-three years after, (A. D. 41,) Herod Agrippa, by the favor of Claudius, reunited the several provinces of Palestine under his own government, and reigned over the whole territory which had formed the kingdom of Herod the Great. (Ibid. xix. 5, § 1.) At his death, A. D. 44, the Roman authority was established over the whole country, which was administered by a Procurator holding under the President of Syria. To the younger Agrippa, however, king of Chalcis, a power was presently intrusted (A. D. 48) of managing the sacred treasury at Jerusalem, superintending the temple, and appointing the Jewish High Priests. (Ibid. xx. 1.)

NOTE XXI., p. 187.

Tacitus sacrifices accuracy to brevity in his sketch of these changes: — "The victorious Augustus enlarged the kingdom given by Antony to Herod. After the death of Herod, one Simon, without waiting for any action on the part of the Emperor, assumed the royal title. Quintilius Varus took possession of Syria, and punished him; and the children of Herod governed the nation thus brought into subjection, dividing its territory into three districts. Under Tiberius, they remained quiet; but afterwards, when they were ordered by Caius Cæsar (i. e. Caligula) to place his statue in the temple, they preferred to take up arms. The death of the Emperor put a stop to this revolt. Claudius, after the kings had either died or been reduced to subjection, intrusted the government of the province of Judæa to Roman knights, or freedmen." (*Hist.* v. 9.)

Elsewhere, he sometimes falls into actual error, as where he assigns the death of Agrippa, and the reduction of Judæa into the form of a Roman province, to the 9th of Claudius, A. D. 49. (*Annal.* xi. 23.)

Dio's notices are very confused. He seems scarcely able to distinguish one Herod from another. (*Hist. Rom.* xlix. p. 405, E.; liii. p. 526, D.; lv. p. 567, B.; and lx. p. 670, B.)

NOTE XXII., p. 187.

See the last note. Tacitus appears, in both the passages, to place the first reduction of Judæa into the position of a Roman province under Claudius, upon the death of Agrippa. Yet he elsewhere notices the procuratorship of Pontius Pilate, *in the reign of Tiberius.* (*Ann.* xv. 44, quoted in Note IV.)

NOTE XXIII., p. 187.

Joseph. *Ant. Jud.* xx. 1, § 3. It has not always been seen that Festus *referred* (ἀνέθετο) St. Paul's case to Agrippa on account of his occupying this position. Dean Alford, however, distinctly recognizes this feature of the transaction. (*Greek Testament*, vol. ii. p. 252.)

NOTE XXIV., p. 188.

It has been questioned whether the Jews themselves had any *right* of capital punishment at this time. (Lardner, *Credibility*, &c., vol. i. pp. 21-48; Olshausen, *Biblischer Commentar*, vol. ii. p. 501.) Josephus certainly represents the power as one which the Romans reserved to themselves from the first establishment of the procuratorship. (*De*

Bell. Jud. ii. 8, § 1; compare *Ant. Jud.* xx. 9, § 1.) But, as Dean Alford remarks, the history of Stephen and of the "great persecution," (διωγμὸς μέγας,) soon after, seems to show "that the Jews did, by connivance of, or in the absence of the Procurator, administer summary punishments of this kind." (*Greek Testament*, vol. ii. p. 75; compare Joseph. *Ant. Jud.* l. s. c.)

NOTE XXV., p. 188.

See Matt. v. 26; x. 29; xvii. 25; xviii. 28; xxvi. 53; xxvii. 26, 27, and 65: Mark vi. 27; &c. The terms, it will be observed, are such as either belong to the military force, the revenue, or the office of governor. They are such therefore as would naturally be introduced by a foreign dominant power.

NOTE XXVI., p. 189.

See Mark vi. 7, and 40; vii. 11; x. 51; xiii. 14; &c. The number of instances might of course be greatly increased. Among the most noticeable are Matt. v. 18, (ἰῶτα ἓν ἢ μία κεραία;[1]) v. 22, (ῥακά;[2]) v. 29, (γέεννα;[3]) vi. 24, (μαμωνᾶς;[4] conf. Luke xvi. 9, &c.;) Mark iii. 17, (βοανεργὲς;[5]) v. 41, (ταλιθὰ κοῦμι;[6]) vii. 34, (ἐφφαθά;[7]) xi. 9, (ὡσαννά;[8]) John i. 43, (κηφᾶς.[9]) Compare also the thoroughly Hebrew character of the Canticles in Luke i. and ii.

NOTE XXVII., p. 189.

Joseph. *De Bell. Jud.* vii. 8, § 1: "For that time was fruitful among the Jews in all sorts of wickedness, so that they left no evil deed undone; nor was there any new form of wickedness, which any one could invent, if he wished to do so. Thus they were all corrupt, both in their public and their private relations; and they vied with each other who should excel in impiety towards God and injustice to men. The more powerful oppressed the common people, and the common people eagerly sought to destroy the more powerful; for the former class were governed by the love of power, and the latter by the desire to seize and plunder the possessions of the wealthy." Compare *Ant. Jud.* xx. 7, § 8; *Bell. Jud.* v. 13, § 6; and 10, § 5.

1 One jot, or one tittle. 2 Raca. 3 Gehenna, (translated *hell.*)
4 Mammon. 5 Boanerges. 6 Talitha cumi.
7 Ephphatha. 8 Hosanna. 9 Cephas.

NOTE XXVIII., p. 189.

Joseph. *Ant. Jud.* xvii. 9, § 3; xx. 4, § 3; *Bell. Jud.* ii. 19, § 1; &c. On one occasion it appears that more than two and a half millions of persons had come up to Jerusalem to worship. (*Bell. Jud.* vi. 9, § 3.)

NOTE XXIX., p. 189.

Ant. Jud. xv. 7, § 8: "In Jerusalem there were two fortresses, one belonging to the city itself, and the other to the temple. Whoever held these had the whole nation in their power; for without the command of these, it was not possible to offer the sacrifices; and no Jew could endure the thought that these should fail to be offered: they were even ready sooner to lay down their lives, than to omit the religious sacrifices which they were accustomed to offer to God."

NOTE XXX., p. 189.

Not only was Caligula's attempt to have his statue set up in the temple resisted with determination, (Joseph. *Ant. Jud.* xviii. 8,) but when the younger Agrippa, by raising the height of his house, obtained a view into the temple courts, the greatest indignation was felt, (*δεινῶς ἐχαλέπαινον.*) The Jews immediately raised a wall to shut out his prospect, and when Festus commanded them to remove it, they positively refused, declaring that they would rather die than destroy any portion of the sacred fabric, (*ζῆν γὰρ οὐχ ὑπομένειν, καθαιρεθέντος τινὸς μέρους τοῦ ἱεροῦ.*) See *Ant. Jud.* xx. 8, § 11; and on the general subject, compare Philo, *De Legat. ad Caium*, pp. 1022, 1023.

NOTE XXXI., p. 190.

Ant. Jud. xv. 8, §§ 1–4.

NOTE XXXII., p. 190.

See Lardner's *Credibility*, &c., book i. ch. 9; vol. i. pp. 110–121.

NOTE XXXIII., p. 190.

Josephus tells us, that when Cyrenius came to take the census of men's properties throughout Judæa, a controversy arose among the

Jews on the legality of submission to foreign taxation. Judas of Galilee (see Acts v. 37) maintained that it was a surrender of the theocratic principle; while the bulk of the chief men, including some considerable number of the Pharisees, took the opposite view, and persuaded the people to submit themselves. (*Ant. Jud.* xviii. 1, § 1.)

NOTE XXXIV., p. 190.

Ant. Jud. xx. 6, § 1: "Now there arose an enmity between the Samaritans and the Jews, from the following cause: The Galileans were accustomed, in going up to the feasts that were held in Jerusalem, to pass through the country of the Samaritans. At this time there was on the road which they took a village called Ginea, situated on the boundary between Samaria and the great plain. When the Galileans came to this place, they were attacked, and many of them killed."

NOTE XXXV., p. 190.

Ibid. xviii. 1, §§ 3 and 4. Note especially the following: Of the Pharisees — "They believe that souls have an immortal vigor, and that beyond the grave there are rewards and punishments, according as they follow a virtuous or a vicious course of life in this world." Of the Sadducees — "But the doctrine of the Sadducees is, that the soul is annihilated together with the body." Compare Acts xxiii. 8.

NOTE XXXVI., p. 190.

Ibid. l. s. c. [The Pharisees] "are very influential with the people; and whatever prayers to God or sacrifices are performed, are performed at their dictation. The doctrine [of the Sadducees] is received by but few; but these are the men who are in the highest authority."

NOTE XXXVII., p. 190.

Bell. Jud., vi. 5, § 4. "But that which most of all roused them to undertake this war, was an ambiguous oracle, . . . found in their sacred books, that at that time a man of their country should rule over the whole earth."

NOTE XXXVIII., p. 190.

Sueton. *Vit. Vespasian.*, § 4: "An ancient and settled opinion had prevailed throughout the whole East, that fate had decreed that at that time persons proceeding from Judæa should become masters of the world. This was foretold, as the event afterwards proved, of the Roman Emperor; but the Jews applied it to themselves, and this was the cause of their rebellion." Compare *Vit. Octav.*, § 94, and Virg. *Eclog.*, iv.

NOTE XXXIX., p. 190.

Tacit. *Histor.*, v. 13: "These things [the prodigies that occurred just before the capture of Jerusalem by the Romans] were regarded by a few as alarming omens; but the greater number believed that it was written in the ancient books of the priests, that at that very time the East, should become very powerful, and that persons proceeding from Judæa should become masters of the world."

NOTE XL., p. 190.

Leben Jesu, § 34; vol. i. p. 220, E. T.

NOTE XLI., p. 190.

See Philo, *De Legatione ad Caium*, p. 1022, D. E. For the portraiture of Josephus, see above, Note XXVII.

NOTE XLII., p. 191.

This passage is given by Wetsten (*Nov. Test. Gr.*, vol. ii. p. 563) and Dean Alford (*Greek Testament*, vol. ii. p. 175) as from Xenophon *De Rep. Atheniens.* I have not succeeded in verifying the reference.

NOTE XLIII., p. 191.

Liv. xlv. 27, ad fin.

NOTE XLIV., p. 192.

How attractive to *strangers* Athens was, even in her decline, may be seen from the examples of Cicero, Germanicus, Pausanias, and others.

(See Conybeare and Howson's *Life of St. Paul*, vol. i. pp. 398, 399.) On the greediness of the Athenians after *novelty*, see Demosth. *Philipp.* i. p. 43, ("Or tell me, do you wish to go about asking each other in the market place, 'What is the news?' And can there be any thing newer, than that the man of Macedon," &c.;) *Philipp. Epist.* pp. 156, 157; Ælian. *Var. Hist.*, v. 13; Schol. ad Thucyd. iii. 38, &c. On their religiousness, compare Pausan. i. 24, § 3, (the Athenians are more zealous than others in the worship of the gods;) Xen. *Rep. Atheniens.* iii. § 1, and § 8; Joseph. *Contra Apion.* ii. 11, ("All say, that the Athenians are the most religious of the Greeks;") Strab. v. 3, § 18; Ælian. *Var. Hist.* v. 17; Philostrat. *Vit. Apollon.* vi. 3; Dionys. Hal. *De Jud. Thuc.*, § 40; and among later authors, see Mr. Grote's *History of Greece*, vol. iii. pp. 229–232.

Note XLV., p. 192.

See the *Life and Epistles of St. Paul*, by Messrs. Conybeare and Howson, vol. ii. pp. 66, et seqq. (1.) The "*Great* Goddess, Diana," is found to have borne that title as her *usual title*, both from an inscription, (Boeckh, *Corpus Inscript.*, 2963 C,) and from Xenophon, (Ephes. i. p. 15: "I invoke our ancestral God, the great Diana of the Ephesians.") (2.) The "Asiarchs" are mentioned on various coins and inscriptions. (3.) The "town-clerk" (γραμματεὺς) of Ephesus is likewise mentioned in inscriptions, (Boeckh, No. 2963 C, No. 2966, and No. 2990.) (4.) The curious word νεωκόρος, (Acts xix. 35,) literally "sweeper" of the temple, is also found in inscriptions and on coins, as an epithet of the Ephesian people, (Boeckh, No. 2966.) The "silver shrines of Diana," the "court-days," the "deputies" or "proconsuls" (ἀνθύπατοι) might receive abundant classical illustration. The temple was the glory of the ancient world[1] — enough still remains of the "theatre" to give evidence of its former greatness.

Note XLVI., p. 192.

Compare Luke xxiii. 2; John xix. 12–15; Acts xxv. 12 and 26; xxvi. 32; 2 Tim. iv. 17; 1 Pet. ii. 13 and 17.

[1] Plin. xxxv. 21; Strab. xiv. 1; Phil. Byz. *De Sept. Orb. Spectaculis.*

Note XLVII., p. 192.

The Roman provinces under the empire were administered either by proconsuls, or legates, or in a few instances by procurators. The technical Greek name for the proconsul is ἀνθύπατος, (Polyb. xxi. 8, § 11,) as that for the consul is ὕπατος. Proconsuls are mentioned by St. Luke in Cyprus, (Acts xiii. 7,) at Ephesus, (ib. xix. 38,) and at Corinth, (ib. xviii. 12, where the verb "to be a proconsul" expresses the office of Gallio.) In every case the use of the term is historically correct. (See below, Notes CIV. and CVIII.) Other officers are not so distinctly designated. Legates do not occur in the history; and the Greek possessing no term correspondent to procurator, such officers appear only as ἡγεμόνες, (governors,) a generic term applicable to proconsuls also. (See Luke ii. 2; iii. 1; Matt. xxvii. 2; Acts xxiii. 24; xxvi. 30, &c.)

The anxiety to avoid tumults may be observed in the conduct of Pilate, (Matt. xxvii. 24;) of the authorities at Ephesus, (Acts xix. 35–41;) and of Lysias, (Acts xxi. 32; xxii. 24.) The governors were liable to recall at any moment, and knew that they would probably be superseded, if they allowed troubles to break out.

Note XLVIII., p. 192.

See especially Gallio's words, (Acts xviii. 14–16.) Compare Acts xxiii. 29; and xxviii. 30, 31. On the *general* tolerance of the Romans, see Lardner's *Credibility*, vol. i. p. 95, et seqq.

Note XLIX., p. 192.

In a Rescript of Severus and Caracalla, (*Digest.* xlviii. 17, 1,) we read, "We have also this law, that the absent must not be condemned; for indeed the rule of justice does not allow any one to be condemned without having his cause heard." Compare Dionys. Hal. vii. 53, p. 441. The odium incurred by Cicero for proceeding without formal trial against the Catiline conspirators, (*Ep. ad Famil.*, v. 2, p. 60, b,) is an indication of the value attached to the principle in question.

Note L., p. 192.

Acts xxii. 28. Dio says of Antony, "He collected money from private individuals, selling to some the right of citizenship, and to others exemption from taxes." And of Claudius, "Since the Romans were, so to speak, in all things preferred to foreigners, many addressed their petitions directly to him, [for the privilege of citizenship,] and others purchased it of Messalina, and of the Emperor's favorites," (lx. 17, p. 676, C.) Citizenship by birth on the part of a foreigner might arise (1.) from his being a native of some colony or municipium; (2.) from a grant of citizenship, on account of service rendered, to his father, or a more remote ancestor; or (3.) from his father, or a more remote ancestor, having purchased his freedom. Dio speaks, a little before the passage last quoted, of many Lycians having been deprived of their Roman citizenship by Claudius. That Jews were often Roman citizens appears from Josephus. (*Ant. Jud.* xiv. 10, §§ 13, 14, 16, &c.)

Note LI., p. 192.

Acts xxv. 11. Suetonius says of Augustus, "The appeals of litigants belonging to the city he referred every year to the prætor; but those of persons belonging to the provinces, to men of consular dignity, of whom he had appointed a separate one over the affairs of each province." (*Vit. Octav.* c. 33.) Pliny probably refers to cases where the right of appeal had been claimed, when he says of the Bithynian Christians, "There were others under the same infatuation; but as they were Roman citizens, I directed them to be sent to the capital." (*Ep. ad Traj.* x. 97.)

Note LII., p. 192.

The *humane* treatment of prisoners is an occasional feature of the Roman system. (See Acts xxiv. 23, and xxviii. 16 and 30.) Lardner (*Credibility*, vol. i. p. 128) observes that the treatment of Herod Agrippa I. closely illustrates that of St. Paul. Soon after his first imprisonment, by the influence of Antonia, his friends were allowed free access to him, and permitted to bring him food and other comforts. (Joseph. *Ant. Jud.* xviii. 6, § 7.) On the death of Tiberius, whom he had offended, Caligula enlarged him further, permitting him to return and *live in his own house*, where he was still guarded, but less strictly than before. (Ibid. § 10: "He commanded that Agrippa should be removed from the camp to the house in which he had lived before he was imprisoned; so that now he was free from anxiety with regard to his situation; for it was, to be sure, one of custody and surveillance, but with much liberty as to his mode of life." Compare the order of Felix with regard to St. Paul — "commanding a centurion to keep him, and to let him have *liberty*," &c. Acts xxiv. 23.)

NOTE LIII., p. 192.

On one occasion we find St. Paul "bound with two chains," (Acts xxi. 33;) but commonly we hear of his "chain" (ἅλυσις) in the singular. (Acts xxviii. 20; Ephes. vi. 20; 2 Tim. i. 16.) Now, it is abundantly apparent from Seneca (*De Tranquill.* 10, *Epist.* 5) and other writers, (*Tacit. Ann.* iv. 28, &c.,) that prisoners were commonly fastened by a chain passed from their right wrist to the left wrist of their keeper. Where greater security was desired, a prisoner had two keepers, and a second chain was passed from his left wrist to the second keeper's right. The keeper to whom a prisoner was bound was called co-bondman.

NOTE LIV., p. 192.

Matt. xxvii. 27; Acts xx. 6; xxiv. 23; xxviii. 1, 16. The military custody (*custodia militaris*) of the Romans is well known to writers on antiquities. Ulpian says, that when a person was arrested, it was the business of the proconsul to determine "whether the person should be committed to prison, or delivered to the custody of a soldier, or placed in the care of his sureties, or, finally, left to take care of himself." (*Digest.* xlviii. Tit. 3. *De Custod. et Exhib. Reor.* § 1.) Examples of the military custody will be found in Tacitus, (*Ann.* iii. 22;) Josephus, (*Ant. Jud.* xviii. 6, § 7;) Ignatius, (*Ep. ad Roman.* v. p. 370;) *Martyr. Ignat.*, (ii. p. 450; v. p. 544,) &c.

NOTE LV., p. 192.

Examining free persons by scourging (Acts xxii. 24) or other torture, was against the spirit, and indeed against the letter, of the Roman law. "The Divine Augustus made a law that the torture should not be applied." (*Digest.* 48. Tit. 18, § 1.) But arbitrary power often broke this law, both at Rome and in the provinces. Suetonius says of Augustus, "And he took Quintus Gallius, the prætor, from the tribunal, and put him to the torture, as if he had been a slave." (*Vit. Octav.* § 27.) Tacitus of Nero, "Thinking that the body of a woman would not be able to endure the pain, he ordered Epicharis to be scourged." (*Annal.* xv. 57.) This examination was in part by scourging.

NOTE LVI., p. 192.

See Livy xxxiii. 36, ("After they had been scourged, he fastened them to crosses;") Val. Max. i. 7, § 4; Joseph. *Bell. Jud.* ii. 14, § 9, ("Florus chastised many with scourges, and afterwards crucified them. He had the boldness to scourge men of equestrian rank before the judgment-seat, and then to nail them to the cross;") &c. These last notices show the practice on the part of the Roman governors of Palestine.

NOTE LVII., p. 192.

The crucifixion of the Orientals has more commonly been impaling, than nailing to a cross. (See Ctesias, ap. Phot. *Bibl.* Cod. LXXII., p. 122; Casuabon. *Exerc. Antibaron.* xvi. 77.) The Romans fastened the body to the cross either by cords or nails. (See Smith's *Dictionary of Gr. and Rom. Antiq.* p. 370.) It is evident from Josephus, that nailing was the common practice in Palestine. (See the last note, and compare *Bell. Jud.* vi.: "The soldiers, through rage and hatred, fastened their captives to crosses, some in one manner, and some in another, in mockery; and on account of the great number, there was not room enough for the crosses, nor crosses enough for the bodies.") St. Augustine speaks as if nailing was the ordinary Roman method. (*Tractat.* xxxvi. in Johann. *Opera,* vol. ix. p. 278: "When men are tormented with very severe pains, they call them ex-*cruciating,* a term derived from the cross, (a cruce.) For they who are crucified, being suspended on the wood, and being fastened to it with nails, undergo a lingering death.")

NOTE LVIII., p. 192.

Plutarch. *de Sera Numinis Vindicta,* ii. p. 554, A.: "And each of the malefactors sentenced to capital punishment, carries his own cross." Compare Artemidor. *Oneirocrit.* ii. 61: "The cross is also a symbol of death, and he that is about to be nailed to it, first carries it along."

NOTE LIX., p. 192.

The practice of attaching a small board or placard to criminals, with a notification of the nature of their offence, is mentioned by several writers, and there are many allusions to it in the poets. The technical name of this placard was in Latin "titulus." (Compare the *title* of John xix. 19.) See Sueton. *Vit. Calig.* § 34: "At a public feast in Rome, when a slave had stolen a piece of silver from one of the couches, he delivered him at once to the executioner, and his hands being cut off, and hanging upon his breast, suspended from his neck, he was led about through the throng of guests at the feast, *carrying before him a title which declared the cause of his punishment.*" *Vit. Domitian.* § 10: "He dragged from the theatre a master of a family, because he had said that a Thracian was equal to a gladiator, but unequal to a master of the shows, and cast him to the dogs in the arenas *with this title*: 'a Parmularian[1] who has spoken impiously.'" Dio Cass. liv. p. 523: "When the father of Cæpio therefore released one of the slaves who had been banished along with his son, because he had tried to defend the deceased, but led the other one, who had betrayed him, through the midst of the market place, *with a writing declaring the cause of his death*, and afterwards crucified him, he was not displeased." Ovid. *Fasti*, vi. 190, 191: "He lived that he might die convicted of a crime against the state. Advanced age conferred upon him this *title*." Compare *Trist.* iii. 1, 47. We have no classical proof that the "titulus" was ordinarily affixed to the cross, unless we may view as such the statement of Hesychius — "A board, a door, a plastered tablet, on which accusations against malefactors were written at Athens. It was also *placed upon the cross*."

NOTE LX., p. 192.

Seneca speaks of the "centurion who had the charge of inflicting punishment" as an ordinary thing. (*De Ira*, c. 16, p. 34.) Petronius Arbiter says, "A soldier watched the crosses, lest some one should carry off the bodies for burial." (*Satyr.* c. 111.)

[1] This word means, "an adherent of the party of the Thracians, who were armed with a small round shield, called 'parma.'"

NOTE LXI., p. 192.

So Alford (vol. i., p. 647) — "The garments of the executed were by law the perquisites of the soldiers on duty." Cf. *Digest.* xlviii. Tit. 20, § 6.

NOTE LXII., p. 193.

Ulpian says, "The bodies of those who suffer capital punishment are not to be refused to their friends. And the Divine Augustus writes, in the tenth book of his life, that he also observed this rule. But at this day, the bodies of the persons in question are not buried, unless permission has first been sought and granted. And sometimes it is not granted, especially in the case of those condemned for treason." (*Digest.* xlviii. Tit. 24. *De Cadav. Punit.* § 1.) And again — "The bodies of those who suffer punishment are to be given to any requesting them for interment." (Ibid. § 3.) So Diocletian and Maximian declare, "We do not forbid that those who are guilty of crimes, after they have been duly punished, should be consigned to burial." The practice of the Jews to take bodies down from the cross and bury them on the day of their crucifixion, is witnessed to by Josephus — "He proceeded to such a degree of impiety, as to cast out bodies unburied, although the Jews took so much care in regard to burials, that they even took down and buried, *before the sun went down*, those who had been condemned and crucified." (*De Bell. Jud.* iv. 5, § 2.)

NOTE LXIII., p. 193.

Among minute points of accordance may be especially noticed the following: — 1. The geographical accuracy. (*a*) Compare the divisions of Asia Minor mentioned in the Acts with those in Pliny. Phrygia, Galatia, Lycaonia, Cilicia, Pamphylia, Pisidia, Asia, Mysia, Bithynia, are all recognized as existing provinces by the Roman geographer, writing probably within a few years of St. Luke. (*H. N.* v. 27, et seqq.) (*b*) The division of European Greece into the two provinces of Macedonia and Achaia, (Acts xix. 21, &c.,) accords exactly with the arrangement of Augustus noticed in Strabo, (xvii. ad fin.) (*c*) The various tracts in or about Palestine belong exactly to the geography of the time, *and of no other.* Judæa, Samaria, Galilee, Trachonitis, Ituræa,

Abilene, Decapolis, are recognized as geographically distinct at this period by the Jewish and classical writers. (See Plin. *H. N.* v. 14, 18, 23; Strab. xvi. 2, §§ 10, 34; Joseph. *Ant. Jud.* xix. 5, § 1, &c.) (*d*) The routes mentioned are such as were in use at the time. The "ship of Alexandria," which, conveying St. Paul to Rome, lands him at Puteoli, follows the ordinary course of the Alexandrian corn-ships, as mentioned by Strabo, (xvii. 1, § 7,) Philo, (*In Flacc.* pp. 968, 969,) and Seneca, (*Epist.* 77,) and touches at customary harbors. (See Sueton. *Vit. Tit.* § 25,) Paul's journey from Troas by Neapolis to Philippi presents an exact parallel to that of Ignatius, sixty years later, (*Martyr. Ignat.* c. 5.) His passage through Amphipolis and Apollonia on his road from Philippi to Thessalonica, is in accordance with the Itinerary of Antonine, which places those towns on the route between the two cities, (p. 22.) (*e*) The mention of Philippi as the first city of Macedonia to one approaching from the east, ("the chief city of that part of Macedonia," Acts xvi. 12,) is correct, since there was no other between it and Neapolis. The statement, that it was "a colony," is also true, (Dio Cass. li. 4, p. 445, D; Plin. *H. N.* iv. 11; Strab. vii. Fr. 41.) 2. The minute political knowledge. (*a*) We have already seen the intimate knowledge exhibited of the state of Ephesus, with its proconsul, town-clerk, Asiarchs, &c. A similar exactitude appears in the designation of the chief magistrates of Thessalonica as "the rulers of the city," (Acts xvii. 6,) their proper and peculiar appellation. (Boeckh, *Corp. Inscr.* No. 1967.) (*b*) So too the Roman governors of Corinth and Cyprus are given their correct titles. (See Notes CIV. and CVIII.) (*c*) Publius, the Roman governor of Malta, has again his proper technical designation, ("the chief man of the island," Acts xxviii. 7,) as appears from inscriptions commemorating the chief of the Melitans, or "Melitensium primus."[1] (See Alford, ii. p. 282.) (*d*) The delivery of the prisoners to the "captain of the (Prætorian) guard" at Rome, is in strict accordance with the practice of the time. (Trajan. ap. *Plin. Ep.* x. 65: "He ought to be sent bound to the præfects of my Prætorian guard." Compare Philostrat. *vit. Sophist.* ii. 32.)

Among additions to our classical knowledge, for which we are indebted to Scripture, it may suffice to mention, 1. The existence of an Italian cohort (the Italian band) as early as the reign of Tiberius, (Acts

[1] The Latin and the Greek are precisely equivalent.

x. 1.) 2. The application of the term Σεβαστὴ (Augustan) to another *cohort*, a little later, (Acts xxviii. 1.) 3. The existence of an Altar at Athens with the inscription, "To the unknown God," (Acts xvii. 23,) which is not to be confounded with the well-known inscriptions to unknown gods. 4. The use of the title στρατηγοὶ (Prætors) by the Duumviri, or chief magistrates of Philippi, (Acts xvi. 20.) We know from Cicero, (*De Leg. Agrar.* 34,) that the title was sometimes assumed in such cases, but we have no other proof that it was in use at Philippi.

Note LXIV., p. 193.

Lardner, *Credibility*, &c., vol. i. p. 60.

Note LXV., p. 193.

See Acts xiii. 5, 14; xiv. 1; xvi. 3, 13; xvii. 1, 10, 17; xviii. 4; xix. 8, &c.

Note LXVI., p. 194.

"Now, in regard to the holy city, there are some things which I ought to say. It is, as I have said, the place of my nativity; and it is the metropolis, not of the single country of Judæa, but of a great many countries, by means of the colonies which it has sent out from time to time, — some to the neighboring countries of Egypt, Phœnice, Syria proper, and that part called Cœle-Syria; — and some planted in the more distant regions of Pamphylia, Cilicia, and many parts of Asia, as far as Bithynia and the recesses of Pontus; in like manner also in Europe, in Thessaly, Bœotia, Macedonia, Ætolia, Attica, Argos, Corinth, and many of the best parts of the Peloponnesus; and not only are the continental countries full of Jewish colonies, but also the most famous islands, as Eubœa, Cyprus, and Crete; not to speak of those beyond the Euphrates. For excepting a small part of Babylon, and of the other satrapies, all the places which have a fertile territory around them have Jewish inhabitants; so that if my country shall receive this favor from thee, not one city only, but ten thousand others, situated in every region of the habitable world, will be benefited; those in Europe, and Asia, and Africa; those on the continents and in the islands, on the sea shore and in the interior. (Philo Jud. *Legat. ad Caium*, pp. 1031, 1032.)

NOTE LXVII., p. 194.

"For no single country contains the Jews, but they are exceedingly numerous; on which account they are distributed through nearly all the most flourishing countries of Europe and Asia, both insular and continental; and they all regard the sacred city as their metropolis." (Ibid. *In Flacc.* p. 971, E.)

NOTE LXVIII., p. 194.

Joseph. *Ant. Jud.* xx. 2; *De Bell. Jud.* vii. 3, § 3; *Contr. Apion.* ii. 36, &c.

NOTE LXIX., p. 194.

Philo frequently mentions the synagogues under the name of "places of prayer." (*In Flacc.* p. 972, A. B. E.; *Legat. in Caium*, p. 1014, &c.) Their position by the sea-side, or by a river-side, is indicated, among other places, in the Decree of the Halicarnassians reported by Josephus, (*Ant. Jud.* xiv. 10, § 23,) where the Jews are allowed to offer prayers by the sea-side, according to their national custom. See also Philo, *Legat. in Caium*, p. 982, D.; Tertull. *ad Nat.* i. 13; *De Jejun.* c. 16; and Juv. *Sat.* iii. 13.

NOTE LXX., p. 194.

Lightfoot, *Hebraic. et Talmudic. Exercitat.*, not. in Act. Apost. vi. 8; *Works*, vol. ii. p. 664.

NOTE LXXI., p. 194.

See *Legat. in Caium*, (p. 1014, C. D.,) where Philo speaks of Transtiberine Rome as *κατεχομένην καὶ οἰκουμένην πρὸς 'Ιουδαίων*,[1] and then adds, *'Ρωμαῖοι δ' ἦσαν οἱ πλείους ἀπελευθερωθέντες*.[2]

NOTE LXXII., p. 194.

Annal. ii. 85: "The question of banishing the sacred rites of the Egyptians and of *the Jews* was also determined; a decree was made by

[1] Occupied and inhabited by Jews.

[2] But the greater part of them were Roman freedmen.

the fathers, that four thousand of the *class of freedmen*, who were tainted with that superstition — those being selected who were of suitable age — should be transported to the island of Sardinia."

Note LXXIII., p. 195.

For the tumultuous spirit of the foreign Jews, see Sueton. *vit. Claud.* p. 25; Dio Cassius, lx. 6; Joseph. *Ant. Jud.* xviii. 8, § 1; 9, § 9; xx. 1, § 1; &c.

Note LXXIV., p. 196.

Annal. xv. 44. Tiberius reigned (as sole emperor) 23 years. (Suet. *vit. Tib.* § 73.) His *principatus*, however, may date from three years earlier, when he was associated by Augustus. (Tacit. *Ann.* i. 3; Suet. *vit. Tib.* § 21.)

Note LXXV., p. 196.

If our Lord was born in the year of Rome 747, (see above, Lecture VI., Note I.) he would have been three years old at Herod's death; and 32 years old when he commenced his ministry, in the fifteenth year from the *associated* principate of Tiberius. This is not incompatible with St. Luke's declaration, that he was *about* thirty years of age (ὡσεὶ ἐτῶν τριάκοντα) when he began to preach; for that expression admits of some latitude. (See Alford's *Greek Testament*, vol. i. pp. 323 and 327.)

Note LXXVI., p. 196.

Joseph. *Ant. Jud.* xiv. 7, § 3; xvii. 8, § 1; Nic. Damasc. Fr. 5.

Note LXXVII., p. 196.

Joseph. *Ant. Jud.* xv. 6, § 7; Tacit. *Hist.* v. 9. "The victorious Augustus enlarged the kingdom given to Herod by Antony."

Note LXXVIII., p. 196.

See Lardner's *Credibility*, vol. i. pp. 148–151; and compare Joseph. *De Bell. Jud.* i. 27, § 1; 29, § 2; 33, § 8; Appian. *De Bell. Civ.* v. p. 1135.

NOTE LXXIX., p. 196.

The cruelties, deceptions, and suspicions of Herod the Great, fill many chapters in Josephus. (*Ant. Jud.* xv. 1, 3, 6, 7, &c.; xvi. 4, 8, 10; xvii. 3, 6, 7, &c.) His character is thus summed up by that writer: — "He was a man cruel to all alike, yielding to the impulses of passion, but regardless of the claims of justice; and yet no one was ever favored with a more propitious fortune." (*Ant. Jud.* xvii. 8, § 1.) His arrest of the chief men throughout his dominion, and design that on his own demise they should all be executed, (ibid. 6, § 5; *Bell. Jud.* i. 33, § 6,) shows a bloodier temper than even the massacre of the Innocents.

NOTE LXXX., p. 197.

Strauss, *Leben Jesu*, § 34; vol. i. p. 222, E. T.

NOTE LXXXI., p. 197.

Strauss grants the massacre to be "not inconsistent with the disposition of the aged tyrant to the extent that Schleiermacher supposed," (*Leben Jesu*, l. s. c. p. 228, E. T.,) but objects, that "neither Josephus, who is very minute in his account of Herod, nor the rabbins, who were assiduous in blackening his memory, give the slightest hint of this decree." (l. s. c.) He omits to observe, that they could scarcely narrate the circumstance without some mention of its reason — the birth of the supposed Messiah — a subject on which their prejudices necessarily kept them silent.

NOTE LXXXII., p. 197.

Macrob, *Saturnal.* ii. 4: "When Augustus had heard, that *among the children under two years of age whom Herod, the king of the Jews, had commanded to be slain in Syria*, there was also one of the king's own sons, he said it was better to be the sow,[1] than the son of Herod." Strauss contends, that "the passage loses all credit *by confounding the execution of Antipater*, who had gray hairs, with the murder of the

[1] There is in the original a play upon the similarity of the Greek words for "hog" and "son," which is partly, at least, preserved in translation by taking license to substitute the feminine for the masculine in this word.

infants, renowned among the Christians;" but Macrobius says nothing of Antipater, and evidently does not refer to any of the known sons of Herod. He believes that among the children massacred was an *infant* son of the Jewish king. It is impossible to say whether he was right or wrong in this belief. It may have simply originated in the fact that a jealousy of a *royal* infant was known to have been the motive for the massacre. (See Olshausen, *Biblsch. Comment.* vol. i. p. 72, note; p. 67, E. T.)

Note LXXXIII., p. 197.

Josephus says, "When Cæsar had heard these things he dissolved the assembly; and a few days afterwards he appointed Archelaus, not indeed king, but ethnarch of half the country which had been subject to Herod, . . . and the other half he divided, and gave it to two other sons of Herod, Philip and Antipas; . . . to the latter of whom he made Peræa and Galilee subject, . . . while Batanæa with Trachonitis, and Auranitis with a certain part of what is called the House of Zenodorus, were subjected to Philip; but the parts subject to Archelaus were Idumea and Judæa and Samaria." (*Antiq. Jud.* xvii. 11, § 4.) Compare the brief notice of Tacitus: "The country which had been subdued, was governed, in three divisions, by the sons of Herod." (*Hist.* v. 9.)

Note LXXXIV., p. 197.

Strauss says, "Luke determines the date of John's appearance by various synchronisms, placing it in the time of Pilate's government in Judæa; in the sovereignty of Herod, (Antipas;) of Philip and of Lysanias over the other divisions of Palestine; in the high-priesthood of Annas and Caiaphas; and moreover precisely in the 15th year of the reign of Tiberius, which, reckoning from the death of Augustus, corresponds with the year 28–29 of our era. With this last and closest demarcation of time *all the foregoing less precise ones agree. Even that which makes Annas high-priest together with Caiaphas appears correct,* if we consider the peculiar influence which that ex-high-priest retained." (*Leben Jesu,* § 44; pp. 300, 301, E. T.)

Note LXXXV., p. 197.

Joseph. *Ant. Jud.* xvii. 11, § 1. "But all who were of the kindred of Archelaus refused to join themselves to him, on account of their hatred towards him." Compare 13, § 2.

NOTE LXXXVI., p. 197.

Joseph. *De Bell. Jud.* ii. 1, § 3.

NOTE LXXXVII., p. 198.

Strauss, *Leben Jesu*, § 48; vol. i. p. 346, E. T.

NOTE LXXXVIII., p. 198.

Josephus says, "Herod the tetrarch had married the daughter of Aretas, and had now lived with her a long time. But having made a journey to Rome, he lodged in the house of Herod, his brother, but not by the same mother. For this Herod was the son of the daughter of Simon, the high-priest. Now he fell in love with Herodias, this man's wife, who was the daughter of Aristobulus their brother, and the sister of Agrippa the Great; and he had the boldness to propose marriage. She accepted the proposal, and it was agreed that she should go to live with him, whenever he should return from Rome." (*Ant. Jud.* xviii. 5, § 1.) And again: "Herodias, their sister, was married to Herod, the son of Herod the Great, who was born of Mariamne, the daughter of Simon the high-priest, who had also a daughter Salome; after the birth of whom, Herodias, in shameful violation of the customs of our nation, allowed herself to marry Herod, the brother of her former husband by the same father, separating from him while he was living. Now this man [whom she married] held the office of tetrarch of Galilee." (Ibid. § 4.)

NOTE LXXXIX., p. 198.

Ant. Jud. xviii. 5, § 2: "Now some of the Jews thought that the army of Herod had been destroyed by God, in most righteous vengeance for the punishment inflicted upon *John, surnamed the Baptist*. For he taught the Jews to cultivate virtue, and to practise righteousness towards each other, and piety towards God, and so to come to baptism. For he declared that this dipping would be acceptable to Him, if they used it, not with reference *to the renunciation of certain sins*, but to the purification of the body,[1] the soul having been purified by righteousness. And when others thronged to him, (for they were profoundly moved at the hearing of his words,) Herod feared that his great influence over the men would lead them to some revolt, (for they seemed ready to do any thing by his advice;) he therefore thought it much better to anticipate the evil, by putting him to death, before he had attempted to make any innovation, than to allow himself to be brought into trouble, and then repent after some revolutionary movement had conmenced. And so John, *in consequence of the suspicion of Herod, was sent as a prisoner to the afore-mentioned castle of Machærus*, and *was there put to death*." The genuineness of this passage is admitted even by Strauss. (*Leben Jesu*, § 48; vol. i. pp. 344–347, E. T.)

NOTE XC., p. 198.

Strauss, *Leben Jesu*, l. s. c. The chief points of apparent difference are the motive of the imprisonment and the scene of the execution. Josephus makes fear of a popular insurrection, the Evangelists offence at a personal rebuke, the motive. But here (as Strauss observes) there is no contradiction, for "Antipas might well fear that John, by his strong censure of the marriage and the whole course of the tetrarch's life, might stir up the people into rebellion against him." Again, from the Gospels we naturally imagine the prison to be near Tiberias, where Herod Antipas ordinarily resided; but Josephus says that prison was at Machærus in Peræa, a day's journey from Tiberias. Here, however, an examination of the Gospels shows, that the place where Antipas made his feast and gave his promise is not mentioned. It only appears that it was near the prison. Now, as Herod was at this time engaged in a war with Aretas, the Arabian prince, between whose kingdom and his own lay the fortress of Machærus, it is "a probable solution" of the difficulty, that he was residing with his court at Machærus at this period. (Strauss, § 48, ad fin.)

NOTE XCI., p. 198.

Philip is said to have retained his tetrarchy till the 20th year of Tibe-

[1] Dr. Burton acutely remarks on this expression, that it is a covert allusion to the Christian doctrine of "a baptism for the remission of sins," and shows the acquaintance of Josephus with the tenets of the Christians. (*Eccles. Hist.* vol. i. p. 199.)

riùs. (*Ant. Jud.* xviii. 5, § 6.) Herod Antipas lost his government in the first of Caligula. (Ibid. ch. 7.)

NOTE XCII., p. 198.

Ant. Jud. xvii. 12; xviii. 1; *De Bell. Jud.* ii. 8, § 1. "Now, when the territory of Archelaus was formed into a province, a certain procurator, of equestrian rank among the Romans, Coponius by name, was sent to govern it, receiving from Cæsar the power of life and death." The procurators for this period, mentioned by Josephus, are Coponius, M. Ambivius, Annius Rufus, Valerius Gratus, and Pontius Pilate. (*Ant. Jud.* xviii. 2, § 2.)

NOTE XCIII., p. 198.

Joseph. *Ant. Jud.* xviii. 6, §§ 10, 11; 8, § 7; xix. 5, § 1; Philo, *In Flacc.*, p. 968, D. E.

NOTE XCIV., p. 198.

Joseph. *Ant. Jud.* xix. 8, § 2: "Now, after he had reigned three full years over the whole of Judæa, he *was at the city of Cæsarea*, which was formerly called Strato's Tower. And there he held public shows in honor of Cæsar, having learned that a certain festival was celebrated at that time, to make vows for his safety. Now, *at that festival there were assembled* a multitude of those who were first in office and authority in the province. *On the second day of the shows, putting on a robe made entirely of silver*, the texture of which was truly wonderful, he came into the theatre early in the morning. When the first beams of the sun shone upon the silver, it glittered in a wonderful manner, flashing forth a brilliancy which amazed and awed those who gazed upon him. Whereupon his flatterers immediately cried out, (though not for his good,) one from one place and one from another, — *addressing him as a god*, — 'Be propitious to us;' and adding, 'Although we have heretofore feared thee as a man, yet henceforth we acknowledge thee to be of more than mortal nature.' *The king did not rebuke them*, nor reject their impious flattery. *A little after*, therefore, looking up, he saw an owl sitting upon a certain rope over his head; and he immediately understood that it was a messenger of evil, as it had formerly been of good; whereupon he was overcome with a profound sadness. There was also a severe pain in his bowels, which began with a sudden violence. Turning therefore to his friends, he said, — 'I, your god, am now commanded to end my life; and fate *immediately* reproves the false shouts that were just now addressed to me: and so I, whom you call immortal, am now snatched away by death. But we must accept the fate which God ordains. And indeed we have not lived ill, but in the most brilliant good fortune.' When he had said this, he was overcome by the intensity of the pain. He was therefore quickly carried to the palace, and the report went abroad to all, that he must inevitably soon die. . . . Being consumed thus for five days *in succession* with the pain in his belly, he departed this life."

Note XCV., p. 199.

Ibid. xix. 9, § 2: "[Claudius] therefore sent Cuspius Fadus as a procurator over Judæa, and all the kingdom."

Note XCVI., p. 199.

Ibid. xx. 5, § 2; 7, § 1; and 8, § 4. Agrippa II. bore the title of king. (*De Bell. Jud.* ii. 12, § 8.)

Note XCVII., p. 199.

Antiq. Jud. xix. 9, § 1; xx. 7, § 3. The evil reports which arose from this constant companionship are noticed by Josephus in the latter of these passages. They are glanced at in the well-known passage of Juvenal, (*Sat.* vi. 155–169.) "That well-known diamond, made even more precious by being worn on the finger of Berenice. This jewel the barbarian formerly gave to that unchaste woman, and Agrippa gave it to his sister, in that country where kings keep the Sabbath festival with naked feet, and an ancient indulgence allows the old men to eat pork." Compare Tacit. *Hist.* ii. 2 and 81.

Note XCVIII., p. 199.

Joseph. *Ant. Jud.* xx. 8, § 8; 9, § 7: "The king had been intrusted by Claudius Cæsar with the care of the temple." In one passage (*Ant. Jud.* xx. 1, § 3) Josephus says that these privileges continued to be exercised by the *descendants* of Herod, king of Chalcis, from his decease to the end of the war. But he here uses the term "descendants" very loosely; or he forgets that Agrippa II. was the nephew, and not the son, of this monarch. (See the note of Lardner, *Credibility*, vol. i. p. 18, note [g].)

NOTE XCIX., p. 199.

The procuratorship of Pilate lasted from the 12th year of Tiberius (A. D. 26) to the 22d, (A. D. 36.) See Joseph. *Ant. Jud.* xviii. 3, § 2, and 4, § 2. Felix entered upon his office as *sole* procurator in the 12th year of Claudius, (A. D. 53,) and was succeeded by Porcius Festus early in the reign of Nero. (*Ant. Jud.* xx. 7, § 1; and 8, § 9.)

NOTE C., p. 199.

The vacillation and timidity of Pilate appear in his attempt to establish the images of Tiberius in Jerusalem, followed almost immediately by their withdrawal. (*Ant. Jud.* xviii. 3, § 1.) His violence is shown in his conduct towards the Jews who opposed his application of the temple-money to the construction of an aqueduct at Jerusalem, (ibid. § 2,) as well as in his treatment of the Samaritans on the occasion which led to his removal. (Ibid. 4, § 1.) Agrippa the elder speaks of the iniquity of his government in the strongest terms, (ap. Philon. *Leg. ad Caium*, p. 1034: "he feared lest they should examine and expose the misdeeds of his former procuratorship, the taking of bribes, the acts of violence, the extortions, the tortures, the menaces, the repeated murders without any form of trial, the harsh and incessant cruelty.")

NOTE CI., p. 199.

Tacitus says of Felix, "Antonius Felix exercised the royal authority in a manner agreeable to the baseness of his disposition, with all cruelty and wantonness." (*Hist.* v. 9.) And again: "But his father, whose surname was Felix, did not conduct himself with the same moderation. Having been a long time governor of Judæa, he thought he could commit all crimes with impunity, relying upon his great power." (*Ann.* xii. 54.)

Josephus gives a similar account of his government. (*Ant. Jud.* xx. 8.) After he quitted office he was accused to the emperor, and

35 *

only escaped a severe sentence by the influence which his brother Pallas possessed with Nero.

NOTE CII., p. 199.

See *Ant. Jud.* xx. 8, §§ 10, 11; *Bell. Jud.* ii. 14, § 1. In the latter passage Josephus says, "Now Festus, having succeeded this man in the office of procurator, relieved the country of its greatest scourge. For he captured a large number of the robbers, and destroyed not a few. But Albinus, who succeeded Festus, did not govern after the same manner. For it is not possible to mention any form of evil-doing which he omitted to practise."

NOTE CIII., p. 199.

See above, Notes C. and CI.

NOTE CIV., p. 199.

Here the accuracy of St. Luke is very remarkable. Achaia, though originally a senatorial province, (Dio Cass. liii. p. 503, E.,) had been taken into his own keeping by Tiberius, (Tacit. *Ann.* i. 76,) and had continued under legates during the whole of his reign. Claudius, however, in his fourth year restored the province to the senate, (Suet. *vit. Claud.* § 35,) from which time it was governed by proconsuls. St. Paul's visit to Corinth fell about two years after this change.

NOTE CV., p. 199.

Seneca says of Gallio, "I used to say to you, that my brother Gallio, (*whom every body loves as much as I do*, although no one can love him more,) while he was free from all other vices, had a special hatred to this." And again: "No other mortal is so *dear* to any one, as he is to all." (*Quæst. Nat.* iv. Præfat.) Statius uses the same epithet, (*Sylv.* ii. 7, ll. 32, 33:) "This is more than to have given Seneca to the world, or to have been the parent of *dear* Gallio."

NOTE CVI., p. 200.

See Joseph. *Ant. Jud.* xvii. 12, § 5; xviii. 1, § 1. "Moreover Cyrenius came also into Judea, which had been annexed to Syria, *to make a valuation of their property*, and to dispose of the money of Archelaus. But the people, although at first they could hardly endure to hear of an *enrolment*, at length submitted," &c. The difficulty with respect to the *time* of the taxing will be considered in Note CXIX.

NOTE CVII., p. 200.

There was a Sergius Paulus who bore the office of consul in the year A. D. 94. Another held the same office in A. D. 168. This latter is probably the Sergius Paulus mentioned by Galen. (*Anat.* i. 1, vol. ii. p. 218; *De Prænot.* § 2; vol. xiv. p. 612.)

NOTE CVIII., p. 200.

Cyprus was originally an imperial province, (Dio Cass. liii. p. 504, A.,) and therefore governed by legates or proprætors, (Strab. xiv. 6, § 6;) but Augustus after a while gave it up to the Senate, from which time its governors were proconsuls. (See Dio, liv. p. 523, B. "At that time therefore he gave up Cyprus and Gallia Narbonensis to the people, as having no further need of his arms; and so proconsuls began to be sent to those nations.") The title of proconsul appears on Cyprian coins, and has been found in a Cyprian Inscription of the reign of Claudius. (Boeckh, *Corp. Inscript.* No. 2632.)

NOTE CIX., p. 200.

Joseph. *Ant. Jud.* xiv. 13, § 3; *De Bell. Jud.* i. 13, § 1; Dio Cass. xlix. p. 411, B. This Lysanias was the son of Ptolemy, son of Mennæus, and seems to have been king of Chalcis and Ituræa, inheriting the former from his father, and receiving the latter from Mark Antony. See the passages above cited.

NOTE CX., p. 200.

Lysanias, the son of Ptolemy, was put to death by Antony, at the instigation of Cleopatra, (Joseph. *Ant. Jud.* xv. 4, § 1, certainly before the year of Rome 719, B. C. 35. (See Dio Cass. l. s. c.)

NOTE CXI., p. 200.

So Strauss, *Leben Jesu*, § 44; vol. i. p. 302, E. T.

NOTE CXII., p. 200.

Ibid. p. 301. "We cannot indeed prove that, had a younger Lysanias existed, Josephus must have mentioned him," &c.

NOTE CXIII., p. 200.

Strauss assumes, without an atom of proof, that Abila (or Abilene) was included in the kingdom of Lysanias, the contemporary of Antony. It is *never* mentioned as a part of his territories. Indeed, as Dr. Lee has remarked,[1] it seems to be pointedly excluded from them. Agrippa the First received "the Abila of Lysanias" from Claudius, at the very time when he relinquished the kingdom of Chalcis, which formed the special territory of the old Lysanias. (Joseph. *De Bell. Jud.* ii. 12, § 8; *Ant. Jud.* xix. 5, § 1.) Thus it would appear that Josephus really intends a different Lysanias from the son of Ptolemy in these two passages. Even, however, if this were not the case, his silence would be no proof that a second Lysanias had not held a tetrarchy in these parts at the time of John's ministry. That Abila formed once a tetrarchy by itself seems implied in the subjoined passage from Pliny — "Tetrarchies, each forming a sort of province, intersect these cities, and bind them together, and these again are united into kingdoms, as the tetrarchy of Trachonitis, of Paneas, of *Abila*," &c. (*H. N.* v. 18, ad fin.)

NOTE CXIV., p. 201.

See above, Notes IV., LXXXIX., and XCIV.

NOTE CXV., p. 201.

Strauss, *Leben Jesu*, § 32; vol. i. p. 301, E. T.

NOTE CXVI., p. 201.

See the *Zeitschrift für geschichtliche Rechtwissenschaft*, vol. vi., quoted by Olshausen in his *Biblischer Commentar*, (vol. i. p. 125; p. 116, E. T.) On the general question, see Alford's *Greek Testament*, vol. i. p. 315.

1 See his *Inspiration of Holy Scripture*, Lecture VIII., p. 403, note 2. I am indebted to my friend, Mr. Mansel, for my knowledge of this excellent work.

NOTE CXVII., p. 201.

Ant. Jud. xviii. 1, § 1. See above, Note CVI.

NOTE CXVIII., p. 201.

Strauss, *Leben Jesu*, § 32, p. 204, E. T.

NOTE CXIX., p. 202.

The following explanations of Luke ii. 2, have been proposed: (1.) It has been proposed to take πρώτη[1] with ἀπογραφή,[2] to regard Κυρηνίου[3] as a genitive dependent on ἀπογραφή,[4] and ἡγεμονεύοντος[5] as equivalent to ἡγεμόνος[6] or ἡγεμονεύσαντος.[7] The passage is then translated, "This was the first assessment of Cyrenius, once governor of Syria." (See Lardner, *Credibility*, vol. i. pp. 173–175.)

(2.) Only slightly different from this is the view of Beza[8] and others, which takes "first" in the same way, but regards ἡγεμονεύοντος Κυρηνίου[9] as a genitive absolute, and renders the verse, "This first assessment was made when Cyrenius was governor of Syria." Both these explanations suppose that Cyrenius made two assessments, one before he was actual President of Syria and one afterwards. The former regards Cyrenius as designated by his *subsequent* title; the latter supposes that he may have been called "governor" when strictly speaking he was not so, but had a certain degree of authority. Two objections lie against both views. 1. The *ordo verborum* does not allow us to take "first" with "taxing." 2. No writer hints at Cyrenius having been twice employed to make a census in Palestine.

(3.) A third explanation is, that πρώτη[10] is for προτέρα,[11] and that the genitive Κυρηνίου[12] depends upon it, the construction used being analogous to that of St. John, ὅτι πρῶτός μου ἦν,[13] (i. 15.) The meaning is, then, "This assessment was made before the time when Cyrenius was governor of Syria." (Lardner, *Credibility*, vol. i. pp. 165–173; Alford, *Greek Testament*, vol. i. p. 314.)

1 First. 2 Taxing, or enrolment. 3 Cyrenius. 4 Taxing.
5 Governing, or being governor. 6 Governor. 7 Having been governor.
8 See Lardner, *Credibility*, vol. i. p. 171, note d.
9 Cyrenius governing, or when Cyrenius was governor. 10 First.
11 Former. 12 Of Cyrenius. 13 For he was before me.

(4.) Finally, it is maintained that ἐγένετο[1] should be regarded as *emphatic* — and that St. Luke means, as I have suggested in the text, that while the enrolment was begun a little before our Lord's birth, it was never *fully executed* until Cyrenius carried it through. Both this and the preceding explanation seem to be allowable — they are compatible with the Hellenistic idiom, and do no violence to history. As Lardner has shown, there is abundant reason to believe that an enrolment was actually set on foot shortly before the death of Herod. (See the *Credibility*, vol. i. pp. 151–159.)

Note CXX., p. 202.

See his *Short View of the Harmony of the Evangelists*, Prop. xi. pp. 145–149.

Note CXXI., p. 202.

Connection of Sacred and Profane History, vol. ii. p. 505.

Note CXXII., p. 202.

Ant. Jud. xviii. 1, § 1. After speaking of Cyrenius as sent from Rome for the express purpose of effecting a census, Josephus adds, "Now Judas, a Gaulonite, of the city named Gamala, taking as his accomplice the Pharisee Sadduc, *rushed into rebellion*, saying that the imposing of the tribute was nothing short of downright slavery, and summoning the people to a struggle for freedom." He then speaks of the success of Judas's efforts, and his formation of a sect, which Josephus puts on a par with those of the Pharisees, the Sadducees, and the Essenes. "Of the fourth of these sects of philosophy, *Judas the Galilæan* became the leader." (Ibid. § 6.)

Note CXXIII., p. 202.

De Bell. Jud. ii. 17, § 8. The followers of Theudas "were scattered and *brought to nought*," (Acts v. 36,) but those of Judas the Galilæan "were dispersed." (Ibid. verse 37.) It is in exact accordance with this distinction that the latter reappear in the Jewish war, while of the former we hear nothing. See Dean Alford's note ad loc.

[1] Was made, or took place.

NOTE CXXIV., p. 202.

Antiq. Jud. xx. 5, § 1.

NOTE CXXV., p. 202.

Ib. xvi. 10, § 4: "But at this time Judæa was agitated by *ten thousand other tumults*, and *many from all quarters* rushed to arms, either in the hope of their own advantage, or out of enmity to the Jews."

NOTE CXXVI., p. 203.

De Bell. Jud. ii. 13, § 5: "But the Egyptian false prophet brought upon the Jews a heavier woe than this. For this impostor came into the country, and persuaded the people that he was a prophet, and assembled about 30,000 misguided men. Leading them about from the wilderness to the mount called the Mount of Olives, he thought he would be able from that position to force an entrance into the city, and having overpowered the Roman garrison, to oppress the people, with the help of the soldiers that would break into the city with him. But Felix, meeting him with his Roman soldiers, anticipated his attack, and all the people joined him in his defensive operations; so that when an engagement took place, the Egyptian fled with a small company, and the *greater part* of those who were with him were either destroyed or captured. But the rest of the multitude were dispersed, and each sought his own home as secretly as possible." Compare *Antiq. Jud.* xx. 8, § 6.

NOTE CXXVII., p. 203.

In the parallel passage of the Antiquities, (l. s. c.,) Josephus says that Felix slew 400 and captured 200 of the Egyptian's followers. If he had really estimated their whole number at 30,000, he would scarcely have said, that "very many (πλεῖστοι) were killed or taken prisoners," when the loss in both ways was no more than 600 men. It has been sagaciously conjectured that the reading τρισμυρίους[1] should be replaced by τετρακισχιλίους,[2] having arisen from the ready confusion of ͵λ[3] with ͵δ,[4] or ͵Λ[3] with ͵Δ.[4] (Lardner, *Credibility*, vol. i. p. 227.)

[1] 30,000. [2] 4,000. [3] The Greek letter which stands for 30,000.
[4] The Greek letter which stands for 4,000.

NOTE CXXVIII., p. 203.

Ant. Jud. xx. 2, § 6. Compare Dio Cassius, lx. pp. 671, 672; Tacit. *Ann.* xii. 43; Sueton. *vit. Claud.* § 18. Eusebius mentions a famine in Greece during the same reign. (*Chronica*, pars. ii. p. 373, Ed. Mai.) Josephus calls the famine in Judæa, to which he refers, "the great famine." (*Ant. Jud.* xx. 5, § 2.)

NOTE CXXIX., p. 204.

Alford, *Greek Testament*, vol. ii. p. 53.

NOTE CXXX., p. 204.

See an article "on the Bible and Josephus," in the *Journal of Sacred Literature* for October, 1850.

NOTE CXXXI., p. 205.

S. Ambrose, *Comment. in Psalm.* cxviii. § 37. (*Opera*, vol. i. p. 1206.)

NOTE CXXXII., p. 205.

Ibid. *Explic. Luc.* x. § 171. (*Opera*, vol. i. p. 1542.)

NOTE CXXXIII., p. 205.

Irenæus, *Advers. Hæres.* iii. 1. (*Opera*, vol. ii. p. 6.)

LECTURE VIII.

NOTE I., p. 207.

Of all our writers on the Evidences, Lardner is the only one who appears to be at all duly impressed with a feeling of the value of *Christian* witnesses. He devotes nearly two volumes to the accumulation of their testimonies. (See his *Credibility*, vols. i. ii. and iii.) Paley does not make any use of Christian writers to prove the facts of Christianity; he only cites them as witnesses to the early existence and repute of our Historical Scriptures. Butler in a general way refers to the evidence of the "first converts," (*Analogy*, part ii. ch. 7, p. 291;) but omits to enlarge on the point. And this is the general spirit of our Apologists.

NOTE II., p. 207.

So Celsus, (ap. Origen. *Contr. Cels.* iii. 44.) Strauss endeavors to diminish the authority of the Apostles, and first preachers of Christianity, by contrasting the darkness of Galilee and Judæa with the enlightenment of "highly civilized Greece and Rome." (*Leben Jesu*, § 13, sub fin.; vol. i. p. 64, E. T.)

NOTE III., p. 208.

Stromata, ii. pp. 464, 489, 490; v. p. 677; vi. p. 770. Clement believes the writer to be the companion of St. Paul. (See *Strom.* ii. p. 489: "I have no need to multiply words, for I have the testimony of the *Apostolic Barnabas*. Now he was one of the seventy, and was a *co-worker with Paul*." He then quotes from the extant Epistle.)

NOTE IV., p. 208.

Contra Celsum, i. § 63; p. 378, B.; *De Princip.* iii. 2, § 4; p. 140, E.

NOTE V., p. 208.

Professor Norton assigns the Epistle of Barnabas to "the middle of the second century," (*Genuineness of the Gospels*, vol. i. p. 347;) but on very insufficient evidence. Lardner gives A. D. 71 or 72 as the probable date of its composition. (*Credibility*, vol. i. p. 285.)

M. Bunsen, while rejecting the view that it was written by the companion of St. Paul, puts its composition "about 15 years before that of the Gospel of St. John," or some time before the close of the first century. (*Hippolytus and his Age*, vol. i. p. 54.)

The genuineness of the Epistle has been well defended by Dr, Lee, who thoroughly exposes the common fallacy, that, if the work of the Apostle, it must have formed a portion of Canonical Scripture. (See his *Lectures on the Inspiration of Holy Scripture*, Appendix E., pp. 472–477.)

NOTE VI., p. 209.

See the subjoined passages — "In fine, by teaching Israel, and *performing such wonders and signs*, and preaching, he showed his great love to Israel. But when he *chose his own Apostles*, to preach his gospel . . . then he showed himself to be the Son of God." (§ 5, p. 15.) "Now the servants who perform this sprinkling, are they who preach to us the remission of sins, and the purification of the heart. For he gave them authority to proclaim the gospel; and they are twelve in number, for a testimony to the tribes; for the tribes of Israel are twelve." (§ 8, p. 25.) "He himself wished to suffer thus . . . for he who prophesied of him said . . . 'Behold, *I have given my back to the scourges, and my cheeks to buffetings.*'" (§ 5, p. 16.) "Then they shall see him in that day, *having* about his body the *scarlet robe reaching down to the feet*, and they shall say, 'Is not this he whom we *set at nought, and crucified*, and pierced, and *mocked?*'" (§ 7, p. 24.) "The Son of God suffered, that his wound might give us life; . . . moreover, when he was crucified, they gave him vinegar and gall to drink." (§ 7, pp. 20, 21.) "And again Moses made a type of Jesus, [showing] that it was necessary that he, whom *they believed to have perished*, should suffer, and should so become the author of life." (§ 12, p. 39.) "What then does the prophet say? 'The assembly of the wicked encompassed me; they surrounded me, as bees around the comb; and they *cast lots upon my raiment.*' Thus were foreshown the sufferings of him who was about to be manifested and to suffer." (§ 6, p. 18.) "Wherefore we spend the eighth day in gladness, on which also Jesus *rose from the dead;* and when he had shown himself, he *ascended to heaven.*" (§ 15, p. 48.)

NOTE VII., p. 209.

Lardner, *Credibility*, vol. i. p. 289, et seqq; Burton, *Eccles. History*, vol. i. pp. 342, 343; Norton, *Genuineness*, &c., vol. i. pp. 336–338; Bunsen, *Hippolytus*, vol. i. pp. 44–47; Jacobson, *Præfat. ad S. Clem. Ep.* p. x.–xvii., prefixed to his *Patres Apostolici.*

NOTE VIII., p. 209.

The following are the passages to which reference is made in the text: "From him (i. e. Jacob) came the Lord Jesus Christ, as to his flesh." (§ 32, p. 114.) "The *sceptre of the majesty of God;* our Lord Jesus Christ came not with noisy boasting and pride, although *he could have done so,* but with humility." (§ 16, pp. 60, 62.) "His *sufferings* were before our eyes." (§ 2, p. 12.) "Especially when we remember the words of the Lord Jesus, which he spake, teaching *gentleness* and *long-suffering.* For thus he spake: 'Be merciful, that ye may receive mercy; forgive, that ye may be forgiven; as ye do, so shall it be done to you; as ye give, so shall it be given to you; as ye judge, so shall ye be judged; as ye show kindness, so shall kindness be shown to you; with what measure ye measure, with the same shall ye be measured.'" (§ 13, p. 52.) "Let us look to *the blood of Christ,* and let us observe how precious to God is his blood, *which was shed for our salvation.*" (§ 7, p. 34.) "For the love which he had to us, our Lord Jesus Christ gave his blood for us, according to the will of God, and his flesh for our flesh, and his soul for our souls." (§ 49, p. 178.) "That there should be a future resurrection, of which he made our Lord Jesus Christ the *first-fruits,* by raising him *from the dead.*" (§ 24, p. 98.) "Now Christ was *sent by God,* and the Apostles by Christ." (§ 42, p. 148.) "With the *full assurance of the Holy Spirit,* the Apostles went forth, preaching that the kingdom of God was about to come. *Preaching thus through many countries and cities,* from the first fruits of their labors, after having proved them by the Spirit, they *appointed bishops and deacons.*" (ibid. pp. 148, 150.) "Through jealousy and envy, the *greatest* and *most just pillars* were persecuted, and came to a violent end. Let us set before our eyes the good apostles. *Peter,* through an unrighteous envy, suffered, not one, nor two, but *many troubles,* and so becoming a martyr at last, he went to the fitting place of glory. Through envy also *Paul* won the reward of patience, *seven times wearing bonds, being compelled to flee, being stoned, becoming a preacher to the East and to the West;* and he gained a noble renown by his faith, *having taught* righteousness to the *whole world;* and having penetrated to the farthest west, he *suffered martyrdom under the emperors,*" &c. (§ 5, pp. 24, 28.)

NOTE IX., p. 209.

Ep. ad Cor. § 47, p. 168: "Take up the Epistle of the blessed Apostle Paul. What did he write to you first, in the very beginning of the gospel. Truly he gave you a spiritual charge concerning himself, and Cephas, and Apollos; for even then ye were given to partialities." Comp. 1 Cor. i. 10–12.

NOTE X., p. 210.

See Burton's *Ecclesiastical History of the First Three Centuries*, vol. i. pp. 197 and 357.

NOTE XI., p. 210.

Ibid. vol. ii. p. 23. Compare Pearson's *Disputatio de Anno quo S. Ignatius a Trajano Antiochiæ ad Bestias erat condemnatus*, (printed in Dr. Jacobson's *Patres Apostolici*,) vol. ii. pp. 524–529. Pearson places the Martyrdom in A. D. 116; M. Bunsen in A. D. 115. (*Hippolytus and his Age*, vol. i. p. 89.)

NOTE XII., p. 210.

Two of these Epistles are addressed to St. John, and the third to the Virgin Mary. They exist in several MSS., and were printed at Paris as early as A. D. 1495. Burton says of them, "Two Epistles to St. John and one to the Virgin Mary, which only exist in Latin, do not deserve even to be mentioned." (*Eccles. Hist.* vol. ii. p. 29, note.) So far as I know, they are not now defended by any one.

NOTE XIII., p. 210.

Lardner, *Credibility*, vol. i. pp. 314, 315; Burton, *Eccles. Hist.* vol. ii. pp. 29, 30; Schröckh, *Christl. Kirch. Geschichte*, vol. ii. p. 341, et seqq.; Neander, *Geschichte der Christl. Religion*, vol. ii. p. 1140; Kiste in Illgen's *Zeitschrift für historische Theologie*, II. ii. pp. 47–90; Jacobson, *Patres Apostolici*, vol. ii. pp. 262–470; Hefele, *Patrum Apostolicorum Opera*, 3d edition, Prolegomena, p. lviii.

NOTE XIV., p. 210.

Euseb. *Hist. Eccles.* iii. 36; Hieronym. *De Viris Illustr.* c. xvi., (*Op.* vol. ii. p. 841, ed. Vallars.) The brief account given in the text of a very complicated matter, requires a few words of elucidation, and perhaps, to some extent, of correction. The twelve Epistles in their *longer* form exist both in Greek and in an ancient Latin version. Eleven Epistles out of the twelve are found in a second Latin version, likewise ancient, which presents numerous important variations from the other, and is in general considerably *shorter*. Of these eleven Epistles, the first seven, and a fragment of the eighth, were found in Greek in the famous Medicean manuscript, which evidently gave the original text of the shorter Latin translation. The seven (complete) Epistles of the Medicean MS. are nearly, but not quite, identical with the seven Epistles mentioned by Eusebius and Jerome. They consist, that is, of six out of the seven (viz., the Epistles to the Ephesians, Magnesians, Trallians, Philadelphians, Smyrnæans, and Polycarp,) together with a letter to a Christian woman, Maria Cassobolita; and there is also in the MS. a fragment of the Epistle to the Tarsians. The Epistle to the Romans, which is placed at the end of the shorter Latin recension, is not in the Medicean MS.; but this is explained by the fact that that MS. is a fragment. As it observes the exact order of the shorter Latin version, and seems to be the text — only somewhat corrupt — from which that version was made, we may conclude, that it contained originally the same eleven letters. Thus we cannot base any argument on the identity of the Eusebian and Medicean Epistles. It is not an exact identity; and the approach to identity is perhaps an accident.

NOTE XV., p. 210.

See Dr. Cureton's *Corpus Ignatianum*, Introduction, pp. xxxiv.–lxxxvii.; Bunsen, *Hippolytus and his Age*, vol. i. pp. 98–103.

NOTE XVI., p. 211.

See Dr. Jacobson's Preface to the third edition of his *Patres Apostolici*, p. liv.; Hefele's *Prolegomena*, l. s. c.; Professor Hussey's *University Sermons*, Preface, pp. xiii.–xxxix.; Uhlhorn in Niedner's *Zeitschrift für historische Theologie*, xv. p. 247, et seqq., and Canon Wordsworth in the *English Review*, No. viii. p. 309, et seqq. The shorter Greek Recension is also regarded as genuine by the present Regius Professor of Hebrew in the University of Oxford.

NOTE XVII., p. 211.

The subjoined are the most important of the Ignatian testimonies to the facts of Christianity: "Come together in one faith, even in Jesus

Christ, who was of the family of *David* according to the flesh, the Son of man and Son of God." (*Ep. ad Eph.* xx. p. 302.) "For Jesus Christ our God *was born of Mary*, according to the appointment of God, of the seed of David, but *by the Holy Spirit.* He was born, and *was baptized,*" &c. &c. (Ibid. xviii. pp. 296–298.) "Three notable mysteries were kept secret from the prince of this world, the virginity of Mary, and the birth and death of the Lord." (Ibid. xix. p. 298.) "How then was he manifested to the ages? *A star shone in heaven, brighter than all the other stars*, and its lustre was indescribable, and the novelty of its appearance caused great wonder." (Ibid. xix. p. 300.) "Our Lord . . . was truly born of a virgin, *baptized by John, that all righteousness might be fulfilled by him*, and was truly *nailed to the cross* in the flesh for us, *under Pontius Pilate and Herod the tetrarch.*" (*Ep. ad Smyrn.* i. p. 416.) "We love the prophets also, because they too announced gospel tidings, and hoped in him, and waited for him; in whom also they believed, and were saved in the unity of Jesus Christ, being holy men, and worthy of love and admiration, to *whom also Jesus Christ bore testimony.*" (*Ep. ad Philadelph.* v. pp. 394–396.) "On this account *the Lord received the ointment upon his head*, that he might breathe upon his church the odor of immortality." (*Ep. ad Ephes.* xvii. p. 296.) "He suffered truly, as he also *truly raised himself from the dead.*" (*Ep. ad Smyrn.* ii. p. 418.) "We no longer keep the Sabbath, but we live a new life *on the Lord's day, on which also our life arose* with him." (*Ep. ad Magnes.* ix. p. 324.) "The prophets looked for him as their teacher: and therefore he whom they justly expected, *when he came*, raised them from the dead." (Ibid. l. s. c.) "For I saw him in the flesh even after his resurrection, and I believe that he still exists. And *when he came to Peter and his companions, he said to them*, '*Take*, and *handle me*, and see that I am not a bodiless spirit.' And *immediately they touched him*, and believed." (*Ep. ad Smyrn.* iii. p. 420.) "Now after his resurrection *he ate with them and drank with them*, as one in the flesh." (Ibid. l. s. c.) "Submit yourselves to the bishop and to one another, as Jesus Christ to the Father, in his human nature, and as *the Apostles to Christ* and to the Father and to the Spirit." (*Ep. ad Magnes.* xiii. p. 328.) "It is necessary therefore to submit to the company of presbyters, *as to the Apostles.*" (*Ep. ad Trall.* ii. p. 334.) "Not *as Peter and Paul do* I command you: *they were Apostles*, I am a man under sentence." (*Ep. ad Rom.* iv. p. 368.)

NOTE XVIII., p. 211.

See Dr. Cureton's *Corpus Ignatianum*, pp. 227–231; and M. Bunsen's *Hippolytus*, vol. i. pp. 92–98.

NOTE XIX., p. 212.

See Jacobson's *Patres Apostolici*, vol. ii. pp. 484–512. This work is admitted to be genuine, even by M. Bunsen. (*Hippolytus*, vol. i. pp. 223–227.)

NOTE XX., p. 212.

See especially the following passages: "Servants . . . walking according to the truth of the Lord, *who became the servant of all.*" (§ 5, p. 494.) "We remember also what the Lord said *in his teaching*, '*Judge not, that ye be not judged: forgive and it shall be forgiven you:* be merciful, and ye shall receive mercy: with what measure ye measure, it shall be measured back to you:' and, 'blessed are the poor, and they who are persecuted for righteousness' sake, for theirs is the kingdom of God.'" (§ 2, pp. 488–490.) "Christ Jesus, who *bore our sins in his own body on the tree;* who did no sin, neither was guile found in his mouth; but he *endured all* for us, that we might live through him." (§ 8, p. 502.) "Whosoever shall not confess the testimony of *the cross*, is of the devil." (§ 7, p. 500.) "Our Lord Jesus Christ, who endured to be brought *even to death* for our sins; whom *God raised*, loosing the pains of Hades." (§ 1, p. 486.) "We believe in Him who raised our Lord Jesus Christ from the dead, and *gave him glory*, and *a throne at his right hand.*" (§ 2, p. 486.) "Whom (i. e. the Lord) if we shall please in this present world, we shall receive also the future world, as *he promised us, that he would raise us from the dead.*" (§ 5, p. 496.) "I beseech you all therefore . . . to exercise *all patience, which also ye see exemplified before your eyes*, not only in the blessed Ignatius, Zosimus, and Rufus, but also in others among you, and in *Paul himself*, and *the rest of the Apostles*. For ye may be assured that none of these ran in vain, but that they are all in the place that is fitting for them, with the Lord, *for whom also they suffered.*" (§ 9, pp. 502–504.) "The blessed and illustrious Paul, who *visited in person* the men that then lived *among you*, and *taught* the word of truth in a correct and certain manner, and also, *when he was absent, wrote you a letter*," &c. (§ 3, p. 490.)

Note XXI., p. 212.

See the Epistle of Irenæus to Florinus, preserved in Eusebius's *Ecclesiastical History*, (v. 20; vol. i. pp. 359, 360:) — "The lessons of childhood are incorporated with the mind, and grow with its growth, so that I can tell even the very place where the blessed Polycarp used to sit and discourse, and his going out and coming in, and the nature of his life, and the appearance of his person, and the discourses which he delivered to the multitude, and how he related *his intercourse with John*, and with the *rest of those who had seen the Lord*, and how he remembered their words, and what he had heard from them concerning the Lord, and *concerning his miracles*; — how Polycarp declared *all these things* in a *manner agreeable to the Scriptures*, as he had received them from those who were eye witnesses of the word of life."

Note XXII., p. 212.

Euseb. *Hist. Eccles.* iii. 3; vol. i. p. 147; Hieronym. *De Viris Illustr.* x. p. 831, ed. Vallars. Compare Origen. *ad Rom.* xvi. 13.

Note XXIII., p. 212.

See the "Canon" published by Muratori in his *Antiquitates Italiæ Medii Ævi*,[1] where the writer (Hegesippus?) says, that "the book of the Shepherd was written very lately, in our own times, by Hermas, while his brother Pius presided over the Roman Church as bishop." And compare Burton, *Eccles. Hist.* vol. ii. p. 104; Alford, *Greek Testament*, vol. ii. p. 441; Bunsen, *Hippolytus*, vol. i. p. 184; and Norton, *Genuineness of the Gospels*, vol. i. pp. 341, 342.

Note XXIV., p. 212.

Hermas mentions the mission of the Apostles — "Such are they who believed the apostles, *whom God sent into all the world to preach*." (*Past.* iii. 9, § 25, p. 122.) Their travels throughout the world — "These twelve mountains which you see are twelve nations which occupy the whole earth. The Son of God therefore is preached among them, *by*

[1] Vol. iii. pp. 853, 854.

those whom he sent to them." (Ibid. § 17, p. 120.) Their sufferings are indicated in the following passage: "I said to him, 'Sir, I wish to know what they have endured.' 'Hear, then,' he said — '*wild beasts, scourges, prisons, crosses*, for the sake of his name.'" (Ibid. i. 3, § 2, p. 78.)

NOTE XXV., p. 213.

See Burton's *Eccles. Hist.*, vol. ii. p. 73 and p. 496.

NOTE XXVI., p. 213.

Ap. Euseb. *Hist. Eccles.* iv. 3; vol. i. p. 230: "Now the works of our Saviour were always conspicuous; for they were real. They who were healed, and they who were raised from the dead, were seen not only when they were healed, and when they were raised, but they were always visible afterwards; not only while the Saviour sojourned among us, but also after he departed, and for a long time, insomuch that some of them have reached even to our own times."

NOTE XXVII., p. 213.

Burton, *Eccles. Hist.* vol. ii. p. 111; Norton (*Genuineness of the Gospels*, vol. i. p. 126) says A. D. 150. So the Benedictine Editors. Bunsen and others date it eleven years earlier, A. D. 139. (See *Hippolytus and his Age*, vol. i. p. 216. Compare Bishop Kaye, *Account of the Writings and Opinions of Justin Martyr*, pp. 11, 12; who, however, declines to decide between the earlier and the later date.)

NOTE XXVIII., p. 213.

Burton, *E. H.*, vol. ii. pp. 128, 129. According to its title, the second Apology was addressed to the Senate only, (to the Senate of the Romans;) but it contains expressions which imply that it was addressed to an emperor, and Eusebius tells us that it was actually offered to M. Aurelius.

NOTE XXIX., p. 213.

Kaye, *Writings and Opinions of Justin Martyr*, ch. i. p. 3.

Note XXX., p. 213.

Paley, *Evidences*, part i. ch. vii. p. 75. Professor Norton remarks, "From these works of Justin might be extracted a brief account of the life and doctrine of Christ, corresponding with that contained in the Gospels, and corresponding to such a degree, both in matter and words, that almost every quotation and reference may be readily assigned to its proper place in one or other of the Gospels."

Note XXXI., p. 215.

The following are among the most important of Justin's testimonies: —

1. "Now Joseph, who was espoused to Mary, wished at first to put away his betrothed, thinking that she had become pregnant by intercourse with a man, that is to say, by fornication. But he was commanded in a dream not to put away his wife; and the angel who appeared to him told him, that what she had conceived was by the Holy Ghost. Struck with awe, therefore, he did not put her away; but when there was an enrolment in Judæa, which then took place for the first time under Cyrenius, he went up from Nazareth, where he dwelt, to Bethlehem, whence his family originated, in order to be enrolled; for his family was of the tribe of Juda, which inhabited that part of the land. And he, together with Mary, was commanded to go forth into Egypt, and to be there with the child, until they should receive divine direction to return to Judæa. Now the child was born at that time in Bethlehem, and since Joseph had not any place to lodge in that village, he lodged in a certain cave, in the neighborhood of the village. Thus, then, it happened, while they were in that place, that Mary brought forth Christ, and put him in a manger; where the Magi from Arabia found him when they came; . . . and when the Magi from Arabia did not return to Herod, as he had requested them to do, but departed into their own country another way, as they were commanded, and when Joseph, with Mary and the child, had already gone into Egypt, as they were divinely directed, Herod, not knowing the child which the Magi had come to worship, commanded the children in Bethlehem to be destroyed without distinction." (*Dialog. cum Tryphon.* § 78, p. 175.)

2. "It was necessary that [the sacrifices] should cease, according to the will of the Father, at the coming of his Son Jesus Christ, who was born of a virgin of the race of Abraham, and the tribe of Judah, and the family of David." (Ibid. § 43, p. 139.)

3. "The power of God came upon and overshadowed the virgin, and caused her, though a virgin, to conceive; and the angel of God, who was sent to this virgin at that time, announced to her glad tidings, saying, 'Behold, thou shalt conceive in thy womb by the Holy Ghost, and shalt bring forth a son, and he shall be called the Son of the Most High, and thou shalt call his name Jesus; for he shall save his people from their sins." (*Apolog.* i. § 13, p. 64.)

4. "Then said Trypho, 'So you grant to us, that he was circumcised, and observed the other rites enjoined by Moses.' I answered, 'I have granted it, and I grant it now.'" (*Dial. cum Tryphon.* § 67, p. 164.)

5. "Now this king Herod inquired of the elders of your people, when the Magi from Arabia came to him, and said 'We have learned, from a star that has appeared in heaven, that a king has been born in your country, and we have come to worship him.' Then the elders said that it should take place in Bethlehem, because it is thus written in the prophet: 'And thou, Bethlehem,' &c. Now when the Magi from Arabia came to Bethlehem, and had worshipped the child, and offered him gifts, gold, and frankincense, and myrrh, inasmuch as by a revelation from heaven . . . they were commanded not to return to Herod," &c. (Ibid. § 78, pp. 174, 175.)

6. "And there (i. e. in Egypt) [Joseph and Mary] remained in exile, until Herod, who slew the children in Bethlehem, had died, and Archelaus had succeeded him." (Ibid. § 103, p. 198.)

7. "Now that the Christ, who was born, should be unknown to other men until he should be grown, as it actually happened, hear what was foretold on this point." (*Apolog.* i. § 35, p. 65.)

8. "Jesus, when he came to Jordan, was supposed to be the son of Joseph the carpenter, and was regarded as a carpenter, for he performed the works of a carpenter when he was among men, making ploughs, and yokes," &c. (*Dial. cum Tryphon.* § 88, p. 186.)

9. "And then, when Jesus came to the river Jordan, where John was baptizing, Jesus went down into the water, and a fire was kindled in the Jordan, and as he came up out of the water, his apostles have testified in writing, that the Holy Spirit, in the form of a dove, lighted upon him." (Ibid. § 88, pp. 185, 186.)

10. "For while John was making his abode on the banks of the Jordan, and preaching the baptism of repentance, wearing only a leathern girdle and a garment of camel's hair, and eating nothing but locusts and wild honey, men suspected that he was the Christ. But he cried out to them, 'I am not the Christ, but the voice of one crying; for he that is mightier than I will come, whose shoes I am not worthy to bear.'" (Ibid. l. s. c. p. 186.)

11. "Now when [Christ] became a man, the devil came to him, that is to say, that power which is called the Serpent and Satan, tempting him, and striving to cause him to fall, by demanding that he should worship him. But on the contrary he was himself destroyed and cast down, for Jesus proved him to be wicked, in demanding, contrary to the Scriptures, to be worshipped as God, whereas he was an apostate from the will of God. For he answered him, 'It is written, Thou shalt worship the Lord thy God, and him only shalt thou serve.'" (Ibid. § 125, p. 218.)

12. "Now that it was foretold of our Christ that he should heal all diseases, and raise the dead, hear the words that were spoken. They were these: 'At his coming the lame shall leap as a hart, and the tongue of the stammerers shall speak plainly: the blind shall see, and the lepers shall be cleansed, and the dead shall be raised, and walk.' Now that he did these things, you can learn from the acts that were drawn up under Pontius Pilate." (*Apolog.* i. § 48, p. 72.)

13. "And from these things we know that Jesus had foreknowledge of what was to be after him, and also from many other things which he foretold as about to occur to those who believed on him, and confessed him to be the Christ. For even what we suffer, in having all things taken from us by our kindred, this he foretold as about to come upon us, so that in no respect does there appear to be any failure in his word." (*Dial. cum Tryphon.* § 35, p. 133.)

14. "For Christ the Son of God, knowing by revelation from his Father, one of his disciples formerly called Simon, gave him the name of Peter." (Ibid. § 100, p. 195.)

15. "For his changing the name of Peter, one of the Apostles, . . . as well as his changing the names of two other brothers, who were sons of Zebedee, and whom he called 'Boanerges,' which means 'sons of thunder, was a significant intimation that he was the Messiah." (Ibid. § 106, p. 201.)

16. "A certain foal of an ass was standing at the entrance of a village, tied to a vine. This he commanded his friends to bring to him at that time; and when it was brought he sat upon it, and came into Jerusalem." (*Apolog.* i. § 32, p. 63.)

17. "The apostles, in the Memoirs composed by them, which are called Gospels, have reported to us that Jesus enjoined this upon them. Taking bread, he gave thanks, and said, 'This do in remembrance of me: this is my body;' and taking the cup likewise, he gave thanks, and said, 'This is my blood.' And he distributed these to them only." (Ibid. § 66, p. 83.)

18. "On the day on which he was about to be crucified, taking three of his disciples to the mount called the Mount of Olives, which lies near to the temple in Jerusalem, he prayed, saying, 'Father, if it be possible, let this cup pass from me.' And after this he said in his prayer, 'Not as I will, but as thou wilt.'" (*Dial. cum Tryphon.* § 99, p. 194.)

19. "The power of this same mighty word . . . had a suspension; . . . for he was silent, and did not wish to answer any one a word, when he was examined before Pontius Pilate." (Ibid. § 102, p. 197.)

20. "Now Herod succeeded Archelaus, and assumed the authority that was conferred upon him. To him Pilate, in order to do him a favor, sent Jesus bound," &c. (Ibid. § 103, p. 198; compare *Apolog.* i. § 40, p. 67, C.)

21. "Now Jesus Christ, when he was crucified by the Jews, had his hands extended, . . . as said the prophet, . . . 'They pierced my hands and my feet,' referring to the nails by which his hands and his feet were fastened to the cross. And after he was crucified, they cast lots upon his raiment." (Ibid. § 35, p. 65; compare § 38, p. 66.)

22. "After he was crucified, and all his friends had forsaken and denied him, — after that, having risen from the dead, and being seen by them, he taught them to study the prophecies, in which it was foretold that all these things should come to pass; and when they had seen him ascend to heaven, and believed, and had received from thence the power which he sent upon them, they went to men of every race, and taught these things, and were called Apostles." (Ibid. § 50, p. 73.)

23. "And when he yielded up his spirit on the cross, he said, 'Father, into thy hands I commit my spirit.'" (*Dial. cum Tryphon.* § 105, p. 300.)

24. "For the Lord remained upon the tree almost until the evening; and towards evening they buried him: afterwards he arose, on the third day." (Ibid. § 97, p. 193.)

25. "For there is no race of men whatever, whether barbarians or Greeks, or by whatsoever other name they may be called, whether living in wagons, or houseless wanderers, among whom there are not offered prayers and thanksgivings to the Father and Maker of all, through the name of the crucified Jesus." (Ibid. § 117, p. 211.)

Note XXXII., p. 215.

See pages 204 and 205.

Note XXXIII., p. 216.

See especially Baur, in the *Tübinger Zeitschrift für Theologie*, 1836, fasc. iii. p. 199; 1838, fasc. iii. p. 149; and in a pamphlet *Ueber den Ursprung des Episcopats*, Tübingen, 1838, pp. 148–185. Also compare his work, *Die Ignatianischen Briefen und ihr neuester Kritiker, eine Streitschrift gegen Hernn Bunsen*, 8vo., Tübingen, 1848. Schwegler and others have followed in the same track.

Note XXXIV., p. 216.

I refer especially to the labors of Signor Marchi and Mons. Perret — the former in his *Monumenti delle Arte Cristiane Primitive nella Metropoli del Cristianesimo*, (4to, Rome, 1844,) the latter in his magnificent work, *Les Catacombes de Rome*, (6 volumes, folio, Paris, 1852–1857.) In our own country two useful little works have appeared on the subject — Dr. Maitland's *Church in the Catacombs*, (London, 1847,) and Mr. Spencer Northcote's *Roman Catacombs*, (London, 1857.) An able Article in the *Edinburgh Review* for January, 1859, (Art. iv.,) — to which I must here express myself as under considerable obligations — has made the general public familiar with the chief conclusions established by modern inquiry.

Note XXXV., p. 217.

See Bishop Burnet's *Letters from Italy and Switzerland in* 1685 *and* 1686, (Rotterdam, 1687,) pp. 209–211.

NOTE XXXVI., p. 218.

Spencer Northcote, *Roman Catacombs*, p. 4.

NOTE XXXVII., p. 218.

See Note IV. on Lecture VII., p. 383.

NOTE XXXVIII., p. 218.

Edinburgh Review No. 221, p. 106.

NOTE XXXIX., p. 218.

The grounds upon which Mr. Spencer Northcote bases his calculation are these: 1. The incidental notices in the old missals and office books of the Roman church, and the descriptions given by ancient writers, mention no less than *sixty* different Catacombs on the different sides of Rome, bordering her fifteen great consular roads. Of these about one third have been reopened, but in only one case has there been any accurate measurement. Father Marchi has carefully measured a portion of the Catacomb of St. Agnes, which he calculates at one-eighth of the entire cemetery, and has found the length of all its streets and passages to be about two English miles. This gives a length of 16 miles to the St. Agnes' Catacomb; and as that is (apparently) an average one — certainly smaller than some as well as larger than some — the 60 Catacombs would contain above 900 (960) miles of streets. 2. The height of the passages varies in the Catacombs, and the layers of graves are sometimes more, sometimes less numerous, occasionally not above three or four, in places thirteen or fourteen. There are also interruptions to the regular succession of tombs from the occurrence of chapels, and monuments of some pretension, (*arcosolia.*) Allowing for these, it is suggested that we may take an average of ten graves, five on each side, to every seven feet of street; and this calculation it is, which, applied to the 900 miles of street, produces the result of nearly seven millions of graves.

NOTE XL., p. 219.

Perret, *Catacombes de Rome*, vol. vi. p. 101, et seqq.; Spencer Northcote, *Roman Catacombs*, pp. 29, 30. For arguments to the contrary, see Maitland's *Church in the Catacombs*, pp. 142–151.

NOTE XLI., p. 219.

Thus we find such inscriptions as the following : — "In the time of the Emperor Adrian, the young man Marius, a general in the army, who lived long enough, since he sacrificed his life for Christ by a bloody death, rested at last in peace; and was buried with merited tears and respect." (Maitland, p. 128.) And, "The wave of death has not dared to deprive Constans of the crown to which he was entitled by giving his life to the sword." (Ibid. p. 129.) And again,

ΘΗCΓωΡΔΗΑΝΥCΓΑΛΛΗΕΝΥΝCΗΥC
ΗΥΓΥΛΑΤΥCΠΡωΦΗΔΕCΥΜΦΑΜΗΛ
ΗΑΓωΤΑQΥΗΕCCΥΝΤΗΝΠΑΚΕ
ΓΕωΦΗΛΑΑΝCΗΛΛΑΦΕCΗΤ

which may be thus explained —

θηc Γωρδηανυς Γαλληε νυνcηυς
ηυγυλατυς πρω φηδε cυμ φαμηλ-
ηα τωτα qυηεσcυντ ην πακε
Τεωφηλα ανcηλλα φεcητ.

Hic Gordianus, Galliæ nuncius,
Jugulatus pro fide, cum famil-
ia tota, quiescunt in pace.
Theophila ancilla fecit.[1] (Perret, vol. vi. p. 152.)

NOTE XLII., p. 219.

The entire inscription runs as follows : — "Alexander is not dead, but lives above the stars, and his body rests in this tomb. He ended his life under the Emperor Antoninus, who, when he saw himself much surpassed in conferring benefits, returned hatred for kindness. For when he was bending the knee to offer the sacrifice of prayer to the true God, he was led away to punishment. O what times!" See Dr. Maitland's *Church in the Catacombs*, pp. 32, 33.

NOTE XLIII., p. 220.

"Dormit,"[2] "quiescit,"[3] "depositus est,"[4] are the terms used; and

1 Here Gordian, the courier from Gaul, strangled for the faith, with his whole family, rests in peace. The maid-servant Theophila erected this.

2 He sleeps. 3 He rests. 4 He is laid away.

from the same idea burial-places are called by the name which has since become common in Christian lands, viz., κοιμητήρια, "cemeteries" or "sleeping-places." See Marchi's *Monumenti delle Arte Cristiani Primitive*, &c., p. 63; Spencer Northcote, *Catacombs*, p. 162. "*In pace*" occurs, either at the beginning or at the end of an inscription, almost as a necessary formula.

NOTE XLIV., p. 220.

Northcote's *Catacombs*, p. 163. The contrast in this respect between Christian and Heathen monuments of the same date is very striking. See Maitland's *Church in the Catacombs*, pp. 42, 43.

NOTE XLV., p. 220.

Northcote's *Catacombs*, pp. 50–64. Compare M. Perret's splendid work, *Les Catacombes de Rome*, where these subjects are (almost without exception) represented. The subjoined are the most important references. Temptation of Eve, (vol. iv. Pl. 31; v. Pl. 12;) Moses striking the Rock, (vol. i. Pl. 34, 57; ii. Pl. 22, 27, 33; iii. Pl. 2, 6; iv. Pl. 28;) Noah welcoming the Dove, (vol. ii. Pl. 53, 61; iv. Pl. 25, &c.;) Daniel among the Lions, (vol. ii. Pl. 42, 61; iii. Pl. 7, 36;) the Three Children, (vol. ii. Pl. 36, 39; iii. 7;) Jonah under the Gourd, (vol. i. Pl. 67; vol. ii. Pl. 22, 28, 39; vol. iii. Pl. 2, 5, &c.;) Jonah and the Whale, (vol. iii. 16, 22; vol. v. Pl. 40, 57;) Adoration of the Magi, (vol. v. Pl. 12;) Magi before Herod, (vol. ii. Pl. 48;) Baptism of Christ by John, (vol. iii. Pl. 52, 55;) Cure of the Paralytic, (vol. ii. Pl. 34, 48;) Turning of Water into Wine, (vol. iv. Pl. 28, No. 67;) Feeding of the Five Thousand, (vol. i. Pl. 27; iv. Pl. 29, No. 73;) Raising of Lazarus, (vol. i. Pl. 26; vol. ii. Pl. 61; vol. iii. Pl. 7, 36; vol. iv. Pl. 25, 31, 32; vol. v. Pl. 13, &c.;) Last Supper, (vol. i. Pl. 29;) Peter walking on the Sea, (vol. iv. Pl. 16, No. 85;) Pilate washing his Hands, (Maitland, p. 260.) To the historical subjects mentioned in the text may be added the following: — The Nativity, (Perret, vol. iv. Pl. 16, No. 84;) the Conversation with the Woman of Samaria, (ibid. vol. i. Pl. 81;) and the Crucifixion, (ibid. vol. i. Pl. 10; vol. iv. Pl. 33, No. 103.) The only unhistorical scenes represented, besides the parabolic ones, are Tobias and the Angel, (Perret, vol. iii. Pl. 26,) and Orpheus charming the Beasts, which is frequent.

NOTE XLVI., p. 221.

Tacit. *Annal.* ii. 39, 40; Suet. *vit. Tib.* § 25; Dio Cass. lvii. p. 613, C. Tacitus indeed says, in speaking of the claim made by Clemens, "credebatur Romæ;" but it was a faint belief, which Tiberius thought of allowing to die away of itself. And though his constitutional timidity prevented him from taking this course, he showed his sense of the numerical weakness of the dupes, by bringing Clemens to Rome, when he might have had him assassinated at Ostia. Nor did his execution cause any tumult, either at Rome or in the provinces.

NOTE XLVII., p. 222.

Norton's *Genuineness of the Gospels*, vol. i. p. 100.

NOTE XLVIII., p. 223.

Martyr. Ignat. § 3, p. 542: "The cities and churches of Asia received the saint, by their bishops, and presbyters, and deacons; and they all crowded around him, that *they might if possible obtain some portion of spiritual gifts.*"

NOTE XLIX., p. 223.

So Eusebius, who had the works of Papias before him, relates. *Hist. Eccles.* iii. 39, p. 224. "[Papias] relates that *a dead man was raised in his time*, and moreover that another wonderful thing occurred to Justus, who was surnamed Barsabas, namely, that he drank a deadly poison, and suffered no unpleasant effects, on account of the grace of the Lord."

NOTE L., p. 223.

Dialog. cum Tryphon. § 88, p. 185: "Among us also you may see both males and females possessing gifts from the Spirit of God." (Compare *Apolog.* ii. § 6, p. 93.) "For many of our Christian people, exorcising in the name of Jesus Christ, who was crucified under Pontius Pilate, have cured, and are even now curing, many demoniacs in your own city and in all parts of the world, though these persons could not be cured by all other exorcists, and enchanters and sorcerers. But ours have overcome and driven out the demons that possessed these men." See also *Tryphon.* § 39, p. 136; § 76, p. 173, and § 85, p. 182.

NOTE LI., p. 223.

Miltiades ap. Euseb. *Hist. Eccles.* v. 17, pp. 351, 352.

NOTE LII., p. 223.

Adversus Hæreses, ii. 32, § 4, (vol. i. pp. 374, 375:) "On this account also his true disciples, receiving grace from him, perform miracles in his name for the benefit of men, as each of them has received the gift from him. For some truly and really expel demons; . . . and others have foreknowledge of the future, and visions, and prophetic utterances. Others heal the sick and make them well, by the imposition of their hands. And even now, as we have said, the dead have also been raised, and have remained with us many years." And v. 6, (vol. ii. p. 334:) "As also we have many brethren in the church having prophetic gifts, and speaking in all foreign tongues, and bringing to light the secrets of men, for a good purpose."

NOTE LIII., p. 223.

See Tertullian, *Apolog.* § 23; Theophilus, *Ad Autolyc.* ii. 8, p. 254, C. D.; Minucius Felix, *Octav.* p. 89. These passages affirm the continuance of the power of casting out devils to the time of the writers. On the general question of the cessation of miracles, Burton's remark (*E. H.*, vol. ii. p. 233) seems just, that "their actual cessation was imperceptible, and like the rays in a summer's evening, which, when the sun has set, may be seen to linger on the top of a mountain, though they have ceased to fall on the level country beneath."

NOTE LIV., p. 224.

The vast number of the Christians is strongly asserted by Tertullian, *Apolog.* § 37: "We are of yesterday, and yet we fill all your places, your cities, islands, castles, towns, courts, your very camps, your tribes, your decuriæ, your palace, your senate, your markets. We have left you only your temples. What wars we might wage, and with what energy, even against superior forces, we who are so willing to be slain, if it was not a part of our discipline, that it is better to be killed than to kill! We might also, unarmed and without making any rebellion, but only disagreeing with you, contend against you with the hostility of separation only. For if so great a multitude of men as we are should suddenly separate from you, and retire to some distant quarter of the earth, truly the loss of so many and such citizens would undermine your dominion: yes, it would even inflict upon you an absolute desolation. Without doubt you would be dismayed at your solitude, at the general stillness, and the dulness as if of a dead world. You would look about for some to command; you would have more enemies left than citizens: but now you have few enemies, in comparison with the multitude of Christians." See also Justin Martyr, *Dialog. cum Tryphon.* § 117, (pp. 210 211,) quoted in note 31, § 25, p. 528

Note LV., p. 227.

The attempts of Strauss to prove variations in the story — irreconcilable differences between the accounts of the different Evangelists — appear to me to have failed signally. See above, Note XXXIII. on Lecture VI., p. 378.

Note LVI., p. 228.

Strauss himself admits this difference to a certain extent, (*Leben Jesu*, Einleitung, § 14; vol. i. p. 67, E. T.,) and grants that the Scripture miracles are favorably distinguished by it from the marvels of Indian or Grecian fables; but he finds in the histories of Balaam, Joshua, (!) and Samson, a similar, though less glaring, impropriety. Certainly the speaking of the ass is a thing *sui generis* in Scripture, and would be grotesque, were it not redeemed by the beauty of the words uttered, and the important warning which they contain — a warning still only too much needed — against our cruel and unsympathetic treatment of the brute creation.

Note LVII., p. 228.

Strauss, *Leben Jesu*, § 144; vol. iii. p. 396, E. T. The entire passage has been given in Note XXVI. on Lecture I.

ADDITIONAL NOTE TO LECTURE V.

On the Identification of the Belshazzar of Daniel with Bil-shar-uzur son of Nabu-nahit.

Since the foregoing sheets were in type, my attention has been called by an anonymous correspondent to a difficulty in the proposed identification of Belshazzar with *Bil-shar-uzur*, son of *Nabu-nahit*, arising from his probable age at the time of the siege of Babylon. If *Nabu-nahit*, (Nabonadius,) as suggested in the text,[1] married a daughter of Nebuchadnezzar *after* his accession to the throne, as he only reigned *seventeen* years in all, *Bil-shar-uzur*, supposing him the son of this wife, could have been no more than sixteen years of age when left to administer affairs at Babylon. This, it is said, is too early an age for him to have taken the chief command, and to have given a great feast to "his princes, his *wives*, and his *concubines*."[2] The difficulty here started does not appear to me very great. In the East manhood is attained far earlier than in the West,[3] and husbands of fourteen or fifteen years of age are not uncommon. Important commands are also not unfrequently intrusted to princes of no greater age; as may be seen by the instances of Herod the Great, who was made governor of Galilee by his father at fifteen;[4] of Alexander Severus, who became Emperor of Rome at seventeen;[5] and of many others. There is thus nothing unusual in the possession of regal dignity, and an establishment of wives, on the part of an Oriental prince in his sixteenth or seventeenth year. If Nabonadius married a daughter of Nebuchadnezzar as soon as he came to the throne, and had a son born within the year, he may have associated him

1 Page 171.

2 Dan. v. 2.

3 "He had now become a *man*," says Mr. Layard of a young Bedouin, "for he was about *fourteen* years old." (*Nineveh and Babylon*, p. 295.)

4 Joseph. *Ant. Jud.* xiv. 9, § 2.

5 Gibbon, *Decline and Fall*, ch. vi. vol. i. p. 182.

in the government when he was fourteen, which would have been in his own fifteenth year. This youth would then, in the seventeenth and last year of his father's reign, have entered on the third year of his own joint rule, as we find recorded of Belshazzar in Daniel.[1]

Another way of meeting the difficulty has been suggested. Nabonadius, it is said, may have been married to a daughter of Nebuchadnezzar *before* he obtained the crown. It is only an inference of Abydenus, and not a statement of Berosus, that he was entirely unconnected with Laborosoarchod. This is undoubtedly true. But the inference, which Abydenus drew from the text of Berosus, seems to me a legitimate one. Berosus, who has just noticed the relationship of Neriglissar to the son of Nebuchadnezzar, whom he supplanted, would scarcely have failed to notice that of Nabonadius to his grandson, if he had known of any relationship existing. At any rate he would not have called the new king, as he does, "a certain Nabonnedus of Babylon," (Ναβοννέδῳ τινὶ τῶν ἐκ Βαβυλῶνος,) had he been the uncle of the preceding monarch.

My attention has been further drawn to a very remarkable illustration which the discovery of Belshazzar's position as joint ruler with his father furnishes to an expression twice repeated in Daniel's fifth chapter. The promise made[2] and performed[3] to Daniel is, that he shall be the "*third* ruler" in the kingdom. Formerly it was impossible to explain this, or to understand why he was not the *second* ruler, as he seems to have been under Nebuchadnezzar,[4] and as Joseph was in Egypt,[5] and Mordecai in Persia.[6] It now appears, that, as there were two kings at the time, Belshazzar, in elevating Daniel to the highest position tenable by a subject, could only make him the *third* personage in the Empire. This incidental confirmation of what was otherwise highly probable, is a most valuable and weighty evidence.

1 Dan. viii. 1. 2 Verse 16. 3 Verse 29.
4 Dan. ii. 28. 5 Gen. xli. 41-43. 6 Esth. x. 3.

INDEX OF AUTHORS,

AND A

SPECIFICATION OF THE EDITIONS QUOTED OR REFERRED TO IN THE FOREGOING NOTES.

A.

B.

C.

D.

E.

F.

G.

H.

I. J.

K.

L.

M.

N.

R.

S.

T.

V.

W.

X.

THE END.

Gould and Lincoln's Publications.

THE HARVEST AND THE REAPERS. Home Work for all, and how to do it. By Rev. HARVEY NEWCOMB. 16mo, cloth. 63 cents.

FIRST THINGS; or, the Development of Christian Life. By BARON STOW, D. D. 16mo, cloth. 60 cents.

CHRISTIAN BROTHERHOOD. By B. STOW, D. D. 16mo, cloth. 50 cts.

LIMITS OF RELIGIOUS THOUGHT EXAMINED. By HENRY L. MANSEL, B.D. NOTES translated for American edition. 12mo, cloth. $1.00.

THE CRUCIBLE; or, Tests of a Regenerate State. By Rev. J. A. GOODHUE. Introduction by Dr. KIRK. 12mo, cloth. $1.00.

LEADERS OF THE REFORMATION. Luther — Calvin — Latimer — Knox. By JOHN TULLOCH, D. D 12mo, cloth. $1.00.

JOHN ANGELL JAMES. CHURCH MEMBER'S GUIDE. Cloth. 33 cts.

——————— *CHURCH IN EARNEST.* 18mo, cloth. 40 cts.

——————— *CHRISTIAN PROGRESS.* Sequel to the Anxious Inquirer. 18mo, cloth. 31 cents.

THE GREAT CONCERN. By N. ADAMS, D. D. 12mo, cloth. 85 cents.

JOHN HARRIS'S WORKS. THE GREAT TEACHER. With an Introductory Essay by H. HUMPHREY, D. D. 12mo, cloth. 85 cents.

——————— *THE GREAT COMMISSION.* With an Introductory Essay by WILLIAM R. WILLIAMS, D. D. 12mo, cloth. $1.00.

——————— *THE PRE-ADAMITE EARTH.* Contributions to Theological Science. 12mo, cloth. $1.00.

——————— *MAN PRIMEVAL:* Constitution and Primitive Condition of the Human Being. Portrait of Author. 12mo, cloth. $1.25.

——————— *PATRIARCHY;* or, The Family, its Constitution and Probation. 12mo, cloth. $1.25.

——————— *SERMONS, CHARGES, ADDRESSES, &c.* Two volumes, octavo, cloth. $1.00 each.

HUGH MILLER'S WORKS. TESTIMONY OF THE ROCKS. With Illustrations. 12mo, cloth. $1.25.

——————— *FOOTPRINTS OF THE CREATOR.* With Illustrations. Memoir by LOUIS AGASSIZ. 12mo, cloth. $1.00.

——————— *THE OLD RED SANDSTONE.* With Illustrations, etc. 12mo, cloth. $1.25.

——————— *MY SCHOOLS AND SCHOOLMASTERS.* An Autobiography. Full-length Portrait of Author. 12mo, cloth. $1.00.

——————— *FIRST IMPRESSIONS OF ENGLAND AND ITS PEOPLE.* 12mo, cloth. $1 00.

——————— *CRUISE OF THE BETSEY.* A Ramble among the Fossiliferous Deposits of the Hebrides. 12mo, cloth. $1.25.

——————— *POPULAR GEOLOGY.* 12mo, cloth. $1.25.

HUGH MILLER'S WORKS. 7 vols. Elegant embossed cloth. $8.25.